Task
and
Organization

WILEY SERIES ON
INDIVIDUALS, GROUPS AND ORGANIZATIONS

Series Editor

Cary Cooper,
Department of Management Sciences,
University of Manchester Institute
  of Science & Technology,
Manchester

Associate Editor

Eric J. Miller,
Tavistock Institute of
  Human Relations,
London

Theories of Group Processes
Edited by Cary Cooper,
University of Manchester Institute
of Science & Technology

Task and Organization
Edited by Eric J. Miller,
Tavistock Institute of Human Relations

Task
and
Organization

Edited by

Eric J. Miller

Tavistock Institute of Human Relations,
Tavistock Centre, London, England

JOHN WILEY & SONS

London · New York · Sydney · Toronto

Library of Congress Cataloging in Publication Data:
Main entry under title:

Task and organization.

   (Wiley series on individuals, groups, and organizations)
   1. Organization—Addresses, essays, lectures.
2. Management—Addresses, essays, lectures.   3. Industrial sociology—Addresses, essays, lectures.   4. Rice,
Albert Kenneth—Bibliography.   I. Miller, Eric John.
HD31.T27   1976   658.4   75–12606

ISBN 0 471 60605 7

Photosetting by Thomson Press (India) Limited, New Delhi,
and printed at The Pitman Press Ltd., Bath

Contributors

BORIS M. ASTRACHAN, M. D.
Professor of Clinical Psychiatry, Yale University School of Medicine; Director, Connecticut Mental Health Center.

A. B. CHERNS, M.A.
Professor of Social Sciences, Head of Department of Social Sciences, Loughborough University of Technology.

P. A. CLARK, B.A., M.I.W.P.
Lecturer in Organizational Sociology, Organizational Analysis Research Unit, Management Centre, University of Bradford.

ARTHUR D. COLMAN, M. D.
Associate Clinical Professor, Department of Psychiatry, University of California Medical School, San Francisco, California; Lecturer, School of Environmental Design, University of California, Berkeley.

J. H. FITCH, B. A., F.B.Ps.S.
Senior Principal Psychologist, Behavioural Sciences Research Division, Civil Service Department. Formerly Principal Psychologist, Prison Department, Home Office.

HULDA R. FLYNN, Ph.D.
Research Associate in Psychiatry, Yale University School of Medicine.

WILLIAM HAUSMAN, M.D.
Professor and Head, Department of Psychiatry, University of Minnesota.

D. G. HEWLINGS,
Controller (Operations), Prison Department, Home Office (formerly Assistant Controller).

RAYMOND G. HUNT, Ph.D.
Faculty Professor, Social Sciences and Administration, and Director, Survey Research Center, University of New York at Buffalo.

GEOFFREY HUTTON, B.Sc.
Reader in Behavioural Sciences, School of Management, University of Bath.

ROBERT L. KAHN, Ph.D.
Director, Survey Research Centre, Institute of Social Research, University of Michigan.

W. G. LAWRENCE, M.A. *Consultant, Tavistock Institute of Human Relations.*

DANIEL LEVINSON, Ph.D. *Professor of Psychology, Department of Psychiatry, Yale University.*

LARS B. LOFGREN, M.D. *Chief, Psychiatric Unit III, VA Hospital (Brentwood), Los Angeles, California; Associate Professor in Psychiatry in Residence, University of California Medical School at Los Angeles, California.*

TOM LUPTON, M.A., Ph.D. *Professor of Organisational Behaviour, Manchester Business School.*

ERIC J. MILLER, M.A., Ph.D. *Consultant, Tavistock Institute of Human Relations.*

BARRY PALMER, M.A. *Chairman, Group and Organizational Studies Unit, The Grubb Institute of Behavioural Studies.*

BRUCE REED, M.A., Th.L. *Director, The Grubb Institute of Behavioural Studies.*

A. K. RICE, M.A., Sc.D. *formerly Consultant, Tavistock Institute of Human Relations.*

KENN ROGERS, Ph.D. *Professor of Psychiatry and Organizational Psychology, New Jersey Medical School, College of Medicine and Dentistry of New Jersey.*

PHILIP SADLER, M.A., F.B.I.M. *Principal, Ashridge Management College.*

ROGER L. SHAPIRO, M.D. *Professor, Department of Psychiatry and Behavioral Sciences, The George Washington University School of Medicine.*

JOHN ZINNER, M.D. *Section on Personality Development, Adult Psychiatry Branch, National Institute of Mental Health, Bethesda.*

Editorial Foreword to the Series

Over the last decade, there has been an enormous growth of interest in the social and psychological aspects of institutional and organizational life. This has been reflected in a substantial upsurge in research and training in the field of organizational behaviour particularly in Institutes of Higher Education and Research throughout the Western World. Attention in this development has focussed on the interrelationship between the individual, the variety of groups to which he belongs and the organizational environment within which he and his group operate.

The purpose of this series is to examine the social and psychological processes of these interrelationships, that is the nexus of individual/personal development, group processes and organizational behaviour and change. Within this context, a wide range of topics will be covered. These will include: the individual, his role and the organization; multiple roles and role conflict; the impact of group processes on personal and organizational development; strategies for 'humanizing' the organizational environment to meet individual and group needs; and the influence of technical and economic factors on organizational life.

The series will attempt to draw together the main schools of organizational behaviour including, for example, the American behavioural science tradition as reflected by Harvard, UCLA and National Training Laboratories, and the British socio-technical and open systems approaches of the Tavistock Institute of Human Relations. It is hoped that this will add significantly to understanding the distinctive characteristics of the various approaches and also provide a link between them through which individual, group and organizational behaviour can be seen in fuller perspective.

CARY COOPER
ERIC MILLER

Preface

This volume is dedicated to the memory of Albert Kenneth Rice, who died on November 15th, 1969, at the age of 61. When those of us who were his immediate colleagues in the Tavistock Institute began to think of ways of paying some kind of tribute to him, our first priority was to see his final writings through the press. A paper, 'Individual, Group and Intergroup Processes' (which is reproduced in this volume), was already with the printers of *Human Relations;* and the manuscript of a book, *The Modern University*, was ready for the publishers: this was brought out by Tavistock Publications in 1970. The manuscript of another book, on family businesses, had been lying fallow for several years, in the absence of permission to publish from one of the client groups with which Rice had been working. They felt that, although the names and locations had been disguised, people associated with them would still be able to identify the family business concerned. When we approached them again in 1970, they still withheld permission: although most of the issues raised by Rice in the consultancy and later in the book had been worked through, memories were still fresh and painful. That book, therefore, remains unavailable.

As another kind of tribute, we conceived the idea of putting together a collection of papers around the theme of 'Task and Organization'. *Primary task* was very much Rice's concept and, although his use of it has been criticized, it has undoubtedly been a valuable tool in the hands of Rice and other practitioners concerned with organizational change. Accordingly, on behalf of my colleagues, I approached a number of potential contributors in Britain and overseas. These fell into three overlapping categories: those who were applying Rice's conceptual framework in particular settings; those who were developing the concepts; and those with a parallel interest in organizational theory but not directly influenced by Rice. The response was positive: indeed, more contributions were offered than could be accepted.

It has nevertheless taken a long time to assemble this volume. The final versions of two or three papers, which were too important to exclude, came very late. There was also delay on my side. For this some rational excuses could be found. Time reserved for the editorial task got diverted into other activities while the last few papers were still to come, and when they finally arrived other commitments took me away from my desk. But I think that in part I was also reluctant to complete my task because to do so was to come to terms with the ending of a relationship that had been more important to me than any other in my working life.

When I first came into contact with Ken Rice in the early 1950's he was part of the lively and vigorous group that had established the Tavistock Institute's early reputation. Others at that time included Tommy Wilson, Eric

Trist, Harold Bridger, Isabel Menzies and Sidney Gray. These had all been together in the army during the war working at practical problems, such as officer selection, morale and resettlement of prisoners-of-war, within a shared framework that viewed mental health in an institutional and social context. This was the nucleus of the group that had conceived the idea of a more permanent peacetime institute dedicated to advancing the social sciences through engagement with clients in tackling the practical issues that they faced.

Rice, though fully committed to the Institute's objectives and approach, had come to it after the war by quite a different route. From the High School at Nottingham, where he was brought up, he went as an exhibitioner to Gonville and Caius College, Cambridge and there read mathematics. He switched to anthropology and after getting his degree joined the Colonial Service in Kenya. Neither then nor later was he a conformist. One gets the impression that he was not popular with his superiors. If he disagreed with their instructions, he either challenged them or ignored them—sometimes both. And he found himself in increasing disagreement with their policy towards the local population, especially the Kikuyu, the tribe with which he worked most closely. On this issue he left the Service—and the tragic uprising among the Kikuyu a decade or so later suggests that Rice had been eminently right to question the Government's policy.

From the Colonial Service he moved to management in England, first as an assistant general manager with a group of department stores, and then, for most of the war, as personnel manager with a London engineering company. Immediately after the war, he became deputy director of the Industrial Welfare Society (now the Industrial Society). It was from there that he first became involved with the Tavistock group. He became a member of the Council of the Tavistock Institute soon after it was incorporated in 1947, but within a year he had resigned from Council to become a staff member. He was then nearly 40, and he made a major imprint on the work and development of the Institute from then until his death 21 years later.

The publications listed at the end of this Preface tell part of the story of his career with the Institute and contribution to it. He was a member of the team for the Institute's first major project, with the Glacier Metal Company (Jaques, 1951). Among the crop of papers that sprang from this work (1950, 1951a, 1951b, 1951c, 1952a, 1952b, 1953a), two were seminal. The first, of which Rice was senior author with Hill and Trist, was 'The Representation of Labour Turnover as a Social Process' (1950). This described a new approach to the study of labour turnover in which the firm was considered as an open system. It demonstrated that the passage of members through it from joining to leaving could be identified as 'a continuous, mathematically coherent process, analogous to organic metabolism'. It also showed that part-institutions displayed their own distinctive processes that were nevertheless related to the institution as a whole. The other paper, 'The Use of Unrecognised Cultural Mechanisms in an Expanding Machine-Shop' (1951c), reflected the influence on Rice's thinking of Wilfred Bion's work on group processes. His membership, first in 1945 and for a longer period in 1947–48, of Bion's groups, which had the task of studying their own behaviour, had been a powerful formative experience. Now in this paper he used Bion's concepts to illuminate, in quite a new way, relations both within and between groups in an industrial situation. These two themes, which for convenience we can label 'open systems' and 'unconscious group processes', were to continue to permeate Rice's thinking and writing for the rest of his life.

In the next set of publications, which arose from Rice's 'Indian phase' (1953b, 1955a, 1955b, 1958, 1963), one finds the third major theme in Rice's work, the concept of 'socio-technical system'. The Tavistock group had formulated this concept as a result of studies of work organization in coal-mining, and Rice immediately set about testing it experimentally in the loom-sheds of a textile company in Ahmedabad. The publication of this 'amazing success story' (to quote Katz and Kahn, 1966, p. 445) gave Rice an international reputation, and the first part of *Productivity and Social Organization*, which describes the experiments, is much more widely known than the second part, which introduced the concept of 'primary task' in relation to open-system theory. The theme of 'unconscious group processes' was not in the forefront of his conceptual scheme of organization at that time, but was explicit in the way he conceived and operated his role as consultant (see especially *The Enterprise and its Environment*).

In 1964 he was awarded the degree of doctor of science at Cambridge University on the merit of his published work to date.

Systems of Organization developed the open-system approach somewhat further; and during 1969, when he was a visiting professor at Yale University School of Medicine, Rice prepared the manuscript of *The Modern University*, in which he applied this framework to the analysis of university organization.

The list of publications includes only one book, *Learning for Leadership* (1965), that describes Rice's contribution to training conferences and courses in group relations. To quote a historian of the Tavistock,

'It was not until 1957 . . . that the Institute, jointly with the University of Leicester, launched the first full-scale experiment in Britain with the "laboratory" method of training in group relations. The original concept of the Leicester Conference owed much to the experience of group psychotherapy pioneered by the Tavistock Clinic and reinforced by the contributions of social psychology and sociology. American experience, notably at the National Training Laboratory in Group Development at Bethel, Maine, had naturally an important influence, but the Leicester Conference was designed to meet the demand for a course of training which harnessed the new knowledge and understanding about groups, yet was rooted in British experience'. (Dicks, 1970, p. 212)

This was the first of a still continuing series of conferences, of which Rice took over direction, at the request of his Institute colleagues, in 1962. *Learning for Leadership* describes how he used his open-systems approach and the concept of primary task to reformulate the task and organization of the conferences themselves. New events were designed and developed in close collaboration with Pierre Turquet, who, as a consultant in the Tavistock Clinic and Institute, has continued to be innovative in this field. What neither this book nor his other publications tell us is how much the new coherence and rigour of conference design and operation owed to the strength of Rice's own leadership—in particular, the example he set of single-minded commitment to the task in hand.

Thus although the publications tell us part of the story, it is by no means the whole. For example a further aspect of his leadership in the conference area was a belief that the Institute could no longer go on subsidizing these training events: he was determined to make them pay their own way, and he succeeded—though he and Turquet in particular had at first to invest a great deal of their own time and energy for no financial reward to themselves. And in the Institute generally, Rice's insistence on facing economic realities more than once helped to avert financial disaster. For his 'business manager's approach' he was at times unpopular with colleagues, who did not always relish being reminded that the fascinating 'pie-in-the-sky' projects they wanted to pursue had to be set on one side in order to earn the fees needed to secure institutional survival. Indeed this was so unpalatable to some members of staff that new internal subgroupings emerged in the early 1960s, and Rice became founder-chairman of a group that was later named the Centre for Applied Social Research.

However, Rice's 'business manager's approach' was only one aspect of his profound, partly intuitive, understanding of the nature of institutions and of processes of institution-building. He carried this into a deep personal commitment to the institutions in which he himself was involved. As a result, he was often pulled in opposite directions by institutional needs and personal loyalties. And, although the personal costs were heavy, it was usually the institutional that won. This institutional sense was reflected too in his insistence on handing over leadership to the next generation. He was justifiably afraid that the institutions he had created would remain too dependent on him and so perish with him; so he pushed leadership at others. Accordingly, in 1968, he stepped down from the directorship of the Leicester conferences and from the chairmanship of the Centre for Applied Social Research and then gave support to the new leadership. In both cases, he remained the most competent person for the job and in both cases he knew that by handing over he would be facing problems of interpersonal rivalry. To hold on to the leadership would have been easier; but he stuck to what he believed was institutionally right.

Again, one only catches glimpses of this in his publications, but there is no doubt that his own experience of such conflicts and the way he resolved them permeated his role as consultant to other organizations. As in his conference leadership, he was setting a personal example. He never demanded greater rigour and integrity of thinking on the part of his clients than he was prepared to apply to himself; and awareness of his own dilemmas and conflicts gave him a sympathetic understanding of theirs. He could accept that their resolution of the dilemma might be different from his; only if they denied the existence of real dilemmas did he lose his patience.

Rice's bibliography also does less than justice to certain areas of his work.

For example, there is only one reference to management selection (1961), even though he did a lot of consultancy in this area, principally for industrial clients. 'Selection', in fact, is a misnomer, for often his main contribution was not in helping to find the right man for the job but in careful clarification of the nature of the role and the relationships involved—a process that often led to redefinition of other roles and to wider organizational changes. In addition, one can recall a number of long-standing relationships with chief executives of companies and groups, through which he helped them to initiate and implement change. A characteristic problem—and there were several instances of this— was that of the young and successful company which had grown rapidly. As it expands, diversifies and perhaps goes public, the founding chief executive has to come to terms with his ambivalence about introducing, and transferring authority to, a new echelon of professional managers. This is a problem that Rice understood.

I have written as if all Rice's work was carried out in industrial and commercial organizations. Indeed, if one excludes the work on training, his posthumous book, *The Modern University* (1970), was his only published study of an organization of a different kind. Until at least the mid-1960s, industrial clients had in fact predominated. The principal factor that changed this was the expansion of training activities. To the conferences came men and women not only from industry, but from education, the church, medicine, the prison service, social work and many other institutional and professional backgrounds. Working with them at trying to understand the application of what they had learned to their own jobs and institutions, Rice and his colleagues found themselves testing the relevance of his conceptual framework to a widening variety of organizational settings. In addition, Rice was active in helping other institutions to develop their own capacity to run conferences. *Learning for Leadership* describes the beginnings of collaborations which still continue with Christian Teamwork (now the Grubb Institute of Behavioural Studies) in England and with the Washington School of Psychiatry in the United States. There were more to follow. To quote Rice:

'We have suggested that if work of this kind is to spread, what is needed is the building of joint institutions staffed in the first place by the collaborating organisation and the [Tavistock] Institute. Subsequently, the collaborating institutions should take over the running of their own conferences or courses, modifying the techniques to suit their own particular needs. Once their own conferences or courses are established, then the joint institutions can be used for the benefit of all collaborating institutions and the Institute to develop new methods and to train new staff'. (Rice, 1965, pp. 173-4).

This has happened. In the United States, for example, where expansion of this work has been rapid, from 1965 onwards Rice directed a series of conferences, some jointly sponsored by the Tavistock Institute and the Washington School of Psychiatry (and initially also the Yale University School of Medicine) and some by the Washington School alone; he took Tavistock colleagues with him, but trained increasing numbers of Americans to take on staff roles, including, ultimately, his own role as conference director; other

American centres developed their own training programmes; the Board responsible for running the annual Mount Holyoke conference—the original joint event—became, after Rice's death, the board of a new A. K. Rice Institute (still within the Washington School), which sponsored or supported a variety of new conferences; and, at the time of writing, the Rice Institute is undergoing a further transformation into what may become a national federation of a set of autonomous institutions in different parts of the United States.

The point I want now to come back to is that the burgeoning of training activities opened many new relationships, both with institutions sending members to conferences and with institutions running events themselves. Many were non-industrial; many were in the United States. *Systems of Organization* (1967) still drew mainly on work with industrial and commercial organizations: at the time that was written, Rice's recent projects with a government-sponsored research unit and with a psychiatric hospital were regarded as unusual. But this changed quite quickly. An independent research institute and a school for delinquent boys—both engaged in re-examining their primary tasks—were added to his list of clients; and in the last year of his life the three projects that took up most of Rice's time were with an Indian management institute, an American university department and an English cathedral.

The papers in this volume testify to a continuation of that trend. The range of organizations discussed is extremely wide, and the authors also write from a variety of standpoints—the theoretician, the consultant and the man on the job introducing changes in his own organization.

The question of role perspectives is discussed in an introductory essay. Then, in Part I, I have assembled three papers—one by Rice himself (1969)—around the theme of the organization and the individual. Organizations provide the means through which the individual can gain security, grow, mature and exercise personal authority; and at the same time the individual is party to organizational processes, sometimes overt and more often hidden and obscure, that submerge individuality itself. The individual's perpetual struggle to avoid submergence within the group on one side and alienation from it on the other is one with which Rice strongly identified. Part II contains nine papers on the theme of designing organization for task performance in a variety of institutions—military, commercial, educational , therapeutic, corrective and religious. Taken together, they offer a considerable contribution to our understanding of the kind of thinking that leads to effective organizational design. The fact that Part III is entitled 'Approaching Organizational Change' does not mean that the earlier papers are not also concerned with change; nor that the four papers in Part III are not concerned with model-building. These four are, however, more directly concerned with strategies for change, through internal initiative, external intervention and education. The papers describe the experience of the authors in innovating; it is left to the reader to take responsibility for deciding what is relevant to him and for making use of it in his own role.

In conclusion there is a number of acknowledgements to be made. My primary debt, of course, is to the contributors themselves, both for submitting their papers and for their subsequent forbearance. Nor do I forget those who offered contributions that could not be used. Among colleagues who have supported me in my task, I want here to single out two. Gordon Lawrence, at a time when I was hard-pressed, produced first drafts of the introductions to Part II and III. Though I have to accept responsibility, and gladly do so, for the final versions, they remain in fact substantially his. I am hoping that he will be developing some of his ideas in another publication shortly. The second colleague is Janet Martin, who has borne the brunt of collating. correcting, retyping, reference-chasing and other similar chores that are part of assembling a volume like this. I am immensely grateful to them both.

E. J. M.

References

Dicks, H. V., (1970), *50 Years of the Tavistock Clinic*, Routledge and Kegan Paul, London.
Jaques, E., (1951), *The Changing Culture of a Factory*, Tavistock Publications, London.
Katz, D. and Kahn, R. L. (1966), *The Social Psychology of Organizations*, Wiley, New York.

Publications of A. K. Rice

1948 Works managers and personnel management, *Engineer, Lond.*, **154**, 667–669.
1949a The role of the specialist in the community, *Human Relations*, **2**, 177–184.
1949b Social factors and industrial morale, *Bull. Inst. Industr. Admin.*, **3**, No. 6.
1950 with J. M. M. Hill and E. L. Trist, The representation of labour turnover as a social process, (Glacier Project–II), *Hum. Relat.*, **3**, 349–372.
1951a with E. Jaques and J. M. M. Hill, The social and psychological impact of a change in method of wage payment, (Glacier Project–V), *Hum. Relat.*, **4**, 315–340.
1951b An examination of the boundaries of part institutions, (Glacier Project–VI), *Hum. Relat.*, **4**, 393–400.
1951c The use of unrecognised cultural mechanisms in an expanding machine-shop, (Glacier Project–III), *Hum. Relat.*, **4**, 143–160.
1952a The relative independence of sub-institutions as illustrated by departmental labour turnover, (Glacier Project–VI), *Hum. Relat.*, **5**, 83–90.
1952b with E. L. Trist, Institutional and sub-institutional determinants of change in labour turnover, (Glacier Project–VIII), *Hum. Relat.*, **5**, 347–371.
1953a An approach to problems of labour turnover, *Brit. Mgmt. Rev.*, **2**, 19–47.
1953b Productivity and social organization in an Indian weaving shed, *Hum. Relat.*, **6**, 297–329.
1955a The experimental reorganization of non-automatic weaving in an Indian mill, *Hum. Relat.*, **8**, 199–249.
1955b Productivity and social organization in an Indian weaving mill, II, A follow-up study of the experimental reorganization of automatic weaving, *Hum. Relat.*, **8**, 399–428.
1958 *Productivity and Social Organization: The Ahmedabad Experiment*, Tavistock Publications, London.
1961 Selection for management, I and II, *Secretaries Chron.*, **37**, 306–308; 352–354.
1963 *The Enterprise and its Environment*, Tavistock Publications, London.
1965 *Learning for Leadership*, Tavistock Publications, London.
1967 with E. J. Miller, *Systems of Organization: Task and Sentient Systems and their Boundary Control*, Tavistock Publications, London.
1968 Management and the nationalised industries, *New Society*, 8th Feb., No. **280**, 189–191.
1969 Individual, group and intergroup processes, *Hum. Relat.*, **22**, 565–584.
1970 *The Modern University: a Model Organization*, Tavistock Publications, London.

Acknowledgments

The editor and publishers wish to thank the Tavistock Institute of Human Relations and Plenum Press for permission to reproduce the paper by the late A. K. Rice from *Human Relations*, **22,** pp. 565–584.

They are also grateful to the following for permission to quote extracts in this volume:—

Tavistock Publications Ltd. and the Tavistock Institute of Human Relations for the quotations from A. K. Rice, *The Modern University* (1970), on p. 170; from E. J. Miller and A. K. Rice, *Systems of Organization* (1967), on p. 174 and p. 333; and from A. K. Rice, *The Enterprise and its Environment* (1963), on p. 191.

The Controller of Her Majesty's Stationery Office for the quotation from *People in Prison* (1969), on p. 243.

The Council of Europe and the author for the quotation from P. J. Woodfield, 'Organization of a system of corrections', A Report presented to the European Committee on Crime Problems, Sixth European Conference of Directors of Criminological Research Institutes, Strasbourg (1968), on p. 245.

The Editor of the *British Medical Journal* and the author for the quotation from P. D. Scott, 'Punishment or treatment; prison or hospital' (1970), on p. 247.

Tavistock Publications Ltd. and the author for the quotation from R. H. Guest, *Organizational Change* (1968), on p. 255.

The New Era and the author for the quotation from M. Milner, 'The sense in non-sense' (1956), on p. 272.

Faber and Faber Ltd., W. W. Norton Inc. and the author for the quotation from E. H. Erikson, *Identity—Youth and Crisis* (1968), on p. 272.

Routledge & Kegan Paul Ltd., Aldine Atherton and the author for the quotations from V. W. Turner, *The Ritual Process—Structure and Anti-Structure* (1969), on p. 276.

The State University of New York Press and the author for the quotation from J. Schulman, *Remaking an Organization* (1969), on p. 315.

The paper by Tom Lupton has appeared in *Personnel Review*, **4,** No. 1, Winter 1975.

An earlier version of the paper by Daniel Levinson and Boris Astrachan appeared in *Administration in Mental Health*, Summer 1974, a publication of the National Institute of Mental Health; Alcohol, Drug Abuse, and Mental Health Administration; U.S. Department of Health, Education, and Welfare.

Contents

PART III. APPROACHING ORGANIZATIONAL CHANGE

Introductory Essay:
Role Perspectives and the Understanding
of Organizational Behaviour

Eric J. Miller

Introduction

This essay is written around the proposition that the study of organization will make only halting progress unless it includes study of the roles from which organization is studied.

It was a rereading of the reviews of *Systems of Organization* (Miller and Rice, 1967) that triggered reflections along these lines. Pronounced differences in judgements of the book seemed to be clearly linked to differences of role—the reviewer's own role or assumptions he was making about the role of his readers. Each role evoked a distinctive, though not always explicit, set of criteria against which the book was to be assessed. These criteria tended to be treated as if they were mutually exclusive rather than complementary. The more general point is that those of us who work in the various areas of the human sciences have found the concept of role to be a useful tool in analysing the behaviour of other people but have perhaps made insufficiently disciplined use of it in analysing our own. While we are quick to recognize the ways in which role can restrict or distort the individual's view of the world around him and can accept at an intellectual level that we are not immune to these processes ourselves, our behaviour often transmits quite a different message: my window on the world provides the one correct perspective from which to observe and understand reality; yours is distorted.

Rice's work is a good starting-point. Like many of his colleagues at the Tavistock Institute, myself included, he was not always modest about the rightness and centrality of his approach. It has been a long-standing Tavistock aspiration to develop an integrated science of human behaviour. The opening sentence of *Systems of Organization* is:

'We try in this book to develop a theory of organization that reconciles tasks, human activities and organization within one general framework.' (Miller and Rice, 1967, p. xi).

The journal *Human Relations*, originally launched by the Tavistock Institute jointly with the Institute for Social Research at the University of Michigan, still carries the subtitle 'Studies towards the Integration of the Social Sciences'. Rice's last paper, published in that journal and now reprinted in this volume, focussed on similarities in the dynamics of intrapersonal, interpersonal and intergroup relationships (Rice, 1969). At the same time, in counterpoint to this evidence of what might be variously described as immodesty, arrogance or omnipotence, Rice always tried to be explicit about the role in which he gathered his data and which thus influenced his theoretical formulations: see, for example, Chapter 1 of *The Enterprise and its Environment* (Rice, 1963, pp. 3–9). This too was part of the Tavistock culture (cf. Jaques, 1951; Sofer, 1961).

There can be no dispute about the social importance of understanding organization, which was Rice's focal interest. As soon as we take on our roles as citizens, of our own countries or of the World at large, however much we may disagree over whether existing social institutions should be conserved and adapted, or destroyed and rebuilt from scratch, we cannot but agree on the need to understand, for our own survival, how to organize ourselves for the problems we have to solve. Nor can there be much doubt that such understanding requires an integration of different approaches. I use the word 'approaches' advisedly. One used to speak of interdisciplinary integration, which was the early Tavistock aspiration. Subsequently there was some tendency in Tavistock and elsewhere to believe that the best hope lay not in the interdisciplinary team but in the multidisciplinary individual. Unfulfillable though this hope was, at least it pointed to the notion that disciplinary boundaries might not be relevant to, and might even stand in the way of, understanding the processes of organization and organizational change. Now, of course, the boundaries of the conventional behavioural disciplines are much more precarious. Within these boundaries newer subdisciplines have been emerging—industrial psychology and organizational sociology, for example—and at the same time quite different approaches, or fields of study, which cut across these boundaries, have taken hold—general systems theory, information theory, decision-making theory, game theory, cybernetics, operational research. These are sometimes called multidisciplines, though March (1965, p. xiv) describes the study of organization as a semidiscipline, which perhaps reflects more accurately its unorganized character. Growing recognition of the complexity of the problems that a manager has to solve has both stimulated and been stimulated by the development of an unwieldy tool-kit of 'management sciences' for his use in solving them.

Instead of interdisciplinary integration, those concerned with practical problems of designing, building and changing organizations often have a picture of interdisciplinary fragmentation. The discrediting of other people's approaches seems sometimes to take priority over the advancement of knowledge.

It is my contention that development of understanding of organization requires much more dialogue among protagonists of the various approaches and further that effective dialogue requires the various types of theorists and practitioners to be quite explicit about their different roles. It is necessary to move away from assertions of the type, 'My perception is correct; yours is distorted', towards the more constructive, 'This is the way in which my role affects my perception'.

In the first part of this essay I illustrate the influence of role on perception by considering reviews of *Systems of Organization*, and I suggest that the nature and content of critiques tend to vary systematically according to the roles assumed by reviewers. In the second part I discuss the role from which Rice himself was operating and try to clarify some aspects which appear to have been found ambiguous. In this way, I hope to clear the ground for discussion in the third part of the conditions for effective dialogue.

Reviews of *Systems of Organization*

It is no surprise to find different reviewers propounding diametrically opposed opinions. For example:

'The section on the family business attracted me more than any other' (Lupton, 1969, in *Sociology*)

and, in reference to the same section:

'These very weak chapters could have been omitted' (Schoenherr, 1968, in *The American Journal of Sociology*).

Or again:

'The book's final part is an unusually effective summary of the authors' basic ideas' (Hunt, 1968, in *Administrative Science Quarterly*),

and:

'The conclusions are short and unsatisfactory' (Lupton, 1969).

In many instances, however, reviewers identified the role or standpoint from which they were commenting, and in a few other cases it could be unambiguously inferred. When these roles are examined, superficial contradictions still remain, but some underlying uniformities become detectable.

Four clusters of roles emerged:

(1) Practising managers and specialists (e.g. personnel managers);
(2) Management teachers, students and research workers;
(3) Students of organization (in which I have included, on contextual evidence, one 'scientific theorist');
(4) Sociologists.

Of these, the third was least sharply defined and may have overlapped with the second and possibly the fourth. Let me consider each of them in turn.

Managers, etc.

For reviewers writing from this standpoint the principal criteria are readability and relevance to the practice of management. The reviewer typically outlines the contents of the book and ends with a clear-cut recommendation for or against reading it, with few supporting arguments. To quote an anonymous reviewer (1968) in *Management Decision*, for example:

'It is an excellently readable book for all who think carefully about their managerial role'.

The editor of a technical weekly summarizes the authors' thesis from the standpoint of 'airline people' and concludes by saying:

'Unless your airline is already perfectly run, I do commend this book to you' (Seekings, 1968, in *Aeroplane*).

A slightly fuller explanation is given by Fox (1968), in *The Journal of Management Studies*:

'... managers with a taste for the abstract will find much of interest and profit in seeing highly diverse task situations analysed in terms of the import-conversion-export framework and the distinction between task and sentient group.'

Two other reviewers express more doubt about managers' powers of comprehension:

'... Only the most academically inclined professional managers will have the stamina to struggle through its language and wrestle with the concepts it presents' (Sadler, 1968a, in *Management Today*)

'... The results and conclusions are never sufficiently coherently expressed, and are obscured by a number of not very helpful diagrams, ... In my view this is not a book for busy personnel managers (even not so busy ones) hoping to find a substantial and significant contribution to the theory of organization' (Baird, 1968, in *Personnel*).

The reviewer in this set who gives the clearest reasons for his recommendation is Macleod (1968), in *Industrial Society*. He begins by stating that 'senior members of management and their specialist advisers who may have to design or reshape the structure of their organizations should be acquainted with the organizational model developed in this book'; he outlines the book's main argument; he warns that Part I 'is a bit of a brain teaser but well worth persevering with' (noting, in contrast to Baird, that 'the explanatory diagrams are excellent'); and says in conclusion:

'By adopting this type of approach to the analysis of the situational demands of an enterprise, management will not necessarily resolve problems of imbalance and conflict, but they should be able to confront them more constructively.'

Management Teachers, etc.

If we turn now to the second cluster of roles around management teaching and research, we find a different and (within the limits of a small sample) consistent response to the book. The criterion here, as one would expect, is whether it contributes to teaching and learning about processes of management. Sadler (1968a) predicts that this category, in contrast to managers, 'will find in it much to stimulate and even excite them.' Duncan (1968), in *Sociological Review*, is also certain that the book 'will be welcomed by students and teachers of management for whom detailed case material is particularly useful and for whom an intermingling of empirical and normative orientations is not inappropriate.'

(That last phrase foreshadows criticisms that Duncan is to make from his role as sociologist.)

Students of Organization

The essential criterion for reviewers in this category is whether the book advances organizational theory. On these grounds too the reception is positive. This can be exemplified by Berry (1968), in *Personnel and Training Management*, who urges a thorough study of the book, emphasizes its contribution to the understanding of organizational boundaries, expresses some hesitations—that the book is over-concerned with change to provide an adequate basis for a *general* theory of organization; that observations are too often clinical, rather than based on measurement; and that 'they rely on data which ethical consultancy prevents revealing'—but nevertheless concludes by endorsing it as 'a highly distinguished contribution to the theoretical literature on organizations'. Hunt (1968), in *Administrative Science Quarterly*, also comments on its 'significance ... for the scientific theorist'.

Sociologists

The criterion adopted here is essentially one of sociological legitimacy. Regardless of whether or not the book adds to understanding of organization, for the manager, the teacher/student of management or the student of organization, the question posed by the sociologist reviewer is whether it fits into a sociological framework. Does it throw light on sociological problems? Do its concepts stand up to rigorous scrutiny from a sociological standpoint?

Users of these criteria greet the book with much more reserve. There are several comments to the effect that the authors have not taken the world of sociology sufficiently into account. Thus Duncan (1968), in *The Sociological Review*, refers to

'their isolation from academic sociology and the restrictive vision imposed by previous consultancy assignments',

While Silverman (1968), in *The British Journal of Industrial Relations*,

'notes with interest the absence of a *sociological* perspective, for instance in relating motivations to the social situations experienced and roles played both inside and outside the organization, or of due attention to the sociological literature' (italics in original).

As Duncan puts it (citing Mouzelis, 1967),

'It is important to distinguish between sociological problems and the problems with which managers are preoccupied. Excessive involvement with the latter inhibits clarification of the former.'

One way in which this manifests itself, according to Fox (1968) (in *The Journal of Management Studies*), is in

'a disinclination to face the facts of power relations and organized group conflict—or by a disposition to reduce them to Kleinian "anxieties" and "hates" within the individual . . . Power is not mentioned in this book.'

Silverman echoes this, commenting that as a result of their 'orientation towards psycho-analysis' the authors take the view

'that there are no basic conflicts of interests which can arise inside organisations'.

(By contrast, Clark (1968), in *The British Journal of Social and Clinical Psychology*, says that the authors' aims 'centre around power relationships'.)

References in the book to psychological factors disturbed other reviewers who do not explicitly identify with the sociological role. For example, Lupton (1969) (in *Sociology*) says that the authors rely too heavily on 'psycho-analytically based speculations' and are guilty of 'confusing the reader with shifts from structural to psychological levels of analysis'. This is also among the reservations that leads Sadler (1968b) (in *Occupational Psychology*) to sum up:

'*Systems of Organization* leaves one with very mixed feelings. On the one hand the quality of the thought, the skill displayed in description and analysis of cases, are streets ahead of most work being produced in this field. At the same time one is compelled to ask, is it social science?'

Two of the sociological reviewers explicitly criticize the authors' concept of *primary task*. To quote Fox (1968):

'The primary task . . . is first defined as the task which the enterprise must perform if it is to survive (p. 25). This is an objective definition. But later it emerges that the leaders of an enterprise or a sub-system within it may define their primary task wrongly and so threaten its survival. This is a subjective definition. We thus have two entities which need to be conceptually distinguished: that which is necessary for organisational survival and that which its members *believe* is necessary. To give them the same name invites confusion.'

Silverman (1970) points to a slightly different difficulty about the concept:

'Thus we are left with a method of inferring the primary task from observations of the operation of various parts of the organisation. Now, quite apart from the problem that separate observers might draw conflicting inferences, we are clearly unable to resolve the difficulties that can arise if, as is quite likely, the behaviour of different groups in the organisation reflects their differing definitions of the situation,'

He goes on to say:

'Thus Miller and Rice once more illustrate the consequences which flow from the reification of organisations through the attribution to them of "goals" or "needs". For the organic analogy requires a *referent* by which to judge the health or disease of a system and, for obvious reasons, such a factor is more readily apparent in a biological than in a social system. This is why such writers feel compelled to get involved in metaphysics about "primary tasks" instead of merely observing the range of ends which are actually pursued within organisations.'

Rice's Consultancy Role

I have illustrated the fairly obvious point that divergent evaluations become more explicable when the various roles from which reviewers are writing are identified. Beyond this, there is a point to which neither the authors nor the reviewers gave sufficient attention: where human behaviour is our field of study no conceptual framework is complete without a statement of the role of the conceptualizer. This is a boundary role, the existence of which implies both a distinction and a relationship between the observer and the observed. The dimensions of what is observed are a function of the role of the observer. If within a group I address myself to a person, I confirm his identity as an individual. If I shift my focus to the group, the notion of the bounded individual, other than as a biological organism, may be seen as a reification: the observable reality is a set of processes, moving towards but never reaching individual autonomy on the one hand and submergence in the group on the other. From here it looks like this; from there it looks like that.

This is reminiscent of Heisenberg's principle of uncertainty. The more accurately the position of, say, an electron is known, the more indeterminate is its velocity; and vice versa. To cope with the inherent indeterminacy of sub-atomic processes, within which electrons and other entities appear to behave sometimes as particles and sometimes as waves, physicists found it necessary to introduce another principle, that of complementarity. As Heisenberg puts it:

'The concept of complementarity is meant to describe a situation in which we can look at one and the same event through two different frames of reference. These two frames mutually exclude each other, and only the juxtaposition of these contradictory frames provides an exhaustive view of the appearance of the phenomena'. (Heisenberg, 1969, quoted by Koestler, 1972)

I take this to imply that the validity of a physicist's statements or theories about the wave-like behaviour of electrons can be tested only by taking into account his role as a student of electrons-as-waves: to question his formulation from the vantage-point of the student of electrons-as-particles would be meaningless. A similar distinction has, of course, long been accepted in the social sciences between, for example, the psychologist and the sociologist. But so far we have no principle of complementarity, and in the study of organization the existence of different vantage-points so often goes unrecognized that the relevance of criticisms may be very difficult to evaluate.

Thus the work of Rice and his colleagues has been perceived in widely divergent ways. The type of role that Rice took has been variously labelled 'prescriptive' (Silverman, 1970; also in a paper by Cherns and Clark elsewhere in this volume) and 'sociotherapeutic' (Sofer, 1961). There are criticisms that the 'Tavistock approach' upholds the vested interests of those in power; yet I have heard the particular form of training conference developed by Rice (1965) for the study of leadership and authority in organizations (and now widely known in the United States as 'the Tavistock model') described as encouraging radical and even revolutionary outlooks, by virtue of its rigorous insistence on examining the boundary relationships of person, role and institution.

These divergent perceptions have arisen in part from false assumptions of similarity in the approaches of different people who are ostensibly engaged in much the same kind of activity. Whereas in psycho-analysis, despite differences of schools and personal styles, there is a recognizable consistency among theoretical frameworks and basic techniques, and practice is controlled by professional bodies, a term such as 'organizational analysis', 'social analysis' or 'sociotherapy' has no consistency of usage and no professional sanction behind it. These are terms that any practitioner can adopt to describe whatever it is that he happens to do.

It has to be recognized too that there has been no unitary 'Tavistock approach'. For example, the role model adopted by Jaques (1951) in the well-known Glacier study has seldom if ever been replicated. Sofer's sociotherapeutic role differed from that of Jaques and in some respects from Rice's. Certainly Rice's thinking about primary task developed over the years, as he himself pointed out (cf. Rice, 1963, p. 185), and only in 1967 was it clearly identified as a heuristic concept. (Before that, Silverman's warning about the dangers of reification would have been more justified.) In addition, the way in which Rice occupied his role was not entirely uniform as between different periods and different clients. Most of us have experienced difficulty at times in establishing our roles in particular situations (Miller and Gwynne, 1972: see especially Chapter 2). This makes it all the more incumbent upon us to describe our roles as clearly as we can.

In fact, although there has been no single Tavistock role-model, Tavistock writers have usually tried to be explicit about their roles. In the case of the Glacier project,

'the Institute had stated that it refused on principle any request for consultation unless not only the management group as a whole were agreed, but representatives of the workers also; such general agreement being regarded as an essential pre-condition of any technically effective and professionally responsible undertaking in this special line of work.'

Accordingly, the project team became responsible to the Works Council, which was taken as being representative of the firm as a whole, and explicit conditions governing the conduct of the project were agreed and followed (Jaques, 1951).

Experience since then has continually reinforced the importance to the effectiveness of the relationship of clarifying who the client is—a firm, a board of directors, a chairman, a project committee—and the nature of the consultant's contract with him. Indeed the process of clarification is in some cases the main work of the consultancy: the working through of relationships which is necessary within the client system in order to enable it to relate to the consultant may give its members the competence to tackle the presenting problems that precipitated the request for external help. When social consultancy takes this form it comes closest to an analogue of psycho-analysis. At the other extreme, some Tavistock work has had the characteristics of the commissioned research project, in which the primary task has been to produce a research report on a defined issue and the working through of implications with the client has been of secondary importance.

In Rice's work, as in Sofer's, the professional role was of first concern. This meant that

'the problem posed by the client was taken as data but not as a mandate. The contract with the client has always been based on an understanding that the effort would be a collaborative one to work through a problematic situation. Often the presenting problem masked a deeper underlying problem . . .'. (Rapoport, 1970, p. 502)

The objective was not simply the solution of a problem, whether presenting or underlying, but also an attempt to leave the client equipped with greater problem-solving competence. As Sofer put it, the consultant's work 'will have defeated its own purposes if he has acquired a vested interest in the incapacities of the organisation and made himself indispensable' (Sofer, 1961, p. 130).

Sofer was also unequivocal in emphasizing that the professional role implied that the social consultant's obligation was to the organization, not to individuals:

'Whatever arrangements are made (to deal with the interests of individuals), it is necessary for him to give absolute priority to the needs of the organisation, to serve its overall interests, and to contribute to its primary task'. (Sofer, 1961 p. 130)

Here, however, 'the organization' and its needs seem to be defined not, as in the Glacier study, by a representative structure, but by the consultant's own conception of what the primary task should be.

A further corollary of the professional role, emphasized by both Sofer and Rice, was that client needs had to take priority over the consultant's research interests. Thus although Sofer was explicit about identifying and conceptualizing the research component of the social consultant's role and distinguishing it from the therapeutic component, he also noted that, of the three projects described in *The Organization from Within*, in two 'the main objectives were therapeutic, and any scientific contributions that emerged had to be regarded as incidental to the main purpose', while in the third, though it 'had formal research objectives as well as operational and advisory aims', nevertheless 'the research–therapy balance tilted in favour of the latter' (Sofer, 1961, p. 115).

Sofer's account of the sociotherapeutic role needs no further elaboration here. Rice appeared to accept Sofer's definition and to attribute any differences in his own approach to differences in personal style rather than in role as such. For example:

'Most of my colleagues would accept that our own feelings of pleasure and pain, anxiety and relief, excitement and sobriety, are frequently the only measures we have available to assess what is real and what unreal in a difficult situation. The use we make of our feelings may differ. Sofer states that he avoided remarks about his clients' feelings towards him and his work "which would have included elements not fully conscious to respondents or displaced from other real and fantasy relationships". By contrast it will be seen that I frequently did make such comments. I used my experience of my clients' attitudes towards me and my feelings about them when I thought that, by so doing, I could illuminate the problems we were discussing'. (Rice, 1963, p. 5)

The Enterprise and its Environment, from which that quotation is taken, documents clearly the way in which Rice actually operated a consultancy role in one setting, and I can confirm from my association with him in some of the work described there as well as elsewhere that the description is not misleading. My purpose here, therefore, is not to repeat or summarize what he has already written, but to focus on certain aspects of the role which relate to his conceptual formulations and which are sometimes misunderstood.

One point that needs to be made is that such effectiveness as Rice had as a change agent did not come from *applying* a general theoretical framework of organization to specific situations. His concept of the primary task and of the enterprise as an open system emerged in the course of working with clients to help clarify their problems. The relevance of such concepts lies mainly in their contribution to this process of clarification for the actors in the situation. For example, in Rice's experience and my own, the concept of primary task has provided an extremely powerful heuristic tool in the consultancy process. He described it as 'a starting-point for making decisions about change' (Rice, 1963, p. 185). First, it has the effect of mobilizing the members of the enterprise with whom one is working into their work roles in the organization and to grapple with its problems from that perspective. Other influences—for example, career aspirations, interpersonal rivalries or external professional affiliations—while not being disregarded, can then be the better separated out and subsequently re-examined as practical constraints on performance of a given primary task. In the meantime, differences in perceptions of the task itself are more accessible for mutual examination. Second, and related to this, it provides the beginnings of a new shared language through which members of the organization can discuss the issues confronting them, initially with the consultant and then with each other. Third, alternative organizational models can be constructed for different definitions of the primary task. Comparison of these with each other and with the existing form of organization then produces the creative dialogue through which critical issues can be identified, assumptions tested (and sometimes discarded) and a more explicit definition of task and constraints can emerge. The dialogue is fundamental to the process, so that the consultant's role here is anything but 'a commitment to a primarily prescriptive frame of reference' (Silverman, 1970, p. 120). The perceived prescriptiveness of the approach may arise from the tendency of a theoretically oriented reader of a book such as *The Enterprise and its Environment* to concentrate on the organizational concepts and to ignore the less systematically described and understood context within which they are used. Tacitly, if not overtly, both that book and *Systems of Organization* invite the reader not to apply the conceptual frameworks as such but to use them as a stimulus and guide in questioning assumptions in organizational settings within which he himself has a role as, for example, a manager or consultant.

The fact that Rice's consultancy model invoked members of the client organization in their work roles needs underlining. Other change agents operate differently. For example, Harrison (1970), while putting forward the proposition that the consultant should 'intervene at a level no deeper than that at which the energy and resources of organization members can be committed to problem solving and to change', nevertheless entertains strategies in which 'core areas of the personality or self are the focus of the change attempt': he says, for example, that 'in order to obtain the information necessary to link organizational goals to individual goals, one must probe fairly deeply into the attitudes, values and emotions of the organization members'. The process of invoking task-related roles will of course at times raise intrapersonal issues for individuals —for example, when social defence mechanisms, to which personal defence mechanisms are linked, are identified and examined. My working hypothesis, which I believe was also Rice's, is that the individual has the responsibility and resources (ego-strength) to work through for himself the personal consequences of the organizational and role issues that are being dealt with and that it is not my job as an organizational consultant to take on the individual's problems. If these are brought to me, I share Sofer's view that 'employment of a colleague for consultations of a more personal character serves a symbolic as well as a practical function in this respect' (Sofer, 1961, p. 109). This is not to say that the boundary between role and personal issues is always clear-cut. Work with family businesses, for example, may require intervention in both family and business relationships and thus expose individuals to emotionally laden issues of role conflict. Again, when the client is a chief executive faced with difficult choices and needing personal support in making them, the consultant may find himself drawn more deeply than he intended into the role of personal adviser. This sometimes happened to Rice. He wrote, for example, of his involvement in his Indian work, where

'my clients and their families became my close friends.' (Rice, 1963, p. 9)

However, he was manifestly aware of the problems this raised and he worked at them. It is likely that members of a client organization learn more from the consultant who works at his problems of staying in role than from one who appears to have no such problems: the latter may be insufficiently involved to be useful.

Just as the consultant role adopted by Rice was not directed towards changing individual behaviour, but related to persons in roles, so (to quote Sofer again)

'there were no attempts to improve relationships for their own sake. In some cases relationships were improved, in the sense that people got on better with each other, in others they were not. This was incidental to the task of helping the group to function more effectively'. (Sofer, 1961, pp. 103–104)

Nor was the aim to reduce conflict but rather, as Rice often said, to ensure that the conflict that occurred was between the right people and about the right issues.

The professional role is partly maintained by a constant preparedness to examine it. It is understood at the outset that both client and consultant are free to end the relationship at any time and the issue of continuation is usually raised explicitly at intervals during a project.

When we consider some of these points together, it is evident that the nature of such a professional working relationship between consultant and client itself sets a model for working relationships within the organization. Friendships there may be, but the work role has priority. Feelings, attitudes, unconscious motives are given full weight, while at the same time it is recognized that they may act as constraints on primary task performance. Definition of the consultant's role is emphasized; correspondingly definitions of task and role become internal concerns. Organizational models around which internal dialogue may be invoked focus attention on boundaries of systems and of roles. Thus between the consultant role and the conceptual framework there is not merely consistency but reinforcement. This concentration on the task-oriented elements of organizational behaviour leads one critic to say:

'My impression is that Rice and Miller are too cognitive and too rational'. (Clark, 1969, p. 87)

In the light of this, the labelling of this kind of approach as prescriptive or normative becomes more understandable. It is not normative in the sense of telling people what they should do, but it does involve drawing attention to factors that the client needs to take into account if he desires to pursue his stated task more effectively; and moreover it is clear that the consultant's behaviour in his role and in pursuit of his own task may be taken as some kind of norm for behaviour within the client system.

Relating Different Perspectives

I now want to refer to one writer whose review of *Systems of Organization* defied simple classification by reviewer role. This was Clark, in *The British Journal of Social and Clinical Psychology* (1969). He opens by drawing attention to

'two complementary developments: first, of increasing sophistication by administrators and specialists about "organisation"; and secondly, of the emergence of a network of social scientists involved in teaching, research and consultancy who are attempting to build "a social science using capacity" into organizations. The importance of this new professional group and of the Rice–Miller book is the focus upon "organisation". (Clark, 1969)

Adducing an earlier role of his own as a social scientist in a department of industrial engineering, he then examines the book by standards used in assessing good work-study practice and finds it wanting in many respects. However, he does not see this as an indictment of the book. On the contrary, he defends

it on the grounds that 'this area is new and imperfectly understood' and complains that

'when scrutinizing such work that has already been done [in this area] social scientists all too frequently don their citizen's hat and tend to take a solely ethical viewpoint. The proper test ... is whether when the authors say this "can be" they are right with reference to a particular case. This can in parts be judged by drawing on the body of social science knowledge ...' (Clark, 1969)

He concludes with the opinion that

'*Systems of Organization* will prove a stimulus to the dialogue within the community of researchers, teachers and consultants interested in organisational analysis. It should prove useful both to managers and trade unionists.' (Clark, 1969)

One would judge that Clark had difficulty in writing this review and his meaning is not always clear: for example, what is implied in the 'solely ethical viewpoint' of social scientists wearing their citizens' hats? Manifestly, his difficulty arises from his recognition that there is no one 'correct' role from which the book can be appraised—for example, in terms of its contribution to sociology as a discipline.

What Clark does recognize is that the book is directed towards building a 'goal-based empirical theory' (as defined by Golembiewski, 1962, pp. 51 ff.). Implicitly, he is commenting on something that I am here trying to make more explicit, namely the need for means through which such theories can be more effectively formulated, tested, compared and developed. I want, therefore, to conclude by postulating the form of 'organization' required to pursue the study of organization. Essentially, this involves trying to implement, in this field, the physicist's principle of complementarity.

To do this, we have to start by acknowledging certain characteristics of the field that I have already mentioned. In many ways it is as unstable as the realm of subatomic physics. Knowledge of human behaviour cannot have an extraneous reality of its own independent of the role of the generator, transmitter or user of the knowledge. When a social scientist carries out research, his vantage-point affects his definition of the situation, just as the definition of other actors in the situation is affected by their respective vantage-points. Moreover, he changes the situation, either in the actual process of collecting data, or later when his findings are transmitted, directly or indirectly, to actors in the situation, or both.

Furtherance of our understanding of organization—especially if one is concerned about the use to which that understanding is to be put—requires a form of dialogue that will facilitate the making of linkages between insights and concepts derived from different roles. For this it is counterproductive to assume that the roles are arranged in a hierarchy of righteousness. Regrettably, some sociologists still aspire to an all-embracing olympian perspective, from which all other (lesser) perspectives are to be explained and understood. Silverman, for example, enquires why social scientists 'should be *reduced* to considering the factors associated with high productivity' (Silverman, 1968,

p. 397, italics added) and describes Lawrence and Lorsch (1967) as having a 'management orientation' that is 'blatant' (Silverman, 1968, p. 395). In the appropriate theory-building environment it is not considered discrediting to be concerned with social as well as sociological problems, but it would be discrediting not to acknowledge one's own role and the limitations that this imposes. In this respect the scholar-sociologist based on a university is no less constrained and no more value-free than any other commentator on society. Given the value systems of society, however, there may indeed be an expectation that what he has to say will be more all-embracing, more authoritative; so perhaps we should not be surprised if he sometimes comes to believe this himself.

If it is assumed that we wish to develop socially relevant theories, then the primary dialectical system for furthering the study of organization invokes those whose roles have to do with the purposes of designing, building, managing and changing organizations. These organizations will be industrial, educational, religious, recreational, therapeutic, governmental—indeed, all forms of purposeful endeavour which require the coordinated activity of sizeable groups of people—and the relevant set of roles will include those within the boundaries of these various organizations who are concerned to clarify and conceptualize what they are trying to do, as well as those outside who relate to them in the processes of clarification and conceptualization. Common to this whole set of roles is recognition and acceptance of the goal-based nature of organizational activity. The need within this system is to develop a shared conceptual framework which, I postulate, has the characteristics of the framework proposed by Rice. Thus, some such concept as primary task is inescapable; so also probably are notions of system and boundary. In addition to and consistent with this framework for examining organization, Rice also proposed a particular framework within which to consider the behaviour of individuals and groups—the essential resources through which organizational tasks are carried out (Rice, 1969).

From the perspective of this system (or rather its set of common and complementary perspectives) other institutions and social processes continue to constitute a more or less turbulent environment, which offers both opportunities for and constraints upon task performance. Members of the organization import some of this turbulence with them into their work roles. However, what appears as turbulence from one standpoint may be perceived from another as a set of phenomena with certain regularities. To take an obvious example, behaviour that seems irrational within the work role becomes comprehensible when external affiliations and their associated values are understood. There is therefore a need for dialogue with other dialectical systems which invoke different foci—for example, that of the scholar-sociologist or the psychologist. Each focus requires a distinctive conceptual apparatus. The concept of primary task, for instance, which may be indispensible to a focus on the enterprise and its boundary transactions, may take on quite a different meaning if the level of analysis is concerned with processes of legitimation of authority.

More generally, any theory in the social sciences may be seen at one level as offering an explanation of human behaviour and at another level as an expression of a particular set of human values—a statement which, while it offers the hope that social theorists will never be out of work, is unpalatable for those who seek an ultimate truth. It follows then that although this dialogue is necessary to those in the primary dialectical system if members of organizations are to maintain sufficient understanding of and control over their environments in order to carry out their tasks, there is always a limit to the understanding that can be transferred from one perspective to another, with the result that environments must remain to some extent turbulent and unpredictable.

I postulate, however, that the capacity of what I have called the primary dialectical system to make use of inputs from other perspectives is contingent on its own coherence as a system within which communication can occur among the parallel and complementary roles. This links again to Clark's reference to a relevant 'network' or 'community'. All, or almost all, the writers in this volume are explicit about the roles from which they approach the issues of task and organization, whether as institutional leaders, consultants or observers; and all, in one way or another, are writing of their predicaments in trying to understand what they see from the position they are in. All of them too relate their position to that of Rice. In that sense this book represents one effort towards building an effective theory-building community.

References

Anonymous (1968), book review of: Miller, E. J. and Rice, A. K., *Systems of Organization*, Tavistock Publications, London, 1967. *In: Management Decision*, Summer, p. 128.

Baird, D. (1968), book review of: Miller, E. J. and Rice, A. K., *Systems of Organization*, Tavistock Publications, London, 1967. *In: Personnel*, March, p. 46.

Berry, D. (1968), book review of: Miller, E. J. and Rice, A. K., *Systems of Organization*, Tavistock Publications, London, 1967. *In: Personnel and Training Management*, March, p. 39.

Clark, P. A. (1969), book review of: Miller, E. J. and Rice, A. K. *Systems of Organization*, Tavistock Publications, London, 1967. *In: British Journal of Social and Clinical Psychology*, **8**, 86–88.

Duncan, P. (1968), book review of: Miller, E. J. and Rice, A. K. *Systems of Organization*, Tavistock Publications, London 1967. *In: Sociological Review*, **16**, 261–262.

Fox, A. (1968), book review of: Miller, E. J. and Rice, A. K. *Systems of Organization*. Tavistock Publications, London, 1967. *In: Journal of Management Studies*, **5**, 241–246.

Golembiewski, R. T. (1962), *Behaviour and Organisation*, Rand McNally, Chicago.

Harrison, R. (1970), Some criteria for choosing the depth of organisational intervention strategy, *Journal of Applied Behavioural Science*, **6**, 181–202.

Heisenberg, W. (1969), *Der teil und das ganze*, München.

Hunt, R. G. (1968), book review of: Miller, E. J. and Rice, A. K., *Systems of Organization*, Tavistock Publications, London, 1967. *In: Administrative Science Quarterly*, **13**, 360–362.

Jaques, E. (1951), *The Changing Culture of a Factory*, Tavistock Publications, London.

Koestler, A. (1972), *The Roots of Coincidence*, Hutchinson, London.

Lawrence, P. R. and Lorsch, J. W. (1967), *Organization and Environment*, Harvard Business School, Boston.

Lupton, T. (1969), book review of: Miller, E. J. and Rice, A. K., *Systems of Organization*, Tavistock Publications, London, 1967. *In: Sociology*, 3, 119–121.

Macleod, K. (1968), book review of: Miller, E. J. and Rice, A. K., *Systems of Organization*, Tavistock Publications, London, 1967. *In: Industrial Society*, April, p. 21.

March, J. G. (Ed.), (1965), *Handbook of Organizations*, Rand McNally, Chicago.

Miller, E. J. and Gwynne, G. V. (1972), *A Life Apart*, Tavistock Publications, London.

Miller, E. J. and Rice, A. K. (1967) *Systems of Organization*, Tavistock Publications, London.

Mouzelis, N. P. (1967), *Organisations and Bureaucracy*, Routledge and Kegan Paul, London.

Rapoport, R. N. (1970), Three dilemmas in action research, *Human Relations*, 23, 499–513.

Rice, A. K. (1963), *The Enterprise and its Environment*, Tavistock Publications, London.

Rice, A. K. (1965), *Learning for Leadership*, Tavistock Publications, London.

Rice, A. K. (1969), Individual, group and inter-group processes, *Human Relations*, 22, 565–584; (for errata see: *Human Relations*, 23, 498(1970)).

Sadler, P. (1968a), Problems from the Tavistock. Book review of: Miller, E. J. and Rice, A. K., *Systems of Organization*, Tavistock Publications, London, 1967. *In: Management*, March, 115–116.

Sadler, P. (1968b), book review of: Miller, E. J. and Rice, A. K., *Systems of Organization*, Tavistock Publications, London, 1967. *In: Occupational Psychology*, 42, 195–196.

Schoenherr, R. A. (1968), Book review of: Miller, E. J. and Rice, A. K., *Systems of Organization*, Tavistock Publications, London, 1967. *In: American Journal of Sociology*, 74, 207–209.

Seekings, J. (1968), comment on: Miller, E. J. and Rice, A. K. *Systems of Organization*, Tavistock Publications, London, 1967. *In: Aeroplane*, February 21st, p. 27.

Silverman, D. (1968), book review of: Miller, E. J. and Rice, A. K., *Systems of Organization*, Tavistock Publications, London, 1967. *In: British Journal of Industrial Relations*, 6, 393–397.

Silverman, D. (1970), *The Theory of Organisations*, Heinemann, London.

Sofer, C. (1961), *The Organisation from Within*, Tavistock Publications, London.

PART I

Organization and the Individual

Introduction to Part I

> *'An individual has ... no meaning except in relation to others with whom he interacts. He uses them, and they him, to express views, take action, and play roles. The individual is a creature of the group, the group of the individual'. (Miller and Rice, 1967, p. 17)*

> *'All institutions provide mechanisms at both conscious and unconscious levels for the satisfaction of human need and for defence against anxiety.' (Rice, 1965, p. 17)*

Many of the papers in this volume are devoted to what Rice called 'organizational model-building' (Rice, 1963, pp. 196 ff). The term 'organization' here refers to 'the patterning of activities through which the primary task of the enterprise is performed' (Miller and Rice, 1967, p. 33). Exercises in model-building explore the consequences of differing definitions of the task of an enterprise and the characteristics of the systems of activity required for performance of the defined task. For any given definition, alternative models may be constructed (Miller, 1959; Trist and coworkers, 1963). Models make it possible to predict the effects, functional and dysfunctional, of drawing organizational boundaries in different ways. To take a simple example, Rice predicts what will happen if the two roles of purchasing (an operating system) and financial control (a regulatory system) are assigned to one person in a manufacturing unit. This, he says,

'Can easily lead to a mutually recriminating circular process. An attack by Sales on the quality of the products—an almost inevitable, if understandable, conflict in a normal industrial enterprise–leads to an attack by Manufacturing on both quantity and quality of raw materials. This can be followed by virulent criticism of sales overheads or manufacturing costs by the Accounts department'. (Rice, 1963, p. 217)

This vignette illustrates three very familiar aspects of organizational life. First, for effective task performance conflict is necessary and appropriate. As Rice indicates, for example, the solutions that are best from the manufacturing viewpoint may pose difficulties for sales, and vice versa, so that conflict between them is constructive in relation to the overall task inasmuch as it leads to an optimum solution for the company as a whole. The solution will not be stable, because of changes both outside and inside: to that extent conflict and re-optimization have to be a continuous process. Positive conflict, however—and this is the second point—also requires each of the parties concerned (in this case Sales, for example) to examine how far a deteriorating position is attributable to his own performance and capable of correction by him. It is easier to try to dump the problem onto someone else (in this case Manufacturing). He, in order to avoid looking at the reality, seeks another scapegoat (Purchasing). The third aspect then is establishment of a collusive system (by allowing the Purchasing man to sidestep into his Accounting role), which has the function of letting the participants avoid the difficulty of examining their own competence, but at the same time eliminates the constructive conflict that might raise the level of performance in the system as a whole.

Here the organization is used to provide defensive mechanisms against anxieties generated by its own task. The salesman's experience of being squeezed between company pressures and market pressure is a straightforward example. In other cases the requirements of the task resonate with deep-seated anxieties within the individual. The classic paper by Menzies (1960) demonstrates that the task of nurses evokes primitive and painful feelings about dependency and death, with the result that the organization is used to provide institutionalized defences against these feelings at the expense of task performance (see also Miller and Gwynne, 1972). Less effective performance of the task itself heightens anxiety and so reinforces the need for defensive structures. But the second quotation from Rice (1965) at the beginning of this Introduction makes a more general proposition. Apart from anxieties that may be aroused by the specific task and form of organization, individuals need and use social systems as a means of maintaining their identity and protecting themselves against intolerable internal conflict. At the same time, the price of protection is distortion of individuality.

Therefore, before we consider the building of organizational models for task performance, it is appropriate to take a more prolonged look at some of these underlying transactions between the organization and the individual. By what processes does the individual shape the organization to meet his needs and, correspondingly, do shared assumptions about the organization mould the behaviour of the individual?

It could be argued that this question is unanswerable, on the grounds that certain aspects of behaviour are unconsciously motivated and therefore inaccessible to explanation. However, the fact that electrons cannot explain to us the basis of their apparently erratic behaviour does not prevent physicists from developing useful theories to explain it. Indeed, it is the absence of plausible alternative explanations for some behaviour that makes it necessary to postulate an unconscious.

Concepts that link individual and group behaviour and that also take unconscious elements into account have been sparse. The object-relations theory of psychoanalysis (cf. Klein, 1959) has provided a useful starting point. It offers the fruitful notion of the individual's internal world being populated by a set of objects and part-objects which are inner representations of his early experience of relationships with others. Klein postulates that the infant is initially unable to distinguish between what is outside and what is inside, between the inherent characteristics of an external object and his own internal feelings about it. His feelings are attributed to the object, or projected onto it; and to cope with the dilemma that the same object—for example, the mother's breast—is at one time satisfying and 'good' and at another time frustrating and 'bad', the infant resorts to splitting: he internalizes two separate representations of the same object, the one good, the other bad. As he develops he acquires a boundary—an ego-function—which enables him to become progressively more capable of discriminating between outside and inside, reality and fantasy, and of managing the relation between them. It nevertheless remains difficult to cling to the mature view that the same object may indeed be partly satisfying and partly frustrating. Primitive processes of splitting and projection recur. Thus an adult encountering a person in an authority position may respond not simply to the realities of what the other says and does, but also to a long-persisting internal representation of authority, which may be benign and dependable or punitive and dangerous.

Bion (1961) built partly on Klein in his contribution to the understanding of small-group behaviour. His postulate is that man, as a group animal, is on the one hand motivated to work, in the sense of engaging with the task, thinking, learning, maturing; but on the other hand is suffused with primitive emotional states, related for example to responsiveness to danger and needs for dependency. At any one time, members of a group collaborate at two levels: at a sophisticated level to work on the task, and at a 'basic assumption' level to share in a particular emotional state of which they are not conscious. Often the basic assumption is functional for task performance, in that it serves to keep at bay (in a postulated 'protomental system') emotions that are inappropriate to the work; at other times, group members go into collusion at a basic assumption level to resist the task.

Both Klein and Bion highlight the struggle for individuation. The rational, mature aspects of individuality have constantly to be asserted against a potential alliance between primitive emotions within oneself and external group pressures. This is a view of man that fitted comfortably with Rice's open system thinking. The same model, of an inner world, an external environment and a leadership as a boundary function mediating between them, could be applied to the individual, the small group and the large group. The individual indeed could be seen in a sense as a 'group', made up of internal objects and part-objects in a dynamic relation with each other, with the ego taking the leadership role. To quote Rice:

'By organisation is meant a set of administrative arrangements to cope with a given task. In this sense individuals and groups have "organisations" which may be more or less disorganised' (Rice, 1965, p. 15)

Rice developed this thinking most fully in 'Individual, Group and Intergroup Processes', the paper that follows. The individual is conceived as 'a multiple-task enterprise' who has to exercise 'management control' in order both to mobilize the internal resources that are relevant to performing his role as a member of a particular task group, and also to regulate those attributes and emotions that are irrelevant or inimical to task performance.

Rice's paper provides a theoretical framework that illuminates processes that occur within and between groups. The connections he makes can be tested against experience. Indeed, here, as in much of Rice's other writings, the reader is implicitly invited to look at these phenomena not simply as a distanced observer but in the light of his own direct experience of struggling to be a self-managing individual in his own groups and organizations.

In the training conferences that Rice helped to develop this has been the explicit message. They are about learning by experience. In his book on the conferences, Rice refers to the distinction made by William James between 'knowing about' and 'knowledge-of-acquaintance' (Rice, 1965, pp. 23–24). The former type of knowledge—erudition—is appropriate where the subject under study is, or is generally perceived to be, independent of the characteristics of the observer. It can be transmitted through words and symbols which will be widely understood in the same way. There are limitations on trying to transmit knowledge about human behaviour as if it were an extraneous, objective entity; and they are very similar to the limitations that Copernicus discovered when he tried to communicate an understanding of what might seem to be a very extraneous relationship, between Earth and Sun. Certain theories, such as Freud's or Skinner's, are accepted or rejected not on the basis of their explanatory or predictive merits, but on the view of man that they imply in relation to pre-existing value systems of groups and individuals. Learning by experience—acquiring knowledge-of-acquaintance—starts with oneself. The conference setting provides a variety of phenomena to be observed, experienced and examined. The conference member is working at the task when he is struggling to understand, in the light of the role he has, the relationship between what is happening around him and what is happening inside. Other people may offer their views of the situation; the responsibility and authority for forming his own view rests with him. He is learning when he catches a glimpse of the way in which the unique patterning of his own internal world is affecting his perception of the phenomena.

It is because learning is defined in this way that the question keeps arising as to whether the aims of the conferences are educational, as they purport to be, or therapeutic. Indeed, in *Learning for Leadership* Rice found it necessary to devote a chapter to this theme (Rice, 1965, Chap. 12). Yet the dichotomy itself is an artefact of the structure of contemporary thought. It is almost as if introspection is legitimate only if one first shows symptoms of mental illness. It is worth bearing in mind that these conferences merely follow a precept that is at least 2500 years old: 'Know thyself'. As a prerequisite of knowing more about the roles and relationships in which I am involved, and about managing myself in them, I have to learn more about me. And inasmuch as these conferences focus on authority relationships, which are crucial in organizational life, I need to learn how far in my relationships I am responding to what the other person is actually saying and doing and how far I am superimposing between us primitive images of a benign or punitive authority that belong to my own internal world. The fact that this is also often a painful process may also contribute to its being defined as a therapeutic activity.

The paper by Astrachan and Flynn takes one type of event in these conferences—the intergroup exercise—and traces links between the structure and process of the event on the one hand and typical problems in external institutions.

They are delineating areas in which participants might be expected to learn something that they can apply to their own jobs.

The intergroup event provides a useful laboratory in which some of the propositions in Rice's paper can be demonstrated. For example, Rice postulates that

'the effectiveness of every inter-group relationship is determined, so far as its overt purposes are concerned, by the extent to which the groups involved have to defend themselves against uncertainty about the integrity of their boundaries' (p. 25).

with the corollary that

'the making of any intergroup relationship carries with it the possibility of a breakdown in authority, the threat of chaos and the fear of disaster' (p. 26).

Astrachan and Flynn's description of 'the mad dash' from the room at the opening of the event and the influence of that on the formation and subsequent behaviour of groups supplies evidence in support of Rice's proposition. But it is support at the level of 'knowledge about'. As the authors imply, 'knowledge-of-acquaintance' occurs only when the participant recognizes and acknowledges his own moments of panic during the mad dash and tries to relate this to his own on-going behaviour: he is then engaging in 'the process of struggling with the experience in order to continue the learning over time'.

It is perhaps worth noting here that as more of the members arrive at these conferences with 'knowledge about' them that they have read and heard, the excitement of observing phenomena that they have been led to expect may become a substitute for actually experiencing the phenomena themselves. If the staff are to fulfil their task of providing members with opportunities to learn, as distinct from meeting members' expectations, they have to keep the design and conduct of events under constant review. At the same time there has been a tendency in the last few years, as this approach to training has proliferated in Britain, the United States and elsewhere, for the form to become ossified and ritualized, as evidenced in such phrases as 'the Tavistock model', 'the Rice model', 'the Bion group', with corresponding stereotypes of how a 'Tavistock consultant' is supposed to behave. Thus I find myself wanting to emphasize that the two structures that Astrachan and Flynn describe are inevitably only illustrative of an approach, not a definitive statement of method. The definitive statement would be a contradiction of what the conferences stand for, which is the continuing struggle to examine the problems of being an individual and a member of an organization.

Kahn's paper, 'Individual and corporation: the problem of responsibility', is also precisely in this area. In discussing the perversion of individual respons-ibility by the enterprise and the individual's collusion in this process, he cites Milgram's experiments, which are perhaps not so well known as they should be precisely because their findings are so disturbing—that there is an Eichmann in most of us. A majority of us will conform to an organizational definition of 'responsibility' even though we are aware that this violates our personal values

24

and that it may involve inflicting pain on another human being. Whereas in the conferences that Astrachan and Flynn describe, it is the individual who is being asked to reconsider what he is doing to others and what others are doing to him in discharging his own role, and to do something about it, Kahn is primarily urging the corporation to take the initiative in bringing about change. He argues that although some experiments—Rice's in India among them—have demonstrated 'that it is possible to create organizational forms in which the meeting of role requirements will be more congruent with personal growth and responsibility' (p. 79), these have been limited and circumscribed. Many assumptions about corporate organization remain largely unquestioned, including the basic hierarchical principle, which fuses status, prestige, power and material rewards.

One cannot but agree with Kahn's conclusion that radical experimentation is required in order to find forms of organization for task performance that provide a better fit with human capacities and needs, and in particular with a conception of man as a self-managing animal.

References

Bion, W. (1961), *Experiences in Groups*, Tavistock Publications, London.
Klein, M. (1959), Our adult world and its roots in infancy, *Human Relations*, **12**, 291–303.
Menzies, I. E. P. (1960), A case-study in the functioning of social systems as a defence against anxiety, *Human Relations*, **13**, 95–121.
Miller, E. J. (1959), Technology, territory and time: the internal differentiation of complex production systems. *Human Relations* **12**, 243–272.
Miller, E. J. and Gwynne, G. V. (1972), *A Life Apart*, Tavistock Publications, London.
Miller, E. J. and Rice, A. K. (1967), *Systems of Organization*, Tavistock Publications, London.
Rice, A. K. (1963), *The Enterprise and its Environment*, Tavistock Publications, London.
Rice, A. K. (1965), *Learning for Leadership*, Tavistock Publications, London.
Trist, E. L., Higgin G. W., Murray, H. and Pollock, A. B. (1963), *Organizational Choice*, Tavistock Publications, London.

Individual, Group and Intergroup Processes*

A. K. Rice

This paper is an attempt to apply to individual and group behaviour a system theory of organization, normally used for the analysis of enterprise processes. The use of such a theory will inevitably concentrate on the more mechanistic aspects of human relationships, but I hope that the approach will help to clarify some of the differences and similarities between individual, group and intergroup behaviour and throw some light on the nature of authority.

To perform a task, activities must be carried out. But however automated their processes, enterprises have to employ human resources for some activities. Such activities seldom, if ever, use the total capacities of the individuals so employed and individuals can seldom, if ever, give to an enterprise only the capacities it requires. If an enterprise fails to provide outlets for the unused capacities, they are likely to interfere with task performance. But to provide them it has to use resources that could otherwise be used for task performance or could be dispensed with. The provision of such outlets inevitably, therefore, reduces the efficiency of task performance, measured as the difference between intakes and outputs. I hope that the application of a system theory of organization to human behaviour will, therefore, not only help to clarify that behaviour, but may also enrich the theory itself and, in time, thus enable enterprises to make better use of their human resources.

I have another minor aim: to try to find concepts and language that can be applied both to institutional processes and to human behaviour. Psychologists and psychiatrists have enormously enlarged our understanding of individual and group behaviour, and anthropologists and sociologists of institutional behaviour, but when we try to use their insights to gain understanding of enterprise organization and institutional processes we are frequently faced with the difficulty of marrying different theoretical frameworks and different languages. The problem is to raise the level of conceptual abstraction; the danger that in so doing we shall not only lose the simplicity and richness of existing descriptive concepts, but lose also ourselves in an arid complexity of irrelevant variables.

My basic propositions are that:

(1) The effectiveness of every intergroup relationship is determined, so far as its overt purposes are concerned, by the extent to which the groups involved have to defend themselves against uncertainty about the integrity of their boundaries,

(2) Every relationship—between individuals, within small groups and within

*Reprinted from *Human Relations*, **22**, No. 6, pp. 565–584.

large groups as well as between groups—has the characteristics of an intergroup relationship.

A corollary to the first proposition is that the making of any intergroup relationship carries with it the possibility of a breakdown in authority, the threat of chaos and the fear of disaster.

In addition to a system theory of organization, I shall also use concepts derived from the object-relations theories of psychoanalysis, and I hope the findings will be consistent with the work of Bion on the nature of small group behaviour (Bion, 1961).

The first part of the paper summarizes briefly the relevant concepts of enterprise and institutional organization. Subsequent parts then apply these concepts to individual behaviour, to group and intergroup relations, and to the role of leadership.

A System Theory of Organization

The Enterprise as an Open System

The theory treats any enterprise or institution, or a part of any enterprise or institution, as an open system. Such a system must exchange materials with its environment in order to survive. The difference between what it imports and what it exports is a measure of the conversion activities of the system. Thus a manufacturing company imports raw materials, converts them and exports finished products (and waste). For the outputs it receives a pay-off, from which it acquires more intakes. The intakes into a university, on the other hand, are students; and the outputs graduates (and failures).

Such intakes and outputs are the results of import-conversion-export processes that differentiate enterprises from each other. But every enterprise has many import-conversion-export processes; a manufacturing company, for example, recruits employees, assigns them to jobs and sooner or later exports them through retirement, resignation, dismissal or death. It imports and consumes power and stores; it collects data about markets, competitors and suppliers' performance and converts the data into plans, designs and decisions about products and prices.

The nature of the many processes and their intakes and outputs reveal the variety of relationships that an enterprise, or part of it, makes with different parts of its environment and within itself, between its different parts. The processes also reveal the variety of tasks that the enterprise performs as a whole and the contributions of its different parts to the whole.

Every enterprise, or part enterprise, has, however, at any given time a primary task—the task it must perform to survive.[1] The dominant import-conversion-export process is that process by which the primary task is performed. It is this dominant process that defines the essential relationship of an enterprise to its environment, and to which other tasks and other throughputs are subordinate.

Boundary Controls

A *system of activities* is that complex of activities which is required to complete the process of transforming an intake into an output. A *task system* is a system of activities plus the human and physical resources required to perform the activities. The term 'system', as it is used here, implies that each component activity of the system is interdependent with at least some of the other activities of the same system, and that the system as a whole is identifiable as being in certain, if limited, respects independent of related systems. Thus a system has a boundary which separates it from its environment. Intakes cross this boundary and are subjected to conversion processes within it. The work done by the system is, therefore, at least potentially measurable by the difference between its intakes and outputs.

What distinguishes a system from an aggregate of activities is the existence of regulation. Regulation relates activities to throughput, ordering them in such a way as to ensure that the process is accomplished, that the different import-conversion—export processes of the system are related to each other and that the system as a whole is related to its environment.

The most important *management* control in any organization is, therefore, the control of the boundaries of systems of activity, since it is only at boundaries that the difference between intake and output can be measured. Task management then is essentially:

(1) The definition of boundaries between task systems
(2) The control of transactions across boundaries.

The boundary of a system of activities, therefore, implies both a discontinuity of activity and the interpolation of a region of control. The location of the boundary control function is shown in Figure 1.

Those systems of activity that lie on the main stream of the dominant import-conversion-export process by which the primary task is performed are the operating systems. Where, in any enterprise, there is more than one operating system, a differentiated managing system is required to control, co-ordinate and service the activities of the different operating systems. This will include the management of the total system, management of each discrete operating system, and also those non-operating systems that do not perform directly any part of the primary task, of the whole, but which provide controls over, and services to,

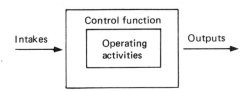

Figure 1. A task system and its boundary control function

the operating systems. An enterprise with three first order operating systems, three control and service functions in the first order managing systems, two second order operating systems, and two second order control and service functions is shown in Figure 2. In it, to avoid complexity the topological form of Figure 1 has been simplified by locating the boundary control region at one point on the boundary of the operating system viz:

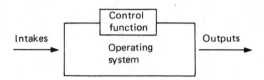

Members of an enterprise occupy roles in these various systems of activity. One member may take more than one role; and one role may be taken by more than one member. In assigning activities to roles and roles to people, the enterprise cannot always predetermine the role-sets that will emerge or the relative *sentience* of the various groups to which each individual will belong. These factors are, nevertheless, relevant to the effectiveness of task performance, supporting or opposing it.

Management of an enterprise requires therefore three kinds of boundary control:

(1) Regulation of task system boundaries (i.e. regulation of the whole enterprise as an import-conversion-export system, and regulation of constituent systems of activity);

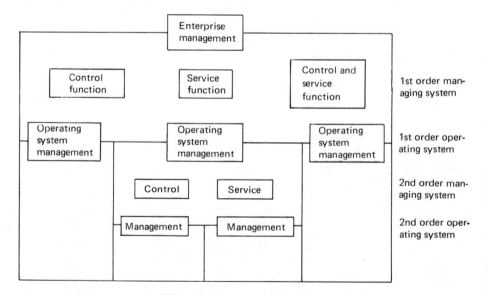

Figure 2. Organizational model

(2) Regulation of sentient system boundaries (the boundaries of the group to which individuals belong, either directly through their roles in systems of activity or indirectly through their consequential role-sets and personal relationships);

(3) Regulation of the relation between task and sentient systems.

Organization Models

Organization is the instrument through which an enterprise assigns activities to roles and roles to individuals and groups. Organization is thus a means to an end and the most appropriate organization is the one that best fits primary task performance. It follows that for every task an organizational model is required, which will define the boundaries of operating systems and the control and service functions that are required to co-ordinate, control and service the operating systems. Such definitions of the boundaries of the systems will determine the roles and role-relationships that provide for effective performance.

In building an organizational model, the starting point is the process flow. The dominant process identifies the nature of the intakes, the activities required to convert these into, and dispose of, outputs, and the human and physical resources required to provide or to facilitate these activities. The next step is to discover the discontinuities in a process that mark the boundaries of systems of activity. These are the appropriate points at which to draw organizational boundaries and these in their turn define management commands.

Since the performance of any task is subject to complex constraints, the actual organization of the enterprise will inevitably be a compromise between the model and the constraints. In the same way, since each part of any enterprise has its own primary task and thus requires an organizational model for itself, the organization for the whole will be constrained by the need to integrate the organizations of the parts, and the organizations of the parts will be constrained by the need to fit into the whole. The model provides a basis against which to examine the reality of the constraints and the consequent compromises.

To the three boundary controls given above, therefore, must be added the regulation of organizational boundaries where these, because of unalterable constraints, do not coincide with boundaries of activity systems.

Task, organizational and sentient boundaries may coincide. Indeed they must coincide to some extent at the boundary of the enterprise if it is to continue to exist. The enterprise may also be differentiated into parts which are similarly defined by coinciding boundaries. There are dangers in such coincidence. One danger is that members of a group may so invest in their identity as a group that they will defend an obsolescent task-system from which they derive membership. One can add the possibility that the identification of change in task-system boundaries, and even the identification of the boundaries themselves, can be made difficult by the existence of group boundaries that are strongly defended.

In general, it can be said that without adequate boundary definitions for activity systems and sentient groups, organizational boundaries are difficult to define and frontier skirmishing is inevitable. It is perhaps a major paradox of modern complex enterprises that the more certainly boundaries can be located, the more easily formal communications systems can be established. Unless a boundary is adequately located, different people will draw it in different places and hence there will be confusion between inside and outside. In the individual this confusion leads to breakdown, in enterprises to inefficiency and failure.

Because an enterprise is an open system, the nature of the constraints within which it operates is constantly changing. Internally, a change in technology may remove old constraints and introduce new ones. Externally, changes may range from a minor statutory requirement to a major shift in definition of the primary task. Such changes, even if they do not demand a redefinition of the primary task of the whole, frequently redefine the primary tasks of parts and modify the strategies through which an enterprise relates its internal and external environments so as to achieve the most effective performance of its primary task. Changes in strategy may not always be explicit; they may be merely reflected in changes in the behaviour of the enterprise. Different forms of organization differ in their capacity to respond and adapt to changes in strategy. Strategic changes, whether or not they are explicit, and even if they do not entail a redefinition of the primary task, may require changes in the form of organization if this is to retain its effectiveness.

Multiple Task Systems

A simplified form of a multiple task system is shown in Figure 3. Theoretically, two tasks, and thus two systems of activity can be identified, but those who perform the tasks—the human resources of the two systems—constitute a single and identical sentient group. Thus the strength of the sentient boundary of the group is affected by what happens in both activity systems, and, by way of the common sentient group, the activities of each task system are affected by those of the other. Involvement of a group in two activity systems may require the coexistence of two different arrays of roles and role relationships that may relate the individual members together in different ways.

System conflict does not arise in conditions of stable equilibrium—in other words, where environmental forces are unchanging or do not impinge too differentially on the three systems. For example, primitive societies often seem to have had relatively closed system characteristics over a long time. A stable equilibrium was established between the different systems of activity in which the tribal group engaged. But in contemporary society with its increasingly rapid social and technological change, disequilibrium is common.

Family businesses provide many examples of disequilibrium because of the differential pressures on the different systems of activity: those pertinent to the family, as a family, and those pertinent to the business as a business. In the kind of business that requires increasing capital to maintain parity with competitors,

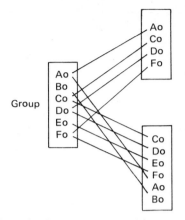

Figure 3. One group—two task systems

it is difficult for any but the most wealthy family to provide enough to maintain control. If, in addition, the business requires increasing numbers of technicians, scientists and managers, to handle the more sophisticated technologies of production, marketing and control, it is unusual for one family to be able to provide them all. As others outside the family are introduced into positions of power in the business task system, they tend to usurp the expected roles of family members, and thus distort role relationships in the family system.

In conditions of social and technical change, the attitudes and behaviour of members of a group to each other, and to the external environment may not only jeopardize the survival of the task systems but put such strain on internal group relationships that group survival is also jeopardized.

Temporary and Transitional Task Systems

By definition temporary and transitional task systems require temporary and transitional organizations (for convenience called *project organizations*). The essential feature of a project type of organization is that the group brought together to perform a particular task is disbanded as soon as the task is completed. The group as a group has no further *raison d'être* in terms of task performance. But the theoretically finite life of a project team is frequently prolonged either as a result of a redefinition of its task or of the accretion of new tasks. A research team, for example, either because it has invented a new technique or because its members have become devoted to working together, generates further problems to which it can apply its technique, or which will keep the team intact—irrespective of whether the generated problems are relevant to the overall task of the research enterprise of which they are a part.

But project groups cannot by definition provide either permanent sentience or career patterns for their members. Or if they do, they become difficult to disband at the conclusion of task performance. A successful project type

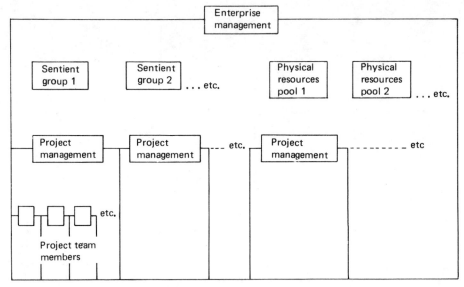

Figure 4. General form of project organization

organization requires, therefore, control and service functions in the managing system:

(1) To ensure that adequate resources, both human and physical, are available for every project undertaken;

(2) To provide sentient groups to which members can commit themselves and to which they can return for reallocation at the conclusion of each project;

(3) To provide pools in which physical resources can be stored and maintained.

The general form of organization is illustrated in Figure 4. In a small enterprise, the total enterprise can be the only sentient system required. But a large and complex enterprise can seldom provide sufficient personal identity, and separate differentiated systems are then essential.

Transactional Task Systems

By definition, a transaction between an enterprise and its environment must take place across the boundary of the enterprise. The activities of the transaction involve those parts of the enterprise and of its environment through which the transaction is made. The task system of the transaction, however temporary, therefore has a boundary which cuts across enterprise boundaries, a boundary that in any genuine two-way transaction cannot be fully controlled by the enterprise. Moreover if the enterprise is large, not all of its members can take part in the transaction and one or more have to 'represent' the enterprise.

This condition inevitably involves the control of boundaries between the enterprise and its representative or representatives.

A simple example is illustrated in Figure 5. It represents a transaction between two enterprises A and B; 'a' conducting the transaction on behalf of A, and 'b', on behalf of B. For the duration of the transaction, the task system (ab) boundary cuts across the enterprise boundaries of both A and B. So far as there is any uncertainty in A, B, a, b or ab about the relative strengths of the A, B, a, b or ab boundaries so will there be doubts about control of transactions across the boundaries between A and a, B and b and a and b. Control of the ab boundary must be sufficiently strong to perform the task of transaction, and yet, if it becomes too strong it jeopardizes control of the Aa and the Bb boundaries, and hence the integrity of the A and B boundaries. Any uncertainty can be exacerbated when either a or b consists of more than one individual. Then not only may there be uncertainty about the Aa and Bb boundary but the intragroup relations of 'a' and 'b' may also cause anxiety.

Examples of difficulty are common. If 'a' is a sales representative of a supplier A and 'b' the buyer of customer B, the management of A will require its representative 'a' to make good relationships with 'b' and, at the same time, to remain loyal to A. A representative who is suspected of favouring 'b' at the expense of A does not usually last long. Similarly a buyer who is believed to use the ab relationships for his own benefit rather than for the benefit of B gets short shrift as soon as he is caught. In the same way, negotiations between groups acting on behalf of institutions, or even nations, may not only create uncertainty about control of the boundaries of the institutions they represent, but different opinions between the delegates of the negotiating groups about the task they are engaged on can threaten the whole transaction.

Some transactions by their nature give power and privilege to one party to the transaction. Most such transactions are governed by social and even legal sanctions. If A in Figure 5 represents the medical profession and 'a' a member of it, B the community and 'b' a patient, very strict rules with legal backing govern the nature of the transactions and the role relationships within the task system boundary. Other professions have equally strict rules.

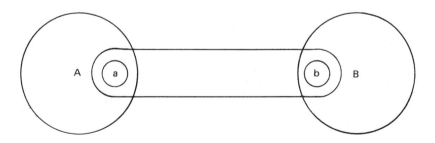

Figure 5. Simple transactional task system

But even in those transactions in which no recognized professions are involved, the (ab) boundary (of the transactional task system) is usually 'controlled by cultural conventions to which both A and B subscribe. In the absence of such conventions, or without acceptance of recognized conventions, much time and effort has to be spent in establishing rules of procedure before performance of the real transaction can start.

More generally, any transaction between an enterprise and its environment introduces some uncertainty into the relative strengths of the boundaries of the enterprise, the environment and the transactional task system. If chaos is defined as uncertainty about boundary definition, or more colloquially, as not knowing who, or what belongs where, then every transaction is potentially chaotic. If we go further and suggest that the major characteristic of disaster is the obliteration of known boundaries (of the guides and directories which govern existence), then every transaction can be said to have built into it the elements of incipient disaster. The doctor who has sexual intercourse with his patient, that is, who allows personal relationships in the task system boundary to obliterate the boundary of the medical profession to which he belongs is, in reality, courting disaster.

The transactional task system is temporary and transitional. When the task has been performed it should be discontinued. If it is prolonged beyond task completion, it uses resources unnecessarily. By so doing it must reduce the efficiency of task performance. It requires therefore a project type organization which may or may not be renewed.[2] At the end of the transaction 'a' is once more enclosed in A; and 'b' in B. But whatever the outcome of the transaction, the relationships of 'a' to other parts of A and to the whole A (and of 'b' to B) are likely to have changed. And it is at this stage that any disagreements within 'a' (or 'b') are likely to affect the formation of future 'project teams' for transactional tasks.

The general point is that, in terms of its transactions with the environment, an enterprise is a multi-task system, forming and disbanding temporary project teams (of one or more) for task performance. For the duration of the transaction a project team operates with the authority of the enterprise. Every transaction tests the integrity of the boundaries of the enterprise and the project team and the control that the enterprise can exercise over its own project team; that is, over the extent to which the project team acts with less, equal or more authority than it has been given. The outcome of every transaction can thus change the nature and strength of the controls.

The common defences against uncertainty of control are the precise definition of terms of reference for the 'project team' and the prescription of rules and procedures for dealing with any unforeseen or unplanned activities in the transaction. But the defences, by adding constraints to the transactional task system, must put limits on performance.

The Individual

The theories of human behaviour and of human relationships are in many ways analogous to those of system theory as applied to institutions. Like an institution, an individual may be seen as an open system. He exists and can exist only through processes of exchange with his environment. Individuals, however, have the capacity to mobilize themselves at different times and simultaneously into many different kinds of activity system, and only some of their activities are relevant to the performance of any particular task.

The personality of the individual is made up of his biological inheritance, his learned skill and the experiences through which he passes, particularly those of early infancy and childhood. A baby is dependent on one person—his mother. He gradually assimilates into his patterns of relationships his father and any brothers and sisters. As he grows into childhood he includes other members of his extended family and of the family network. The first break with this pattern is usually made when the child goes to school and encounters for the first time an institution to which he has to contribute as a member of a wider society. It is his preliminary experience of what, in later years, will be a working environment.

The hopes and fears that govern the individual's expectations of how he will be treated by others, and the beliefs and attitudes on which he bases his code of conduct derive from these relationships and are built into the pattern that becomes his personality. They form part of his internal world. Besides the skills and capabilities he develops, this contains his primitive inborn impulses and the primitive controls over them that derive from his earliest relations with authority, together with the modifications and adaptations he incorporates as he grows up.

In the mature individual, the ego-function mediates the relationships between the external and the internal worlds and thus takes in relation to the individual a 'leadership' role and exercises a 'management' control function. The mature ego is one that can differentiate between what is real in the outside world and what is projected on to it from 'inside', between what should be accepted and incorporated into experience and what should be rejected. In short the mature ego is one that can define the boundary between what is inside and what is outside and can control the transactions between the one and the other. Diagramatically the individual can be represented at any one time, therefore, as a system of activity. The ego-function is located in the boundary control region, checking and measuring intakes, controlling conversion activities and inspecting outputs. It uses the senses as instruments of the import system; thinking, feeling and other processes to convert the intakes; then action, speech or other means of expression to export the outputs.

But the individual is not just a single activity system with an easily defined primary task. He is a multi-task system and capable of multiple activities. The activities become bounded and controlled task systems when they are directed to the performance of a specific task, to the fulfilling of some specific purpose. The difficulty then is the control of internal boundaries and dealing with activities that are not relevant to task performance. And these controls are the result of the built-in attitudes and beliefs, born of previous experience, which may or may not be relevant to the specific task or system of activities required for its performance.

To take a role requires the carrying out of specific activities and the export of particular outputs. To take a role an individual could be said to set up a task system; and the task system to require the formation of a 'project team' composed of the relevant skill, experience, feelings and attitudes. Different roles demand the exercise of different skills and different outputs. The task of the ego-function is then to ensure that adequate resources are available to form the 'project' team for role performance, to control transactions with the environment so that intakes and outputs are appropriate, and to suppress or otherwise control irrelevant activities. When the role changes the 'project team' has to be disbanded and reformed.

The individual as a multiple task enterprise is shown in simplified form in Figure 6. Task systems I (t_1) and II (T_2) require the individual to take roles 1 and 2 (R_1 and R_2). R_1 and R_2 overlap to the extent that they use some, but not all, of the capabilities of the individual. The task systems are related to different but neighbouring parts of the environment. The management controls required will also therefore be similar, but not necessarily the same. In contrast, task system III (T_3) requires the individual to take role 3 (R_3). This requires quite different capabilities, is related to a quite different part of the environment, and hence requires a different kind of managerial control. In practice, such complete splits are not usual (except in the schizophrenic), but it is possible to recognize, on the one hand, those individuals who are always the same no matter what the situation is or with whom they are in contact; and, on the other, those who appear to be quite different people in different situations.

More generally we can say the ego-function has to exercise different kinds of authority and different kinds of leadership in different roles and in different situations. Dislike of the role and of the activities or behaviour required in it,

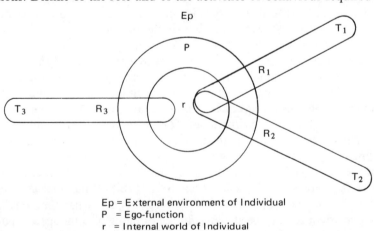

Ep = External environment of Individual
P = Ego-function
r = Internal world of Individual
T_1 etc. = Tasks
R_1 etc. Roles

Figure 6. The role system of the individual

and the demonstration of the dislike by attempts to change the role or modify the behaviour, or the intrusion of feelings or judgments that contradict role requirements, inevitably distort intakes, modify conversion processes, and can only result in inappropriate outputs. It is as though the management of a multiple task enterprise, with an organization such as that outlined in Figure 4, were to set up a project team for the solution of a particular problem but not only could not be sure whether the team was working on the right problem but could not even control membership of the team or the resources they used or squandered.

In effect, I wish to suggest that the general diagram of a project type organization, as shown in Figure 4 can be used, however crudely, to represent the individual as a role-taking but sentient being. In the individual, the sentient groups and resource pools of the enterprise become the repositories of the capacities of the individual to fill different roles. The resource pools hold the intellectual power, cognitive and motor skills, experience and other capabilities; the sentient groups the attitudes, beliefs and feelings—the world of objects and part-objects—resulting from up-bringing. In effect, because a role demands specific skills and the exercise of specific authority in a particular context it is unlikely to require every personal attribute of a given individual. Some attributes and some skills will always be unused by any given role. Maintaining a role over a long time leads therefore either to the atrophy of unused attributes, or to the need to find other means of expressing them.

I recognize, of course, that for human beings, the many import-conversion-export processes cannot be so easily defined as the previous paragraphs might suggest, and that 'productivity' is seldom a simple measure of the difference between known intakes and known outputs. I hope, however, that this way of thinking about an individual will help to clarify some of the problems of role-taking when we have to consider group and intergroup processes.

Before moving on to consider the group, however, I would like to use the concept of a transactional task system as an example of a pair relationship. When an individual takes a role and makes a relationship with his environment the parts of him that are 'used' are the equivalent of the representative team 'a' of Figure 5 acting on behalf of the whole A. If the other party to the transaction is another individual, then Figure 5 represents a transaction between project teams a and b on behalf of A and B. In the same way as for a transaction between two institutions, uncertainties about the relative strengths of A, B and ab boundaries can interfere with the effectiveness of the transaction, as, of course, can uncertainties about the 'a' and 'b' boundaries. In an 'ideal' pair relationship of the kind frequently imagined by the more romantic novelists, all parts of the personality are invested in the relationship and the A and 'a' and the B and 'b' boundaries coincide, and the ab boundary is the AB boundary. No relationships ever achieve such a romantic ideal, and the effectiveness of the pair relationship is frequently diminished by the relationships of other parts of A with 'a', with 'b' and with other parts of B as well as by the many other roles taken by A and B in relation to others.[3]

The ego-function has therefore to control not only transactions across the individual/environment boundary but also between role and person. When the ego-function fails to locate boundaries precisely and fails to control transactions across those boundaries, confusion is inevitable, confusion in roles and in the authorities exercised in roles. Authority and responsibility appropriate in one role are used inappropriately in other roles. To be continuously confused about the role/person boundaries or completely unable to define and maintain boundaries is to be mentally sick.

The Group

The internal world of the individual includes the objects and part-objects derived from the relationships he has made, particularly in his early life. His attitudes towards authority, both of his own and that of others, are conditioned by his earliest experiences of authority, usually that exercised by his parents. 'Individual' has, therefore, little meaning as a concept except in relationships with others. He uses them and they him, to express views, take action and play roles. The individual is a creature of the group, the group of the individual. Each, according to his capacity and experience, carries within him the groups of which he has been and is a member. His experiences as an infant, child, adolescent and adult within his family, at school and at work, and the cultural setting in which he has been brought up will thus affect, by the way in which they are moulded into his personality, the contemporary and future relationships he makes, in his family, his work and his social life.

A group always meets to do something. In this activity the members of the group co-operate with each other; and their co-operation calls on their knowledge, experience and skill. Because the task for which they have met is real, they have to relate themselves to reality to perform it. The members of the group have, therefore, to take roles and to make role relationships with each other. The work group is now a task system. It may or may not have very much sentience depending on the extent to which its members are committed to each other. Even as a sentient system it may, or may not, support task performance. Controls are then required:

(1) To regulate transactions of the whole, as a task system, with the environment and of the constituent systems with each other.
(2) To regulate sentient group boundaries.
(3) To regulate relationships between task and sentient groups.

But, in the discussion of the individual, I wrote that the role taken by each member of a group is also a 'task system' and the 'management' of each of these (the ego-function) has to control the relations between the 'task' and 'sentient' systems of the individual. So long as the role taken by each individual member is supported by that member's own individual 'sentient' system, so the task group and sentient group tend to coincide. But individual members may not be aware of all the elements either of their own individual or of total group sentience, even if such exists. To put this another way: task roles are unlikely to use all attributes of every member's personality; the unused portions may or may not support role- and hence group-task performance, but neither individual member nor group may be aware of the discrepancies between individual and group sentience or of changes over time.

More importantly, the unused attributes of individuals may themselves have such powerful sentience attached to them that they have to be expressed in some way. That is, an individual, though a member of a task group, may be unable to control those personal attributes that are not relevant to task performance and may seek other outlets for the emotions and feelings that the unused attributes and the inability to control them, gives rise to. This represents a breakdown in the 'management control' of the individual so far as role performance is concerned. Group task leadership may still so be able to control group sentience, as not only to overcome individual discrepancies but also to harness group emotions and feelings in favour of group task performance. The charismatic leader, for example, can be said to attract to himself as a person the unused sentience of group members and, since he is concerned with task performance, can thus control any group opposition to that performance. If task leadership cannot either harness group feelings in favour of task performance or contain opposing feelings by personal leadership, then other 'groups' consisting of some or all of the task group members may be formed to express opposing sentience. Such groups may seek and 'appoint' other 'leaders'. If the other 'group' gets support from all other members of the task system, however unaware they may be of this support (since individual management control has broken down), then the other 'group' can become more powerful than the task group.

Bion postulated that a group always behaves on two levels: the sophisticated level and the basic assumption level (Bion, 1961). He also postulated a proto-mental system in which the inoperative basic assumptions were held. He described three basic assumptions which determine group behaviour:

(1) Dependency : to obtain security from one individual;
(2) Fight/Flight : to attack or to run away from somebody or something;
(3) Pairing : to reproduce itself.

He suggested there may be others. He could not at the time define them. He showed that when the basic assumption was appropriate to task performance, the group culture was a powerful reinforcement to that performance, when it did not there was conflict of such an order that it could lead to task distortion or redefinition.

In the terms used here, Bion describes the situation in which the sentience of the roles taken by the members of a group in the task system may or may not be stronger than other possible sentient systems. If the sentient systems of the individual members coalesce, that is individual members find a common group sentience, then the group can be said to be behaving as if it had made a basic assumption. If the common group sentience is opposed to task performance, that is the control is not maintained by task leadership, other leaders will be found.

I now feel that Bion's concepts describe special cases which are most easily observable in small groups, because they are large enough to give recognizable power to an alternative leadership, and yet are not so large as to provide support for more than one kind of powerful alternative leadership at any one time. As Bion points out, the capacity for co-operation among the members of a task group is considerable; that is role sentience in a task group is always likely to be strong. Hence, while the group maintains task definition the strength of the sentience supporting task performance at the reality level makes the life of leadership opposing task performance precarious.

A pair who have met to perform an agreed task can hardly provide alternative leadership and remain a task system. With three, an alternative leader is rapidly manifest and either immediately outnumbered or at once destroys co-operation in task performance, i.e. the three cannot easily remain a task group. (Two is company, three is none.) A quartet can provide some support for alternative leadership by splitting into pairs, but cannot sustain the split for very long without destroying the quartet as a task system. In groups of five and six, the interpersonal transaction systems are still relatively few and task leadership can be quick to recognize alternative leadership, usually before it can manifest powerful opposition to task performance. Above six, the number of interpersonal transactions becomes progressively larger, and hence it may be more difficult to detect their patterning.

In general, the larger the number of members of a group there are, the more members there are to find an outlet for their non-task related sentience, and hence the more powerful can be its expression, and the more support can an alternative leader obtain. Equally, because of the large number, the more futile and useless can group behaviour appear when there is no sentient unanimity among the membership either in support of, or in opposition to, group task performance. In other words, the larger the group the more opportunities members have to divest themselves of their unwanted or irrelevant sentience, by projecting it into so many others.

But the individual is a multiple task enterprise, and his various sentient systems can be in conflict with each other. When he joins a group to perform a group task, he must by his very joining to some extent commit himself to take the role assigned to him, and hence to control irrelevant activities and sentience. Mature individuals thus find themselves distressed and guilty when in any attempt to reassert 'management control' over their own individual boundaries they recognize, however vaguely, the number of different hostages they have given to so many conflicting sentient groups.

The situation of the group can be roughly approximated symbolically:

Let the members of a group be: $I_1, I_2, I_3 \ldots$
Each is capable of taking many roles: $R_1, R_2, R_3 \ldots R_n$

Each role, in the way the term is used here, is a task system in itself. It comprises a number of specific activities together with the necessary resources for its performance. The resources should include not only the skills, but also the appropriate attitudes, beliefs and feelings derived from the individual's 'sentient' groups. But not all individuals are capable of taking all roles, and role performances by different individuals in the same role also differ.

If the role performance is represented by IR then:

$$I_1R_1 \neq I_2R_1 \neq I_3R_1 \ldots \text{etc.}$$

and

$$I_1R_1 \neq I_1R_2 \neq I_1R_3 \ldots \text{etc.}$$

Ideally a task system requires only activities and we could then write

$$T = f(R_1 + R_2 + R_3 \ldots R_n)$$
$$= f\Sigma(R) \ldots$$

But because roles are taken by individuals, we have to write

$$TP \text{ (task performance)} = f(I_1R_1 + I_2R_2 + \ldots + I_nR_n)$$
$$= f\Sigma(IR) \ldots \qquad (1)$$

assuming R_1 to be taken by I_1, R_2 by I_2 ... etc. But when an individual takes a specific role not all his aptitudes are likely to be used, and his performance in any specific role is likely to be reduced by the amount of 'energy' he devotes to other aptitudes and to other sentience. If we represent these other irrelevant activities and their related sentience by R°_1, $R^\circ_2 \ldots R^\circ_n$ then any given role performance R_1 by an individual I_1 will have to be written:

$$I_1R_1 - I_1(R^\circ_1 + R^\circ_2 \ldots R^\circ_n)$$

in which R°_1, R°_2, etc. can have zero, or positive values so far as they do not affect or oppose I_1R_1. (I assume that all task supporting sentience is included in R_1.) Equation (1) therefore has to be written:

$$TP = f[\Sigma(IR) - I_1(R^\circ_1 + R^\circ_2 + \ldots R^\circ_n) - I_2(R^\circ_1 + R^\circ_2 \ldots R^\circ_n)$$
$$\ldots - I_n(R^\circ_1 + R^\circ_2 + \ldots R^\circ_n)]$$
$$= f[\Sigma(IR) - \Sigma(IR^\circ)] \qquad (2)$$

Even if $\Sigma(IR^\circ) \neq 0$ and has a positive value it can still be small enough to be controlled either because of the discrepancy between the many different roles taken by the different I's or because the combinations of different numbers are themselves small. Nevertheless, the sentience invested in the R°'s can still produce such disagreements between I's that a sense of futility can grow as I's spend more time and energy trying to find agreement between themselves in roles irrelevant to TP than in R_1, R_2, etc. that are relevant. If overtly or covertly they all agree on a role that is irrelevant to TP (say R°_m) then equation (2) becomes:

$$TP = f\left[\Sigma(IR) - R^\circ_m \Sigma(I)\right] \qquad (3)$$

If equation (3) is written out more fully:

$$TP = f\left[(I_1R_1 + I_2R_2 + I_3R_3 + \ldots + I_nR_n) - R^\circ_m(I_1 + I_2 + I_3 + \ldots + I_n)\right] \quad (4)$$

It can be seen that because R°_m is taken by all group members it can become a considerable threat to TP which requires different members to take different roles. If R°_m is large enough and is a consciously agreed role, there is revolt; if members are both unaware of their agreement and of the role they have agreed upon, they are then behaving 'as if' they have made a basic assumption opposed to task performance.

It can also be seen that the more I's there are the greater the threat of $R^\circ_m(I_1 + I_2 \ldots I_n)$ but, at the same time, the more difficulty there is likely to be in getting agreement on R°_m. It can also be seen why, with small numbers, alternative leadership is difficult to sustain without immediate destruction of task performance. From equation (4) $TP = f\left[(I_1R_1 + I_2R_2) - R^\circ_m(I_1 + I_2)\right]$ for a pair. If now R°_m has a large value, and is reinforced by $I_1 + I_2$ it will almost certainly give TP a negative value.

Intergroup Process

I have tried to show that all transactions, even the intrapsychic transactions of the individual, have the characteristics of an intergroup process. As such they involve multiple problems of boundary control of different task systems and different sentient systems and control of relations between task and sentient systems. Each transaction calls into question the integrity of boundaries across which it takes place and the extent to which control over transactions across them can be maintained. Every transaction requires the exercise of authority and calls into question the value of and sanction for that authority.

In the examination of a simple intergroup transaction between two groups in which individuals represent the two groups (as in Figure 5), account has to be taken, therefore, of a complex pattern of intergroup processes: within the individuals who represent their groups, within the transactional task system, between the groups and their representatives, within the groups and within the environment that includes the two groups. Even a simple intergroup transaction is, therefore, affected by a complex pattern of authorities, many of which are either partially or completely covert. If I now extend the analysis to more than two groups and each with more than one representative, the pattern becomes still more complex. A meeting of pairs of representatives from four groups is illustrated in Figure 7. It will be seen that in the meeting of representatives alone transactions across 17 different pairs of boundaries have to be controlled: four pairs for each pair of representatives, and one pair for the group of representatives as a group.

To understand the nature of the authority of a representative, or of a group of representatives, appointed to carry out a transaction on behalf of a group, involves, therefore, the understanding of multiple and complex boundary

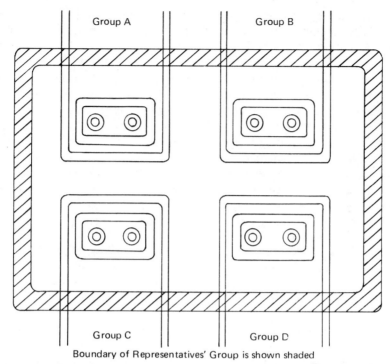

Boundary of Representatives' Group is shown shaded

Figure 7. Meeting of representatives' group—one pair from each of four groups

controls. In other words, the appointment of a representative or representatives is never just a simple matter of representing a task system to carry out a task-directed transaction with the environment. To put the same thing more colloquially: representatives are invariably chosen not only to carry out the specific transaction, but also to convey the mood of the group about itself and about its representative, and its attitude, not only to the specific part of the environment with which the transaction is intended, but to the rest of it as well. And not all the 'messages' are explicit and overt; many, if not most of them, are implicit and covert.

But the representative has his own intrapsychic processes, and his own intrapsychic 'group' has had to make 'intergroup' relations with the group he represents. The same mixture of transactions, overt and covert, have, or should have, taken place before he starts the intergroup transaction for which he has been appointed. The results of these transactions can seldom endow the representative with personal attributes that he did not previously possess, at least latently. The choice of representative(s) therefore offers important data, about the group attitude not only towards its task, but also towards itself and its environment. Further important data can be gathered from the extent to which the representative is given the authority to commit his group, and by his status within the group.

One further dimension of complexity has to be mentioned: time. I have spoken about the problems of the control of the representative's own boundaries, of the boundaries between the representative and his group and of the relative strengths of the individual, group and transactional task system boundaries. It is surely rare for them all to be perfectly controlled in the interests of task performance. Even if they are, a transaction takes time, and during the transaction the representative cannot be in continuous communication with the group he represents, not, that is, if he is anything more than a relay system. During the transaction the individual, group and task system sentiences may change. Indeed, in any critical negotiation they are almost bound to change, as hopes and fears of the outcome increase and decrease.

The past, during which decisions were made, attitudes formed and resources collected is always the past; a transaction is the present and if it is to have any meaning, must determine a future. Individuals and even groups with strongly defended boundaries can, by staying firmly within them, occasionally live in the past; intergroup relations never.

The number and complexity of the boundary controls required for even comparatively simple transactions between groups might make one wonder how any negotiation is ever successful, how any salesman ever got an order for anything. The reality is, of course, that the preponderance of intergroup transactions takes place in settings in which the conventions are already established and mutual pays-offs understood. Nevertheless, I suggest that it is this complex authority pattern, imperfectly understood and imperfectly comprehended, together with the need to defend each of the boundaries in the multiple transactional systems against uncertainty, chaos and incipient disaster, that give rise to the futility of so many negotiations and to the unexpected results that often emerge. The conventions and pay-offs for the majority of intergroup transactions are defences against chaos and disaster. In new kinds of negotiations without established defences, the fear of chaos and disaster often makes procedure more important than content.

There is perhaps small wonder that international negotiating institutions find it so difficult to satisfy the hopes of their creators. Indeed, unless the boundary of the negotiating group itself becomes stronger than the boundaries that join the representatives and those they represent, there seems little hope of successful negotiations. But this means that not only the group of representatives but the groups they represent, have to invest the representative task system with more sentience than they invest in their own groups. The United Nations cannot, in other words, be fully effective, until not only the members of its Council, but the nations they represent, invest more sentience in the United Nations than they do in their nationalisms.

The Role of Leadership

Finally, I turn to the role of leadership, which can be conceived of as a special case of representation: representation with plenipotentiary powers. Conceptually, it is irrelevant whether the role is taken by an individual or by a group. For convenience, I shall discuss it in terms of an individual leader.

As a member of a task group every individual has to take a role and through it control his task transactions with his colleagues individually and collectively; as a person he also has to control his own person/role transactions as well as his interpersonal relationships with his colleagues. In addition to these, a leader has to control transactions between the group and relevant agencies in the environment in the interests of task performance; without such control task performance is impossible. In this sense, the role taken by the leader and boundary control function of the group must have much sentience in common. For the leader, at least, sentient group and task group *must* reinforce each other. So far as task performance is unsatisfactory, either by reason of inadequate resources or of opposing group sentience, transactions with the environment are likely to be difficult and the task sentience of the leader weakened if not destroyed.

If I return to the notation I used earlier and let R^L represent the role of leader taken by an individual I then leadership task performance can be written:

$$TP = IR^L - I\,(R^\circ_1 + R^\circ_2 + R^\circ_3 + \ldots R^\circ_n)$$
$$= I\,(R^L - \Sigma R^\circ)$$

For the leader at least ΣR must be close to zero. What he has to provide is an IR model that is task oriented. The model, however, must be a credible one. A leader who puts all his energy into IR^L (with $\Sigma R^\circ = 0$) is hardly credible and gives no reinforcement to group members in controlling their own ego boundaries; on the other hand, a leader who puts too much energy into ΣR° encourages his followers to do the same and their $\Sigma(IR^\circ)$ may only temporarily take the same form as his with consequent detriment to task performance.

More generally, since transactions with the environment can only be based on adequate task performance, the leader's authority has to be based on sufficient group sentience that is supportive of such performance. It follows that the mobilization of group sentience for any other reason than task performance, for example personal loyalty, friendship or ideology, always leaves a task group vulnerable. It also follows that any change in the group task, by change either in the environment or in the group, changes not only the internal transactions between the members but also those with the environment, and hence the role of leadership and the appropriate sentience that has to be mobilized.

In practice, groups use all kinds of feelings and attitudes to maintain co-operation in task performance: love, affection, friendship, hatred, dislike and enmity as well as commitment to the group task. So far as a group is committed to its task, contrary sentience including the leadership's own can be contained and controlled within the group; so far as commitment is tenuous, so far will the group find it impossible to control the contrary sentience. Under such circumstances, task leadership is castrated, the task redefined or irrelevant transactions with the environment have to be used to cope with the discordant feeling and attitudes.

46

Notes

1. For a fuller description of this concept and the system theory of organization see Miller and Rice (1967), Rice (1958 and 1963).
2. In this conceptual framework the calls made by a sales representative are seen as separate 'projects', between calls he 'returns' to his sentient group within his company.
3. I am perhaps using 'role' in a rather limited sense in this context. I am ignoring for example the difference between overt and covert expectations, and between anticipated and realized interactions as elements of 'role' and role relationships.

References

Bion, W. R. (1961), *Experiences in Groups*, Tavistock Publications, London.
Miller, E. J. and Rice, A. K. (1967), *Systems of Organization*, Tavistock Publications, London.
Rice, A. K. (1958), *Productivity and Social Organization: the Ahmedabad Experiment*, Tavistock Publications, London.
Rice, A. K. (1963), *The Enterprise and its Environment*, Tavistock Publications, London.

The Intergroup Exercise: A Paradigm for Learning about the Development of Organizational Structure

Boris M. Astrachan and Hulda R. Flynn

Introduction

Man is born in a group, he lives in groups, works in them and finds pleasure and pain in them. Even when he is alone, man carries his groups with him (Bion, 1961; Etzioni, 1968; Rice 1969). Each group serves to help the individual define himself by insisting that he fill some role necessary for the group's functioning, that he adopt or at least give lip service to the group's attitudes, values and behaviours. In each important group to which the individual belongs (family, peer group, work group, political organization, sex, religion or racial groups, etc.) the individual begins to learn something about the ideals and behaviours that are expected of him, and to explore whether the conditions of membership are worth the cost. Each person discovers that there are some groups to which he may belong, some to which he *must* belong and some which will not have him. He learns that behaviours that are acceptable or even necessary for membership in one group may not be tolerated by another.

The challenges of multiple group membership with the attendant multiple demands on an individual's commitment and loyalty to group ideals may either confound a person or help him develop a sense of his own individuality. Paying the price of membership to one group (whether willingly or not) may effectively deny the individual entry into other groups. A person may belong to multiple groups which reinforce the values, ideals and behavioural expectations of one another (e.g. neighbourhood, church, political group and family values may reinforce one another). He may be inadvertently caught up in conflict between the diverse groups in which he has membership or he may even deliberately seek out such conflict in order to clarify for himself the conditions of his membership in the various groups to which he elects to belong. In this process the individual may be seeking to cope effectively with multiple realistic external demands or he may be searching out differing groups with diverse value systems in order to 'act out', without attempted synthesis or resolution, aspects of his internalized conflict.

Each individual carries within himself the potential for intergroup conflict and collaboration. In all intergroup activities, questions of divergent priorities and demands for loyalty are apparent. Multiple group demands on the individual must be handled by the individual. He may seek to affiliate himself with groups that have similar value systems; he may withdraw as much as possible from any group involvement; or he may define one group as having highest priority and then identify primarily with its values (e.g. a religious or political group) holding all other values secondary, even perhaps inferior. The individual also has the potential of defining his relationship to the multiple groups in which he is a member and, with obvious difficulty, to insist upon his ability to manage divergent loyalties, either by constantly regulating and reevaluating the priorities he will assign to the diverse claims on him, or by ignoring conflicting priorities and compartmentalizing (i.e. on six days a week I steal, on the seventh I pray).

Man, the group animal, organizes his activities and develops structures and institutions in which to live and work. Rice (1963) and others have addressed the ways in which organization serves task performance. But individual member wishes to maximize personal choice are often in conflict with needs to accomplish specific tasks and protect the rights of others (Dahl, 1970). It is repeatedly demonstrated in the intergroup exercises that we shall describe that individuals tend to develop incipient organizations in order to cope with the dilemma of being alone and of facing the difficulties of making choices without any clear directions as to how those choices are to be made. (For example, is there any *one* group available to me, that will have me and with which I can identify?) Without a structure the individual must confront his multiple group membership without any clear ideas as to how he should establish priorities. By developing an organizational structure, the individual can allow priorities to be established on what then is regarded as some 'rational' reason. The priorities of the organization are then seen as logically following from the definition of the organization's task.

Durkheim (1893, trans. 1964) over a half a century ago, focused on man's propensity for organizing himself into groups with other men. The division of labour in society serves not only task performance but perhaps even more importantly, unites men in interdependent ways to other men, defining their 'moral' obligations to one another. Individual and organizational energies can be freed for 'task' performance, if mechanisms can be found for ordering priorities, binding up conflicts and developing procedures to provide mutual guarantees for minority and majority groups. Organizations may develop political structures to carefully deal with the complex problem of priority allocation while providing some mix of attention to task performance and individual, group and intergroup needs; or magical solutions may be sought which seek to simplify, to limit choice, to avoid complexity by establishing a 'moral' order, to provide preestablished answers to even unanticipated questions. This wish to simplify, to develop structures which contain and constrain may lead to the development of organizations which may only poorly accomplish task while limiting group and individual choice.

Men, having organized themselves into groups, must then cope with their own internalized intergroups. (Have I made the right choice, does this group serve me best, would some other group serve me better, ought I leave, can I leave, etc?). In order to do work groups must mobilize the requisite skills and resources to accomplish task performance. They must also sufficiently commit skilled individuals to the goals of the group. When individual sentience[1] conflicts with group task, the potential exists that individuals will seek to gratify their important human needs elsewhere, ignoring or even interfering with group task performance.

The need for regulation of individual, group and intergroup activities if work is to be done, has been repeatedly described (Rice, 1963, 1969; Schaar, 1970; Zaleznik, 1970). Whether such regulation carefully attends to conflicting priorities and attempts to understand and manage these within the context of a continually changing and open system, or rigidly defines the manner in which priorities will be ordered depends upon the way in which the individual, group or organization understands and utilizes power, authority and leadership.

The intergroup exercises designed by the late A. K. Rice (1965) and his colleagues at the Tavistock Institute provide the participants with opportunities for learning through first-hand experience about the bases and processes of group formation as well as the development of group structure both to achieve goals and as a defence against the members' anxiety. The exercises provide an opportunity for observation of the development of authority relations both within groups and between groups and challenge the participants to examine their own and others' behaviour in the face of situations which present in microcosm individual, group and organizational issues and illustrate common intraorganizational strains.

These intergroup exercises and the kinds of behaviour they elicit will be described with the purpose of illuminating a number of phenomena that are common to most social situations in which groups interact. A singular advantage of the exercises for this purpose is the fact that herein the processes of group formation and intergroup relations may be studied without the extra baggage of the issues of real power, authority, and group and individual status in the actual organizations in which the members work and live. Certain phenomena, especially those behaviours that are least rational and which spring most clearly from the emotional needs and fears of individuals and groups, stand out in stark relief.

The intergroup exercises pioneered by Rice and his associates ordinarily take place within the context of a residential conference and as part of a carefully planned series of group experiences that include opportunities to study behaviour in small groups and in larger groups.[2] The conference members, typically well-educated and drawn from a variety of occupational backgrounds, usually have positions of responsibility and leadership in the organizations in which they work 'back home'; they are already concerned in their daily lives with issues of group and intergroup behaviour, but they may vary widely in their degree of knowledge and sophistication about group behaviour.

The conference itself, consisting of members of the conference and the staff which provides the learning opportunities, may be viewed as a temporary organization with certain tasks and with its own history and development. The fact that the historical process is compressed into a fortnight or a week or even a week-end serves to highlight some of the phenomena that develop more slowly in the life of most organizations.

The staff of the conference functions as the management of the organization and, like management everywhere, has the task not only of dealing with the outside environment and controlling transactions across organizational boundaries (Rice, 1963; Miller and Rice, 1967), but has also the responsibility of monitoring and helping to clarify the events taking place within conference boundaries. Staff is constantly preoccupied with the success of the conference as an educational enterprise, with assessing the learning opportunities it offers and the actual learning that takes place.

The task of the membership is that of taking advantage of the opportunities provided in order to learn about the behaviour of groups and of individuals in group settings. The extent to which members are committed to the task will vary among the members. Some persons may be required by their organizations to attend the conference; others may be there primarily for the enhancement of self-understanding. For the most part, however, experience has shown that the vast majority of conference members feel a commitment to learn about group relations. The dedication of staff to its own tasks provides a model for members.

In the present paper, we shall focus on three specific issues that relate to group development and intergroup behaviour and that can be profitably explored and examined in the intergroup exercises. First, what influence does the manner in which a group initially forms have on its subsequent development? Second, how do authority relationships develop within the group and between groups? And third, can the intergroup exercise be profitably viewed as an organizational model, as a prototype of actual organizational behaviour?

It should be stressed that the manner in which any one of these issues is dealt with by groups and by individual members has consequences for the way in which the other issues will develop and be dealt with. No *one* issue is *the* intergroup issue or the central theoretical question.

Intergroup Exercise I

IGE I typically begins in a large meeting room. Seats are arranged for as many members as are expected and—in the version described here—for one staff member. On the chair of each member is a one-page mimeographed sheet which gives a simple description of the task of the exercise and the resources available. Typically the task is defined as, 'to study relations between groups as they happen'. The numbers of the rooms that are available for the exercise are listed as are the names of the staff consultants to the rooms.[3] It may be noted that each consultant will be accompanied by a non-participant observer, a staff member.[4] Additionally, the room in which the members initially meet is defined as that area available for any 'plenary' and intergroup meetings; the staff member in attendance at the initial meeting is defined as the consultant to plenary and intergroup meetings. The time periods available for the conduct of the intergroup exercises are listed. The last line on the mimeographed sheet reads, 'The intergroup exercise has now started'. It is not at all unusual to see members immediately get up, dash out of the plenary room and begin searching for a group to join. Some more sophisticated members may attempt to stop the mass exodus by insisting that members remain together and decide how to split into groups rationally. In residential conferences, members who have either heard of, or who have had some prior experience in such exercises, may even attempt to develop some organizational structure of the membership prior to the beginning of the exercise. Whether the members bolt from the plenary room or try to remain there, they are faced with the requirement of forming groups. Choices are occasionally made on the basis of the particular consultants available or prior friendships or the wish to avoid some people. Even more rarely, choices may be based on some perception of how best to accomplish the specific task of learning more about the study of relations between groups as they occur.

Members often report that they sought a room where the assigned consultant seemed to offer a safe haven from an anxiety-provoking experience or, conversely, that they welcomed what they viewed as a risky, new experience with a consultant unknown to them. Members may be torn by the conflict between the wish to stick together in already formed, safe social groupings and the feeling that this provides an escape hatch that smacks of evasion of the task and is faintly unethical. Many members either directly or indirectly appeal to authority—'What are we *supposed* to do?' For many members, this initial experience in the exercise is deeply revelatory of their own and others' irrationality under stress and of the primitive tendency to appeal to authority on the one hand and to escape anxiety by group formation on the other.

Eventually (usually sooner, rather than later), the membership splits into groups. The consultant to each particular room attempts to help 'his' group to understand the manner in which it came together. What were the reasons that individuals chose to come together into that particular group? Some groups may spend time in attempting to understand why they formed, others will immediately begin insisting that they develop some organizational structure.

During this initial phase, a few members of the conference may be totally unable or unwilling to enter into any group. Having delayed past the time spent by most of the membership in choosing a room, they may become 'displaced persons' because no group will then accept them, because they are unable to make choices about joining any group or, sometimes, because they deliberately elect to play that role. Regardless of their motives, as the exercise progresses, these individuals will find it increasingly difficult to enter into any group. Groups may respond to these displaced individuals with guilt or even with anger or scorn. In any case, the groups will soon learn that regardless of the nature of their response, it is impossible to ignore these people without casting them out of the total exercise. The consultant insists that the groups consider the problem posed by these 'displaced' individuals rather than settling them in areas where they and the problems they represent might be forgotten.

Within the groups the processes of structuring begins. Leaders are often chosen not so much to facilitate the task of the group, but rather to bring order out of chaos. Strong, angry leaders are preferred in some groups; friendly, non-threatening leaders are preferred in others. Some groups carefully define their territorial boundaries. They deliberately limit their openness. They may post guards or gate-keepers at their doors to limit the entry of representatives of other groups or of the 'displaced' persons. Other groups may insist upon remaining open, democratic or even anarchic. They may discover that they they are unable to do any work, that they are inundated by conflict within the group and by inputs from other groups or individuals.

During this phase of creating organizational structure, the consultant attempts to confront the group with his observations about how and why the group is organizing. He continually encourages it to consider what structure is necessary to accomplish the task of learning about relations between groups.

One group may organize itself most rapidly and it may send out observers or even representatives who will attempt to stimulate interaction between groups. In response to this activity, all of the groups will rapidly begin to develop some structure. At this stage some beginning of intergroup activity is evidenced as groups begin defining themselves in relationship to other groups. During this phase the primary task of the exercise is frequently lost sight of as member groups begin viewing themselves in a win–lose situation vis-à-vis other member groups. 'We–they' responses become common; some groups may recognize that they formed primarily to reassure one another and chose leaders who would give comfort and protection against anxiety and chaos. They may hurriedly reorganize and choose a new kind of structure and even new leadership. The new leader who may be chosen during this phase is apt to be one who demonstrates some competence in organizing activities. The purpose of this reorganization may be less for study of behaviour than for purposes of competition with other groups. Group representatives are elected, appointed or simply volunteer, and begin the process of transacting with other groups. Groups define activities and begin to insist that their representatives successfully complete those activities. Members begin to experience themselves as leaders, as followers, as delegates and as those who participated in delegating. Members begin to share in the group.

As group representatives meet with individuals representing other groups, the representatives begin to form their own special group. Representatives may become conflicted about their loyalties. What must they do for their original group in order to keep them content and assure them that they are adequately represented? And what must they do in order to facilitate the work of the new group of representatives? Member groups may become increasingly concerned about the behaviour of their representatives and may insist that representatives, even when transacting with others in a continually changing situation, be bound by positions that were promulgated within the original member groups at some time in the past. Issues of trust become paramount. Some groups require that their representatives act simply as messengers with no power to act for the group, while others may confer plenipotentiary powers. Occasionally, a representative may return to his group only to find that the group has undergone a complete reorganization in his absence and that agreements he has made will not be honoured. In examining these phenomena, members may learn how their own behaviour may undercut the group's learning task or may even totally avoid that task.

In the competition and hostility between groups that develop in the course of the exercise, individual members experience difficult dilemmas. Often they must choose between loyalty to a group as it is constituted and their individual wish to further the learning task of the exercise. The fears and frustrations associated with the need to make open, forced choices can be intensely experienced and explored.

Occasionally, in the intergroup exercise, individuals experience the dilemma of too many choices, too much conflict over priorities of group membership. At times individuals may behave in ways analagous to those seen in peak experiences obtained with drugs, in religious conversion or even psychosis. The boundaries around the individual may become fluid, new possibilities seen as practicable (even when this is not so) and prior restraints ignored. In this process, other group members may not intervene or may even collude to allow an individual to misidentify reality.

Individual behaviour which is seen as bizarre, as evidencing boundary confusion, may be interpreted in terms of, for example, the needs of the membership to use one of their members to represent all of the chaos. Rumours, however ill-founded, may run rampant throughout the conference membership as to management's intention of extruding from the exercise a member whose deviant behaviour has actually resulted from being egged on by the group. The interaction of individual membership characteristics and group and intergroup forces may be utilized to begin illustrating the manner in which groups, and even individuals collude to produce deviants or scapegoats.

Throughout all of this activity the consultant to the group continues to focus on the task and the manner in which he perceives that the individual group is attempting either to pursue or to avoid that task. The more the group gets involved in its own activity, the less likely it is to attend to the comments of the consultant. However, when groups find themselves in crisis, when they feel that they are being inundated or overwhelmed by other groups, they may then turn to the consultant not as someone whose purpose is to help them attend to the task of learning, but rather as someone who can provide them with a degree of safety and comfort.

The exercise typically ends in a plenary session, whose format is often planned hastily under great time pressure by agreement between group representatives after long, arduous and painful preliminary negotiations between groups. Members attempt to come to grips in the plenary with at least some of the learning. Some individuals and groups attempt to 'package' their learning, wrapping it up neatly and defining some limited area in which some learning has occurred. Other individuals or groups feel overwhelmed by the experience and seem unable to develop any concepts. For most individuals, the learning will go on long after the experience has concluded.

Intergroup Exercise II

In IGE II the staff group, functioning as a management body, interacts as a group with the membership. This exercise generally takes place within an overall conference structure, but may also be run as an independent exercise during, for example, a long weekend. A typical opening is described here.

The exercise begins in a large group setting with the staff sitting in a row as a group facing the assembled membership. The director of the staff reads a statement to the assembled group. He describes the task of the exercise, defines the territory and time periods available and points to the fact that there are two main groups within the exercise. He describes one as the conference faculty or staff and the other as the conference membership. He notes that the faculty is an organized body and that all faculty or staff members have plenipotentiary power. That is, each of them may commit the total faculty to any action he individually takes. Consultants are supplied to member groups in the defined rooms only at the request of the member groups. The director then notes that the membership is unorganized, representing a diversity of groups and that before it can interact effectively as a group, it may need to develop some organizational structure. He goes on to define the terminology that staff will use to refer to different types of representative. Observers are defined as persons who may be sent to view the activities of another group, who may obtain information but who are not sanctioned to interact with that group. Delegates are representatives sent out by the group to transmit or receive messages for their groups or take a specific action on the group's behalf. The actions of delegates are limited by their instructions; they have no sanction to modify their stance. Delegates must, when faced with an unforeseen situation, always obtain additional instructions from their groups. Plenipotentiaries are defined as representatives who have full power to act for the group. The policies of the group are known to the plenipotentiaries and they do the best they can for the group in terms of those policies. The director concludes by noting that the staff is the conference management in terms of structuring the exercise, but that the responsibility for learning belongs to the members. He notes further that rules apply to the staff and that the staff will abide by them. If there are no questions from the membership, the staff as a group arises, and moves to its assigned space.

If this exercise is held in the context of an overall conference in which the members have had experience in IGE I, there is often an aborted attempt to divide the membership into groups in some reasonable manner. However, members ordinarily discover that although their attempts at division may be rational, there is nonetheless great difficulty in convincing the *entire* membership to elect any one plan for division into groups. Thus, in the early phases, many of the same difficulties experienced in IGE I are experienced for a second time. Member groups may, however, be able to organize somewhat more rapidly and effectively. Confusion and chaos may be somewhat better controlled, but the same behaviours seen in IGE I may be repeated in IGE II.

Some experienced members may have decided in advance to avoid the chaotic, anxiety-provoking and frustrating scene in the large meeting room. Having formed a core group, they may depart in a body for one of the designated rooms, leaving the rest of the membership to struggle over issues of division and the consequences of their leaving.

Member groups that form often act as though their task is relating more effectively to one another. They may ingore the new task of the exercise, relating to staff as a group. The staff group may be avoided and staff consultants are frequently not called until late in the exercise. Members have a great deal of difficulty in believing that the staff would in any way assist them in developing an organizational structure so as to confront staff. Member groups may attempt to dominate one another, to manipulate the exercise, to develop control over other groups, but rarely attempt to develop and truly collaborative relationships so that the total membership can learn through the experience of interaction with the staff.

In this exercise there is frequently a testing of the staff rules. Members may organize groups in territories outside of those defined by staff as available to groups in the exercise. Although the staff does not interfere in such activities, it abides by its own rules and will refuse to send consultants to those territories. Members begin to insist that the staff give up its 'arbitrary' position which 'dominates the behaviour and interaction of the entire membership'. This preoccupation with staff rules for staff may allow for the beginning of membership organization. That is, although staff rules are clearly defined as applying only to staff, the members can begin to organize themselves as they insist that these rules are meant to define the behaviour of members and are enormously inflexible and constrictive. The authority of the staff and the visibility of the staff begin to allow the development of some incipient organizational structure within the membership. There is considerable ambivalence about these events and, at times, very powerful subgroups or individual member groups attempt to serve in a priestly function. They strongly identify with staff, espouse what they believe are staff values and even begin to act as they envisage staff might want them to act. Conflict among member groups may develop in order to avoid any conflict with the staff. More rarely, the membership may eventually unite in order to confront the staff, only to find that the staff is willing to hear them out and even to attend to their concerns. Such attention to member concerns may indeed lead to total breakdown of the organizational structure of groups, structure which had been attained largely as a reaction to the perceived authority of staff.

As in IGE I, this exercise also concludes with a plenary session and many of the same behaviours occur that were described earlier. Some members may feel overwhelmed by the experience and unable to think. Some refuse to think, preferring to wallow in the experience. Others may attempt tightly to structure and order their thinking in order to bind the experience up, to insist that the anxiety and the chaos were worthwhile and that some learning had occurred. Still others may begin the process of struggling with the experience in order to continue the learning over time.

Discussion and Application

As we indicated earlier, our discussion of the issues of individual and group behaviour and experience that are encountered in the intergroup exercise will focus on three theoretical questions without claiming that these are the only questions that could be examined in the context of the exercise and without assigning degrees of importance or centrality. Obviously, all of them are interrelated.

The Influence of a Group's Initial Formation on its Subsequent Development

The anxiety that is generated by facing individuals with their own multiple group memberships and insisting upon choice may cause individuals precipitously to form into groups. The mad dash of 'sane, rational', respected professionals out of the plenary room and into a group space—any group space—is eloquent testimony to the intensity of the initial experience. In unplanned for ways, groups develop to reorder individual priorities. The issues around which groups begin to form has dramatic impact on ways in which they will structure themselves, will allow roles to be defined and will permit the intragroup definition of leadership and authority. Within the defined context of forming groups in order to study behaviour in an intergroup exercise, groups may form in order to pursue a diversity of other purposes. The need to form groups to avoid individual anxiety and individual choice often interferes with the effectiveness of groups in developing structure to learn from the exercises.

Individuals may join with one another to accomplish a task which will unite them (e.g. 'get even' with the staff, form a 'woman's liberation' group, develop a 'revolutionary group', etc.). They may seek to reconcile divergent ideologies or tasks (e.g. engage in activity as contrasted to reflecting upon behaviour, join together domineering women and hypermasculine men, etc.). Groups may even form to contain the dysphoria of making choices (e.g. form a loving, caring or therapeutic group, or a group exposing democracy in order to avoid conflict and decision-making). The need to cope with the task of forming groups usually overrides any learning task. The development of structures, role relationships, etc. that are specifically oriented to forming a group may interfere with the task of learning.

Groups which form in order to accomplish some explicitly defined unifying task (regardless of the nature of the task) may rapidly organize around that task, assign roles, define the nature of authority in the group and begin their work. Of course, in this process the group may almost completely lose sight of the goal of learning. It is very likely to resist all efforts to have it examine its own behaviour (although it may energetically explore its impact upon the behaviour of others).

In one such conference, a group, very early in its history, decided to pursue as its task the kidnapping of a prestigious member of another group. A group leader was chosen who had the ability to integrate and coordinate the activities of others. Representatives dispatched to other groups were chosen for their interpersonal skills and they were expected to confuse, dazzle and amuse other groups. Observers sent to other groups were chosen on the basis of their ability to melt into the background of the observed group. Indeed, one observer was even taken for a minimally participating member of the group being observed. The most attractive women in the group were chosen to interact with and, it was hoped, seduce the 'victim', etc. Other members served as the part of the group who reflected upon and tried to understand the exercise—although they usually felt as though they were not influential in the group's decision-making activities.

Under the impetus of a 'task', roles were easily assigned, authority defined and accepted. An organization was developed which facilitated the work that the group had decided upon (even to conducting most work in secret, out of the bounds of the exercise, and then allowing other groups to observe openly what were in fact essentially meaningless deliberations). Members experienced their behaviour as effective, competent and as evidencing 'leadership'. They had difficulty in studying the consequences of their actions either for their own group or for others and in facing up to the conclusions that they had organized for war and had then gone on to insist that their war was in the service of scholarship. Indeed, in the final plenary session the group presented a concise report of its activities in an aggressive manner, delighting more in the impact of their presentation on the staff and other groups than in its content.

Groups which form primarily to reconcile divergent ideologies or tasks may become incapacitated through their need to reconcile without actually negotiating internal compromise. No authority may be allowed, lest one ideology prevail, or a rudimentary parliamentary structure may be developed in order to assure 'fairness'. Quite frequently, groups may form in an attempt to reconcile wishes to do something and to study something. As the group struggles with wishes to be active or reflective, it often loses sight of potential compromise (e.g. decide on that which can be both studied and acted upon) and becomes caught up in its own elaborate structure and rules. It may even begin to view itself as 'the best', 'the most effective' or 'most democratic' group. It may begin to behave as if its major tasks were to give 'grades' to other groups and to discover how it is rated by others. Task roles are defined, but the basis for defining role performance does not lie in the need to perform a task but in the need to bind up conflict.

Groups which form in order to avoid the pain of making choices (i.e. by forming caring or therapeutic groups, or forming groups based on pre-existing relationships to consultants or to one another) are frequently trapped in their origins and their history, demanding of the exercise continuing justification for their existence. Therapeutically-oriented groups demand casualties to heal and are furious at staff and other members for being heartless. Groups oriented around consultants demand the reconstitution of small groups (either with or without a staff member), in order to return to work they already know, rather than moving into new areas.

There are certainly many more ways in which groups may be formed. As each group forms, it tends to see itself as, at least, a microcosm of the exercise. It sees itself as most critical (or its relationship to the staff group in IGE II as most critical) to the conduct of the exercise. It assumes that the task it has chosen is most important, and it seeks reassurance that its status is recognized by other member groups and by staff. Thus groups, ostensibly formed to pursue a task, develop structures to bind up member anxiety and thereupon become preoccupied with developing and maintaining their status. In this process, the groups may even contribute to members' development and learning, but it frequently seems as if this task becomes secondary.

Group organization which ostensibly served the performance of a specific task may readily by subverted to serve the needs of certain members for stability, security and rectitude. In this process original task goals are generally ignored. Individuals and groups faced with new tasks assume that old skills and organizational patterns are relevant. The possibilities for applying these learnings to organizational life are legion.

As an example we may consider the requests made of psychiatric facilities for the development of treatment or counselling services in other institutions. The psychiatric institution, valuing its skills and personnel, often assumes that its techniques are universally applicable. It rarely explores whether such activities are relevant to the requesting organization's needs or whether they will facilitate task accomplishment.

Within the United States, large numbers of individuals arrested for 'minor crimes' are unable to obtain legal counsel or sufficient funds to pay 'bond'. Additionally, because of significant delay in the legal system, many such individuals wait for extended periods in city and state jails prior to trial. Since these individuals have not been convicted or sentenced they are ineligible for rehabilitative programs. In some localities attempts have been made to provide services for such 'pre-trial' prisoners. Mental health professionals approached for advice and services are not unnaturally appalled by the conditions under which such prisoners live, and their disconnectedness from family, friends and even from parts of the prison system. Programs of psychiatric counseling have at times been proposed ignoring the critically important and unaddressed system tasks (e.g. obtaining legal counsel, speeding up the trial process, etc.).

The organization of such psychiatric programs might give the professional practitioners a renewed sense of their own morality, concern for others and might reify for them the importance of their work. However, they would in no way address the real problem faced by this prison population and the fact that significant resources would have to be appropriated for psychiatric programs that might have been utilized in legal aid activities.

Authority Relationships Within and Between Groups

As we have pointed out, authority develops in groups in relation to the tasks defined, and in terms of the need to form a cohesive group and keep it together. The authority of the consulting staff in the exercises is omnipresent and serves as a focus for exploring extragroup authority.

The two intergroup exercises can serve to constrast the manner in which groups both seek out and simultaneously reject external authority. In IGE I, each group or sector has a consultant. Although his function is to facilitate the work of the exercise, the members often behave as though he should provide leadership for the particular group with whom he is associated. If he ignores his task (which is to focus on the work of the group) and colludes with the group, he can become their own demi-god. If he focuses on the group's work and its behaviour in relation to other groups, he is often denigrated and is generally ignored. At the same time, he may be seen as the representative of management and the members of the group may feel scrutinized, monitored and evaluated by him and by the non-participant observer. The consultant cannot shed his identity as a member of the staff and members may find it hard or impossible to believe in his role as facilitator. Thus they often reject the authority of his expertise and render him impotent to make his skills count for anything.

Each group experiences its own needs as most pressing, its work as most important. Intergroup meetings are often failed activities. Groups send delegates without understanding the purpose of intergroup meetings and without being willing to invest the delegates with any authority. Groups experience one another as manipulative, untrustworthy and usually enough actual evidence is generated to give each group good reason to suspect all others. Intragroup needs to preserve assumptions about the status of one's own group in relation to other groups begin to take precedence over meaningful interaction. In order to relate to one another and come together, the groups need to develop some mechanisms for meeting but no group is willing to be dominated by others. Even as coalitions begin to arise, some groups insist on withdrawing from interaction. Members are distressed to experience intense hostility and violent urges towards colleagues. Occasionally, even in this 'game-like' atmosphere, episodes of physical confrontation do occur. Representatives find themselves distrusted by their own groups, who fear they will 'give something away'. Group leaders may find themselves in conflict with group goals. Delegates attending intergroup meetings may seek to develop yet another isolated small group (the group of representatives) and the authority of any group, of any representatives, of any expertise is rejected.

An individual in everyday back-home life who has made a choice of belonging to a group, on whatever grounds, or who willy-nilly has been forced into a group by virtue of his profession or his work identity, often finds himself angry and full of scorn at the group's behaviour or the behaviour of its leadership or its representatives. As in the intergroup exercise, he finds himself faced with painful choices. Shall he attempt to depose leadership? Shall a commitment to excellent work override being sorry for the inept leader or group representative? Is it 'fair' to cajole or bully the group through the exercise of one's special skills?

Ethical issues also present themselves in that the individual asks himself if he rejects incumbent leadership on reasonable grounds or because of the baser wish to kill off leadership and assume it himself. If the member becomes sufficiently disaffected with the group or its leadership, he may feel compelled to withdraw. To do so, he learns, he must be able to bear the wrath or contempt of the group. If he is unable to do so, he must learn to stay in the group but not be truly of it, to find refuge in cynicism and imaginary withdrawal yet with the secret knowledge of his own failure of responsibility. A group which contains a number of such members will tend to be paralysed and ineffective. Only a change in leadership can save it. In the intergroup exercise, few members will leave the conference but in everyday life groups lose members and groups themselves die from inability to solve their leadership problems.

In IGE II, a group with authority is defined in the exercise. The staff exists as a group. The members do not have to struggle to develop a concept of a fantasized potent group; they have hired one.[5] The authority of the staff serves the members. They may develop organizational structures as a response to it. They may use its structure as a model (although the task of members and staff are different). In every IGE II with which we have been associated, some members and some member groups view staff as repressive. Members may wish to replace, destroy or eagerly accept staff authority, but they never ignore it. Groups may delay confronting staff as a group or calling upon consultants, but the presence of staff in the exercise dominates the exercise. The very presence of staff as a group implies that members must respond to it in some fashion. Members are also brought face to face with complex feelings of anxiety towards and guilt about confronting a group which holds authority in the exercise.

The staff sets rules for its *own* behaviour and some members insist that the staff oppresses the members with its rules. Not only has the staff different tasks from those of the membership, but it also has a different organizational position. Its concern is with the total exercise, with each group, and how the groups singly and together represent the exercise. Most of the fury of the members is related to the presumed special expertise and position of the staff.

An important part of members' learning is that of experiencing the advantages and disadvantages of being in a group which must relate to another group which has more skill and experience, a clearer task and a more central position in the exercise. At times, member groups relate to staff as a 'part of the whole' to the 'head'. Staff wisdom is assumed and even when members deny information to the staff, they tend to assume that staff remains omniscient. Staff failures to be completely informed are perceived as evidence of intolerable incompetence. Thus members often deny the reality of their own position in the exercise, their own authority and their knowledge that the staff cannot behave effectively unless members provide them with sufficient information. Each member group's status is a constant concern, staff group status is repeatedly challenged, and issues of status determine group action more than needs for task performance. In this process the complex interrelationships of member group to member group and to the staff are often ignored.

Issues as to who represents a group and the problems of representation, problems with accepting authority in a group, searching for external authority, attempts to avoid intragroup conflict by insisting that problems are between a group and external authority are demonstrable in the exercise and may be used to illuminate common problems in intergroup experiences in member's work lives.

The following examples may serve to highlight some of the applied learnings about authority in intergroups that are addressed in the intergroup exercises.

Problems about representation are common experiences for all of us. Our groups and organizations give imprecise messages about their expectations and the limit of representative authority. A community health board early in its history invited health agencies serving that community to be represented on the health board. Most agencies sent low-level representatives who functioned more as the 'eyes and ears' of the agency in the community, than as individuals who could truly represent and commit their organizations in discussion of agency policies that influenced health care in the community. When the community health board attempted to insist that agency members could not simply serve as 'spies', but needed to be able to speak for their agencies, one agency director noted that in that case he could speak only for himself since he had no formal charge to enter into any discussions with the community his agency was ostensibly serving. This statement was greeted by the community as evidence of either bad faith or lack of policy within the agency, a position that quite obviously surprised the agency director, who seemed quite unaware of the issues of his responsibility and authority to speak for his group.

A group's inability to accept the authority that it may legitimately assume can lead it to search out external authorities (as the staff in the IGE) who will be responsible for decisions and who can be given authority beyond their needs, wishes or charge, and who can be ambivalently admired and despised. A child welfare agency responsible for making recommendations to the court in cases of child abuse routinely sought psychiatric examination of the abusive parents. Although it accumulated masses of evidence it expected psychiatric consultants to evaluate and make recommendations about parental ability to function as caring individuals or as individuals who might be motivated for change (at a time when the threat of legal action had obvious impact on expressed parental attitudes). When psychiatric consultants protested their inability to provide meaningful consultation, they were described as old fashioned, interested in preserving archaic views of professional competence and as unwilling to serve the rights of children. However, new, more relevant consultants were immediately sought (we believe, to take responsibility for recommendations the agency was far more qualified to make).

Questions concerning the legitimacy of authority are recurrently raised in these exercises and reflect current concerns about organizational tasks and goals, as well as demonstrating the real difficulties experienced in combining both emotional and task investments in modern institutions (Schaar, 1970).

The Intergroup Exercise as an Organizational Model

The group and individual phenomena that are observable in the course of the intergroup exercise are applicable in the analysis of the organizational life of institutions in the world outside the confines of the exercise and the conference. For members, one of the most important lessons of the exercise may be this simple and apparently self-evident proposition.[6]

Almost every organization or institution is a group of groups. Even those institutions that profess a self-image of a 'happy family' or a 'therapeutic community' have, in order to perform work at all, divisions of labour and of functional role within the organization. Groups form themselves within the organization on many diverse bases, some of which are work-related ('we secretaries', 'we physicians' or 'we fund-raisers') and some of which may have only such a fortuitous basis as a common territory ('we in the south wing', 'all of us on the third floor'). A common enough division is, of course, between those in authority, including often those who feel they can influence management decisions, and those who feel left out of the decision-making processes of the organization. In the intergroup exercise, these common organizational phenomena stand out by virtue of the absence of the usual organizational ties of purpose and policy.

The conduct of intergroup relations is one of the most familiar tasks in the everyday organizational life of almost all the members of the conference. In his 'back-home' world, the member has a comfortable expertise in behaving as a member or a leader of a work team or section, a professional group or a community committee. While he has come to the conference to learn about problems of leadership and management of groups and of institutions, he often comes with some degree of sophistication about the covert processes that operate in groups and some knowledge of such phenomena as ambivalence towards authority, loyalty towards one's own group and hostility towards out-groups. Nevertheless, each member most commonly discovers that in the intergroup exercises he feels helpless and deskilled. He finds himself in a situation in which the task is defined only as 'the study of group relations as they happen', and in which the groups that form themselves are based on little commonality of purpose. The individual member finds himself stripped of his usual professional or organizational role and his usual habits of behaving in work groups. His only clear role in the temporary organization that is the conference is that of 'conference member' of 'learner'; the only firm boundary at the start of the intergroup exercise is that between members and staff—all else is fluid and becomes crystallized only in the historical development of the groups and their efforts at relating to one another.

This phenomenon of individuals being deskilled occurs in most small groups within these conferences;[7] in the intergroup exercise the groups that form find themselves deskilled in relating to one another. In order for groups to have some sense of their own expertise, they must first define their unique skills and test them out. In the situation where each group feels threatened by the other, there is an unwillingness to let any group develop or demonstrate real skills.

The groups behave as though they had no sense of their connectedness, no sense that they all act for each other. The unique skills and range of behaviours of each group are frequently measured by status criteria, and the groups' interrelatedness is not considered. Real or potential contributions that groups may offer to one another are either ignored or greatly distrusted. Indeed, groups which begin to develop a sense of the exercise as a whole may well develop grandly manipulative schemes, attempting to fit all groups together into a plan they have developed, without considering the wishes of others (Johnson and Lewicki, 1969).

The analogy to organizational behaviour is most apparent in organizations or institutions that are undergoing massive change, in which old roles and fixed, ritual interactions have been broken down. The transition from a traditional, custodial mental hospital to a therapeutic community model or from a therapeutic community hospital model to a mental health model are cases in point. Role changes both for patients and the several categories of staff are involved; issues of group loyalty and the struggle to retain or achieve status may be paramount. Discipline groups (physicians, nurses, social workers) may experience themselves as suddenly deskilled. Similar phenomena occur when a management succession takes place; when a new university president or hospital superintendent is appointed, old groups and old coalitions between groups may become suddenly meaningless. New groups form on new bases that may range from the simply affiliative to the avowedly manipulative.

Questions of 'who speaks for what group' may be of central importance in any organization. To be heard by other groups, a group must have a voice, but to be able to permit itself to have a voice may be impossible unless and until a group develops a common policy upon which it agrees. In the intergroup exercise, representatives of groups engaged in negotiating with other representatives often find the agreements they have reached repudiated by the group they presumably represented. The group has meanwhile changed its policies or strategies and left its representative impotent and without sanction. It is often crucial in organizational life for negotiators to assess the degree to which a given representative can truly commit a group. Does he act only for himself or a clique or can he really carry his group with him? Often a representative will endeavour to create the impression of a powerful, committed group for which he speaks and endeavour to conceal the fact that all that he represents is chaos.

The staff of the conference has the same kinds of issues to deal with as does the management of any enterprise or organization. The major problem confronting staff is to insure that those managerial decisions that are made during the exercises serve the task of learning. Members may, on occasion, attempt to challenge the very nature of the conference and threaten disruption of the conference's boundary with its environment (e.g. through behaviour that would obviously cast disrepute on conference management). Such threats obviously call into question management's ability to stick to the task of providing a structure in which learning can occur. Some staff may collude with part of the membership to insist that direct action must be taken to assert staff authority. This situation is obviously similar to those in organizations in which a variety of both internal and external pressures may be exerted to get the organization to give up its task, and move in new directions which are not mandated.

Efforts to get an organization to redefine its primary task often come from groups within the organization. These groups may be perceived by management as subversive or disloyal while the groups perceive themselves as acting in the larger interest of the organization's survival. For example, efforts to change a university curriculum (Black Studies programs, for example) on the part of groups of students and faculty members may be seen by the administration as a threat to its authority in defining the tasks of education. The challenging groups believe that the institution must change or lose 'relevance' and eventually die. A task for management is that of arriving at a correct appraisal of the realities of the situation it faces and deciding whether or not the dissident groups reflect issues that are truly emerging as social realities or whether the groups represent only passing fads. In the former case, the administration will enter into a serious consideration of educational issues; in the latter, it will attempt to defuse and kill off the dissident groups through the mobilization of other groups that support administration. Or it will attempt to coopt the dissidents through token consideration of their demands and elaborate but meaningless negotiations and manipulation of 'task forces', 'study committees' and the like. In order to take *any* action under conditions of threatened redefinition of task, management must be sure of the correctness of its task definition and of its own commitment to behave in a steadfast manner consistent with that definition.

In a similar fashion, if the pressures for task redefinition are external to the enterprise, e.g. from groups that threaten to withdraw monies or material support if the task is not redefined, management may find that it either has to accept the redefinition or resign. The managers of enterprises that are subject to the continued changing pressures of successive political administrations of a city, state or nation find themselves not infrequently in this position. For the individual member, whether he be leader or follower, complex issues of group, enterprise and task commitment arise, issues which may become for the individual matters of serious personal conflict and choice of priorities of commitment. Just as in the intergroup exercise, the individual is forced into facing his painful personal responsibilities for the behaviour of those to whom he delegates leadership and authority as well as for the consequences of his own behaviour. In the intergroup exercise, it is difficult to sweep these issues under the rug and members report that these lessons, once learned, are carried over into everyday organizational life so that one is never again quite the same person who 'just works here'.

A critical problem for staff in the intergroup exercises is to develop a sense of the progress of the exercises as a whole, to fit staff and member groups into a meaningful whole and to communicate this sense of the exercise in a way which facilitates the learning of members. To achieve this end implies the ability of staff to obtain relevant information about the manner of each group's forming, the special abilities present in groups, the strains groups experience in relating to one another and finally the ability to present this material so that it will not be seen as closing off learning or as forcing one form of learning, or even as a staff ploy to avoid challenges to staff authority.

Identifying and making available information for learning about the relationship of parts of the system to one another, the way in which task activities are related to each other, the manner in which sentient group boundaries have formed and the relationships between task and sentient groups is directly related to learning about the functions of management. Rice defined these as:

'(a) to regulate transactions of the whole, as a task system, with the environment and of the constituent systems with each other; (b) to regulate sentient group boundaries; (c) to regulate relationships between task and sentient groups'. (Rice, 1969, p. 577)

It is, for example, possible that within an intergroup exercise staff might identify in the way groups formed significant conflicts between diverse tasks and sentient needs. Staff might postulate that each group would contain elements of the exercise in it,[8] that it would represent conflicting wishes to seek safety and pursue new experience, to reject and master the exercise, to passively accept and to angrily blame authority, to avoid learning and to use past learning, etc. In attempting to present this material to members, staff must be aware that it might well be misheard as attacking member group activities and as representing a punitive, angry authority structure.

In very much the same fashion, the management of an organization engaged in examining organizational structure and function with a view to changing it may find it difficult to obtain a sufficient flow of relevant information upon which to base decisions. Informational blocks may range all the way from a simple lack of appropriate channels of communication to deliberate sabotage.

So, also, statements by the management of an organization undergoing change and struggling to redefine functions may be seen by sections or groups within the organization as doing injury to them. The view in the section, like that of the group in the intergroup exercise, tends mainly to be concerned with the narrow interests of the section rather than with the larger, overall needs of the organization as a whole. A task of management is to take account of the multiple consequences for groups and individuals of decisions made at higher levels. Of course, in actual organizational life, redefinition of the functions of a group or section may in fact result in actual economic or psychological injury. The section may simply be abolished as a section if management, under pressures of technological development, sees it as obsolete. Even if other jobs are found for members of the section, anger and sadness at the loss of one's work identity and the dissolution of a sentient group are inevitable.

No organization is an island. In addition to the various transactions with its environment that are necessary for it to perform its task, it also is subject to the changing moral and political climate of its time and place. In the intergroup exercise, issues that preoccupy the membership, or a section thereof, in their daily lives at a particular moment in history have their impact on the formation of groups and on the manner in which groups relate to one another and to the management as a group. Thus, at one conference, the issue of 'participatory democracy' and 'sharing authority and decision-making with staff' was a primary issue in the intergroup exercise. In another, the issue of 'black power' and in a third, the issue of 'woman's liberation' took precedence. Obviously, these phenomena have their counterparts in the interaction of institutions with changing environments, as for example, manufacturing companies which must respond to community groups concerned about environmental pollution, or universities which must relate to consumer groups demanding new curricula or changed admissions policies. When a particular issue has once arisen, for whatever specific historical or economic reasons, the organization often finds that the larger social issue is reflected in intraorganizational regroupings as like-minded people seek each other out and attempt to influence management policy as a pressure group from within. Changing social priorities and values embolden new groups to endeavour to change the organization's priorities, rock the organizational boat or even, to use Ralph Nader's term, to 'blow the whistle' on an organization.

Summary

The intergroup exercises designed by A. K. Rice and his colleagues have been described in order to illuminate a number of phenomena that are common in social and organizational situations in which groups form and interact with one another.

In the context of the intergroup exercises, groups form on a number of bases. For example, group formation may occur primarily as a defence against members' anxiety or, in contrast, as a means to task or goal achievement. In any case, the manner in which individuals come together to form a group will influence the group's subsequent development and the way in which it will deal with issues of organizational structure and of leadership.

Authority relations within the groups and between member groups and the staff group are highlighted as issues both for the individual member and for the groups. Individuals and groups in the exercise are forced to examine the ambivalent, co-existing wishes for and rejection of the authority of others. Since issues of real power and authority are minimal in the context of the exercise, members are brought face to face with their anxieties and their fantasies about authority.

The intergroup exercise has been examined as an organizational model. We have described a number of phenomena that are analogous to those that occur in organizations. These include the in-group loyalties that develop; the hostility toward out-groups; the frequent distrust of a group's own leaders and representatives; the problems of negotiations; and the problems for management both in handling boundary issues and in obtaining a flow of relevant information for decision-making.

Notes

1. Miller and Rice (1967) chose the term *sentient* to 'denote the groups with which human beings identify themselves, as distinct from task groups, with which they may or may not become identified'. A sentient group 'demands and receives loyalty from its members...'. This concept is closely related to the concept of reference group. The latter concept points to the individual's tendency to self-appraisal through comparing himself with a particular social group or groups; reference groups also serve as a source of the individual's norms, attitudes and values (Hyman, 1968; Merton, 1957). Thus a professional society (of engineers, psychologists, etc.) serves as a sentient group and a reference group for individual professional men and women (Miller and Rice, 1967).
2. Intergroup exercises have, however, been conducted in non-residential settings and without members having either prior or concurrent experience in studying small groups.
3. Ordinarily, conference members have already become familiar in the exercises with the role of 'consultant'. His task is to help the group examine its own behaviour.
4. The role of observer is not essential to the exercise. Staff members filling this role have the opportunity to discuss the process of consultation with the sector consultant and to prepare themselves to become IGE consultants.
5. For this reason, some have suggested that IGE II is a more appropriate introductory exercise, since the presence of a staff group at least stimulates member group organization. This model then may be subsequently explored in an exercise without staff as a group (IGE I.)
6. For some members, the anxiety generated by the chaotic experience of the intergroup exercise is responded to by treating the whole exercise as an elaborate game. By adopting a stance of 'gamesmanship' the member can deny that the events of the exercise and his own behaviour have relevance to the outside world. He can avoid the painful issues of choice and of his own responsibility for the consequences of his own and the group's behaviour.
7. When leadership and authority are ambiguous, members tend not to allow any one to take action for another. Thus no one may demonstrate the expertise he has in any area. The equality expressed in the small group becomes based on all members being equally unskilled rather than an equality based on mutual respect and the expertise of individuals in many areas. (See Klein and Astrachan, 1971; Astrachan and Redlich, 1969).
8. Higgin and Bridger (1964) described how different groups in an IGE reflect several operative basic assumptions, and how these basic assumptions may be mobilized in the service of work.

References

Astrachan, B. M. and Redlich, F. C. (1969), Leadership ambiguity and its effect on residents' study groups, *International Journal of Group Psychotherapy*, **19**, 487–494.
Bion, W. R. (1961), Experiences in groups, and other papers, Tavistock Publications, London.

Dahl, R. A. (1970), *After the Revolution: Authority in a Good Society*, Yale University Press, New Haven.

Durkheim, E. (1893 trans. 1964), *The Division of Labor in Society*. Free Press, New York.

Etzioni, A. (1968), *The Active Society*, Free Press, New York.

Higgin, G. and Bridger, H. (1964), The psychodynamics of an intergroup experience, *Human Relations*, **17**, 391–446.

Hyman, H. H. (1968), Reference groups, *in: International Encyclopaedia of the Social Sciences*, Vol. 13, McMillan and Free Press, New York, pp. 353–361.

Johnson, D. W. and Lewicki, R. J. (1969), The initiation of superordinate goals, *Journal of Applied Behavioural Science*, **5**, 9–24.

Klein, E. B. and Astrachan, B. M. (1971), Learning in groups: a comparison of study groups and T groups, *Journal of Applied Behavioural Science*, **7**, 659–683.

Merton, R. K. (1957), Continuities in the theory of reference groups and social structure, *in* Merton, R. K., *Social Theory and Social Structure*, Rev. ed., Free Press, Glencoe, Ill.; 1957, pp. 281–386.

Miller, E. J. and Rice A. K. (1967), *Systems of Organization*, Tavistock Publications, London.

Rice, A. K. (1963), *Enterprise and its Environment*, Tavistock Publications, London.

Rice, A. K. (1965), *Learning for Leadership*, Tavistock Publications, London.

Rice, A. K. (1969), Individual, group and intergroup processes, *Human Relations*, **22**, 565–584.

Schaar, J. H. (1970), Legitimacy in the modern state, *in:* Green, P. and Levinson, S., Eds., *Power and Community: Dissenting Essays in Political Science*, Pantheon Books, New York.

Zaleznik, A. (1970), Power and politics in organizational life, *Harvard Business Review*, **70**, May–June, 47–60.

Individual and Corporation: the Problem of Responsibility*

Robert L. Kahn

Introduction

The language of open systems is perhaps 20 years old in the biological sciences, and considerably less than that in social science (von Bertalanffy, 1950; Emery and Trist, 1960, 1965; Katz and Kahn, 1966; Miller, 1965; Miller and Rice, 1967; Rice, 1958, 1963). In very recent years, however, the open-system view of human organizations has become interesting and persuasive to organizational scholars, and a once-esoteric conceptual language has become commonplace.

It is possible, of course, that the long-term influence of open-system theory or, more properly, meta-theory will be mainly terminological. I believe, however, that the open-system approach leads to important and neglected areas in theory and research, and I intend this paper as an illustration of that function.

Let us begin with the implications of openness as a concept. If an organization is open to inputs from its environment, it must be in some degree altered or influenced by them. To understand the nature of the organization and its changes over time, we must therefore study not the organization alone but the organization-in-environment. We therefore become concerned with organizational boundaries and with the transactions across them. We become concerned with the unique quality of organizational membership that has been described as segmental or partial inclusion (Allport, 1933): people are members of the organization with only part of themselves and for only part of their time. They carry into the organization attributes formed and reformed in the outside environment.

As we think in these terms, we become increasingly interested in a class of problems having to do with goodness-of-fit. The goodness-of-fit problem is traditional in organizational and industrial psychology in one form: that is, as a problem in selection and placement, a problem cast in terms of the individual's ability or motivation to conform to the requirements of a particular role in the organization.

But there is also a long tradition of concern, especially among sociologists, for goodness-of-fit at a different level: the organization in relation to the larger environment in which it must exist. Weber's thesis (1904) about the Protestant ethic and its ramifying effects can be interpreted as a statement about changes in economic organizations undertaken to bring them into better

*An earlier version of this paper was read at a symposium, 'The Corporation in Mid-Century America', held at the University of Michigan, March 19, 1969. It was sponsored by the Western Electric Company.

fit with a set of ideas in the larger culture. The following quotation serves to illustrate the point:

'One of the fundamental elements of the spirit of modern capitalism, and not only of that but of all modern culture: rational conduct on the basis of the idea of the calling, was born—that is what this discussion has sought to demonstrate—from the spirit of Christian asceticism ...'

'The Puritan wanted to work in a calling; we are forced to do so. For when asceticism was carried out of monastic cells into everyday life, and began to dominate worldly morality, it did its part in building the tremendous cosmos of the modern economic order. This order is now bound to the technical and economic conditions of machine production which today determine the lives of all the individuals who are born into this mechanism, not only with those directly concerned with economic acquisition, with irresistible force. Perhaps it will be so until the last ton of fossilized coal is burnt.' (Weber, 1904, p. 21)

Marx, of course, saw technology as the prime mover, but for him also the changing form of human organizations was an exercise in accommodation, by which they came to assume properties required for good fit with the (techno-logical) characteristics of the larger society. The following quotation is taken from a letter written in 1846:

'Assume a particular state of development in the productive faculties of man and you will get a corresponding form of commerce and consumption ... Men never relinquish what they have won, but this does not mean that they never relinquish the social form in which they have acquired certain productive forces. On the contrary, in order that they may not be deprived of the result attained, and forfeit the fruits of civilization, they are obliged, from the moment when the form of their commerce no longer corresponds to the productive forces acquired, to change all their traditional social forms ... Thus the economic forms in which men produce, consume, exchange are transitory and historical. With the acquis-ition of new productive faculties men change their mode of production and with the mode of production they change all the economic relations which have been merely the necessary relations of this particular mode of production.' (Marx, 1846, pp. 35, 36)

Whether one thinks of formal organizations as altering primarily in response to external facts of technology or ideology, or as engaged in more reciprocal transactions with agencies in their environment, the problem of goodness-of-fit persists. However, it is a concept and an implied hypothesis surrounded by some lingering uncertainties of definition. For example, how shall we assess the goodness-of-fit between a given organization form and the larger technology and culture in which it is embedded?

I do not believe that social science has yet proposed an adequate answer to this question. The concept of the organization as a socio-technical system (Emery and Trist, 1960), which has been central to the work of the Tavistock group, indicates recognition of the problem rather than a solution. The field experiments of Rice (1958, 1963), Trist and Bamforth (1951), Trist and co-workers (1963) and others represent large-scale efforts to improve the fit of social structure to technological requirements and human needs. The dimensions on which goodness-of-fit must be assessed, however, have yet to be specified.

In this connection, it is instructive to look at the role requirements and norm of formal organizations in comparison to the professed norms and values of the larger society. For one conceptual dimension at a time, we can ask whether the definitions and associated value judgments within formal work organizations are compatible with those outside. Let us attempt something along these lines for the concept of responsibility, and do so in terms of the following questions:

(1) What is the nature of the corporation as a large-scale organization?
(2) What is the meaning of individual responsibility?
(3) Are these two—corporation and individual responsibility—compatible?
(4) Can we conceive of organizations in which individual responsibility is vastly increased, and can we learn to create such organizations? In other words, can we get there from here?

The Nature of Large-Scale Organizations

The open-system approach to organizations taken here has been fully described elsewhere (Katz and Kahn, 1966), and we need reiterate only the points relevant to the issue of responsibility.

We think of the organization as an open system which receives certain inputs from the environment, transforms or combines them in some way, exports them into the environment, and for doing so is somehow enabled to receive new inputs and thus continue the cycle. The corporation is open because of its continuing dependence on its environment: to obtain inputs of manpower, capital, steam, electricity and raw materials the corporation must engage in transactions with agencies outside itself, as it must do so also in order to dispose of its product. The openness of the organization and the cyclical nature of its operations are obvious in the case of the private corporation, which must sell its product or service to get the money with which to buy inputs to continue to function. The cycle is less obvious in the case of universities, charitable organizations or agencies of government, but it is not less applicable to them.

To call the corporation an open system, however, does not distinguish it sufficiently from other entities. Plants and animals show similar cycles of input, transformation and output. Even some artifacts meet the broad definitions of open systems: the automobile requires inputs of air and fuel and lubricants; it transforms these into transportation and such assorted by-products as carbon dioxide, water, an impressive array of more toxic chemicals and the unintended deaths of 53,000 citizens each year in the United States alone.

Biological and mechanical structures have a physical boundedness that social structures lack, however. When the animal dies or the automobile stops running, the physical parts are still there, connected to each other as before, and the mechanic or pathologist can perform a postmortem analysis. Organizations, on the other hand (corporations included), have no structure apart from the patterns of behaviour that are also their internal functions. When these patterns of behaviour stop, the organization ceases to exist, and its traces (buildings and equipment) give few clues to its nature in life. In other words, what is organized in human organizations is human behaviour—events, happenings.

The implications of this view of human organizations are many. For example, if organizations are essentially patterns of behaviour, it follows that they are contrived; they are of human construction and they are infinitely susceptible to modification. It follows also that organizations do not conform to the laws of growth and death that characterize biological organisms; there is no particular size and shape they must attain, or life cycle that they must follow. The cement that holds them together is psychological; people must be motivated to engage in the stable recurring patterns of behaviour that define the organizations and give them continued existence.

The most useful concept for describing the patterns of behaviour in organizations and for understanding their motivational basis is that of role, and large-scale organizations can be understood as systems of interrelated roles. The behaviour of individuals in organizations cannot be understood as the spontaneous expression of biological needs or attributes of personality. Nor can the interdependent behaviour of pairs and groups of people in organizations be understood in terms of their liking for each other or their enjoyment of the joint effort they make. Rather the behaviour of people in organizations is determined by their position in a network of related positions, and this is what we mean by role behaviour. It is motivated not by instinct and immediate gratification, but primarily by external rewards and penalties, although many other motives enter into the process. There is intrinsic satisfaction in the successful and skillful meshing of one's own efforts with those of others, particularly if the process of doing so includes the opportunity to use valued abilities or acquire new ones. The basic process, however, is learning the expectations of others as they are directed to the position one occupies, accepting those expectations as legitimate and behaving in ways that fulfill them.

The reliability of such role behaviour is the intrinsic requirement of human organizations. It is the unavoidable demand that the organization makes on its members. To state that demand in terms that point out one of the paradoxes of individual responsibility in the organizational context, we can say that every organization faces the task of somehow reducing the variability, instability and spontaneity of individual human acts.

The success of organizations in achieving this reduction is available to the most superficial observer. Within an organization (when they are 'in role', so to speak), people behave in ways which they would not do outside it. They may wear special uniforms or costumes. They are likely to follow certain styles and formalities in dealing with others. Above all, their behaviour in organizations shows a selectivity, a restrictiveness and a persistence which is not to be observed in the same persons when outside the organization.

The most elementary forms of behaviour in organizations illustrate this point. Consider, for example, the regularity in the arrivals and departures of employees of a corporation. Some minutes before the appointed hour in the morning workers begin to stream through the plant gates and move to their places, in most plants pausing at the time clock en route. Just before the required hour, the traffic through the gates hits its peak (the timing reflects the superb assurance of long practice), and then there is an abrupt reduction in flow. A small proportion of workers come a few minutes late, and then the traffic stops altogether until the complementary surge outward in the afternoon.

The same employees, were we to survey their preferences for hours of waking and sleeping or their behaviour on weekends and vacations, would show the distribution of human differences typical on almost any characteristic—height, weight, intelligence or what you will. The distribution of such attributes over a large population almost always generates that bell-shaped curve that reminds us of the variability of human preferences and characteristics, the bulking up of most cases in the middle ranges and the symmetrical tapering off to both extremes.

The behaviour of employees in the organization, however, shows a different configuration. The extreme cases reduce in number, the bell shape sharpens to a peak, and the distribution becomes asymmetrical; it is more permissible to be early than late. The normal curve is transformed into the J curve, the curve of conformity that is characteristic of organizationally-determined acts (Allport, 1933, 1934). As the organization becomes larger, more complex, more specialized in its parts, the behaviour patterns required of members are not merely uniform. The generalized requirement of conforming to the requirements of one's role and the expectations of the people who constitute one's role set continues, however.

Indeed such conformity is a more insistent and vital requirement in sophisticated organizations than in primitive ones, precisely because of the greater interdependence in the complex organizations. If one field hand in a group of 100 fails to meet the requirements of his role, total productivity is reduced from 100 per cent to 99. If one assembly-line worker in a group of 100 stops performing, not a single completed unit is produced. The total amount of work done may drop by only one percentage point, but the completed product has dropped to zero. Small wonder that the essential corporate requirement on the individual is for dependable role performance, that the employee who so performs is called responsible, and that deviation from meeting role expectations is defined as irresponsibility.

The effects of encountering each day the demands of a particular position in a corporation, a particular pattern of role expectations, are not limited to overt behaviour on the job; the individual changes in other ways. Some time ago the Survey Research Center collected data about the beliefs and attitudes of some 2500 industrial workers—regarding management, labour unions, wage incentives, seniority and other matters (Lieberman, 1956). About a year later the measures were repeated. The people were the same, but in the meantime some of them had been promoted to foremen, some had been made union stewards and the rest had remained rank-and-file workers.

The workers who became foremen also had become more favourable toward management, more critical of the union, more favourable toward the principle of incentive pay and more critical of the union-sponsored seniority system. The workers who became stewards, on the other hand, had become more critical of management and of the management-sponsored incentive system and more favourable toward the union and the principle of seniority. Those who remained workers throughout the period showed no such changes. Moreover, the future foremen had not differed from the future stewards a year earlier, when they were all workers.

Still another year later, the research group returned again to the same plants, and the same men. Those who had remained foremen were now even more different in attitudes and beliefs from those who had remained stewards. For example, all the foremen thought the company was a good place to work, but none of the stewards thought so. All the stewards thought the union should have more say in setting labour standards, but none of the foremen thought so.

On 16 questions relating to the company, the union and the work situation, the future foremen and future stewards showed an average difference of only 0·1 of a percentage point at the time when they were all rank-and-file workers. About a year after they had been in the role of foreman and steward, respectively, the average difference was 48 percentage points, and in another year or so average difference had grown to almost 63 percentage points.

If there was any doubt that these changes were produced by the role, by the day-to-day experience of meeting the specialized set of expectations that go with the position of foreman or steward, that doubt was dispelled by some further information from the same research. Some of the workers who had been promoted to foremen did not remain so; a drop in the demand for the product resulted in their being returned to the rank and file, and some of the stewards were not continued in office. Almost without exception the return to the old role of worker was accompanied by a return to the old attitudes and beliefs as well.

Other studies extend these findings, and demonstrate that meeting the demands of one's corporate role is not merely a matter of behaviour on the job (Mott and coworkers, 1965). That is primary and intended. Secondary and often unintended is the transformation of the person and the inevitable effects on his extra-organizational life.

To the corporate officer as citizen, statesman or management philosopher such issues may be of great concern. To the same officer in his corporate role, and to the corporation as an ongoing system, these issues are at best of secondary concern. A distinguished Englishman long ago, on seeing a steam engine for the first time, remarked to his friend, 'It is a giant with a single idea!' Personification is a dangerous intellectual habit, but something along the same lines could be said of the corporation. It is a giant, and its pervasive idea is dependability of performance in the appointed tasks or roles. From that dependability stems productivity of the corporation as a whole, profitability, growth and survival itself. Small wonder that acting responsibly in the corporate context means fulfilling such role requirements completely and dependably, and having a great deal of responsibility means seeing that other people do the same.

The Nature of Responsibility

Responsibility is one of the many words we have taken from the Latin; it comes from a verb meaning to answer and by extension to promise, that is to commit oneself to giving a future answer. Thus, the root meaning of responsibility has to do with causality in the past and commitment for the future. When we ask who or what is responsible for a particular condition or event, we mean who or what caused it. In the failure of some expected event, the question of responsibility asks who prevented it or failed to cause it.

To cause something to happen in turn implies the power, knowledge and resources to make it happen. Responsibility implies the possession of such power, and more; it implies intent, awareness and freedom of choice in the use of power. On those points philosophers and laymen, psychologists and lawyers are in some agreement. We do not consider people responsible for everything they cause, or at least we distinguish qualitatively different meanings of the word. We distinguish, for example, between murder, manslaughter and accidental death primarily on the basis of intent.

But responsibility implies more than intent. It also implies awareness of one's acts and their reasonable consequences, and ability to refrain from an act as well as to commit it. Hence the legal plea of insanity or even extreme passion mitigates the responsibility of a person for his acts, on the grounds that he was at least temporarily unaware of them or unable to control them, that is unable to choose not to act as he did. The decision to commit an act or refrain from doing so, freedom of choice, is the most difficult of the ideas involved in the concept of responsibility. It is difficult because freedom of choice implies viable alternatives, and that plunges us into a new and intricate problem. One can argue that the individual who is able to act and is aware of his actions can always choose to avoid or refuse a particular action. There is always an alternative even if the alterntive is death.

We do not ordinarily hold people responsible for acts they perform under threat of death, although there are exceptions and the line is sometimes difficult to draw. Recent inquiries into the behaviour of American soldiers in Viet Nam (for example, the surrender of the ship *Pueblo* by Commander Bucher and the killing of civilians in the village of My Lai) raised this issue among others, and the Nuremberg trials had raised it a quarter of a century earlier. The defence of Adolf Eichmann raised almost all the issues of responsibility we have mentioned; Eichmann argued that he was not invested with the power to refrain from acting in organizationally-required ways, that he was not aware of the consequences of his acts and that in any case refusal to obey would have meant hardship or death.

The judgment in these extreme cases illuminates an additional issue in the definition of responsibility—responsibility to what set of principles or to what people. This specification is an essential part of the definition in any pragmatic situation. Eichmann and many of the Nuremberg defendants argued that they were acting responsibly in relation to their organizational superiors and to the principle of hierarchical authority and obedience. The judgment invoked the question of responsibility to the population of victims and the principle of humanity.

The example, of course, is so monstrous that one is reluctant to make the translation to everyday life in the relatively benign organizations in which most people get their living. But some recent experiments have illustrated the docility with which people respond to instruction, even when the source of the request has not really established his authority and when the requests themselves are in apparent conflict with the individual's own wishes and values. Stanley Milgram (1965), deeply concerned with what he called the Eichmann phenomenon, devised a series of experiments to answer this question: If a person is told to hurt another, under what conditions will he go along with the instruction, and under what conditions will he refuse to obey? In Milgram's experiments the question became: If an experimenter tells an experimental subject to hurt another person, under what conditions will the subject go along with this instruction, and under what conditions will he refuse to obey? The subjects in the initial experiments were adult men of varied ages and occupations, all in the area of New Haven, Connecticut. As the subjects arrived they were told by the experimenter that scientists knew very little about the effects of punishment on memory, and that the subjects were going to participate in experiments to learn more about this matter. They were also told that they would work in pairs, one as teacher and the other as learner. They drew lots to determine who would be the teacher and who the learner in each pair, but the experimenter had arranged things so that the teacher was always the true or naive subject and the learner always an instructed confederate of the experimenter.

The experiment proceeds. The learner (confederate) is taken into an adjacent room and strapped into an electric chair. The teacher, next door, is told that it is his task to teach the learner the proper responses to a list of words, and that he is to administer punishment to the learner whenever he makes a mistake. The punishment is administered by electric shock, controlled by the teacher. The teacher sits next to a simulated shock generator, with indicated voltages ranging from 15 to 450 and labels ranging from 'slight shock' to 'danger: severe shock'. The learner, who is the experimenter's confederate, gives many wrong answers, according to plan. The teacher is instructed to administer one shock for each error, and to increase the voltage one step for each error. Needless to say, no electric shock is actually applied. The responses of the victim (that is, learner) are standardized. Starting with 75 volts, the learner begins to grunt and moan. At 150 volts he demands to be let out of the experiment. At 180 volts he cries out that he can no longer stand the pain. At 300 volts he refuses to provide any more answers to the memory test, insisting that he is no longer a participant in the experiment and must be freed. The experiment ends whenever the teacher-subject refuses to give the next higher level of shock.

More than 1000 people participated in these obedience experiments. Before the results were available, 40 psychiatrists were asked to predict the number of persons who would administer each of the increasing levels of shock. The psychiatrists predicted that most subjects would not continue the shocks after the victim made his first request to be freed (at 150 volts). They also predicted that only one subject in 1000 would obediently administer the highest shock on the board. In fact 62 per cent of the subjects (620 out of 1000) obeyed the voice of authority, met the requirements of their organizational role, and administered (as they thought) shocks of 450 volts to a moaning, protesting and then ominously silent subject.

In a variation of the experiment in which such sounds from the victim were not audible, virtually all subject-teachers, once commanded, went on to the end of the board, in spite of the labels 'extreme shock' and 'danger: severe shock'. The proportion of subjects who behaved so obediently dropped to 62 per cent when the moans and protests of the learner could be heard, dropped a little more when the teacher could also see his victim, and dropped to 30 per cent when the teacher was compelled to touch the victim in order to administer the shock. Significant numbers continued to administer shock even when the victims claimed heart trouble.

Only one point need be added about these experiments. The teacher-subjects were not acting without feeling. On the contrary; they expressed tension, conflict of conscience, sympathy for the learner, dissatisfaction with the experiment and the research organization. But they continued to administer shocks.

Were they behaving responsibly? Certainly they were acting with intent, with awareness of what they were doing and without extreme compulsion; no threat of punishment attached to their refusing to continue the experiment. But responsibility also implies acting in accordance with some kind of principle; were they acting thus? The answer depends upon the principle we choose as our frame of reference. The subjects in this experiment performed faithfully their organizational role; they did the job; they obeyed the requests of their superior in the organization. By those standards they behaved responsibly. But they inflicted pain (so far as they knew) on another human being; they did so over his protests and his expressed wish to terminate the entire activity; moreover, they did so in spite of their own values and their observable discomfiture at violating those values. By those standards they behaved irresponsibly. They betrayed themselves and their fellows.

The power of organizational role expectations to influence individual behaviour can perhaps be accepted without further evidence. To answer the question of compatibility between corporate life and individual responsibility, we must therefore consider what the corporation requires of most employees and within what terms of reference responsibility is defined in the corporate context.

Compatibility of Corporate and Individual Responsibility

In my view, corporations require most of their members to act without responsibility in the broad terms we have just considered; still worse, most corporations subvert or restrict the meaning of responsibility and define it in terms of fulfilling a role set by one's superiors in the hierarchy. The division of labour into fractionated repetitive tasks, the content and method of which is determined by others, minimizes the responsibility of the individual worker. His task, his methods, his tools, the pace at which he is to work, the judgment of whether the quality of his performance is adequate are all decided by others — typically without consultation with him. The information that comes his way through formal channels is limited, on the grounds that information about the larger questions of organizational life are not functionally required for him to do his job. Decisions about new product lines, new design, new methods, new locations for plants, mergers, layoffs or overtime work, rates and the like are defined as outside his realm of influence.

One of the characters in the Caine Mutiny (Wouk, 1951) remarks that 'the Navy is an organization designed by geniuses to be run by idiots'. Argyris (1957), in a passage I still find compelling, contrasts the requirements of human maturation with the requirements of the typical industrial job. He proposes that as a person grows from childhood to maturity, he shows change along several dimensions; he moves from passivity as an infant to increasing activity as an adult, from der dence on others to relative autonomy and independence, from a limited ι. rtoire of behaviour to a wide range of potential behaviours, from shallow and quickly-dropped interests to deeper commitments, from a short time perspective to a longer one, from a subordinate position to one of equality among others, and from obliviousness to self-awareness and self-control. There is a serious and pervasive incompatibility between those characteristics of the mature adult and the demands of non-supervisory jobs in most corporations. They require the passive acceptance of the task as defined by others, a continuing dependence on one's hierarchical superiors for approval and rewards, the repetitive practice of a limited set of skills, a time perspective that is limited to the task of the moment, and the acceptance of a position subordinate in status, rewards and decisions about one's own work.

In short, the corporation through its line and staff defines the roles (jobs), the role requirements, the standards of evaluating role performance and the various safeguards to prevent failure of performance. It defines responsibility in terms of meeting such role requirements, and not letting one's own values intrude if they would urge other behaviour. In a recent study of executive selection and promotion, for example, we found that some executives who were not themselves prejudiced nevertheless discriminated against members of minority groups because, as they explained to us, the job required it. Conversely, we found some prejudiced executives who did not act on their prejudices because they knew that policy forbade it (Quinn, Kahn and coworkers, 1968; Quinn, Tabor and Gordon 1968).

The paradox is clear. If responsibility means acting autonomously in accordance with one's own values, corporations tend to prevent responsible behaviour on the part of most of their employees, except in the restricted sense of performing dependably on the job. To reject the job or any of its major requirements, to refuse to do something out of conscience, or to propose some major modification in the work—these constitute the organizational counterpart of civil disobedience.

The Nurturance of Responsibility

I believe that it is possible to increase very greatly the responsibility and commitment that workers feel for the organizations in which they earn their living. Or, to put it more precisely, I believe that it is possible to create organizational forms in which the meeting of role requirements will be more congruent with personal growth and responsibility. Social and psychological research of the past 25 years in organizations gives clues to some of the possible solutions, for there is more than one. Almost all this research emphasizes the importance to the worker of increased availability of information about the enterprise, increased breadth of experience, increased participation in decisions of importance, increased involvement in a functional work group and increased autonomy in his own work. We could sum up these research results by saying that if you want people to behave more responsibly, you must give them responsibility.

How can this be done within the corporate structure as we know it? To some extent by decentralization, because small units linked together into a federated corporate structure produce by definition a broader distribution of responsibility. A number of specific proposals of this type have been developed, differing in detail but sharing an emphasis on decentralization, delegation of authority and group decision-making at all levels in the organization. The best known of such managerial alternatives are McGregor's *Theory Y* (1960) and Likert's *System 4* (1961, 1967).

Both these should be regarded, however, as variations on the basic hierarchical design of corporations, rather than as completely different structures of governance and production. The familiar pyramid of hierarchical organization is maintained, with its fusion of status, prestige, power and material rewards. It is a truism that as we ascend the corporate pyramid, all these increase and reach their maxima at the pinnacle of the hierarchy. The president of a corporation typically receives the largest salary, enjoys the greatest prestige, can commit the organization to new policies or veto such commitment. Within the limitations of law and collective bargaining, he can hire a man into any job in the organization or fire him; he himself cannot be hired or fired by any other person in the corporation, although he may be answerable to an outside board of directors.

Particularly important to the nature of hierarchical organization is the increase in power of different kinds that characterizes each successive level in the hierarchy. Power is not only executive, having to do with the implementation of policies and goals; it is also legislative, having to do with the origination of policy and the setting of goals. In short, hierarchical power includes not only the operation of the corporation as it exists; it includes the determination of whether the corporation shall be different in policy and structure tomorrow than it is today, and the determination of what individuals shall play the various organizational roles. Corporations are not only run from the top; they are defined at the top.

The hierarchical model is so familiar to us that it seems not only natural, but inevitable. Indeed, when American workers are asked to describe the ideal distribution of power in a corporation, they envisage a significant increase in the influence of the rank and file, but not a basic change in the relative distribution of control. They consider it appropriate that the major decisions be made at the top (Tannenbaum, 1966, 1968).

In theory, however, we can contrast the hierarchical model with the democratic. The democratic model differs from the hierarchical in three main respects—the separation of legislative from executive power, the locus of the veto and the means by which leaders are selected. Executive power in a democratic organization is usually distributed in accordance with the pyramidal structure of authority. Legislative or policy-making power, however, is widely shared among the members of the organization, a principle that reaches its fullest expression in the familiar slogan 'One member, one vote!' A second criterion of democratic structure is the location of the veto, because it implies the locus of ultimate power in the organization. By whom can a decision be overruled, or a conflict be finally resolved? In a corporation the presentation of an unresolved issue to successively higher levels of authority leads ultimately to the president's office; in a democratic organization, the same process leads finally to the membership or to their representatives.

The third criterion for distinguishing democratic from hierarchical organizations is the basis on which selection, tenure and dismissal of staff are determined—especially for key positions. It is a characteristic of hierarchy that each level has the power to name the persons who shall hold positions at the next lower level. The democratic model, on the other hand, implies that each person shall be named to membership and office by his peers or by the body politic, that officers are named to office for limited terms, and are subject to recall by those who have elected them.

All this is not to say that corporations should be run in the fashion of political democracies. The appropriateness of democratic and hierarchical structures to different human purposes and conditions is still unsettled. Moreover, it is not at all obvious that, even in a democratic society, *all* organizations should be democratic in structure. A nation of mini-democracies, from family to national government, is neither easy nor encouraging to visualize.

The contrast serves to remind us, however, that the search for ever-better organizational forms probably has not ended with the corporation. The corporation has been called appropriately a socio-technical system (Emery and Trist, 1960), that is a combination of technology and social arrangements. As a social invention, it dates from the 19th century, although the American corporate form is a 20th century phenomenon. (It was an invention, by the way, that included the express purpose of reducing responsibility, as the British term *limited* reminds us.) During the years of corporate growth the technology of production has changed very rapidly and continues to do so. There have been no changes of comparable magnitude in the organizational structure of corporations, and we now face the question of whether the social and technical aspects of corporate life—the two aspects of the same organization—are congruent and appropriate to each other.

The usual solution to such questions has been given by a rather crude and costly process. Industry has moved ahead with promising technological innovations and then waited to see what discontinuities in social arrangements might be inadvertently introduced along with new inventions and processes. If the difficulties were compelling, there would then be an attempt to cobble or modify organizational policy and structure to contain more comfortably the new technology. The process has been crude in many respects, but it has generated a new degree of affluence and productivity. That very affluence allows us the possibility of innovation and experiment with different forms of productive organizations. By that proposal I mean merely to apply to the dilemmas of human organization the approaches that have been so successful in the basic and applied sciences.

For example, Scanlon has developed a complete plan for corporate decision-making with major participation at all levels, and a method of financial rewards that supports and motivates the process (Scanlon, 1948; LeSieur, 1958). More recently, Forrester (1961) has described a new corporate design in which the superior–subordinate relationship is substantially eliminated and each worker becomes a profit centre. The proposals of McGregor and Likert have already been mentioned, and others could be added. What is needed is not argument but experimentation, pilot operations, small-scale trials and objective evaluations of new and varied corporate arrangements. We do this with technological innovations, because we consider their advantages and weaknesses to be secular questions, subject to empirical evaluation. When it comes to the social aspects of organization, however, we tend to treat the issues as sacred rather than secular, as matters of faith rather than observable evidence—in short, as untestable and therefore properly untested.

There are a few encouraging exceptions—Trist and Bamforth's work on the socio-technical structure of coal mining (1951); Morse and Reimer's experimental reorganization of a large clerical operation (1956); Rice's sustained experimental efforts at Ahmedabad (1958, 1963). The list could be extended, but not to great length, and most of the experiments cited were circumscribed by traditional prerogatives of management. Many principles of corporate organization remain unexamined.

Those countries of the World that live on the edge of the Malthusian razor perhaps cannot afford the applied science of trial and evaluation in these matters, and it would be at least uncharitable to urge it on them. When starvation looms large, questions of individual responsibility and self-actualization are secondary. But with the wealth and productive success of the nations called 'developed', such questions become primary. They can afford to concentrate on improving the quality of work experience and the quality of human life.

American society has been called by many names in recent years, by authors who struggled to grasp its essential attributes. It has been called 'the other-directed society' by Riesman (1950), 'the affluent society' by Galbraith (1958), 'the temporary society' by Bennis and Slater (1968), 'the active society' by Etzioni (1958), 'the mass-consumption society' by Katona (1964), 'the unprepared society' by Michael (1968) and 'the great society' by a recent president.

We can imagine another title, not yet formulated nor yet deserved by any nation—perhaps the experimental society, to signify commitment to discovering or inventing, measuring and evaluating new and better organizational forms. Or perhaps the chosen society—chosen not by God above others, nor by some accident of sociological evolution, but chosen by search for and evaluation of organizational forms that enhance the quality of human life. Such qualities may be in the making. I hope so, for I predict that when the future has become history, the era in which the search for ever-better organizational forms began in scientific earnest will rank with the discovery of continents and the exploration of space.

References

Allport, F. H. (1933), *Institutional Behaviour*, University of North Carolina Press, Chapel Hill, N. C.

Allport, F. H. (1934), The J-curve Hypothesis of Conforming Behaviour, *Journal of Social Psychology*, **5**, 141–183.

Argyris, C. (1957), *Personality and Organization*, Harper, New York.

Bennis, W. G. and Slater, P. E. (1968), *The Temporary Society*, Harper and Row, New York.

Emery, F. E. and Trist, E. L. (1960), Socio-technical systems, *in Management Science, Models and Techniques*, Churchman, C. W. and Verhulst, M., Eds., Vol. 2, Pergamon, Oxford.

Emery, F. E. and Trist, E. L. (1965), The causal texture of organizational environments, *Human Relations*, **18**, 21–32.

Etzioni, A. (1968), *The Active Society*, The Free Press, New York.

Forrester, J. (1961), *Industrial Dynamics*, M. I. T. Press and New York: Wiley, Cambridge, Moss.

Galbraith, J. K. (1958), *The Affluent Society*, Houghton Mifflin, Boston.

Katona, G. (1964), *The Mass Consumption Society*, McGraw-Hill, New York.

Katz, D. and Kahn, R. L. (1966), *The Social Psychology of Organizations*, Wiley, New York.

LeSieur, F. G. (1958), *The Scanlon Plan*, Wiley, New York.

Lieberman, S. (1956), The effects of changes in roles on the attitudes of role occupants, *Human Relations*, **9**, pp. 385–402.

Likert, R. (1961), *New Patterns of Management*, McGraw-Hill, New York.

Likert, R. (1967), *The Human Organization*, McGraw-Hill, New York.

Marx, K. (1846), A letter to P. V. Annenkov, *in* Karl Marx and Frederick Engels (1962), *Selected Works, Vol. 2*, Foreign Languages Publishing House, Moscow. Excerpts reprinted in Burns, T. Ed., (1969), *Industrial Man*, Penguin Books, Baltimore, pp. 35–36.

McGregor, D. (1960), *Human Side of Enterprise*. McGraw-Hill, New York.

Michael, D. N. (1968), *The Unprepared Society: Planning for a Precarious Future*, Basic Books, New York.

Milgram, S. (1965), Some conditions of obedience and disobedience to authority, *Human Relations*, **18**, 57–76.

Miller, E. J. and Rice, A. K. (1967), *Systems of Organization*, Tavistock Publications, London.

Miller, J. G. (1965), Living systems: cross level hypothesis, *Behavioural Science*, **10**, 380–411.

Morse, N. and Reimer, E. (1956), The experimental change of a major organizational variable, *Abnormal Social Psychology*, **52**, 120–129.

Mott, P. E., Mann, F. C., McLoughlin, Q. and Warwick, D. P. (1965), *Shift Work: the Social, Psychological, and Physical Consequences*, University of Michigan Press, Ann Arbor.

Quinn, R. P., Kahn, R. L., Tabor, J. M. and Gordon, L. K. (1968), *The Chosen Few: a Study of Discrimination in Executive Selection*, Survey Research Centre, Ann Arbor.

Quinn, R. P., Tabor, J. M. and Gordon, L. K. (1968) *The Decision to Discriminate: a Study of Executive Selection*, Survey Research Center, Ann Arbor.

Rice, A. K. (1958), *Productivity and Social Organization*, Tavistock Publications, London.

Rice, A. K. (1963), *The Enterprise and its Environment*, Tavistock Publications, London.

Riesman, D. (1950), *The Lonely Crowd*, Yale University Press, New Haven.

Scanlon, J. N. (1948), Profit sharing under collective bargaining: three case studies, *Industrial and Labor Relations Review*, **2**(1), 58–75.

Tannenbaum, A. S. (1966), *Social Psychology of the Work Organization*, Wadsworth Publishing Co., Belmont, California.

Tannenbaum, A. S., Ed. (1968), *Control in Organizations*, McGraw-Hill, New York.

Trist, E. L. and Bamforth, K. W. (1951), Some social and psychological consequences of the longwall method of coal-getting, *Human Relations*, **4**(1), 3–38.

Trist, E. L., Higgin, G. W., Murray, H. and Pollock, A. B. (1963), *Organizational Choice*, Tavistock Publications, London.

Von Bertalanffy, L. (1950). The theory of open systems in physics and biology, *Science*, *III*, 23–9.

Weber, M., (1904), *The Protestant Ethic and the Spirit of Capitalism*. Translated by T. Parsons, Allen and Unwin, 1930. Excerpts reprinted in Burns, T., Ed., 1969, *Industrial Man*, Penguin Books, Baltimore, pp. 15–22.

Wouk, H. (1951), *The Caine Mutiny*, Doubleday, Garden City, N. Y.

PART II

Organization for Tasks

Introduction to Part II

The central theme pursued by the authors of the papers in this section is exploration of actual and potential relationships within and between organizations, as the participants act on their varying percepts of tasks and interact with the reality of their organization and its environment as they have defined them. In this, the writers reflect the major preoccupation of A. K. Rice and for the most part they use, but develop in the light of their own experience, the heuristic concepts that he and his Tavistock colleagues formulated.

The organizations studied include RAF units, marketing enterprises, a school, therapeutic institutions, the prison service and local churches of the Church of England. Like Rice's, the insights of many of the authors and their theoretical constructs of organizations are based on their direct experiences of working in consultancy or action-research roles with members of enterprises. Others have been members of institutions within which they have taken on a leadership role by examining the reality of their own enterprise as constructed both by themselves, their colleagues and other interested parties. From whichever role their thinking is derived, they hold in common a commitment to comprehend, and enable others to appreciate, the complex realities of an organization, this being a necessary preliminary to exercising some choice as to what form the organization ultimately ought to take. Organizational choice is currently an issue of some importance (Child, 1973), and the following chapters may therefore contribute to the debate.

Since Rice's thinking about organizations has influenced many of these papers, it is useful to start by setting this thinking in context. Central to it was an open-system model of organization which he understood to be a socio-technical system, for he recognized the interrelatedness of social–psychological, technological, economic and political factors present in a work enterprise, and also its interdependence with its environment.

The system concept has been a major landmark in organizational theory-building. While it may be that systems theory and its variations will become obsolete, its introduction marked a major conceptual shift in understanding the reality of organizations. When the co-ordination of work in comparatively large, centralized enterprises started to become seriously problematic as a result of the first industrial revolution, the solutions were a product of the salient knowledge of the times. The rationalist and positivist spirit was applied to organizations. It was thought that an organization, such as a manufacturing enterprise, could be designed as a machine to carry out prescribed and bounded tasks and that any deviation from the predicted forms of organization was attributable either to engineering inadequacy or to the fallibility of man (Bennis, 1959). According to Mayntz's concise description:

'The classical model of organization was basically static. The organization appeared as a calculated, rational instrument, its goal fixed and stable, its formal structure the translation of this goal into means activities, and its integration based on hierarchical authority. Hence, goal-setting processes, self-maintenance, environmental interaction and adaptation were not seen as problematical'. (Mayntz, 1964, p. 96)

This 'machine theory of organization' was conceived of as having universal application.

With the discovery of 'human relationships' within industrial and other enterprises, as a result of the Hawthorne experiments, this essentially pre-scriptive model of organization was recognized as being at variance with the empirical reality. Resulting from that, the salient conceptualization of organiz-ations became an admixture: classical organizational prescriptions were now designated as the formal aspects of organization, to which was added a new emphasis on the social and psychological factors present in any work situation, which became known as the informal organization. While this 'human relations approach' made a very real contribution to the understanding of organizations, initially the data generated by such studies were a product of the same mode of thought and conception of science, as had undergirded the first industrial revolution. Essentially, this mode of thought was atomistic and rationalistic: knowledge, it was believed, could be advanced by partializing reality. In such a process, however, 'the nature of the very reality is distorted' (Hartman, 1970, p. 468). The resultant organizational *gestalt* has been remarkably persist-ent. (For an extended discussion of this issue see the paper by Lupton.) One possible explanation for the survival of this kind of 'admixture' model is that it provides the practitioner, be he manager or consultant, with a set of independ-ent variables to be manipulated. Despite empirical studies, for example by Woodward (1965), the technology of organizations is often understood to be immutable, and therefore the only variables left for manipulation are the human ones. For example, the notion that organizations can be changed if the 'style of management' is altered is one still held by a great number of managers. A more fundamental explanation for the persistence of these ideas may be that the place of conflict and its creative resolution, seen as related social processes, are both misunderstood and undervalued in organization, and so are perceived as having to be either socially and psychologically 'engineered' out of existence, or delimited to certain specified areas, such as pay and rewards, so that compliance and consensus can reign through the use of exogenous factors. This, of course, leaves the phenomenal nature of authority within organiz-ations unexamined.

With the introduction of a systems concept of organization, a drastic change in thinking about organization became possible: there was a transition in modes of thought from the linear and analytical to the transactional and synthet-ic. If, as Thomas Kuhn has argued in *The Structure of Scientific Revolutions* (1970), science is not cumulative but collapses and is rebuilt after each major conceptual shift, the systems concept of organization has this potentiality, for it enables practitioners to deal with infinitely more data and their relationships.

The major thrust of a systems concept is that it 'helps us to think about the unthinkable' (Hartman, 1970, p. 468), which must be a necessary preliminary to formulating testable theories of organizations.

It is this thinking about the unthinkable that the majority of the authors here demonstrate, and they have done so for the most part as consultants. Again, it may be useful to note how the systems concept was used by Rice in his consultancy role. The concept, of course, rests on the assumption that enterprises are in critical respects analagous to organisms. One problem is that this metaphor can sometimes be used so literally that it curtails understanding and truncates perception; 'a way of seeing is also a way of not seeing' (Poggi, 1965, p. 284). This is particularly apparent when use of the organic analogy results in organizations being reified, as when they are conceived as having to adapt to certain 'functional imperatives', or when a concept such as 'homeostasis', adumbrated by Cannon (1932) as essential for understanding the various control systems within the human body, is applied indiscriminately to organizational theory-building. This illustrates the difficulty of using any highly abstract model. Confusion arises when a particular framework, such as the socio-technical system approach to organization, is used as an absolute model of empirical reality, rather than a conceptual model, composed of a number of related heuristic concepts, which the observer can use to frame questions, as a means of disentangling the complex reality he is attempting to understand and so extending his construction of reality. Rice always quite explicitly used his socio-technical approach to organizations as a means of enabling him, as a consultant, to build models of the different import-conversion-export relationships present, on the basis of different assumptions about the environment and about change in relations between the enterprise and its environment. The aim was to compare different models with each other and with the existing organizations (Rice, 1958 and 1963).

Rice's development and use of the heuristic concept of 'primary task' was mentioned in the Introductory Essay. So also were some criticisms of it, by Fox and Silverman. To these may be added a comment by Brown:

'There seems to be an implicit assumption at times that all strata within an enterprise will be agreed about the enterprise's primary task, or at least that such agreement is possible'. (Brown, 1967, pp. 45–46)

In response to the first part of Brown's criticism, it has to be pointed out that the concept can be used in three different ways for examining the reality of an organization. First, it can be used by the consultant or action research worker to make a hypothesis about what the primary task appears to be, judging by the behaviour of the participants. Second, in order to understand what social action the participants subjectively believe themselves to be engaged in, the concept can be used to help them to articulate their perceptions. In this way the differing constructions of the reality of an organization, held in the minds of its members and structuring their conduct within the organization, can be exposed for mutual examination. It becomes possible then to differentiate between what is shared and what is idiosyncratic and, as important, to postulate what conscious and unconscious factors make such constructions difficult to examine. Third, the consultant or action-researcher may make a formulation of primary task which is clearly a value-judgement (for example, Miller and Gwynne, 1972). Through discussion of these different formulations, members of an organization can decide what their primary task is and ought to be.

In response to the second part of Brown's criticism, we must note that as a consultant Rice believed that agreement on the primary task of an organization was possible, for he subscribed to the particular conception of man that is expressed in his essay, 'Individual, Group and Intergroup Processes' above. What can be taken out of his discussion of individual personality is the view that the mature individual has the capacity to transact external and internal realities across his personal boundary, and can thus manage his feelings, sentiments and constructions of reality in a way that enables him to take on a role for the pursuance of a particular task. Rice's discussion of the regulatory transactions across the boundaries between the individual's inner and outer worlds, between person and role, individual and group, leader and followers, group and enterprise, enterprise and environment, leads on to the notion that every individual has the potentiality for self-management in roles of both leadership and followership within organizations. In both types of role, the individual exercises authority. The value of this formulation is that it provides a theoretical bridge between the individual and his organization, a meeting-point between social system and social action perspectives. The individual brings to his organization values, orientations and sentiments from the wider society that can influence his social action within it, in whatever way he consciously decides to deal with them. He can thus be seen as negotiating or managing his own sentiments and his definitions of the reality of his organization—its social and political structure, technology, task and environment—in relation to others' definitions, so as to construct a shared reality. As already indicated, therefore, the concept of primary task can be used in both an heuristic and maieutic fashion to bring forward into consciousness what the action is about. This development has become available through combining psycho-analytic, social-psychological and sociological perspectives on organization.

Clearly, Rice believed that through the use of a socio-technical approach to organizations it was possible to think through to a more sophisticated view of enterprises, a view more accurately reflecting their complex reality. As important, he also recognized that men have to take responsibility for what they perceive and for the organizations they design to co-ordinate their activities in the pursuit of goals which individually they could not realize.

The authors of the papers in Part II further explore the relationship between tasks and organizational structures. The theme of the Part is stated in the first two papers: Hunt's 'On the Work Itself: Observations Concerning Relations between Task and Organizational Processes', and Lupton's '"Best Fit" in the Design of Organization'.

The complexity and interrelatedness of tasks is the subject of Hunt's paper.

Organizations (which fundamentally are ways of arranging for the co-ordinated performance of tasks) are taken to be purposive, open-decision systems which, while faced with uncertainty, can be subject to rational criteria. His aim is to develop a conceptual framework for explicating the implications of task for organizations, and so to unravel the complexity of tasks, which appear in different forms and are interrelated with a wide variety of other organizational phenomena, from which they have to be distinguished. As he discriminates among different kinds of tasks, he makes the point that, no matter how defined organizationally, tasks are construed and defined by individuals idiosyncratically; hence account has to be taken of the phenomenology of the tasks which is 'redefined' by the individual. Because it is always this phenomenal task that is actually performed, the design of organizational task models and their associated control systems has to take the actors' definitions of the situation into account. He describes a logical sequence of steps which begins with task and runs through the formulation of particular task models, which are then integrated into larger extended models, to end in output. He shows how this basic task structure can be co-ordinated with planning and control systems and with the various administrative support arrangements. He then attempts to explain how this whole structural process depends on and is relative to tasks, and is co-ordinated to organizational goals and technologies. Hunt, however, makes clear that this logical sequence will not necessarily result in one organizational form or design. Rather, he is concerned to provide a taxonomy of tasks and their interrelationships with organizational phenomena so that mangers can better take decisions on the form of their enterprises.

Organizational design is the subject of Lupton's paper, in which he distinguishes three contrasting approaches and offers extended critiques of two of these: the 'human relations approach' and the 'classical structuralist approach'. Lupton proceeds to make a case for a contingency approach. This is based upon an open-system view of organizations which sees enterprises as patterns of human tasks and relationships which are so shaped as to allow the growth and development, or at least the survival, of organizations in environments which can be seen as offering opportunities as well as constraints. This requires that both the individual and the organization have to be taken into account in organizational analysis and design. In his concluding section, Lupton discusses two examples of published work to illustrate the 'best fit' approach to organizational design and outlines procedures for introducing design changes.

Cherns and Clark, in 'Task and Organization: Military and Civilian', also focus on organizational design, using their direct experiences in both civil and military enterprises. Their work falls into the category of action research, which they see as being of value in exploring the limits of a particular approach to organizational analysis and for suggesting new directions for basic research. They do not view themselves as organizational theorists, but as being concerned to develop organizational models for the better functioning of enterprises. Their framework, they claim, can be placed in that school of organizational design currently being recognized as the task analysis approach, or the contingency theory of organizational design. Having made explicit their role, they note the objectives of such an approach and the criteria which may be used to evaluate it. The charge that the task analysis approach is a form of 'technological determinism' is, they argue, misplaced, for the task perspective does not seek to refer to all behaviour in organizations. While this perspective proved useful in their projects, they also found it necessary to undertake studies of the cultural system and, therefore, utilized the concept of sentient groups (Miller and Rice, 1967). This has implications for the choice of control system in an organization and for the allocation of people to roles within it. They describe an opportunity to test the value both of the approach derived from task analysis and of the concept of sentient groups when they undertook a project on Royal Air Force training units.

The major focus of the relationship between task and organization has tended to be in production enterprises. Sadler, however, in his paper, 'Task and Organization Structure in Marketing', addresses himself to marketing operations. He tries to isolate the main factors that differentiate between types of tasks in marketing, and to identify some of the major constraints that these impose on decisions about organization. Sadler postulates that:

'The primary task of a marketing organization is to manage the relationship between the organization as a whole and the actual and potential users of its output in such a way that over the long term the primary task of the organization as a whole is achieved.'

He discusses five main respects in which organizational structure in the marketing functions of business enterprises appear to vary. Having outlined the constraints, both internal and environmental, which have to be taken into account when constructing a model of organization so as to give the best organizational fit for task performance, Sadler argues that although analysis of the task should be the starting point when designing or redesigning an organization structure, other factors need to be taken into account before managerial decisions are made.

As the title of his paper implies—'Environment, Cohesion and Differentiation in a Secondary School'—Hutton attempts to analyse some of the relations between the organization of a school and its environmental demands and constraints. These are treated not in a global fashion, but as being located in differentiated subenvironments. Hutton shows how environmental pressures on the school influenced not only policy, task formulation and task organization, but also internal culture.

As a result of this piece of work, Hutton suggests that a general conceptual difficulty is that of attempting to match ideal situations, based on a clear definition of task and the establishment of criteria against which the efficacy of performance can be assessed, to real-life organizational processes. The structure of an organization, he argues, is merely a set of abstract statements. The social action of the participants has also to be taken into account, for one person's perception of the structure may not coincide with another's. The question he asks, therefore, is: How is it possible for an organization to change? His hypothesis is that if it makes sense to talk about individual behaviour as being organized so as to maintain the integrity of self-image or self-representation, by analogy there might be operating in an enterprise, in the minds of the members, something which might be called a 'structure representation'. If an organization changes, the structure also overtly changes, but a 'structure representation' might persist within the organization, acting as a further constraint on the task of the organization being realized.

The importance of the concept of boundaries in Rice's organizational thinking has been referred to already. Briefly, the boundary between an organization and its environment has two functions. First, it separates the organization from its environment by demarcating what is within the organization from what is external to it. Second, a boundary has a transactional function, for the less closed the organization is, the more dynamic has to be the interaction between the system of the enterprise and its environment. A boundary is therefore to be regarded as not merely a barrier or encapsulating device, but as a region or space in which vital regulatory functions are carried out as the organization imports and exports persons, ideas and materials, etc. from and to the external environment. The significance of boundaries and their management is the concern of Levinson and Astrachan. Although the example they use is the community mental health centre, the issues they raise have application to any organization concerned with health, education or welfare. They point out that markedly little attention has been paid to the problems of the design, functioning and evaluation of entry systems, even though they are regarded as being important. Consequently, they aim to develop a more systematic view of the entry system both as an intraorganizational task and as a link between the organization and its community context. In this they take a combined clinical-organizational approach, for while clinical considerations are of critical importance in a mental health centre, the development of an effective entry system requires an organizational perspective. Very often, Levinson and Astrachan observe, authority over the entry system is either located in a position of limited organizational authority or is so diffused that no one knows who is responsible. They argue that if the management of an organization has two crucial tasks, of ensuring that the 'conversion' processes are being carried out effectively, and that external boundaries are regulated in ways to promote the survival and continued growth of the organization, the former can be conducted by second and third levels of management, but the regulation of boundaries must be the first priority of top management, both through their own direct involvement and through the creation of effective boundary systems.

The relationship between an organization and its environment is often recognized, but not so often identified precisely. Here, it is argued that multiple external groups and forces are also involved in establishing the service priorities of an organization such as a community mental health centre. Such groups and forces are local political pressures, larger scale political pressures and the needs and demands for the services of the centre as identified through market research. The management of boundary arrangements has to be such, they argue, that there is possibility of fruitful collaboration and negotitation at the interface of the organization with other systems in its community environment. The managerial outlook required to further this organization-community perspective is termed 'proactive pluralism'. Such an outlook, they argue, enables an organization to exchange information with other groups and systems in its environment so that the organization, while defining its own values and goals and means to attain them, is prepared to accommodate to its turbulent environment.

Lofgren, in 'Organizational Design and Therapeutic Effect', examines the subtle interplay between the disturbed individual and the design of the organization into which he has been admitted for treatment. He argues that the assessment of therapeutic efficiency is hindered by a lack of criteria of adequate personality functioning. He uses 'boundary' as his central concept to develop such criteria. He argues that the personality system can be understood as an entity separated from its environment by a boundary across which intake and output of perceptions, feeling states and ideas can be made. Hence, states of mental health can be defined in terms of the functioning or non-functioning of personality boundaries. When the individual personality encounters complex reality situations, there may be a temptation to regression, which means a move in the direction of malfunctioning boundaries. These have to be re-established and reinforced if progression is to take place. Using this general insight, Lofgren distinguishes between the gross disturbances of boundaries that occur in isolated personality systems, and the boundary difficulties that appear only in interactional systems such as the family, where personal boundaries between a husband and wife may be incomplete. The postulate is made that if the general therapeutic task is the re-establishment of boundaries, whether socially specific or socially non-specific, or the creation of conditions whereby they can remain functional, the therapeutic intervention has to be geared to the solution of boundary problems; and further that it should be possible to devise an organization which works with these problems as the common denominator. Lofgren goes on to postulate, on the basis of previous empirical work, that there are certain minimal skills necessary in order to continue to live in any social institution. These are a measure of independence, some ability to make decisions and some capacity for interpersonal exchange in simple situations. His argument is that a therapeutic institution therefore has to enable the patient to move from a state of dependence to independence, through the clarification of individual boundary functioning. In this respect his stance is quite different from the 'proactive pluralism' of Levinson and Astrachan. Whereas their thinking is in terms of providing an array of therapeutic resources to deal with individual patients' needs, he focuses on a single problem—re-establishment of the individual's boundaries—which is common to a diverse patient population.

He describes how these notions have been put into operation in a psychiatric inpatient unit in California. The patient's successful discharge is a result of the pressure from the adaptational requirements of the institution which enables him to regain his own previously held values of independence when his boundaries were functioning. Once this occurs he can no longer fit into the dependent patient culture, and as he cannot become a staff member his continued stay in the institution becomes impossible—there is no role for him—so he moves to discharge.

'Organization and Training for the Task of Treatment in the Prison Service' is the subject of the paper by Fitch and Hewlings. Traditionally, prisons have had a custodial function, but over the years treatment activities have been added. Nowadays, prisons have both treatment and custodial goals, which should not be seen as mutually exclusive, but rather as interdependent. The problem is that the conflict between these two goals is likely to produce chaos in social relationships, both among the staff, who may be pursuing the two goals separately, and between staff and inmates. One solution has been to apply the community model approach to the prison situation, to avoid members of the institution thinking that treatment is only conducted by certain staff in certain places at certain times, while the remainder pursue their custodial tasks. Instead of keeping treatment and security separate, now the aim is to have 'treatment within security'. The introduction of the community model approach, however, suggests that the basic working tool must be the relationship between those in authority (the staff), and those under authority (the inmates). Fitch and Hewlings describe and analyse the group and intergroup relations thrown up by this dynamic relationship. Having defined the treatment task within a prison as the setting up of an intergroup situation between staff and inmates so that the former may facilitate the learning of the latter and encourage in them a desire for self-help, they spell out the implications for the training of basic grade staff and staff in managerial roles.

The final paper, entitled 'The Local Church and its Environment', is by Reed and Palmer. It is an attempt to use an open-system model to understand the organization of local churches within the Church of England. Taking the distinctive primary task of the local church as provision of opportunities for worship, they explore the meanings the act of worship can have. The service of worship provides individuals with an environment and a role in which they can behave in a way which expresses a modulating relationship with an unseen person addressed as 'God'. They argue that the individual in going to church experiences a change in his state of mind, in that he adopts attitudes and behaviour expressing a condition of dependence. For the authors, this term has no pejorative loading, as it expresses a state of mind which also can be found, for example, in friendship and in nursing, and is a means by which normal people can find restoration, a sense of being real and an experience of re-creation. The external environment of the church is referred to as the profane world, in contrast to the sacred world which is created in worship. Having described the qualities of these contrasting worlds, Reed and Palmer posit that if a local church can provide worship which allows for controlled regression to dependence, this enables the worshipper to cope with the anxieties engendered by the profane world. They go on, therefore, to postulate that the primary task of a church is:

'to contain, or render manageable, anxieties associated with the activities of the profane world, so that individuals and institutions are able to carry out the tasks on which the survival and well-being of their society depends'.

If the local church fails to realize this primary task, the individual worshipper is denied the opportunity to experience controlled regression to dependence, which means that he is less able to pursue freedom, truth and justice in the outside profane world.

The cumulative importance of the papers presented in this section is that they provide the practitioner, whether his role is in management, consultancy or action research, with examples of the application of the socio-technical framework to a variety of enterprises. The insights from one kind of enterprise, such as a hospital, may help illumine the social processes in a school or a prison. None of the papers, however, claims to be prescriptive, nor are the solutions, either advanced or implied, universalistic. They are all statements of attempts made by practitioners to advance the understanding of the complex reality of organizations.

One value of the papers may be in helping managers and others to recognize that while an organization is an abstraction held in the mind, it is equally not a 'thing' outside them. Organizations are instruments of men for the pursuance of tasks, and as such can be formed and shaped as a result of considered choice and political decision. Organizations may be potentially immortal, but their destiny is controlled by mortal men. What is clear through the sustained application of a socio-technical framework is that contemporary organizations can no longer be conceptualized, if ever they could, as closed systems cut off from the environment. All the papers in this section have emphasized the relationship of an organization to its environment. The challenge now is to enable participants within organizations to cope more realistically with the necessary innovations to allow their organization not merely to react to their environment but to act back upon it.

References

Bennis, W. G. (1959), Leadership theory and administrative behaviour: the problem of authority, *Administrative Science Quarterly*, **4**, (3), 259–301.

Brown, R. K. (1967), Research and consultancy in industrial enterprises, *Sociology*, **1**, (1) 33–60.

Cannon, W. B. (1932), *The Wisdom of the Body*. Norton, New York.

Child, J. (1973), Organization: a choice for man, *in*: J. Child, Ed., *Man and organization*, Allen and Unwin, London.

Hartman, A. (1970), To think about the unthinkable, *Social Casework*, October, pp. 467–474.

Kuhn, T. (1970), *The Structure of Scientific Revolutions*, 2nd ed., University of Chicago Press, Chicago.

Mayntz, R. (1964), The study of organizations, *Current Sociology*, **13**, (3), 95–156.

Miller, E. J. and Gwynne, G. V. (1972), *A Life Apart*, Tavistock Publications, London.

Miller, E. J. and Rice, A. K. (1967). *Systems of Organization*, Tavistock Publications, London.

Poggi, G. (1965), A main theme of contemporary sociological analysis: its achievements and limitations, *British Journal of Sociology*, **16**, 283–294.

Rice, A. K. (1958), *Productivity and Social Organization: the Ahmedabad Experiment*, Tavistock Publications, London.

Rice, A. K. (1963), *The Enterprise and its Environment*, Tavistock Publications, London.

Woodward, J. (1965), *Industrial Organization: Theory and Practice*, Oxford University Press, London.

On the Work itself: Observations Concerning Relations between Tasks and Organizational Processes

Raymond G. Hunt

Epitomized by Frederick W. Taylor, those mainly historical figures, whom March and Simon (1958) called 'physiological organization theorists,' gave a prominent place to the 'work itself' (i.e. task properties) as a distinctive factor pertinent to both performance and modes of organizing. For all its 'system' protestations, however, the rise of so-called modern organization theory (see W. G. Scott, 1961) has been accompanied by something of a decline of concern for the work itself as a *variable* in organizational analyses, even if it still is an *object* of sometimes lively interest to systems analysts and operations researchers. The contemporary neglect of general research into organizational consequences of tasks, a neglect upon which Porter (1969), too, recently remarked, has caused conceptualization of the organizational role of work to continue in a peculiarly underdeveloped state, which is more than mildly ironic because of course, whatever else they may be, fundamentally organizations are ways of arranging for the co-ordinated performance of tasks.

Since organizations do literally exist for the doing of tasks, it is eminently reasonable for one to expect basic effects upon their processes and outputs that can be traced to variations in the properties of the tasks they are performing. Indeed, J. D. Thompson (1967), for one, has called attention to diverse assumptions about the nature of tasks that are implicit in familiar models of organization design or structure.[1] Scientific management-type theories, Thompson suggests, operate from the tacit assumption that tasks are uniformly repetitive; administrative management models presume tasks which are susceptible to specialization and departmental grouping. Such models also assume detailed knowledge of production tasks while bureaucratic organizational designs are founded on the bedrock idea that the tasks to be done are essentially stable and routinizable.

Expectations of interdependency between tasks and group processes also have empirical justification. From his exemplary review, Hackman (1969b) has concluded that, '...certain task factors control up to 50 per cent of the variance of behavior and output of small laboratory groups' (Hackman, 1969b, p. 436). To be sure, Hackman based his conclusion on small group studies done mostly in 'purified' experimental environments, but there is no reason to suppose *a priori* that things are drastically different in formal organizations. In fact, the reverse is true; but, in any case, sparse as it is, we shall see that data sustain the judgement that at least there are parallels between the two kinds of settings. So, because we think it basic to a comprehensive theory of organization that it include a coherent perspective on the nature and functions of tasks, in this essay we propose, as a kind of preface to such an eventual accomplishment, to explore the relations between organizational phenomena and task properties—the 'work itself'—inquiring into the nature of tasks and how they can be expected to determine or otherwise affect organizational and managerial events.

Task Effects in Organizations

We have said that contemporary interest in task phenomena has not been widespread (in organizational settings anyway); but neither has it been totally lacking. Hackman's and Thompson's work has been noted and task concepts have been important to the thinking of others as well. Miller and Rice (1967), for example, explicitly direct attention to task processes in organizations, and the development by the 'Tavistock group' of the now widely familiar concept of the socio-technical system expresses dedication to the end of discerning the interplay of operational and organizational processes (see, e.g., Miller and Rice, 1967; Rice, 1963; Trist and coworkers, 1963).

The task has also been evident in recent studies of associations between technology and organization (see, e.g., Woodward, 1965; Perrow, 1967; Hunt, 1970). Joan Woodward, one of the most substantial contributors to these endeavours, for instance, has described what she calls a 'task analysis approach' to the study of organization that is premised on the idea that '. . . useful comparisons of behaviour at the organizational level may be made by taking as a starting point the task to which an organization is committed' (Reeves, Turner and Woodward, 1970, p. 3).

Recent empirical papers, by Brown, Tickner and Simmonds (1969), and by O'Brien and Owens (1969), to name only two, have demonstrated clear-cut task effects on work performance. The latter showed an interaction between task properties and operator ability and the former analysed variations in quality of performance as a function of competitive demands from concurrent tasks. Naylor and Dickinson (1969) also have shown tasks to affect performance; in their research more structured tasks yielded better performance than did unstructured ones. Weick (1965) and Hackman (1969a) provide other comparable illustrations of task influences upon performance, albeit drawn mostly from studies done in laboratory situations.

Relatedly, March and Simon (1958) have discussed how the effects of the organizational dimension of 'close supervision' may be moderated by the complexity of the task involved. In the same vein, Alderfer (1969), analysing how complexity affects 'satisfaction', noted that reactions to 'job enlargement' depended on the context of its introduction; for instance, reactions were often negative in the task setting of continuous process technologies. Porter and Lawler (1965), after a searching literature coverage, offer the judgement that, except perhaps as regards organizational rank, no *generally* consistent relations can be found between either performance or attitudes and *any* organizational property (such as centralization versus decentralization, tall versus flat designs, etc.). If it does not prove the point, this finding at least strongly suggests that the effects of different organizational designs are relative to the tasks being done in them.

Moreover, it is possible to show that organizational structures themselves are not independent of task features. Hall (1962), for one, has demonstrated variation in the degree of bureaucratization of intraorganizational units and, although he did not analyse it intensively, he adduced evidence that type-of-task was an important determinant of differences in organizational structure. As Thompson's analysis might have led one to expect, Hall found that departments characterized by non-uniform or social tasks were less bureaucratized than were those involved with uniform or 'traditional' tasks.

Line-staff differentiations can also be seen as more or less task-relative (cf. Allen, 1963), and Guetzkow (1965) ends his review of interrelations among tasks and organizational communication nets by posing for further research the question of just how such nets interact with 'task requirements'. He thereby makes plain the prior conclusion that they do in fact interact.

Finally, Katz and Kahn (1966) have hypothesized that the degree of organizational task interdependence is a major consideration in choosing a suitable authority structure. Actually any view of organizations as role system—Katz and Kahn's is a specimen—almost necessarily prompts questions about the extent to which those systems are basically constrained by task properties and their directly derivative activity networks. But be that as it may, task-performance-structure linkages seem clearly enough established as genuine organizational phenomena.

Even from our rather cursory summary, it is apparent that tasks may have two distinguishable kinds of effect: what Reeves, Turner and Woodward (1970) have termed 'operator level' effects—i.e. constraints on action—or, what they call 'organizational-level' effects—i.e. constraints on administrative modalities. Then, too, task effects may be either direct or indirect. Weick (1965) and Hackman (1969a) provide examples of the former, as do the studies of operator-level task effects by Brown and coworkers (1969) and by O'Brien and Owens (1969). Direct organizational-level effects can be exemplified by Hall's (1962) previously mentioned work on bureaucratization.

Indirect effects of tasks may be found in their moderation of relations between other organizational variables. March and Simon's (1958) analysis of the effects of supervisory style in relation to task complexity is an illustration. Another would be indirect task impact at the operator-level brought about by performance control associated with administrative structures which themselves are task-relative.

All this goes to show plainly that task phenomena have not been ignored in organizational studies; but, as this brief gloss is meant to suggest, their handling in the modern organizational literature has mostly been global or macroscopic in character. Attempts at the identification of task dimensions and theoretical specification of the forms and mechanisms of their actual or prospective relations with organizational process and structure has not been frequent among present-day scholars. Therefore, in the sections that follow, we shall survey some instructive thinking about tasks, casting a hopeful eye to the ultimate object of arriving at a conceptual framework serviceable in explicating their implications for organizations. Our stress will be on relations between tasks and organization structure, but along the way we shall tender some remarks about output too.

On The Nature of Tasks

As is often true, sheer ubiquitousness makes it easy to think of tasks as essentially simple to understand when in fact, and especially in organizations, they are complex, multidimensional things, not at all simple to describe or define. Tasks appear in many different forms and they interconnect with a wide variety of other basic phenomena and constructs from which they need to be discriminated, but not isolated.

Task and Situation

Firstly, tasks belong among the stimulus phenomena broadly classified as 'situational' influences upon behaviour (see, e.g., Hackman, 1969a; Bass, 1968). They may thus be linked-up with the larger class of what Udy (1965) calls ecological influences upon performance (and, by implication, organizing). The anticipation that task properties will have immediate effects on behaviour plainly follows from such a categorization. However, though it may not require saying, tasks are not the only situational influences on behaviour and so can hardly be depended upon as exclusive causes of organizational events. (Hackman (1969a) makes the same point.)

Task and Activity

By the same token, whereas task performance quite obviously requires 'activity', task and activity are not the same thing [see, Weick (1965) for an extended discussion]. In the first place, the latter (activity) references ways of implementing the former (task). Tasks and their performances would need to be kept analytically separate even if one did wish eventually to hazard the dubious proposition that task performance is wholly determined by task properties. It may be generally useful, as we believe it is, to construe tasks behaviourally, but 'activity' must be understood to denominate a generic of which 'task' is a special case. Specifically, tasks have the quality of being 'imposed' and so can be understood as aspects of activity 'responding to expectancies of others' (Bakke, 1959). That is to say, tasks possess an inherently *interactional* nature not necessarily found in all forms of activity; as Weick puts it, tasks are to be found 'embedded in a complex network of relations' (Weick, 1965, p. 228).

Tasks, Goals and Divisions of Labour

Finally, notice should be taken of Trist and coworkers (1963) urgings that tasks should not be confused with organizational goals or 'missions'. Trist and coworkers illustrate the utility of this distinction by showing how task phenomena can be illuminated by being studied in relation to separately defined goal systems. In much the same spirit, Naylor and Dickinson (1969) discriminate between task and work structure, the former having to do with tasks, as such, and the latter with their organizational distribution—the division of labour. Thus, we shall have made some progress if we understand that tasks are related to, but are not to be equated with, situations, activities, goals and divisions of labour. But, important as they are, by themselves such distinctions still leave the phenomenon itself unspecified.

Task Defined

A good place to begin a more thorough specification of task phenomena is with the very general definition of 'task' that has been synthesized by Hackman. He states that:

'a task may be assigned to a person (or group) by an external agent or may be self-generated. It consists of a stimulus complex and a set of instructions which specify what is to be done vis à vis the stimuli. The instructions indicate what operations are to be performed by the subject(s) with respect to the stimuli and/or what goal is to be achieved'. (Hackman, 1969a p. 113)

From within a more explicitly organizational frame of reference, Weick (1965) has presented a similar definition. Paraphrased, his four-part statement runs as follows:

(1) Tasks are imposed either by agencies external to a system or by consensus within the system itself;

(2) Task performance reflects influences additional to those directly imposed by its 'physical' properties;

(3) Tasks include goals plus prescriptions of means for their attainment (although these prescriptions may not always be highly explicit);

(4) 'Tasks vary in the individual and the group processes which they make salient.' This fourth point relates the task to performance and organization as a direct determinant.

It is not certain that as Hackman seems willing to do, Weick would accept as 'tasks' wholly self-generated specifications. (Bakke (1959) would probably describe them as 'acts'.) Nor is the matter a mere quibble. For purposes of organizational analysis, expressly directing attention to the interactional character of organizational tasks, as Weick does, has considerable merit. It also suits well the mission of this essay by highlighting the ramified *social* implications of task prescriptions. Aside from this point of emphasis, however, basically Weick's and Hackman's definitions are quite compatible. Both underscore the multidimensional complexity and instrumental nature of tasks, and both make plain that tasks include performance programs as well as stimulus properties. Of course, these definitions are highly abstract. The kind of total description they imply rarely is achieved or attempted in any concrete organizational setting. But, as good definitions should, they point nonetheless clearly to the basic dimensions for actual operational task description.

Task Description

We earlier suggested that tasks rarely are easy to pin down. Description and classification of group tasks is difficult at best and it is not made any easier by the current absence of any viable taxonomy (cf. Davis, 1969) or standard procedures. Hackman (1969a), for instance, has identified four different 'customary' approaches to the basic problem of task description. Tasks, he says, may be described '*qua* task', i.e. in terms of their physical nature—their stimulus properties. Or, tasks may be specified in terms of behavioural requirements, i.e. the kinds of responses (including interactions) *expected* of their performers. A third approach to task description involves spelling-out what people *actually* do (as distinct from what they are supposed to do) when performing them. And fourthly, tasks may be described in terms of 'ability requirements', i.e. the skills or talents necessary to performance (see also Jaques, 1967).

The first of these approaches to task description is often impracticable, Hackman believes, owing to such inconveniences as excessive numbers of descriptive dimensions. The third approach, that is simply describing what people do in performing tasks, is certainly interesting, but it does not, in fact, specify the task; it amounts instead to delineation of a dependent variable class. Such description would state performance events that still would need explanations—explanations which might, of course, be found among the otherwise specified properties of the task being done. Description of tasks as ability requirement, Hackman argues, is epistemologically equivalent to description as behaviour. Therefore, three of the four main approaches to task description seem to exhibit serious liabilities, liabilities which lead Hackman to propose as most useful task descriptions set forth as behavioural requirements—what activities, exactly, an operator is expected to display.

On practical, and to some extent on conceptual grounds, Hackman's preference is understandable. Describing tasks as behaviour requirements has the important virtue of relating the task concept to the functional properties of organization where our principal interests usually lie. Still, there is something to be said for encouraging efforts to describe tasks *qua* task if one is ever to understand the bases for performance constraint or expectation in task performance. And, too, Hackman's use of the term 'ability' in connection with the fourth mode of task description promotes an overly narrow view of that approach and hence, perhaps, underestimation of its merits. If, instead of 'ability', one stresses a broader idea of *resources* (human and other) required and/or available for performance, this approach neatly complements behaviour requirement modes of description. Moreover, as we shall indicate shortly, it is in the convergence of tasks and resources that the crucial task-technology link is found. It seems clear, then, that combining various approaches to task description can result in fuller specification of an organization's task structure and so provide a firmer base for examining wider organizational ramifications of that structure.

Weick's (1965) approach to task description—this one within an expressly organizational, if still laboratory-based frame—is also instructive. He proposes that tasks may be described in terms of: (a) required actions; (b) stimulus processing; and (c) group information processing. The first of these entails primarily a straightforward behavioural analysis largely unrelated to the goals or results of task prescription of performance. The second comes down, in essence, to a cognitively oriented functional analysis of task requirements, some of the general dimensions of which can be found reviewed in Fitts and Posner's (1967) useful little book. The same can be said for description of group information processing, although, consistent with Weick's characteristic posture toward tasks, it places a heavier emphasis on patterns of cooperative interaction.

Weick's approach to task description in terms of required actions and Hackman's description of task-as-behaviour-requirement seem essentially indistinguishable—if, that is, one defines 'behaviour' and 'action' as synonyms for simple activity. If one chooses not to do that, then required actions might be taken to constitute only one element of a more general behaviour description. In that case, it, together with Weick's other two approaches, might be taken to be subsumed as fuller explication of 'behaviour requirements' in Hackman's sense.

Task Structure

Implicit in the foregoing is the idea that tasks have varying properties that are combined in different ways to constitute a 'synthetic' task. In effect, this synthetic task is both the starting point for analysis and, in some sense, the basis for perceptions by the organization's members of the things that need doing. A bit later we shall have more to say about the phenomenology of tasks; just now we wish to point out that decomposing the synthetic task, via the descriptive approaches reviewed above, for example, serves to reveal its 'structure'—its elements and their modes of relation—and can presumably help to illuminate basic task 'units' and 'rules' for their combination.

At least two writers, Naylor and Dickinson (1969), believe they have already succeeded in identifying the fundamental structural dimensions of tasks (see also W. E. Scott, 1966). Their nominations for the basic dimensions are: complexity, organization and redundancy. By complexity Naylor and Dickinson mean the information-processing or memory-storage requirements of a task; organization refers to similar demands imposed by task component interrelations. Redundancy signifies the overlap among the demands of the various task components.

Clearly this formulation ignores physical properties of tasks in favour of functional ones. It may consequently be regarded as incomplete; nevertheless, as a partial paradigm it has much intuitive appeal (and some empirical support as well). What makes Naylor and Dickinson's ideas particularly interesting is that they help to focus attention on the variable cognitive burdens associated with tasks; those burdens dictate that tasks and their organizational impacts will depend upon the ways in which they are conceptualized, and that in turn, must be relative to human and organizational capabilities for doing so, something Taylor (1965) has considered at length in connection with decision-making and problem-solving.

Task Models

Conceptualizing a task can be construed as a process of 'modelling' and task models can be defined as representing an 'insistent set of perceptions of what the task is and how it should be performed' (Haberstroh, 1965, p. 1173). Task modelling is thus a process of trying to specify the nature and requirements of a task and of elaborating ways of doing it. At the level of the individual, task modelling signifies much the same psychological processes as are implied when one speaks of the 'phenomenology' of the task. Task phenomenology, however, also suggests something about how people relate themselves to tasks—about the meanings tasks have for them. These personal meanings will surely affect the attitudes a person holds toward tasks and will inevitably influence his performance of them (cf. Steiner, 1966; also W. E. Scott, 1966).

In the end, tasks will always be construed more or less idiosyncratically by their performers. (We shall have more to say about this presently in connection with task redefinition.) But *organizational* task modelling is an effort to control and restrict the variance in this process by standardizing specifications of task structure and providing correlated performance programs. Steiner (1966) may be consulted for a review of various types of task model (e.g. additive, disjunctive, etc.), but, whatever they may be, an organization's task models depict its formalized understanding of its work, and of the most suitable ways of doing it. On either or both counts they (the models) may be more or less detailed and precise; how detailed and precise will depend not only on the nature of the task, but also on the material, psychological and social resources available for their conceptualization and performance, orchestrated with the enterprise's current constructions of its objectives. It is for these reasons presumably that Haberstroh (1965) characterizes task models as aspects of an organization's structure highly relative to both its goals and its technology.

Technology Any separation of tasks from the resources pertinent to them is to some extent arbitrary—certainly it is in any concrete setting (see Hickson and coworkers (1969) for an excellent treatment of various aspects of technology). If Woodward, for instance, can speak loosely of 'the work and its technology' (see Reeves, Turner and Woodward, 1970), it must nevertheless be obvious that, as it enters task modelling, technology is integral to any conception of tasks and their doing.

On the one hand, the nature of the task may determine the relevance of resources (cf. Steiner, 1966); but at the same time, perceptions of the nature of the task will depend heavily on the technological perspectives brought to bear on it. These perspectives tend to control not only global perceptions of tasks, but also abilities to analyse and comprehend task structures and awareness of means of identifying and mobilizing resources for performance. Furthermore, technological facility can work literal reconstruction of a task. By way of illustration: the availability of computing machinery can, in a manner of speaking, simplify tasks by reducing their complexity (as Naylor and Dickinson define it) via augmentation of the total system's information processing, memory storage and retrieval capacities. What is more, since technology may be divided into material and social varieties, it necessarily impacts on provisions for organizing task interaction and hence the entire process of organizing for goal achievement (cf. Olsen, 1968).

Goals and the Primary Task   Informed by the larger concept of the socio-technical system, the idea of the 'primary task' expresses the principle that, among tasks as among the animals, some are more equal than others. By definition, primary tasks are those necessary to the survival of the enterprise (cf. Miller and Rice, 1967; Rice, 1963; Trist and coworkers, 1963). They may vary in their nature from organization to organization and from time to time; they may even vary between subparts of the same organizations, but they are necessarily central to the interests of the system and they derive their significance from their relations to the system as a whole.

Rice (1963) has been especially careful about distinguishing the primary task from the organization's mission, yet it is clear that orientations toward tasks must reflect a system's goals as they are construed at a point in time. This is no more than saying that, within an organization, tasks are 'prioritized' and that the bases for assigning priorities are the system's objectives or desired outputs. These may change with states of the system and, as we have said, they may even vary intraorganizationally, but they will still always constitute basic guideposts in processes of task modelling. Indeed, the primary task(s) will be nuclear elements around which operational systems—what we shall call extended task models—are constructed, and they will be the chief focus of system control structures.

Extended Task Models

Organizations, even simple ones, involve multiple interrelated tasks. Consequently a simple conception of singular discrete task models is insufficient. Individual tasks must be allocated and integrated into larger designs—divisions of labour—purposively oriented to yield determinate system outputs. Because, in a very real sense, they constitute elaborations or extensions of the unit-task models, these designs can be regarded as *extended task models*. They define the comprehensive system-wide plans according to which the organization's work is to be done. They are fundamental task-based elements of overall organization structure, pivoting on the system's conception of its primary task(s).

Extended task models are analogous to Naylor and Dickinson's (1969) 'work structures' (which are similar to Trist and coworkers' (1963) 'activity structures'). Defining work structures in terms of the ways task components are distributed among work group members, Naylor and Dickinson hypothesize that actual task performance will be some combined function of task structure (see above), work structure and a third element, communication structure. This last element is self-explanatory and, in any case, is viewed by Naylor and Dickinson as dependent on and constrained by the other two elements. It is, in other words, a group creation, given the task and work structures. However, the extended task model (or any task model for that matter) implies a planning and control system (see Anthony, 1965), plus an array of supportive and administrative provisions that describe other components of organization structure. (Collectively these elements—extended task model, planning and control system, staff and administrative provision—can (together with their linkages) be taken to define the totality of organization structure.)

Planning and Control

Organizations differ greatly in the extent to which their planning functions are formalized. Nevertheless, some kind of planning activity is necessarily basic to formulation of the system's task models, and even more so to their revision as results from performance feedback are processed.

All task models, and especially elaborate extended forms, have obvious regulatory requirements. They depend operationally on a control system and an authority structure to legitimize it (cf. Haberstroh, 1968; Tannenbaum, 1968). Models require interpretation, monitoring and, often, modifying. It is the function of the control and associated managerial systems to assure these things (cf. Whyte (1969) who nominates channelling activity in suitable directions as one of the chief responsibilities of management). Like task modelling, the design and execution of control systems will be relative to organizational purpose(s) and to available material and social technology. In any case, the critical organizational significance of control provisions is highlighted by the phenomenon of 'task redefinition'.

Task Redefinition and Control Task modelling operating systems is a continuous process. Whenever a person begins work on a task he also begins to redefine his initial model of it: to re-evaluate it, reconceptualize it and make new decisions about his performance of it (see Hackman, 1969a; Weick, 1965). At the level of individual behaviour, this process is inevitable, because of the presence of incidental cues or stimuli; accumulated experience with the same or similar tasks; or 'situational embarrassments'—special threats, extraneous involvements, or uncertainty (Weick, 1965).

Since task models represent organizational attempts to generate salutary forms of task definition and performance programming, it follows that control over *informal* redefinition will be organizationally vital (as will provision for *formal* redefinition, if the organization's adaptability to change is to be guaranteed). One function of training or socialization in an organization is dissemination of its formal task models; complementing it is supervision and worker evaluation calculated to 'standardize' and constrain processes of task redefinition—that is to say, to render redefinition organizationally and functionally innocuous by conforming it to a prescribed model.

It is thus possible to make a succession of discriminations about tasks: between 'objective' tasks, modelled tasks and redefined tasks. Like the 'real world', objective tasks are ontological assumptions. Modelled tasks constitute formally stated and technologically based task prescriptions. Redefined tasks are informal, even idiosyncratic, self-definitions of tasks. They are the phenomenal tasks. Task models will be a partial function of 'objective tasks' and so will redefined tasks. The latter, however, can also be constrained by standardized models and control methods. A major function of organizational control systems, therefore, is to minimize disparity between task models and redefined (phenomenal) tasks.

The Problem of Uncertainty

Task refefinition is inevitable and control systems will vary in their ability to cope with it. It will, of course, always be the phenomenal redefined task that is actually performed, and the problem organizationally is that it may be quite difficult to predict performance outcomes solely from knowledge of formal task models. Informal, operator-determined task redefinition introduces a more or less heavy dose of uncertainty and instability into organizational affairs. Dubin (1959) has provided a stimulating treatment of some of the larger aspects of this problem. He stresses the importance of the structure of interrelationships among jobs and prompts a special focus on organizational linkage systems (i.e. on extended task models).

Uncertainty is reducible to the extent that task models *and* their associated control systems can be specified and programmed to yield targetted outputs. Briefly, this seems to depend upon three factors:

(1) Task stability.
(2) Levels of social and material technological development coupled with an understanding of their interrelations—which is to say that in a socio-technical system a major challenge is to relate or mesh social and material technologies.
(3) Environmental stability.

Uncertainty or difficulty in programming performance will tend to increase inversely with changes in the levels of these three factors. Obviously 'changeful' tasks must be largely unprogrammable and programming will likewise be problematic when the performance context is in flux. Similarly, task programming is heavily dependent upon technological considerations (cf. Hunt (1970) for a fuller discussion of these points). It might be borne in mind, in this connection, that tasks, *per se*, and the control systems applied to them are, like technology, to a degree separable. Therefore, as Woodward (1970) points out, carefully constructed control systems may be able to decrease somewhat uncertainty associated with the task system itself. In any event, an important result of programming difficulties—i.e. uncertainty—is that they tend to increase the salience of the individual task, a circumstance vividly depicted in J. D. Thompson's analysis of the 'synthetic organization' (1967). Such a state of affairs tends, in turn, to eventuate in a more task-centred, loosely integrated system oriented more toward 'problem-solving' than toward routine performance.

Uncertainty and Organizational Form

After an earlier review of relations between technology and organization we concluded that the organizationally decisive factor mediating these relations was the extent to which an organization's task systems can be programmed (Hunt, 1970; see also March and Simon, 1958). We especially stressed the significance of the system's capability for dealing with 'exceptions' to its performance routines, since no performance program can anticipate every possible contingency. For one reason or another some uncertainty will always remain, even though the amount may be highly variable.[2]

We went on in that paper to differentiate two basically different kinds of organization: *performance* and *problem-solving*. The former may be epitomized by the mass-production factory, whereas the latter is exemplified either by the research laboratory on one extreme *or* an automated oil refinery at another extreme. The reasoning on which this distinction was based ran like this:

'In a unit production firm, e.g., the laboratory, the system deals almost entirely with exceptions and its problem-solving modes are likely to be unroutinized ... In automated continuous process organizations, whether exceptions are frequent or not, they will be critical when they occur so that such systems, too, are likely to be structured as problem-solving or trouble-shooting affairs. Thus unit production organizations ... *and* continuous process organizations are both likely to be similarly structured as organic problem-solving systems. Other operations facing fewer exceptions and less vitally affected by ones that occur are likely to be differently structured as mechanistic performance systems'. (Hunt, 1970, p. 247)

Speaking of the matter of alternative methods for dividing work, Dale (1963) has also portrayed technology as imposing organizational constraints; moreover, he, too, attached significance to contrasts between segmental operations and computer guided continuous processes that had to do with the extent to which the viability of the system depended on human decision. We might note, too, that Dale gives various criteria for 'optimizing' divisions of work, the basic ones of which all are task-relative. His discussion of tasks, however, is mainly in broad functional terms. Most of the ones he identifies, e.g. policy making, really are 'meta-tasks' or rubrics. The fact that he discerns considerable uniformity in their organization suggests that psychologically these 'meta-tasks' are essentially similar cross-organizationally. They all are of the problem-solving, non-routine variety.

Uncertainty and the Primary Task

Earlier we commented on the nuclear role of the primary task in elaboration of extended task models; that concept is also germane to the present discussion. Considering task effects and other performance constraints, Rice noted that primary tasks can be defined with varying precision, but that the more precisely they are defined, the greater will be the task constraint on performance (presumably because precise definition permits detailed performance programming). In principle '...the most appropriate organization for any enterprise is that giving a best fit to primary task performance' (Rice, 1963, p. 16); but task priorities change. The more fluid is the priority system, therefore, the more fluid, or at least 'open', is organization structure likely to be. It follows, too, that task heterogeneity across the subparts of organizations (e.g. production and marketing) will necessitate a good deal of compromise in organizational-level modelling, compromise up to and including some pretty stringent segregation of organization subunits (see Hunt and coworkers, 1970). Such organizational 'divisionalization' tends to occur because 'a model for the organization of a whole enterprise must...take account of the differences in the primary tasks of the parts' (Rice, 1963, p. 17). Thus, indefiniteness about the primary task appears as a particularly important special case of task uncertainty, and prospects for intraorganizational variability in its specification, like more general task diversity, pose a clear potential for problems in the overall integration of heterogeneous organizational subsystems.

Rice (1963) has spoken of this last point, suggesting that in an integrated complex system, some tasks in certain subsystems may constrain others in different subsystems. Specifically he proposes that:

'In general, the greater the differentiation of a complex organization, the more constraint will be imposed on each subsystem; and the more subsidiary the subsystem, the greater the force of constraint on task definition and methods of performance.' (Rice, 1963, p. 191; also see Hunt, 1970, for a review of some other implications of task and technological diversity in organizations.)

These ideas, implying task hierarchies and control, will be recognized as basic to the concept of the integrative extended task model that is fundamental to coherent organizational process.

Thus the 'specifiability' and 'programmability' of organizational tasks, separately and in interaction, can be viewed as their crucial feature insofar as organizational impact is concerned. This is not just a question of the magnitude of that impact, however; it is also a question of its kind. Our general thesis is that task 'salience' increases with uncertainty, and the more important the task, the more this will be true. When tasks are vague they will exert little *direct* influence on the particulars of performance, but they will tend to be nearer the centre of organizational attention. Implied by this is the existence of rather different organizational structures, like those we described above, and it is quite possible that vague tasks will have relatively little direct effect on modes of performance and relatively more on modes of organizing, whereas the opposite is true of well-defined tasks. As Rapoport and Horvath have commented, 'The organization of a system is simple if the system is a serial or an additive complex of components, each of which is understood' (Rapoport and Horvath, 1968, p. 73). Under other conditions organization cannot be such a simple matter.

Put generally, what, in effect, we are talking about is the ease and extent to which tasks can be modelled and performance control transferred, so to speak, from the operator to the task—i.e., to what extent can human decision be reduced or routinized by articulated performance programs capable of directing discrete operations and of co-ordinating and integrating system-wide output.

We have tried to stress that this is not just a matter of tasks, *per se*:

'... Tasks and jobs are not simple technological "givens"—they are capable of being controlled and altered by human inputs into the organization'. (Porter, 1969 p. 417)

Task influences upon human organization we take as inescapable fact; but the processes of influence are neither mechanical nor unidirectional. Indeed, Woodward has argued that how a task is controlled and not just the nature of the task will determine organizational behaviour. Writing with Reeves and Turner, she posits work programming and control as the basis for most organizational constraint on performance and goes on to propose the hypothesis that control system properties may be the 'underlying variable linking organizational behaviour with technology' (Reeves and coworkers, 1970). She agrees that task uncertainty is a major determinant of the way a task can be controlled, but she also perceives control systems as able to reduce or increase what we would construe as the net amount of uncertainty in the task model. In other words, methods of control, which are integral to task models, are relative to tasks, but they also depend on resources and technologies at least partly independent of the tasks themselves.

This observation underscores the wisdom of avoiding simplistic conceptions of task-organization relations. Tasks exist in systems of human and technological relations, the components of which can affect one another in a variety of ways. Steiner (1966) has quite correctly pointed out that group achievement depends on the joint effects of tasks, resources, motivations and co-ordinations, and Sommer (1967) has described a variety of ways in which task performance can be affected by even such elementary provisions as spatial arrangements. Task phenomena, recognized or not, are the fundamental points of reference around which organizational affairs are oriented, but it will take some sophisticated theorizing to comprehend their workings in any truly satisfactory way.

Task Constraint on Management Decision

Persistent Calvinist exhortations to the contrary notwithstanding, work never has had a really good name. For all its greater rectitude, it has not typically been perceived to be as much fun as play, for instance. For management theorists to be disinclined in their thinking about the determinants of organizational matters to accord a serious standing to work and to favour instead more exotic and even self-congratulatory ingredients is, therefore, understandable. And anyway, the very throught of some kind of situational constraint on social design and action somehow tends to offend our ingrained human sense of freedom and rationality (cf. Buckley, 1968, especially Part V, Sec. A). Among managers this attitude is typically manifest in the illusion that, subject only to their personal wisdom and insight, they are perfectly free to shape organizational affairs in whatever ways they wish. Unfortunately for this viewpoint, the moral of our story is that, if not completely determined, organizational processes are importantly constrained by influences associated with the tasks on which they work. It follows, therefore, that managers will have something less than an infinite number of degrees of freedom in making decisions; many ostensible choices will be functionally foreclosed. Illustrative is Lawler's (1969) analysis of the linkages between job design, motivation and performance. Among other things, he strongly implies that task structure may severely limit prospects for job enlargement (cf. also Hackman and Lawler, 1971; Ford, 1969).

The range of managerial choice may vary, obviously, from a little to a lot—for instance, Reeves and Woodward (1970) suggest that choices among control systems seem to be greater in large batch and mass production firms than among others—but the chief way by which they (managerial choices) can be expanded, or, if not expanded, 'optimized', and, in any case, intelligently made, is by careful analysis of task-organization relations. Putting it bluntly, to change an organization one must change its task model(s) (see Golembiewski, 1965; Scott, 1966).

There are, we said at the beginning, two sides to the coin of task constraint in organizations: task effects on behaviour and task effects on organization. Here we have concentrated on the latter; Hackman (1969a, 1969b), on the other hand, has stressed the former. In his discussion of task influences on job behaviour he outlines various mechanisms by which tasks may influence performance. Briefly, there are four classes of variables (all of which we have touched on) at the 'core' of the task performance process: (a) the task itself; (b) ideas of the performer about how to do it; (c) the performer's actual activities; and (d) performance outcomes (Hackman, 1969a). The task and the performer can be conceived as 'interacting' sequentially along four dimensions that may be schematized (after Hackman) as follows:

Task ⟵————— Hypotheses re performance
⟍⟍ Motive arousal
⟍ Behavioural activation
Process-outcome links

Tasks, then, are occasions for the formulation by operators of ideas about how they (tasks) are to be done; they serve, too, in various ways to engage performer motives (together with estimates on his part of his prospects for satisfying them, cf. Vroom, 1964); they prompt states of 'behavioural readiness' (see Scott (1966) on the subject of activation effects); and, over time, they are the touchstones of episodes in which performers come to learn what consequences (outcomes) follow from various modes and aspects of task performance (process). But, if sequential at a point in time perhaps, these interactional dimensions are not segmental. They are facets of mutually influential cycles of events. To give just one illustration: the motives aroused by tasks will not necessarily be the same on first exposure as they are after the performer has had time to learn something about linkages between task processes and outcomes; and, once this has happened, his hypotheses about task performance will necessarily be affected. These are dynamic affairs, and the importance to them of learning process-outcome links is nicely captured in Hackman's (1969b) appraisal:

'... as the performance process begins, a substantial portion of the behavioral variance will be controlled by those aspects of the task which lead subjects to ... hypotheses about what they ought to do. As performance continues ... the performer learns what outcomes result from particular patterns of behavior, and he finds, perhaps, that he can change his outcomes by changing his behavior. What he is doing ... is *learning the nature of the process-outcome links* ... Ultimately, the performer may base his behavior entirely on what he has learned about the process-outcome links, virtually ignoring the demands of the objective task ...' (Hackman, 1969b, pp. 442–443, italics in original)

If desired, various other attributes of the performance setting can be incorporated into Hackman's model as additional interactional dimensions. Also, there are points of emphasis in his assertions with which one might choose to quarrel: it is important, for instance, not to become excessively 'psychologistic' and allow the 'objective task' to slip completely from view; after all, everything starts with it and, if it sometimes recedes into the background, its importance in the total task-performance-organization process still needs to be held in mind. But these qualifications aside, the ideas expressed by Hackman are essentially consistent with the more general task modelling conceptions we have outlined above. Learning process-outcome links and translating them into hypotheses about task performance, in effect, is task modelling. With regard to *performance*, then, it seems evident that the *task model* is basic.

Shifting back again to the matter of *organization* (structure), we have described a central sequence of events beginning with tasks, running through the formulation of particular task models which then are integrated into larger extended models, and ending in output. Coordinated to this basic task structure are planning and control systems together with various administrative support arrangements; we have tried to show how this whole structural process depends on and is relative to tasks and is coordinated to organizational goals and technology. Our discussion of task-organization relations can be summarized with another simple schematic diagram:

Task (T) .... Model (M) ...., Extended Model (E)—Output (O)

(X)   (X)   (X)

This diagram will be recognized as a system-level formulation. Output events, for instance, would also occur at numerous subsystem levels. Indeed, without them the feedback essential to the operation of control systems would be lacking. It will also be understood that in any real operation there will be at least many task models (M) as there are tasks (T) and that it is a function of the extended task model (E) to coordinate these.

The diagram suggests a more or less integrated flow of events beginning with tasks (T) and ending with output (O). It also suggests at least partial continuity and sequential determination. However, the broken links are intended to indicate that each step is partially disjunctive relative to the others. New inputs (e.g. technological, policy) can be introduced at any save the last. In other words, each partial break in the sequence defines a 'decision point' and, as the 'externalities' (X) in the diagram imply, at each point there is opportunity for input to the process from sources other than those in the main line of the schematic.

Systems will vary considerably in the extent to which actual decision can or does occur at the junction points. A highly integrated system is one which has succeeded in programming not only its task models but also the bridges between the steps in the performance cycle. (And, of course, a maladministered system is one in which such success has not been achieved, but managers act as if it had.) *Ad hoc* organizations often define an opposite pole where pauses for decision are necessary at each step, and task models must be formulated 'on the spot'. Intermediate between these two are systems having more or less well developed, routinized task models, but discontinuities and noise from 'externalities' in the bridges or relations among them, as for example, in many functioning bureaucracies.

A Final Thought

In this essay we have followed the course of what J. D. Thompson (1967) aptly terms 'The Simon–March–Cyert stream of study'. This course is premised on a view of organizations as purposive, open decision systems, faced with uncertainty, but 'subject to criteria of rationality'. Achievement of rationality (bounded or other) is the primary responsibility of managerial subsystems mediating between the 'technical core' of the system and its environment in respect of both inputs and outputs. In addition to operational decision making and policy formulation, managers must make decisions about the designs of their organizations. We have here been concerned with the latitude available to management in making such decisions and with the reference points in the determination of those decisions.

What we have argued is that, if the relations are ofen complex, task properties nevertheless have a great deal to do with performance and organizing.[3] Indeed, we quite literally have identified the latter with the ways resources are deployed for task performance. Consequently satisfactory theories of organization and management await fuller detailed understanding of the organizational role of task phenomena.

In the meantime one thing is sure: since tasks vary, there can exist no one best way of organizing (cf. Lichtman and Hunt, 1971). Furthermore, the idea that a principle of equifinality (see Katz and Kahn, 1966) applies to relations between means and ends in organizational systems, suggests that even task-relative 'optimal' organizations may be hard to find. Pointed illustration of this is to be seen in Trist and coworkers' (1963) demonstration of different, but all successful, spontaneous organizational task-shift rotation systems in British coal mines (see Chapter 18).

It does not follow from this, of course, that for a given set of tasks or a particular task environment, some organizational forms may not be better than others. It is by no means clear, for instance, from the example just cited that each of the three task-shift rotation systems described by Trist and coworkers was equally 'good' from all standpoints. It can only be claimed that each was 'successful'. On the other hand, if, as Guetzkow (1965) maintains, congruence of tasks and communication nets enhances system efficiency, one might argue that over the long-run there should be some optimal adaptation of structure to task. Plausible as it sounds, however, such an expectation assumes an improbable degree of contextual stability. And, in any case, there is no reason, *a priori* why more than one 'optimum' cannot exist.

But neither is there any reason why congruence and hence efficiency cannot be studied and improved. As Trist and coworkers have observed, '...in most technical situations there are possibilities for different kinds of work organization and...the alternatives vary in the extent to which they help or hinder the completion of the primary task. It is important therefore to identify characteristics which facilitate this objective' (Trist and coworkers, 1963, p. 284).

Organizations can undoubtedly be made more effective in a number of ways. We would only argue that enhanced effectiveness seems most likely to flow from better understanding of the essential task-based nature of organization. Such understanding then can eventuate in development of what Kenneth Rice (1963) called 'task-fitted organizations'—managerial models suitably adapted to the task properties of the organizations to which they are to be applied.

But still and all, the truly wise manager will always remain acutely conscious of Rice's cautionary injunction that any organization, 'if it is to remain viable and contribute to the effective use of technology, (must) also satisfy the basic needs of those who work within it' (Rice, 1963, p. 274). We may not have had enough of technology, but we have had enough of technocracy.

Notes

1. See also Golembiewski (1965); for other relevant discussion one might consult W. F. Whyte (1969), who offers an extensive review of classifications of activity, distinctions between work and non-work and relations of task properties to behaviour (see especially pp. 117ff), and also W. E. Scott (1966), wherein can be found airings of relations among task behaviour, sentiments and activation notions.
2. Jaques (1967) has proposed the concept of 'time-span of discretion' as an index of job rank; but it also is pertinent to issues such as these. The concept refers to the elapsed time between operation performance and supervisory review—the longer the interval, the greater the discretion. Highly programmed tasks reduce the time-span of discretion to near zero and, as Jaques comments, 'reduction of the discretionary content of a job to near zero is to dehumanize it. It can be better done by a machine'. (p. 81).
3. We have not, of course, broached the 'causes' of organization or the 'motives' for it. An extended and provocative reflection on the latter may be found in Stinchcombe (1965). As for the former issue, Durkheim long ago (1933) argued that tasks may serve as bases for organization designs, but that they are not the root causes of organizing. Olsen (1968) provides an excellent and more contemporary treatment of these seminal issues, and J. D. Thompson (1967) is cogent, too.

References

Alderfer, C. P. (1969), Job enlargement and the organizational context, *Personnel Psychology*, **22**, 418–426.
Allen, L. A. (1963), Identifying line and staff, *in* J. A. Litterer, Ed., *Organizations: Structure and Behaviour*, Wiley, New York, pp. 94–104.
Anthony, R. N. (1965), *Planning and Control Systems*. Harvard University Press, Cambridge, Mass.
Bakke, E. W. (1959), Concept of social organization, *in* M. Haire, Ed., *Modern Organization Theory*, Wiley, New York, pp. 16–76.
Bass, B. (1968), Interface between personnel and organizational psychology, *Journal of Applied Psychology*, **52**, 81–88.
Brown, I. D., Tickner, A. H. and Simmonds, D. C. V. (1969), Interference between concurrent tasks of driving and telephoning, *Journal of Applied Psychology*, **53**, 419–424.
Buckley, W., Ed., (1968), *Modern Systems Research for the Behavioral Scientist*, Aldine, Chicago.
Dale, E. (1963), The division of basic company activities, *in* J. A. Litterer Ed., *Organizations: Structure and Behavior*, Wiley, New York, pp. 83–94.
Davis, J. H. (1969), *Group Performance*, Addison-Wisley, Reading, Mass.
Dubin, R. (1959), Stability of human organizations, *in* M. Haire, Ed., *Modern Organization Theory*, Wiley, New York, pp. 218–253.
Durkheim, E. (1933), *The Division of Labor in Society*, (G. Simpson, Trans.), Free Press-Macmillan, New York.
Fitts, P. M. and Posner, M. I. (1967), *Human Performance*, Books/Cole, Belmont, Cal.
Ford, R. N. (1969), *Motivation through the Work Itself*, American Management Assn., New York.
Golembiewski, R. T. (1965), Small groups and large organizations, *in* J. G. March, Ed., *Handbook of Organizations*, Rand McNally, Chicago, pp. 87–142.
Guetzkow, H. (1965), Communications in organizations, *in* J. G. March, Ed., *Handbook of Organizations*, Rand McNally, Chicago, pp. 534–574.

Haberstroh, C. J. (1965), Communication in organization, *in* J. G. March, Ed., *Handbook of Organizations*, Rand McNally, Chicago, pp. 1171–1213.

Haberstroh, C. J. (1968), Control as an organizational process, *in* W. Buckley, Ed., *Modern Systems Research for the Behavioral Scientist*, Aldine, Chicago, pp. 445–448.

Hackman, J. R. (1969a), Toward understanding the role of tasks in behavioral research, *Acta Psychologica*, **31**, 97–128.

Hackman, J. R. (1969b), Nature of task as a determiner of job behavior, *Personnel Psychology*, **22**, 435–444.

Hackman, J. R. and Lawler, E. E., Jr. (1971), Employee reactions to job characteristics. *Journal of Applied Psychology*, **55**(3), pp. 259–286.

Hall, R. H. (1962), Intra-organizational structural variation: application of the bureaucratic model, *Administrative Science Quarterly*, **7**, 295–308.

Hickson, D. J., Pugh, D. S. and Pheysey, D. C. (1969), Operations technology and organization structure, *Administrative Science Quarterly*, **14**, 378–397.

Hunt, R. G. (1970), Technology and organization, *Academy of Management Journal*, **13**, 235–252.

Hunt, R. G., Rubin, I. S. and Perry, F. A., Jr. (1970), Federal procurement: A study of some pertinent properties, policies, and practices of a group of business organizations, *National Contract Management Journal*, **4**, 245–299.

Jaques, E. (1967), *Equitable payment*, Penguin, London.

Katz, D. and Kahn, R. L. (1966), *Social Psychology of Organization*, Wiley, New York.

Lawler, E. E. (1969), Job design and employee motivation, *Personnel Psychology*, **22**, 426–435.

Lichtman, C. and Hunt, R. G. (1971), Personality and Organization Theory; a Review of some Conceptual Literature *Psychological Bulletin* **76**, pp. 271–294.

March, J. G. and Simon, H. G. (1958), *Organizations*, Wiley, New York.

Miller, E. J. and Rice, A. K., (1967), *Systems of Organization: the Control of Task and Sentient Boundaries*, Tavistock Publications, London.

Naylor, J. C. and Dickinson, T. L. (1969), Task structure, work structure, and team performance, *Journal of Applied Psychology*, **53**, 167–178.

O'Brien, G. E. and Owens, A. G. (1969), Effects of organizational structure on correlations between member abilities and group productivity, *Journal of Applied Psychology*, **53**, 525–530.

Olsen, M. E. (1968), *The Process of Social Organization*, Holt, Rinehart, Winston, New York.

Perrow, C. A. (1967), A framework for the comparative analysis of organizations, *American Sociological Review*, **32**, 195–208.

Porter, L. W. and Lawler, E. E. (1965), Properties of organization structure in relation to job attitudes and job behavior, *Psychological Bulletin*, **64**, 23–51.

Porter, L. W. (1969), Introduction: effects of task factors on job attitudes and behavior (a symposium), *Personnel Psychology*, **22**, 415–418.

Rapoport, A. and Horvath, W. J. (1968), Thoughts on organization theory, *in* W. Buckley Ed., *Modern Systems Research for the Behavioral Scientist*, Aldine, Chicago, pp. 71–75.

Reeves, T. K., Turner, B. A. and Woodward, J. (1970), Technology and organizational behaviour, *in* J. Woodward, Ed., *Industrial Organization: Behaviour and Control*, Oxford University Press, London, pp. 3–19.

Reeves, T. K. and Woodward, J. (1970), The study of managerial control, *in* J. Woodward Ed., *Industrial Organization: Behaviour and Control*, Oxford University Press, London, pp. 38–56.

Rice, A. K. (1963), *The Enterprise and its Environment: a System Theory of Management Organization*, Tavistock Publications, London.

Scott, W. E., Jr. (1966), Activation theory and task design, *Organizational Behavior and Human Performance*, **1**, 3–30.

Scott, W. G. (1961), Organization theory: an overview and an appraisal, *Academy of Management Journal*, **4**, 7–27.

Sommer, P. (1967), Small group ecology, *Psychological Bulletin*, **67**, 145–152.

Steiner, I. D. (1966), Models for inferring relationships between group size and potential group productivity, *Behavioral Science*, **11**, 273–283.

Stinchcombe, A. L. (1965), Social structure and organization, *in* J. G. March, Ed., *Handbook of Organizations*, Rand McNally, Chicago, pp. 142–194.

Tannenbaum, A. S., Ed., (1968), *Control in Organizations*, McGraw-Hill, New York.

Taylor, D. W. (1965), Decision making and problem solving, *in* J. G. March, Ed., *Handbook of Organizations*, Rand McNally, Chicago, pp. 48–87.

Thompson, J. D. (1967), *Organizations in Action*, McGraw-Hill, New York.

Trist, E. L., Higgin, G. W., Murray, H. and Pollock, A. B. (1963), *Organizational Choice*, Tavistock Publications, London.

Udy, S. H. (1965), The comparative analysis of organizations, *in* J. G. March, Ed., *Handbook of Organizations*, Rand McNally, Chicago, pp. 678–710.

Vroom, V. H. (1964), *Work and Motivation*, Wiley, New York.

Weick, K. E. (1965), Laboratory experimentation with organizations, *in* J. G. March Ed., *Handbook of Organizations*, Rand McNally, Chicago, pp. 194–261.

Whyte, W. F. (1969), *Organizational Behavior: Theory and Application*, Irwin-Dorsey, Homewood, Ill.

Woodward, J. (1965), *Industrial Organization: Theory and Practice*, Oxford University Press, London.

Woodward, J. (1970), Technology, management control and organizational behaviour, *in* J. Woodward, Ed., *Industrial Organization: Behaviour and Control*, Oxford University Press, London, pp. 234–243.

'Best Fit' in the Design of Organizations

Tom Lupton

Introduction

It is useful to distinguish, very broadly, three contrasting approaches to organizational design. The first of these argues, straightforwardly and persuasively, that to design for organizational efficiency, one must begin from a knowledge of the properties of the individual person. The assumption that lies behind the approach is that to the extent that the individuals who work in an organization are committed to its goals, so will they find ways to work effectively towards those goals. The problem for the designer is how to remove the obstacles that prevent commitment. Since, so the argument continues, individuals are similar with respect to the factors that blunt or sharpen their commitment, then it should be possible to produce a common design procedure for all organizations. I refer to this approach as the 'human relations' approach.

The second approach, which I refer to as the 'classical/structural', is also simple and attractive. Organizational design, to the classicists, of whom there are a great many, is a matter of roles, rules and routines. On this view, the designer must attend to matters such as the span of control, the division of 'line' and 'staff' functions, the development of precise job descriptions, efficient control procedures, coherent and visible career and salary structures, etc. Above all the designer must achieve a rational allocation of authority and responsibility in relation to the purposes of the organization as these are defined, for the time being, at the policy apex of the organization. The classical/ structural approach assumes that all organizations have similar problems, and offers a set of practical procedures for solving them that will apply universally.

The first and second approaches are not mutually exclusive. 'Management by objectives' may be taken as an example of an ingenious attempt to combine both in one design.

The third approach is based upon an 'open-system' view of organizations. Such a view is incompatible with either of the first two approaches, or with the M.B.O. hybrid. From the 'open-system' standpoint, organizations are seen as patterns of human tasks and relationships shaped so as to allow at least survival, at most growth and development, in environments which constrain; but which also offer opportunities. These environments could include customers/clients, competitors, resource markets and the requirements of the law. The environment of any one organization is likely to differ to a greater or lesser degree from that of every other organization. The designer who takes the 'open-system' view must therefore make his design *contingent* upon the circumstances of a

122

particular case; he must search for a combination of design features that ease the particular organization's problems of adaptation, that is those that 'fit' both structurally and psychologically.

In the first part of the paper I consider the 'human relations' and 'classical/ structure' approaches. This section will be much more critical than the second part, in which the design implications of an 'open-system' approach are discussed and exemplified. I shall not disguise my partiality for a 'contingency' approach.

Human Relations

Herzberg and Job Enrichment

Organizations come in all shapes and sizes, locations, contexts and types of activity. The human relations 'school' underestimates the significance of this, except perhaps to attribute to bigness and complexity some special problems for man-in-organization. For example, in the investigations carried out by Herzberg and his colleagues (Herzberg and coworkers, 1959; Herzberg, 1966) and since replicated by others (cf., for example, Wall and Stephenson, 1970, Wall and coworkers, 1971) individuals were asked to recall the circumstances in their job-history which had caused them to feel satisfied or dissatisfied with a particular job.[1] They were not limited in their description to their present job, nor were they asked specifically to detail the circumstances surrounding the jobs described, nor their extra-job roles and the circumstances attending these. Of course, in recalling satisfying or unsatisfying episodes during their occupational careers, individuals will offer information of this kind. What is relevant to my present argument is: (*a*) that this type of information is not often collected, with the result that one individual's job context and extra-work context cannot be systematically compared with another's and (b) that even where such information is available it is not possible to compare the respondent's own account of the effect of his job context on his feelings about his job, with an observer's account of the design of the job, and the context of technology, work-flow administration, reward system, etc.

Given this approach, suggested improvements in organization design must centre on the job and its immediate context. In Herzberg's case, the research findings point clearly to the design of the individual job as the positive source of motivation. If the individual feels that the job itself is 'stretching' him, and offering a challenge, e.g. to his pride in workmanship, or his professional competence, or his capacity to carry responsibility, he will be moved to perform it well and be delighted when he has done so. By contrast the quality of interpersonal relationships in the organization, the fringe benefits, the working conditions, etc., although important, will not positively move people to perform well. These factors may, however, act negatively in blunting a man's interest in his job. Hence the concern of Herzberg and his colleagues, in their role as proselytizers and consultants, with 'job enrichment' (Paul and coworkers, 1969).

What I take Herzberg and coworkers to be saying in general, to managers, is this:

If you wish (as employer or manager) to have an efficient organization, you must set to work to improve the performance of the individuals who presently work in it. It does not matter who the individuals are, what they are, what they can do, what they are doing, what the organization does, how it does it or where it is, there will always be scope for redividing and redesigning its tasks so as to enrich them, and for so arranging the context of administrative procedure, supervision, and interpersonal relationships that they will not inhibit motivation and satisfaction.

Statements of this kind are, in the present state of knowledge, little better than speculation. There is no evidence that I know of that demonstrates a *general* link between individual job design and performance and organizational performance, showing that the redesign of the jobs in some way causes the organization performance to improve (or worsen); although the statement has a plausible ring. A demonstration from one organization, or even a number of them, that certain specified changes in job design are associated with improvements in individual motivation and satisfaction, and that organizational performance has also shifted in the expected direction, cannot be admitted as valid evidence for the general proposition, Indeed, unless a causal link can be established between changes in the job behaviour and job attitude of individuals on the one hand, and changes in a set of operationally defined indicators of organizational performance on the other, even the statements about particular organizations, let alone the generalizations, have to be accepted only somewhat tentatively. A more promising strategy for research and for action might be to examine particular organizations in detail using (and developing in use) a common framework and a common set of techniques for recording observed behaviour, for characterizing and measuring the performance of individuals and organizations. Such an approach, however, would produce, indeed has produced, quite different sorts of generalization (cf. Trist and coworkers, 1963; Rice, 1963).

Likert and System 4

When Herzberg and similar workers seek to derive prescriptions from their data about attitudes, they assume single unidirectional chains of causation that start with individual states of mind (as reported by the individuals themselves) and end with the performance of organizations. Likert and his coworkers have made these chains very explicit. In his most recent major work Likert (1967) argues that improvements in the performance of organizations will follow if they are redesigned to resemble a model he calls System 4. System 4 is a member of a fourfold classification of organizational models. The four models are distinguished by their scores on 43 profile dimensions representing the variables Likert considers significant in differentiating one organization from another, and including performance variables. The variables are grouped as follows: Motivation, Communication, Interaction, Decision-making, Goal setting, Control and Performance.

The measures used for 'scoring' along each dimension, with the exception of the performance dimensions, relate either directly to states of mind of individuals, as derived from attitudinal data, or to the implied effect on these states of mind of attempts by some individuals (managers) to influence the behaviour of others (other managers, workers). For example, the level at which certain kinds of decisions are made in organizations, and the amount and kind of information available at the point they are made, are held to influence states of mind and hence behaviour. When decision-making is widely diffused and integrated, says Likert, and accurate information flows freely, then if other influences such as individual motivation, and the formal processes for defining aims and controlling and reviewing performance, are positioned appropriately along the relevant profile dimensions, then the scores on the performance dimensions will be in the required direction, i.e. productivity will be high, waste low and labour turnover low. In brief the organization being described will resemble System 4 (Participation/Group) as contrasted to System 1 (Exploitative/Authoritative), 2 (Benevolent/Authoritative) and 3 (Consultative).

Likert's profiles are more than 'check-lists' of factors. They represent systems, since the 'score' on each variable or group of variables (as represented by a profile 'dimension (s)') is assumed to be influenced in some way by, and in its turn to influence in some way, every other variable. The pattern of causation is, realistically, assumed to be complex, but the chain of causation is, as in the Herzberg case, assumed to be single and unidirectional. Variations in leadership style are seen as causally related to variables of productivity/performance *via* their influence on subordinate attitudes. The argument resembles Douglas McGregor's in many ways—System 4 corresponding to Theory Y management (McGregor, 1960).

Again we are confronted by a claim, this time with impressive empirical support, that certain mental attributes of persons are the basic cause of organizational efficiency or inefficiency, no matter what kind of organization.

However, when Likert surveys the research literature for confirmation of his notion that productivity is always better in those organizations with the collection of related elements of attitude structure, and procedure, that characterize his System 4, he uncovers:

'discrepancies in findings obtained by social science investigators in the relationship of such variables as leadership style (causal), subordinates' attitudes (intervening) and individual or organizational productivity (end-result)' (Likert, 1967, p. 97.)

These discrepancies are explained, at some length, largely by reference: (*a*) to the point in the time-cycle of organizational development when the findings were made, and/or (*b*) to the fact that the effects of some variables moving in direction of a System 4 leadership style might be masked by the effect of other variables having (temporarily) a contradictory effect on employee attitudes, and hence, on productivity.

In what, for the purposes of my argument is a significant and revealing series of passages, Likert refers to the effects of two variables that he does not include in his profiles—namely 'size' and 'kind of work'. Thus:

'. . . The relationships observed may reflect the influence of differences in size as much or more as they reflect the true relationships actually existing among the causal, intervening and end-result variables. The kind of work done by a department influences the relationships among the variables since the time intervals between the changes *(i.e. from style to performance via attitudes (T. L.))* tend to be much shorter for complex and varied tasks, such as research, than for routine, machine-paced operations'. (Likert, 1967, p. 97)

The reader might reasonably expect this passage to be followed by an examination of evidence showing the effects of size and nature of task on the duration and sequence of the causal series postulated in the model. The expression 'true relationships actually existing' might weaken the expectation, but even if the effects of size and task are 'false' in some sense to be determined, they surely merit exploration. These expectations are frustrated; we learn instead that

'although both size and kind of work may influence the relationship which may be found among the causal, intervening, and end-result variables in a particular study, let us ignore them for the moment to keep our illustration from becoming too complex'. (Likert, 1967, pp. 97–98)

Unfortunately, these variables continue to be ignored completely after the moment has passed. Likert explains that

'the interrelationships amongst these variables *(i.e. causal, intervening, end-result (T. L.))* are much more complex and are affected by many more factors than was originally anticipated. Nevertheless . . . the available evidence indicates that there are consistent and dependable relationships amongst the causal, intervening and end-result variables. When all the relevant factors are taken into consideration, especially time, and the proper analysis made, consistent, positive relationships can be expected among the causal, intervening and end-result variables in every organization.' (Likert, 1967, pp. 98, 99)

This statements is little more than an assertion that variables representing attitudes and interpersonal relationships are stronger in their influence on performance (given an undefined period of time to take effect) than variables like size and technology/product. It is also possible to assert, from other 'available evidence', that size and technology/product exert an influence of some permanance, directly or indirectly, on attitudes and interpersonal relationships, and hence on performance. If one combines the two assertions, the interesting possibility arises of a model of mutual interdependencies of structural, attitudinal and behavioural variables. From this model propositions could be generated stating that performance would be contingent upon the existence of a particular pattern of mutual influence amongst organizational variables. Organizations differ in size, technology and location. This means that although a description of the adaptive processes that influence performance, and (importantly) are influenced by it, could be universally valid, the redesign of a particular system so as to improve its performance would depend on a detailed examination of that system. The main shortcoming of Likert's approach is that in order to make his system universally applicable he partially closes it up and makes his

126

causal chains run one way—a doubtful procedure but one entirely consistent with a kind of 'psychological myopia', which is, sadly all too common.

Blake and the 'Managerial Grid'

Likert is to be applauded for his respect for evidence, in the sense that the empirical basis of his assertions is mostly well displayed. His book was meant for an audience of academics as well as managers. Blake writes (Blake and Mouton, 1964) for an audience of managers. The mode of presentation therefore differs greatly from that adopted by Herzberg and Likert, yet Blake's position as to theory and prescription is almost identical. Because it is presented for a lay audience in the guise of a straightforward procedure for organizational improvement based upon apparently self-evident propositions, the theoretical position emerges more starkly.

The 'managerial grid' is a classification of styles of management, based upon two factors: 'concern for people' and 'concern for production'. Given nine degrees of concern for people and nine degrees of concern for production, presented as a 'matrix' or 'grid', we arrive at 81 styles. That is really more than is needed for practical purposes, so those in the middle and those at the four corners are taken, giving five main managerial styles in all.

'Style of management', as I understand it, means the beliefs about his society, his subordinates, his colleagues and his job, that a manager holds; and the way he expresses these in his behaviour at work. A 1/1 manager (see Figure 1)

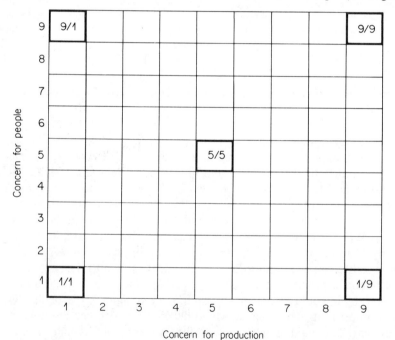

Concern for production

Figure 1. The managerial grid

would be a man who showed no concern for anything, neither the well-being of his subordinates, nor the efficient use of the non-human resources given in his charge. A 1/9 manager would be the tough, no-nonsense fellow, who expects people to get the stuff out of the door on target, and will use any stick or carrot to push or pull them in that direction. The 9/1 manager is the softy who lets production slide in case he offends anyone. The 9/9 man is the type who seems to command the confidence of his subordinates, is solicitous as to their welfare and personal development, but at the same time can deploy his human and non-human resources in ways that lead to high operating efficiency. The man in the middle is on the right lines but has a long way to go; the honest trier.

Confronted with this classification, it is difficult at first, even if one were so inclined, to muster points of criticism. Consider what Blake is saying. He is asking us to accept that the analysis of organizational efficiency ought to begin by examining managerial styles. He is also asking us to accept that we ought to put our observations about management style into a predetermined fivefold framework based upon two factors. We are also being asked to acknowledge one of the five styles as better than all the others and to be aspired to. If our critical faculties are not in good shape there is no difficulty at all in accepting this. We have always admired the man who effortlessly brings his people happily along with him to prodigies of performance, felt contempt for the layabout and for the softy, and tempered awe of the toughy; and should not the honest trier be praised and encouraged? When all this, deeply embedded as it is in the values of our cultural tradition, is set down systematically as a classification of management styles, there is little wonder that it is widely accepted.

If a manager will try, using a step-by-step method of self-questioning devised by Blake to identify his own style, he will most likely identify himself as occupying a box somewhere just north east of 5/5, an honest trier with potentiality. Which is comforting, but slightly guilt-making. What do I have to do, he asks, to become a 9/9 man? Blake's answer would be: Once the managers in an organization have identified their style on the grid, then it ought to be possible to get discussion going about what is stopping the progress to 9/9. And now (and I am still paraphrasing Blake) if the managers in the organization have let their hair down sufficiently to discuss frankly the shortcomings of their styles of management then the time will soon come when they can without inhibition or defensiveness begin to discuss how to get organized to improve the way their organization operates.

A moment's serious examination of this logical edifice reveals glaring cracks. Why should anyone accept without question that, in seeking organization efficiency and human satisfaction, everything stems from the analysis of managerial style? Is it not just possible that the circumstances in which a manager finds himself are the major influence on the style that he evolves to cope with them, and that an attempt to change to another style would be either to produce inefficiencies or intolerable frustrations? Which, put another way, is to suggest that the style of management is a product of the situation, and not the other way around. The test would be to take Blake's classification and establish, in relation to carefully defined measures of operating efficiency and job satisfaction, whether 'bad' styles of management are necessarily correlated with high scores on efficiency and job satisfaction. So far as I am aware, that has not yet been done.[2] Blake dismisses the difficulty either with assertions about an evolutionary process that shows up successful organizations with bad styles as historical anomolies, or by arguments that what appears as bad style in a successful organization must really be a facade, that, on removal, will reveal the true style of its management and underpin Blake's argument.

Blake's reasoning throughout is suspect, e.g.

'While there are numerous factors in any concrete situation which may point toward the use of a style other than 9/9, the general picture seems to be one where, *to the degree that operating requirements permit*, 9/9 is the more mature managerial style.' (Blake and Mouton, 1964, p. 317, italics added)

Nowhere do Blake and Mouton define exactly the nature of the 'operating requirement' for which a particular style is appropriate, nor do they describe how and to what extent this may permit or not permit a particular managerial style to develop. We are given no operational definition of 'maturity of style' either. The argument is very similar to Likert's—namely that the causal sequence: (*a*) style, (*b*) attitudes, (*c*) behaviour and (*d*) organization performance, may be influenced by other variables, but is likely to persist despite this—except that Blake might think the undefined particular circumstances might make a mature style difficult to implant. The relationship: (*a*) actual style, (*b*) particular circumstances and (*c*) organizational performance is not analysed. We are left to judge how plausible all this seems, with precious few yardsticks. How much more convincing might it have been had Blake proceeded as follows:

(1) Define managerial style.
(2) Classify managerial styles.
(3) Build a model relating style to other managerial variables (including 'operating requirements').
(4) State propositions deriving from the 'model', e.g., (*a*) whatever the state of the other organizational variables all high performers approximate to a 9/9 style; (*b*) organizational performance varies with the distance from a 9/9 style that is found amongst managers in that organization. The extent to which it does so will depend on the state of variables other than those included in the definition of style and performance. If this can be demonstrated, then the situations in which styles other than 9/9 are associated with high performance— if such exist—may be defined; and it will now be possible to specify the effects of attempting to introduce a 9/9 style (or any other) into such situations.

In the absence of such a procedure it is difficult to take seriously the usual claims for 'grid training' based upon examples of companies who have undertaken it and now claim to be more successful than they would have been. We have no idea whether the claim that the one is a major cause of the other is valid unless the patterns of causation linking them are elucidated, and this is not possible using Blake's procedure. To change it to include such a validation procedure would entail taking up a position where the possibility that the style of management most likely to be compatible with high economic performance and social satisfaction is contingent upon the exact circumstances of a particular case. This is very far from being Blake's position, or Likert's, or Herzberg's or McGregor's. They are saying, with a few weak caveats, that it is *universally* the case in organizations that improvements in productivity, economic performance and personal satisfaction with work arise from changes in the context of interpersonal relationships in which individuals work whatever the context of size, product or client environment, form of ownership, location, cultural and social structural setting, technology, etc. The degree of dogmatism with which this proposition is asserted various from writer to writer, but one is justified in describing the position of all of them as *psychological universalism.*

Argyris and 'Self-Actualization'

In some ways Argyris shares the same viewpoint on organizational design as Herzberg, Blake and Likert. Like them he seeks to support a view that it is the manner of individual behaviour in interpersonal relationships in organizations that causes differences in the performance of those organizations and in the personal satisfaction and development of individuals in their work. None of these writers, least of all Argyris, neglects to say that to some extent interpersonal relationships are shaped by the way in which authority is allocated and exercised, by the structure of decision-making, by the content and channels of communication, by the systems of administrative control and by the product/technology, i.e. the kind of work that is done and the way that it is done. Argyris gives a good deal more emphasis to these matters than do the others, noting at the same time that the constraining effect some of them may have on behaviour diminishes as one moves away from the 'lower levels' of organizations.

Argyris also draws attention to the effects of size and technology. He notes a widespread belief that as organizations grow larger, and as their technologies become more complex, tighter controls, more rigid rules and more rational procedures for communication become necessary. The actual structure of most modern large scale organizations is testimony to the extent and power of this belief amongst managers. However, he argues, these are the very modes of social control that inhibit free and frank interpersonal relationships, that generate fear to expose feelings: 'there's no room for sentiment in business, keep emotion out of this', etc. These inhibitions are, he argues, barriers to personal and interpersonal effectiveness, they put individuals into relationships of hierarchy, and of anxious dependency.

'Managerial controls tend to create intergroup rivalries, force groups to think for their own, and not others' problems, reward an overall point of view rarely, and place groups in win–lose situations in which they are competing with each other for scarce resources'. (Argyris, 1970, p. 63).

And:

130

'These barriers to effectiveness are rarely potent when the system is dealing with routine, programmed and nonthreatening information. The barriers become especially difficult to identify and overcome when the system is dealing with innovative, nonprogrammed, and threatening information.' (Argyris, 1970, p. 63)

However, if I have understood him aright Argyris is saying that quite apart from their incapacity to adapt to change, the social controls implied by the 'classical' authority system and 'rational' administrative controls of money, movement and information, also have a deadening effect on individual motives, and obscure the connection between the individual's efforts and the economic success of the enterprise. Most of all they inhibit 'self-actualization' by denying to the individual opportunities to realize to the full his own potential. Organizations are getting bigger, and more bureaucratic. At the same time they are under pressure to adapt to changing circumstances. It is apparent then that there is a problem of organization inefficiency, and of waste of individual talent, and even worse, of adverse psychological effects on individuals who have become 'cogs' in the machine, or who are hanging on grimly in the rat-race, or 'playing the politics' of organization for personal and group advantage.

Argyris does not see the chain of causation running all one way, from 'style', via attitudes, to performance. He argues that while it is necessary to change management styles if one is to change organizations, it is also necessary to create the kind of structures that maintain and reinforce the better style. He would like to restructure in such a way that the problems of the organization are systematically tackled by teams of managers pooling their varied expertise— the so-called 'matrix organization'. The 'matrix-type' organization will not produce results efficiently nor, overnight, create a new 'style' unless the style of management is already moving in that direction. This would be unlikely in an 'heirarchical-rational' organization; so something has to be done to change the style as well, towards a much more honest, open, confronting mode. Whoever sets out to change organizations in the direction of being more effective, will do well, says Argyris, to train managers to work with others so that they will be sensitive to the existence of the interpersonal barriers preventing high levels of cooperative effort. A change from one 'rational' structure to another, even if that were a 'matrix' pattern, will not by itself heighten personal understanding of, and commitment to, the need to work with others toward goals that all have had some hand in setting.

All this sounds most attractive. Flexible, adaptive individuals, truly outgoing, generous and frank, willing to pull their weight, working with like individuals in flexible, adaptive groups, expecting support in pursuit of common aims from those with access to greater resources, would seem to be a splendid recipe for efficiency, and for individual self-actualization, not to speak of speed of response to change.

Like the others so far mentioned, however, Argyris is a universalist. His recognition of the constraining effect of managerial controls and technology on the 'lower levels' does not lead him to offer a procedure for identifying what these might be in a particular case, and how matters might be altered, except by influencing the way managers comport themselves in their relationships with each other, and with workers, in defining the job and getting it done.

The Classical/Structural Approach

The doctrines of so-called 'classical theory', and of 'scientific management' are well known. As we have seen, they are unloved by the human relations school. Their detractors allege that their designs crib and confine the individual and set up obstacles to organizational change. Classical theory and scientific management (Taylor, 1947; Fayol, 1949; Urwick, 1956) hold that efficiency in organizations follows from the centralized regulation of behaviour by formal rules and procedures, a hierarchical and functional division of labour and formal rewards and sanctions centrally administered. Scientific management stresses the detailed specification of job targets, the formal requirements for cooperative behaviour and social control by cash carrots and sticks. Scientific management is 'classical' organization structure worked out in detail.

Despite the obvious points of criticism there is a reluctance to abandon the idea that organizations must be designed 'from the top down'. Give a typical group of British managers the task of describing their own organization and they will usually start by drawing an organization chart, showing how (notionally) authority and responsibility are allocated from the top (where policy is made) through various hierarchical levels. They will usually discuss also the various systems they have for exercising control over managerial and operator behaviour. They will be very familiar with expressions such as 'chain of command', 'span of control', 'delegation', 'leadership',...This is the language of classical theory. The assumptions of *structural universalism*, as we shall call this approach, are that organizational efficiency is best achieved by following certain injunctions, such as:

(1) Make sure that all the jobs are carefully defined;
(2) Make sure that every man knows to whom, and for what, he is responsible, and who is responsible to him for what;
(3) Make sure that promotion is based on merit, not on favour, and that the grounds for promotion are known and understood;
(4) Make sure no-one has more than one boss;
(5) Specialists must be on 'tap', never on top;

and that all this must be so to be efficient, whatever and wherever the organization.

Comments on 'Human Relations' and 'Classical' Approaches

The view that increasing organizational scale and complexity must be met, for efficiency's sake, by stricter adherence to a classical design is plausible, so much so that recent heavy attacks on it have left it still firmly established.

The attraction of a classical design, from the point of view of top management, is that it seems to offer them control. As they must see it, the bigger and more complex the task, the more fragmented the division of labour, the greater the need for specialization and the greater the chance of breakdown and inefficiency. Therefore, to ensure order, continuity and success, the processes of work allocation and coordination must be built in to the design of the organization. They cannot be left to the whim of individuals or groups, and they must be run from the top (centre) even if the modes of allocation and coordination imply decentralization, as in the 'product group' or 'cost centre' approach.

'Human relations' approaches, although seemingly at odds with the 'classical approach', share some assumptions with it, as well as its universalism. For one thing, they share a view that conflict can be 'designed out'. They do not jettison the principle of hierarchy either. Likert, for example, always represents the organization as a hierarchial organization chart. However, he is at pains to emphasize that the mechanisms for coordination provided by such an arrangement are far from adequate and he would wish to add patterns of participative interpersonal relationships that cut across the formal lines of hierarchy and department. Argyris, as we have seen, envisages some weakening of hierarchy and a strengthening of 'matrix' groups but even he does not seem to envisage a flat organization. The distinguishing feature of the 'human relations' approach is its emphasis on the individual, that of 'classical theory' is its emphasis on the organization. Both are *universalistic*.

Contingency Approaches to Organizational Design

Woodward and the Influence of Technology

Organizations differ one from another in size (however size is measured); they also differ as to the products or services they provide, the kind of resource markets they operate in, the types of human skills they use, the machinery and plant they deploy, their location, etc., and the same organization may differ in all or any of these respects from time to time. It seems not unreasonable therefore to suggest that the identification and measurement of such factors might be a good starting point for organizational design, if only on the ground that a form of organization adequate for one set of tasks would be inadequate for another.

Studies made in recent decades underline the point. Woodward (1958, 1965) investigated 100 firms in Essex. Her findings suggested a relationship between technology, the structure of managerial and supervisory positions, and the success of an organization; such that the extent to which an organization is successful is *contingent* on the 'match' between its structure and its technology. Woodward postulated, as a result of her researches, the kind of structure (defined in classical terms, spans of control, number of hierarchial levels, extent of functional specialization, etc.') that would be appropriate for a given type of technology, if the organization were to be successful.

'Successful firms in each production category tended to cluster round the median for that category as a whole, while the figures [10 scores on structural characteristics. T. L.] of the firms classified as "below average" in success, were found at the extremes of the range ... The fact that organizational characteristics, technology, and success, were linked together in this way suggested that not only was the system of production an important variable in the determination of organizational structure, but that one particular form of organization was most appropriate to each system of production.' (Woodward, 1965, pp. 70–71).

It is unnecessary to discuss Woodward's work in detail here. Her research has been criticized on the ground that, because of the way the problem was defined, and the data collected and organized, its findings cannot be taken to be conclusive. To pursue this line of criticism would not be germane to my purposes in this paper. I am much more concerned to discern, as I attempted to do for Likert and the others, what is assumed to be causing what. Unlike them, Woodward is saying, in effect, that the nature of the organization's product or client market, as interpreted by those who transact on behalf of the organization in that market, greatly influences the choice of technology. For example, high quality bespoke tailoring obviously demands a 'one-off' technology so as to meet each customer's requirements as and when he specifies them; multiple tailoring for a mass market calls by contrast for a 'large-batch' or 'mass-production' technology, and in this case the customers' requirements are anticipated and production takes place *before* the sale. Different technologies demand different mixes of skills, different administrative procedures, and different relationships of authority and subordination, functional dependence, etc. The chain of causation therefore is seen to start with the organizations' perceptions of the situation in the product/client market. If it is to survive, to grow, to develop, the organization must respond by changing its products and services and the method by which it produces them. These actions in their turn lead to changes in organization structure and then to behaviour and attitudes.

The significant unit of analysis for Woodward is the organization, not the individual manager or worker. It is the *organization* that responds to its environment, and has a technology, and an organization structure chosen so as to make that response effective. So far, the chain of causation looks just as linear and unidirectional as Likert's did, but in a different direction. Individuals are not omitted altogether from Woodward's scheme; they appear as managers who choose, within certain constraints, what technology, and what organization they think appropriate. To the degree that their choices are appropriate, so will the organization be successful in adapting to its product/client environment. A simple diagram of the causes of organizational performance as suggested by Woodward's work looks something like Figure 2.

It is logically impossible to derive from Woodward's work a universal prescription for organization design, of the kind advanced by the classical theorists, which states principles that are to be adhered to whatever the organization is doing and however it is doing it. Her work was expressly designed in fact to discover whether the principles of classical theory, when applied, would *in all cases* lead to organizational success as measured by reference to economic

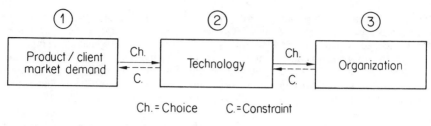

Figure 2.

indices, employee statisfaction and public image; and it led her to the conclusion that the association of the classical model with organizational success was only to be found in a limited range of technologies, namely, 'large-batch' and 'mass-production' engineering technologies.

Implicit in Woodward's work, as in all the work of what might be called the *structural relativists*, is the assumption that the individual's attitudes and behaviour are strongly influenced by the roles assigned to him in a set of structured relationships, that is by the expectations of other individuals in other related roles, and by his own beliefs learned in the process of child and adult socialization and from experience in the particular organization, as to what behaviour is appropriate to the occupational role. Since, on this view, structures are influenced strongly by technology, and technology by the product/client environment, then any attempt to influence attitudes and behaviour must take account of their structural determinants. To give a rather obvious example: if the procedures for cost control, quality control and production control in a manufacturing unit, working in a highly competitive product market, specified or implied heavy sanctions on the supervisor for failure to meet quality standards and time deadlines, he would probably have great difficulty in engendering a relaxed and participative relationship with those for whose work he carries responsibility. Any attempt to influence his behviour via a change in his attitudes, without changing the context in which he was acting, would probably increase the supervisor's difficulties. The *extent* to which, in this instance, the deadlines and standards could be changed to give scope for a changed style of relationships would depend on the competititve situation of the firm. It is quite possible, of course, that the competitive pressures could be met by choosing technical and administrative procedures that make possible a participative style of relationships. This is, however, quite a different way of posing the organizational design problem from those we met in the first part of the paper, and we shall discuss it in more detail presently.

Burns and Stalker, and Rates of Change

Like Woodward, Burns and Stalker (1961) may be characterized as *structural relativists*. They see the rate of change in the environment of the organization, rather than the technology, as the significant influence on organizational structure. If an organization has been offering the same product or group of products, to much the same customer, in much the same quantities, for a considerable period of years, and there appears to that organization no reason to believe that the market will greatly and rapidly expand, or that customer tastes will shift markedly, or that competitors will enter the field, then, say Burns and Stalker, a highly structured organization, with centralized policy making, rigid hierarchial ranks, strict administrative routines, tightly drawn boundaries as between departments, etc., would probably be appropriate—*a mechanistic system*. When the opposite condition exists, namely, when the environment is highly volatile, a rigid system of ranks and routines would damagingly inhibit the organization's speed and sensitivity of response, and threaten its survival. Therefore, they continue, this kind of situation demands a flat hierarchy, colleague relationships instead of boss–subordinate relationships as the predominant mode, short-lived and flexible administrative routines, and shifting departmental boundaries—*an organic system*.

'We have endeavoured to stress the appropriateness of each system to its own specific set of conditions. Equally, we desire to avoid the suggestion that either system is superior under all circumstances to the other. In particular, nothing in our experience justifies this assumption that mechanistic systems should be superseded by organic in conditions of stability. *The beginning of administrative wisdom is the awareness that there is no one optimum type of management system.* (Burns and Stalker, 1961, p. 125, italics added)

Despite their differences of emphasis as to causation, Woodward and Burns and Stalker share a perception of the organization as an open-system of human relationships. The organizational forms that are chosen in a given organization as means to reach and maintain high levels of human cooperation in pursuit of the tasks of the organization, may or may not be well designed to cope with the problems posed by the organization's environment. Whether they are or are not is from this viewpoint contingent to the nature of the relationship between a particular organization and its particular environment. There is no structure or style of behaviour that can be referred to as being appropriate (i.e. adaptive) for all organizations and environments, in all places, at all times and in all cultures.

Rice, Trist and Socio-Technical Systems

It will by now be obvious that this paper is concerned with *work organizations*, i.e. corporate entities owning land, buildings and equipment, and engaging people for pay, to cooperate with others who have been similarly engaged in activities that are more or less formally and explicity stated, and which are related to the pursuit of objectives.

Rice (1963), in common with other open-system theorists, sees work organizations as being engaged in transactions at their boundaries with other organizations and with individuals. These transactions are so organized as to procure inputs of material resources and human competencies, and to dispose of the outputs created by the combination of those resources to consumers and clients. In disposing of their outputs organizations attempt to create a surplus with which to procure further resources so that they may continue in existence, grow by addition, or develop organically. The human social activities that we commonly call production processes, and which transform resource inputs into disposable goods and services are described by Rice as a socio-technical system. That is to say, there exists a technical system—the machinery, the buildings and the formal administrative controls. The social system, that is the pattern of interpersonal relationships, and the norms which govern them, is built on a framework provided by the technical system and is heavily influenced by this framework. Yet this social system has an independent life which may, in turn, influence the operation of the technical system. The hyphen in the term socio-technical system should really be a double headed arrow, expressing a relationship of mutual dependence. Most sociological studies of workshop behaviour (e.g. Roethlisberger and Dickson, 1939 and 1964; Roy, 1954; Lupton, 1963; Cunnison, 1966) describe the relationship well. The well-known study by Trist and coworkers (1963) of mechanization in the coal mines of North West Durham, uses the socio-technical system concept explicitly in its analysis of the complex culture of non-mechanized mining and the disturbances which followed from the introduction of a division of labour and a reward system thought by management to be appropriate to the new longwall technology. The analysis throughout emphasizes the need, when changes are being made in technology, to choose carefully from amongst the alternatives open, a division of labour, a reward system and a set of working practices, which, while enabling the new technology to be effectively exploited, does not at the same time too seriously threaten the existing social system. Otherwise, not only will productivity probably fall below expectations, but, as in the instance reported by Trist, voluntary absenteeism, the accident rate and labour turnover may increase.

Here again, this time at the level of the working group, it is difficult to imagine how the redesign of a production unit for effective performance could safely ignore the connections of *mutual* dependence between attitudes and relationships on the one hand, and product and technology on the other. The connection is obviously a complex one, as Likert somewhat unhelpfully points out, but if the search for simplicity has to disregard what is crucial, then surely that search has to be abandoned in favour of something that is probably more messy and elusive, but for that very reason perhaps, a better approximation to the truth of the matter. Always assuming, of course, that the aim in all this is a practical one. I am not greatly concerned here with the gentle academic art of abstract theory-building, to which many social scientists are particularly drawn, where logical edifices of great elegance are often perched precariously on an unstable pile of unrealistic assumptions and are of little practical consequence.

The authors whose work I have chosen to discuss are mostly scholars with a practical interest, who would agree that all design prescriptions, of whatever school, must be subject to the same test, viz. whether in fact they produce the practical results they promise.

How to Design for 'Best Fit'

It is not necessary to choose *either* the individual *or* the organization as the unit of analysis/diagnosis. To explain organizational structure and functioning, and to design or redesign for effective operation, both must be taken fully and equally into account. However, it is essential to the argument being pursued in this paper, that when both take their proper place, the design prescriptions that follow must necessarily be contingent upon the circumstances of the particular case.

Three questions now arise:

(1) How may 'the circumstances of a particular case' be operationally defined, and what measures of those circumstances may be used, so as to identify precisely the differences between one organization and another?

(2) How may the design features be identified, that are appropriate to the particular circumstance as defined and measured?

(3) Having identified the need for changes in design, in a particular case, how are the changes to be implemented?

The answers to these questions have not yet been fully worked out. Perhaps it would be truer to say that the work has only just started. In this concluding section I choose two examples of published work to illustrate briefly the 'best fit' approach to organizational design. I also outline a procedure for introducing design changes.

The Design of Organizational Structures

Woodward emphasized the influence of technology on organization structure, Burns the influence of the rate of environmental change. Lawrence and Lorsch (1967) point out that organizations differentiate themselves structurally so as to cope with differentiation of various kinds in their environment. Consider rate of change: the product/client environment might be subject to rapid change, the state of knowledge relevant to the organization's products and processes might be changing very slowly or not at all, the labour market might be extremely volatile and the technology static. If this is so, then one imagines that somewhat flexible structures might be appropriate at the interface with the customer and the competitor and with the labour market, whereas the efficient way of managing the manufacturing operations might be to introduce routines, and emphasize formal authority. One might also expect that the style of interpersonal relationships and individual attitudes appropriate for one kind of structure might be inappropriate for another. This point was recognized by Likert in the passage cited earlier in this paper but was not taken up and developed, although, from the point of view of organizational design and performance it would seem to be quite fundamental, since it may pose the kind of problems that 'matrix organization' is a device for solving.

Lawrence and Lorsch assume that complex and differentiated environments require complex patterns of structural segmentation, and these in their turn create a demand for structural integration, if the organization *as a whole* is to adapt efficiently to the environment *as a whole*. There is a number of known integrative mechanisms—hierarchial authority, committees, co-ordinators, project teams, conflict resolving machinery and modes, styles of management, reward systems etc., each or a number of which may be appropriate for a given pattern of structural differentiation.

Lawrence and Lorsch propose some measures of the extent of environmental differentiation in respect of three environments they consider to be characteristic of all work organizations, namely—the market environment, the technological environment (i.e. the manufacturing system) and the research and development environment. They propose a hypothesis that scores on dimensions measuring the state of each environment will indicate the set of structural expedients and modes of interpersonal relationship that are appropriate to cope effectively with each environment. To the extent that the environments differ along the dimensions used, so will the requirements for integration change, and the requisite sophistication of the mechanisms. Organizations with highly differentiated environments will not, on this view, function efficiently with a set of classical/structural expedients. Lawrence and Lorsch propose sets of conditions under which certain classes of integrative persons and mechanisms are likely to function effectively.

Using the framework proposed by Lawrence and Lorsch, we can answer our first question, viz., 'How can the circumstances be defined?' as follows:

The circumstances of a particular case can be defined by reference to the existing state of three environmental segments. These may be measured and differentiated along such dimensions as rate of change, uncertainty and the time lapse before information is received as to the economic and social outcomes of action by the organizations personnel.

Our second question, viz., 'How may the design features be identified?' we answer thus:

The methods of task allocation, superior/subordinate and peer relationships, normative controls, styles of management and supervision, and mental orientations, appropriate to cope with a particular set of environment conditions may be fairly accurately defined. It is now possible to say whether the set of organizational/psychological expedients that presently exist to cope with an environmental segment are appropriate or not and in what respects, and to indicate where changes should be made. The resulting design for structural differentiation defines the requirement for integration, and following guidelines derived from the literature of organizational psychology and sociology, the appropriate integration mechanisms may be specified.

With this step the design process as proposed by Lawrence and Lorsch is complete.[3] Research to test their hypothesis has so far been encouraging (Lawrence and Lorsch, 1967).

Lawrence and Lorsch do not propose an answer to the third question, namely, how is a new design to be introduced? My own proposal for dealing with the problem of implementation can await the discussion of the second example of a design procedure.

The Design of Reward Systems

Whatever their theoretical orientation or practical stance, social scientists and managers alike are agreed on the significance of the reward system(s) as an item(s) or organizational design. The theoretical and prescriptive literature is vast, and the field is filled with warring factions. Regrettably, once again the individual/organization dichotomy inhibits fruitful discussion. The question is often put: What are the influences that move individuals to work hard and effectively? The assumption is that if psychological research can answer that question, then we can design reward systems that will produce hard and effective work. There is agreement that persons are moved by a variety of stimuli; the promise of more money or a more interesting and better paid job, the moral obligation to keep contracts, the sheer interest and challenge in the job, the fear of sanctions, a sense of social obligation. Most reward systems evolve into a package designed to activate a number of these motives. One way then of desiging a reward system, a very commonly adopted way, would be to ascertain or to guess what the motives of individuals *in general* are, and design a 'package' to encourage them. The result is that some packages are highly complex structures, based consciously and deliberately on some general theory of multiple motives (see, e.g., North and Buckingham, 1969), others have evolved out of processes of bargaining and accommodation, others are based on simple prejudices such as 'men are moved by greed' or 'by fear' or 'by the prospect of getting ahead'. Whether simple or complex, or theoretically, well- or ill-founded, such packages are by implication thought of as being of general application. The need for a contingency procedure is implicitly recognized when people speak, as they do, of 'tailor made' compensation packages but is seldom acted upon. What *is* the nature of the relationship between individual motivation and the socio-technical system, and what is the relevance of that relationship to the design of reward systems?

Consider the following example. A team of female operators is working on the assembly of a waterproof garment. Each of them carries out a different operation on the garment, and the work is passed from one to another until the garment is completed. Each operator is paid a price for completing her own operation, i.e. the operation for which she has been trained and which she normally carries out; the more pieces completed, the more pay. Each set of cutting delivered to the team has attached to it a sheet of adhesive stamps, and on each stamp is printed the order number of the batch of garments currently being produced and the number and price of the operation that the stamp represents. On completion of each operation the operator responsible tears off a stamp and attaches it to the stamp card at the corner of her work bench. The psychological theory of the incentive scheme is that the operator, by watching the rate at which her stamp card is filling up, will be able to see her earnings minute by minute. On the assumption that she wants her earnings to grow rapidly she will be encouraged to work hard and effectively (reinforcement, feedback of results and so on).

However, the rate at which the stamps on the operator's card build up is affected by other things than the operator's effort and ingenuity. All operators depend very much on those prior to them in the sequence of operations for a supply of parts to work on. Since the (production) system is not perfectly balanced, and since not all of the operators are equally skilled there are points in the process where gluts and shortages occur. The supervisor, from time to time, finds it necessary to move operators from one operation to another, so as to clear up a bottleneck. But when an operator is moved temporarily from an operation with which she is familiar, and on which she has developed a high rate of working, to another with which she is not familiar, she observes that the rate at which her stamps accumulate falls off rapidly. She then tries to avoid being transferred. One way of doing this is to contrive to be absent from the team so that someone else gets transferred, but this only increases the difficulties of the supervisor, worsens relationships, and reduces the output of completed garments. To add to the difficulty, the rate of absenteeism amongst female operators is usually quite high and also unpredictable. So, the supervisor every morning has to decide on the best dispositions of persons to operations so as to optimize the output of the whole team, and once again the capacity to earn of some individuals will be affected, usually adversely. Since the operators have an expectation as to what is the proper relationship between the monetary rewards they receive from the firm, and the skill and effort they expend, they try to manipulate the situation so as to maintain this relationship, by trying to exert influence on the supervisor, by going absent when deployment looks imminent, and so on. This of course makes the supervisor's job difficult, and affects her relationship with the operators in general, and some operators in particular. To some she appears to press, to boss, to harass.

There is another problem. Garments are produced in batches, so as to satisfy the needs of customers. Every week or so, the team changes over to a new garment. Although the operations on all garments have similarities, e.g. sewing in sleeves, the operation on every new batch is slightly different. For this reason, it will probably have a slightly different price. There is a period of relearning when the rate of earnings tends to fall, and there is the possibility that the price may be regarded as 'tight', so that more parts have to be produced each day for the same daily earnings. In this case, an operator may settle for a lower daily rate of earnings while the particular garment is in production, expecting to make up on the next batch of garments. But the low rate of production might create 'part starvation' further up the line, where another operator might have decided that, on her operation, with a favourable price, she was going to raise her rate of output. In this case, the chargehand might intervene, and delays might occur while arguments ensued about the price for the job, or whether an operator should be deployed to make up shortages.

We observe here a number of structural factors acting in the situation to affect the response of the operators to the rewards offered by the payment system. Firstly, the product market, the response to which gives rise to the batch problem, which in turn gives rise to the relearning problem. Then there is the technology and the design of the work flow which give rise to difficulties of balancing, and give the chargehand a deployment problem, which in turn affects her relationship with the operators; or if you like her 'style' of supervision. Certainly this in turn influences the relationship between operators. The choice of women to perform this operation was clearly influenced by the nature and traditions of the local labour market, but this choice compounded the deployment problem via absenteeism.

I dare say that if one were interested in trying to improve the productivity of the team, the quality of the relationship between the chargehand and the operators and between the operators, the operator's job satisfaction and the level of voluntary (policy) absenteeism, one might start by trying to change the style of management and supervision, and get the operators involved. But one would also be wise to see whether the product batches might be made larger, the layout, manning and balancing of the production line improved, different kinds of training schemes introduced and the incentive scheme redesigned. So the redesign of this unit for higher productivity and job satisfaction would involve tackling *at the same time* the structural and psychological factors that have emerged from the diagnosis.

Confronted with this example, which is only one of hundreds that one might have culled from the literature (see, e.g., Roy, 1954; Lupton, 1963; Lupton and Cunnison, 1957; Klein, 1964; Cunnison, 1966), it is difficult to imagine how any general psychological prescription for the design of a pay system, a pay structure, a job enlargement program or whatever, could except by sheer accident be appropriate to the circumstances of a particular case. So the question arises, what is the best pay system for a particular case? Or, and this is an equally valid question, in what way and to what extent could the circumstances of a particular case be altered so as to make the pay system (or whatever design item one were considering) appropriate in terms of whatever objectives the designer has set himself?

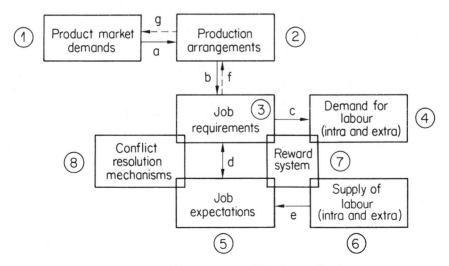

Figure 3. Reward systems as equilibrating mechanisms

I now describe briefly procedure designed to answer these questions. Figure 3 states a hypothesis about the functions of a reward system in an organization. The demands of customers, and the strategies and tactics of competitors, give rise to certain decisions as to what is to be produced, in what quantities, at what dates and times, and by what method. This is represented by the black arrow joining Box 1 and Box 2. It will be readily apparent that a range of choices is possible. There is no unique solution, but a choice from a set of possibilities. Similarly, when the deployment of people around the technology is being considered, there are choices to be made and these will surely be influenced by the availability of people with certain skills at certain wages in the labour market. So there is a causal link between the boxes marked 'job requirements', 'supply of labour' and 'demand for labour'. People come into jobs with certain ideas about what ought to be expected of them, and what they can, and ought to contribute; and these are affected by the state of the labour market. What can be done to give these ideas effect is also influenced by the state of labour supply, as against the demand of the firm for labour deriving from the state of the product market and the choices about production arrangements (Box 2). It will also be influenced by the formal procedures for ensuring that the job requirements are in fact met, e.g. the arrangements for setting work standards, for monitoring performance and for allocating jobs. There is a process of continuous adjustment taking place between 'job requirements' and 'job expectations'. Procedures for bargaining and consultation are mechanisms for handling the conflicts that arise in the relationship between what the firm requires its workforce to do, and the rewards it wishes to offer on the one hand, and what the workforce is prepared to contribute in return for a given set of inducements on the other. I have named these 'mechanisms for conflict resolution'.

A firm when formulating job requirements will be influenced by what it believes to be the current state of job expectations, and will make some adjustments accordingly. The reward system is highly significant mechanism in the adjustment process as between requirements and expectations. It is the mechanism that maintains equilibrium between: (a) the requirements which derive in the first place from the product market, (b) the supply and demand situation in the labour market and (c) the relationship between job requirements and job expectations. Equilibrium might occur at a position when the technology is underutilized, high labour cost is experienced with consequent price disadvantages in the product market and difficulties are encountered in meeting promised delivery dates. The remedies for such a situation might involve decisions about changing the product mix, adopting different production requirements, adjusting the stock of the product held, changing the job definitions, attempting to influence operator attitudes, changing the payment system and the structure of the pay packet, improving recruitment and training procedures, and changing the bargaining and consultative machinery.

In order to decide what has to be adjusted, and in what way, let us start by trying to classify payment systems. Let us define payment systems as those

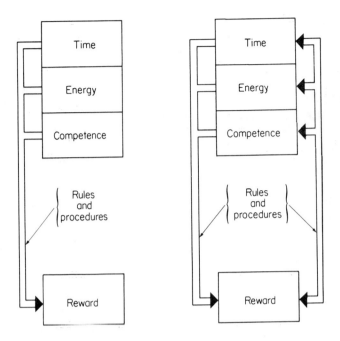

Nonreciprocal		Reciprocal		
Time	Nonreciprocal = TNR	Time	Reciprocal	= TR
Energy	Nonreciprocal = ENR	Energy	Reciprocal	= ER
Competence	Nonreciprocal = CNR	Competence	Reciprocal	= CR
			(Reciprocity may be immediate or deferred.)	

Figure 4. Types of effort–reward relationship

arrangements that link effort of some kind to reward of some kind via a set of formal rules and procedures. We may begin by making a broad twofold classification (as illustrated in Figure 4) between reciprocal and non-reciprocal systems. The difference rests merely in the fact that the rules and procedures in reciprocal systems specify that more effort will bring forth more reward, whereas in non-reciprocal systems the rules and procedures make no such statement. Figure 4 also classifies effort in three ways: (a) *time effort*, where the rewards are offered for time spent at work, (b) *energy effort*, where the rewards accrue for measurable inputs of physical effort and (c) *competence effort*, where the rewards are related to the availability of already acquired skills and competencies. If we allow for two kinds of reward for energy, one for group effort and one for individual effort; and the two modes of reciprocity already distinguished, we have a twelvefold classification table as illustrated in Figure 5. I have inserted in each box an empirical example of the analytical type.

Reward

<table>
<tr><td rowspan="2"></td><td colspan="2">Reciprocal</td><td rowspan="2">Non-reciprocal</td></tr>
<tr><td>Immediate</td><td>Deferred</td></tr>
<tr><td colspan="2">Time</td><td>TRI
(e.g. time rates with overtime and shift premium)</td><td>TRD
(e.g. time rates with deferred equivalents)</td><td>TNR
(e.g. pay by hour or day)</td></tr>
<tr><td rowspan="2">Energy</td><td>Individual</td><td>ERI (ind.)
(e.g. piecework, incentive bonus)</td><td>ERD (ind.)
(e.g. monthly production bonus)</td><td>ENR (ind.)
(e.g. measured day work)</td></tr>
<tr><td>Group</td><td>ERI (grp.)
(e.g. group piece-work or incentives)</td><td>ERD (grp.)
(e.g. group production bonus)</td><td>ENR (grp.)
(e.g., labour contracting)</td></tr>
<tr><td colspan="2">Competence</td><td>CRI
(incentives for craftsmen)</td><td>CRD
(work simplication)</td><td>CNR
(incremental sales)</td></tr>
</table>

Effort (row label on left side)

Figure 5. Types of effort–reward relationship

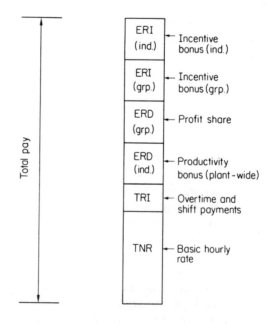

Figure 6. The pay packet contains a number of different types of effort–reward relationships

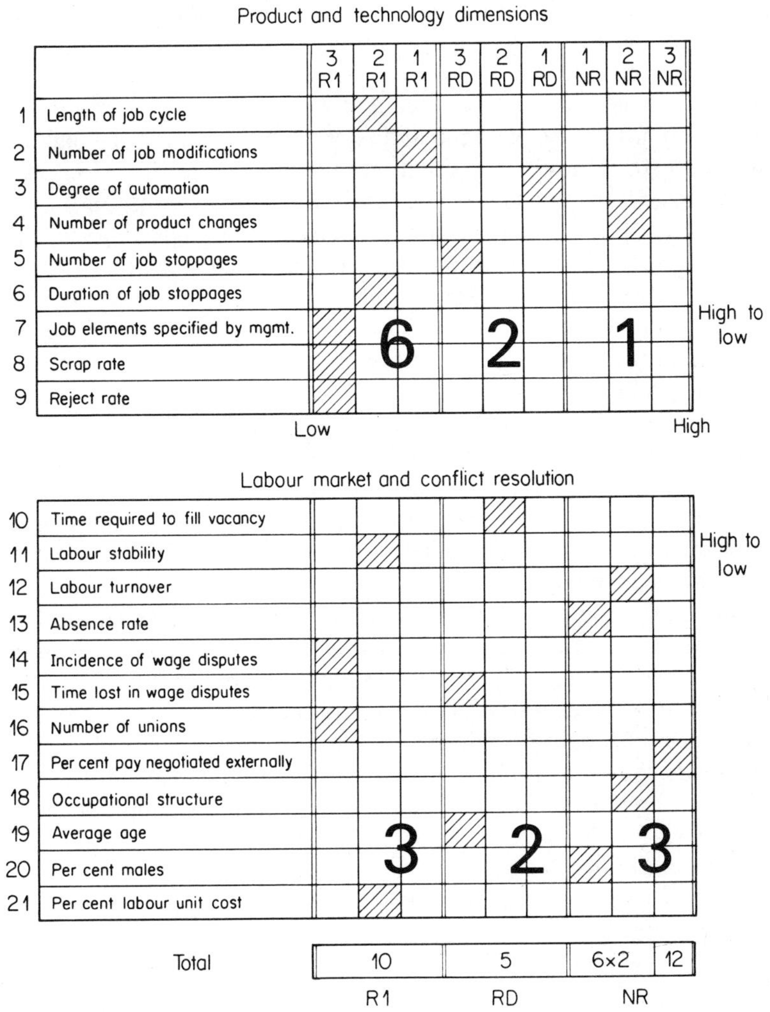

Product and technology dimensions

		3 R1	2 R1	1 R1	3 RD	2 RD	1 RD	1 NR	2 NR	3 NR	
1	Length of job cycle		▨								
2	Number of job modifications			▨							
3	Degree of automation						▨				
4	Number of product changes								▨		
5	Number of job stoppages					▨					
6	Duration of job stoppages		▨								
7	Job elements specified by mgmt.	▨									High to
8	Scrap rate	▨	**6**		**2**			**1**			low
9	Reject rate	▨									

Low   High

Labour market and conflict resolution

		3 R1	2 R1	1 R1	3 RD	2 RD	1 RD	1 NR	2 NR	3 NR	
10	Time required to fill vacancy				▨						
11	Labour stability		▨								High to
12	Labour turnover								▨		low
13	Absence rate							▨			
14	Incidence of wage disputes	▨									
15	Time lost in wage disputes					▨					
16	Number of unions	▨									
17	Per cent pay negotiated externally									▨	
18	Occupational structure								▨		
19	Average age			▨							
20	Per cent males	**3**			**2**			▨ **3**			
21	Per cent labour unit cost		▨								

Total	10	5	6×2	12
	R1	RD	NR	

Add prefix for type of effort: T, E, or C. Decide unit of accountability: Ind., Grp., or Plant.
Basic Design of Optimum Pay Packet

Figure 7. The situation 'profile' (with example)

Now, any reward system (in this case we shall be especially concerned with rewards for manual work) is made up of a number of different types of effort–reward relation. Figure 6 shows a fairly typical pay packet for a manual worker, and includes six boxes from the analytic table.

One problem that arises in designing a reward system is to decide which combination of elements, and in what proportions, would be appropriate for a given situation, and one device for deciding this is illustrated in Figure 7.

The boxes in Figure 3 above are represented in the 'situation profile' by a number of dimensions. It is possible to 'score' any production unit, however large or small, by shading in the appropriate box on each dimension. In the example given, the unit that is illustrated has a short job cycle, is fairly highly automated, changes its product frequently, leaves little discretion to the operators, and has a very low scrap and reject rate. The unit has a high labour stability and high turnover in a situation in which labour is not very easy to come by. It loses little time in wage disputes, which are few; there is one union, and much of the pay of the operators is negotiated at a level higher than the unit itself. The occupational structure of the whole organization of which the unit is a part is complex, the working force comprises mostly men with a medium average age, and the process is fairly capital intensive. The reason for choosing these particular measures, and the nature of the scales, is explained in Lupton and Gowler (1969).

The boxes from the analytical table are arranged along each dimension. The rationale for this arrangement is also explained in Lupton and Gowler. It is sufficient here to say that the rationale is derived from research findings in this field. In the example given, where it is assumed that energy effort is typical of the operation, a short job cycle would indicate *for that dimension* a reciprocal immediate payment system. However, a production system with a large number of product changes poses certain problems for a reciprocal immediate scheme, as we saw in the case of the waterproof garment workshop, so that *for that dimension* a non-reciprocal system would be appropriate. However, and this is to be emphasized, if matters could be arranged so that the number of product changes could be reduced, then the shaded area would shift to the right, towards the reciprocal deferred or reciprocal immediate area of the table. The technology and product market scores in this example suggest that much of the pay packet in this case could appropriately be represented by some kind of payment by results scheme. The scores on other dimensions suggest a more even distribution across the table. The basic design of the pay packet appropriate to this situation is suggested by the totals in Figure 7, so long as the situation represented by the scores on the profiles remains the same.

There are other ways of approaching the problem of pay-packet design, one of which is a mathematical procedure which has been published in Bowey and Lupton (1970).

Both these examples of procedures for organizational design might seem to do too little justice to the psychological variables, but they are certainly able to take them adequately into account. For example, if a program of job enrichment were to be introduced into the production unit in our garment workshop example, the effects could be fairly well predicted and would alter the structure of the appropriate pay packet. The job cycle score would move to the right, the score on degree of automation would probably shift back to the left, the percentage of job elements specified by management would decrease, moving the score to the right. The labour market scores would probably shift. The time required to fill a vacancy would probably increase because of increased training time and so on. The indications are that with such a program, the wage-packet structure would have to be changed to include a lesser proportion based on a reciprocal immediate principle. The tendency would be for most of the elements to move, mostly to the right. All this indicates once again that there is a complex relationship of mutual dependence between the psychological and structural variables, and that to design them into an optimum arrangement requires that they have to be dealt with *at the same time*, and within the same frame of reference. And this means once again that the design is contingent upon the situation.

It is one thing to create a new design for an organization structure, or a crucial part of its processes such as a reward system, and to define the environmental constraints. It is yet another to give effect to the new design. There is no space in this paper to discuss in detail a procedure for making changes, but I shall use the same ideas as I have used in analysing the design problem briefly to discuss implementation.

Implementation of a New Design

If the reader will refer again to Figure 3 he will see that the process of implementation of a new organizational design, whether it be a formal structure of responsibilities and authority, a new payment system or the introduction of a job enlargement program, will disturb the complex relationship of a number of variables. It will be apparent, for example, that a change in what I have called the 'production arrangements', e.g. the introduction of new machinery, a new office procedure, a method of production planning, or a reorganization of the salesforce, a change in the reward system or of the mechanisms of conflict resolutions, will have an impact on the relationship of mutual accommodation between job expectations and job requirements. A significant object of those who are effecting the changes will surely be to minimize the disturbance to this relationship given that the relationship as it exists is not already inhibiting the organization's capacity to cope with its environment. If it is so inhibiting then it might be desirable to attempt to restructure job expectations, for example via training, or to change some of the factors affecting job requirements that seem to be inhibiting an optimum adjustment. To return to the example of the garment-assembly shop, one might be inclined to make alterations to the shop layout so as to produce a better balanced line, and also to train the operators to do more than one job on the line, reducing the need for redeployment or to cushion the effects of it in a situation where absenteeism is likely to be high. Or one might restructure the situation in ways that make it possible and economical to draw labour from different markets. Or one might think of reducing the number of product changes by adjusting stockholding policies or moving into different markets.

In short, at whatever point in the system one starts to implement design changes, one would, if operating with this model, see that the crucial matter to be managed is the job requirements–job expectations relationship. The change must not work *either* with one or the other, but must change *both and the relationship*. Firstly, he must have a knowledge of the present state of the relationship, and of the factors that are affecting both sides of it; secondly, he must have a way of predicting the effect of changes in these factors, and thirdly, he must understand the reward system and the mechanisms for coping with conflict that are required to keep the relationship in balance, given the state of the labour market.

Just as the argument underlying the case for developing a new design for 'best fit' stressed the need to work simultaneously, in diagnosis, both at the level of the organization and the individual, so also must the argument for an implementation strategy. In order to work in this way, one must look at individual behaviour in the context of a set of task relationships. Since each set of relationships that people enter into in work organizations is the outcome of an active interplay of expectations and formal requirements, and since these requirements and expectations are related *inter alia* to the state of product markets, labour markets and technology, and since, further, these states differ from organization to organization, then it is difficult to see how an approach to the preparation and installation of a design for organizational efficiency can feasibly be other than an attempt to find a 'best fit'. Surely future research must be directed to the development of models and practical procedures which improve the skills that can discover 'best fit'. It would seem also that such research would have to be interdisciplinary in the sense that economists, psychologists, sociologists and engineers will be working towards the development of common models of organization. The pursuit of such research might well result in the creation of a new sort of discipline of organizational analysis. Some of the tools for such a discipline are ready to hand.

Notes

1. A balanced and detailed critique of recent job-attitude research following the Herzberg studies may be found in Wall and Stephenson (1970) and Wall and coworkers (1971).
2. Studies of what happened after 'grid' training are inconclusive (see, e.g., Smith and Honour (1969).
3. A more detailed exposition of the design process as derived from the work of Lawrence and Lorsch may be found in Lupton (1971).

References

Argyris, C. (1970), *Intervention Theory and Method: a Behavioral Science View*, Addison-Wesley, Reading, Massachusetts.

Blake, R. R. and Mouton, J. S. (1964), *The Managerial Grid*, Gulf Publishing Company, Houston.

Bowey, A. M. and Lupton, T. (1970), Productivity drift and the structure of the pay packet, *in Journal of Management Studies*, Part I, Vol. 7 (May) pp. 156–171 and Part II, Vol. 7 (October) pp. 310–334.

Burns, T. and Stalker, G. M. (1961), *The Management of Innovation*, Tavistock Publications, London.

Cunnison, S. (1966), *Wages and Work Allocation: a Study of Social Relations in a Garment Workshop*, Tavistock Publications, London.

Fayol, H. (1949), *General and Industrial Management*, Pitman, London.

Herzberg, F, Mansner, B. and Snydeman, B. B. (1959), *The Motivation to Work*, Wiley, New York.

Herzberg, F. (1966), *Work and the Nature of Man*, World Publishing Company, Cleveland.

Klein, L. (1964), *Multiproducts, Ltd.: a Case Study on the Social Effects of Rationalized Production*, HMSO, London.

Lawrence, P. R. and Lorsch, J. W. (1967), *Organization and Environment*, Harvard University, Graduate School of Business Administration, Boston, Mass.

Likert, R. (1967), *The Human Organization: its Management and Value*, McGraw-Hill, New York.

Lupton, T. (1963), *On the Shop Floor: Two Studies of Workshop Organization and Output*, Pergamon Press, New York.

Lupton, T. and Cunnison, S. (1957), The cash reward for an hour's work under three incentive schemes, *in: The Manchester School of Economic and Social Studies*, **25**, (3) pp. 213–269.

Lupton, T. and Gowler, D. (1969), *Selecting a Wage Payment System*, Kogan Page, London.

Lupton, T. (1971), *Management and the Social Sciences*, Penguin Books, Baltimore.

McGregor, D. (1960), *The Human Side of Enterprise*, McGraw-Hill, New York.

North, D. T. B. and Buckingham, G. L. (1969), *Productivity Agreements and Wages Systems*, Gower Press, London.

Paul, W. J. Jr., Robertson K. B., Herzberg, F. (1969), Job enrichment pays off, *Harvard Business Review*, March–April, pp. 61–78.

Rice, A. K. (1963), *The Enterprise and its Environment*, Tavistock Publications, London.

Roethlisberger, F. J. and Dickson, W. J. (1939), *Management and the Worker*, Harvard University Press, Cambridge, Mass.

Roethlisberger, F. J. and Dickson, W. J. (1964), *Management and the Worker*, Wiley, New York.

Roy, D. (1954), Efficiency and 'The Fix': informal intergroup relations in a piecework machine shop, *American Journal of Sociology*, LX (3) November pp. 255–266.

Smith, P. B. and Honour, T. F. (1969), The impact of Phase I Managerial Grid Training, *in Journal of Management Studies*, **6**, October pp. 318–330.

Taylor, F. W. (1947), *Scientific Management*, Harper, New York.

Trist, E. L., Higgin, G. W., Murray, H. and Pollock, A. B., (1963), *Organizational Choice: Capabilities of Groups at the Coal Face under Changing Technologies*, Tavistock Publications, London.

Urwick, L. F. (1956), *The Pattern of Management*, University of Minnesota Press, Minneapolis.

Wall, T. D. and Stephenson, G. M. (1970), Herzberg's two-factor theory of job attitudes: a critical evaluation and some fresh evidence, *Industrial Relations Journal*, **1**, (3), 41–65.

Wall, T. D., Stephenson, G. M. and Skidmore, C. (1971), Ego-involvement and Herzberg's two-factor theory of job satisfaction: an experimental field study, *The British Journal of Social and Clinical Psychology*, **10**, (2) June. pp. 123–131.

Woodward, J. (1958), *Management and Technology*, HMSO, London.

Woodward, J. (1965), *Industrial Organisation: Theory and Practice*, Oxford University Press, London.

Task and Organization: Military and Civilian

A. B. Cherns and P. A. Clark

Introduction

In this chapter we examine selected issues which are faced by the organizational analyst when tackling problems in the area of the design of organizational systems in civilian and military enterprises. For these purposes we have selected two problems which have been of great importance for us in the work which we have undertaken in a variety of contexts—industrial, public service, military. First, we consider the kinds of analytical frameworks which are relevant for the organizational analyst. We examine this topic initially without reference to the kinds of problem which arise when attempting to work jointly with non-social scientists to tackle practical problems. Second, we give some consideration to the requirements for devising frameworks which are of utility to the non-social scientist. The latter's interests are twofold: to have a general understanding of the social scientists' activities, and to be able to carry out some kinds of analysis without advice or assistance.

The problems which we have been working on all broadly fall under the heading of organizational design. For example, they include the kinds of organizational system which are appropriate to different kinds of military task (Cherns, 1967); the design of organizational systems to fit the requirements of an enterprise which was replacing several existing factories with one new one that was to be technologically advanced (Clark and Cherns, 1970; Clark, 1972); the establishment of effective forms of co-ordination for the process of hospital design. In general we shall neglect the concern of social scientists for achieving greater understanding of organizational structures and processes. Rather we shall seek to appraise how far current developments may be found to be fruitful in dealing with actual problems. In this way we expect to learn more about both organizational analysis and the organizations we have been working with, but we make no claims that it is possible to undertake action research and simultaneously make contributions which directly further the development of organizational analysis. It seems more likely that action research will be best considered as an opportunity to explore the limits of a particular approach and suggest new directions for basic research.

Analytical Frameworks

The involvement of the social scientist in tackling the problems of the choice

152

of appropriate control systems for enterprises employing several thousand persons introduces demands on the kinds of analytical frameworks which are relevant that rarely occur when the unit of analysis is the work group or small department. It requires the social scientist to develop an overall concept of the organization, and also to be able to take account of the complexities of its internal differentiation. This is especially so when the project is undertaken in situations of major technological product and administrative innovation.

Given the extensive nature of the kinds of project which we were undertaking, we were concerned to adopt analytical perspectives which were focused upon the enterprise, or at least the major part of it, as the entity for analysis. Any frameworks we selected had to be able to accommodate social and organizational facets which were related to the technological dimension as well as deal with hierarchical-strata aspects and the horizontal interdepartmental relations. Three obvious sources of ideas were the socio-technical framework (Emery, 1959), and the early work of Woodward (1958, 1965), and Burns and Stalker (1961). Though these frameworks have been somewhat castigated in recent commentaries on organizational analysis the main thrust of such criticisms has been that the concepts and propositions developed are prescriptive. Since this was our objective, and it would seem to us also to have been the objectives of their 'inventors' (cf. Silverman, 1970), it was natural that we should consider their relevance.

We did not find, nor have our researches observed, that organizational analysts use only one conceptual framework (Clark and Ford, 1970). The choice of framework is dependent upon the definition of the problem to be tackled. Thus, we found the socio-technical framework as adumbrated by Emery (1959) and developed at the 'Lincoln Conference' in 1966 to be useful as a means of organizing our own thinking when attempting to identify the implications of increased mechanization and automation for the existing control systems as operated by management. We found it less useful when identifying the implications of these technological changes for the social organization of the particular departments which were affected (Clark, 1972). Here it was necessary to carry out investigations which were similar to the many studies which are found in industrial sociology (e.g. Eldridge, 1968; Crozier, 1964).

Organizational design requires the reconstruction on paper of the configuration of activities and interactions which would be required to sustain a particular bundle of tasks. An important element of such a reconstruction is the estimation of the kinds of linkage which are likely to be established between characteristics of the product market, the production technology and the control system. For this kind of exercise it might be considered that the conventional input of systems analysts would suffice. However, systems analysis, as Mumford and Banks (1967) so clearly demonstrate, is principally concerned with the non-social facets of the organization. Similarly, one cannot expect experts in research and development to be concerned with spelling out the kinds of connection between market factors and production systems which are suggested in the researches of Woodward (1965). Yet it is just that kind of connection which is important to organizational design. For example, it is quite possible for marketing to be planning changes in 'concept' which would transform a placid market with an ordered rate of innovation that permits large-batch production into a more highly competitive fragmented market with a number of speciality brands. All this can proceed whilst engineers are designing a production system which is based on the previous market concept, and systems analysts are similarly designing an integrated and highly formalized control system. The reconstruction of the future organizational structure requires not only the consideration of the import of non-social factors for the social structure, but also a facility for incorporating the design of social and non-social facets into one entity. Miller and Rice (1967) in a significant examination of the issues involved in organizational design suggest that technical and organizational aspects need contemporaneous examination. This can only be achieved by adopting a perspective which includes concepts and propositions that refer to this area. If such concepts and propositions require the crossing of the disciplinary boundaries established for teaching and career purposes in universities, then such a journey is required and is appropriate to the problem.

We have already hinted at the kind of role we see for the kind of perspective set out by Burns and Stalker (1961), but we should like to illustrate one point from a project undertaken in a large foundry where this was particularly useful. The problem we were attempting to conceptualize for ourselves was of a site which was to be affected by two kinds of change. First, it was another project in which the action research was concerned with a situation in which a new factory with a more mechanized and automated technology was replacing an existing factory. In that sense it was somewhat like an earlier project (Clark, 1972). However, there was one additional factor. The second kind of change, which cut across and included the first, was that the company operating the foundry was in the process of carrying a major product innovation which was more far reaching than any previous product innovation. In simple value terms the sterling cost of the new innovation was more than ten times the selling price of the previous major product innovation. Thus we found ourselves entering a field situation in which we were trying to identify ongoing changes in organization and reconcile these with a more general concept of the appropriate organizational systems. Here we made an assumption about organizational learning derived from the work of Dill (1962). We made the working assumption that the members of the foundry would attempt to handle the innovation by adopting the forms of organization which had been successful in handling the last major innovation some time previously. We then attempted to identify the likely changes in management system by adopting the mechanistic-organic continuum (Burns and Stalker, 1961). It can, of course, be objected that such a perspective is naive or irrelevant. Against this it must be observed that the perspective sensitizes the analyst to a great deal more than would otherwise be the case. Further, it forces the analysis to account for changes in organizational structure over time on the same site. As Clark (1965, 1972) argues, this dimension is crucial to action research, even if it can be omitted from mainstream research in organizational behaviour!

The main feature of the perspectives we have referred to so far is that they may all be placed within one particular school of thought about organizational design. Each gives some recognition to 'something' which is termed the 'task', and each proposes certain relationships between a particular configuration of task dimensions and an 'organizational system'. This school is increasingly recognized as the 'task analysis approach'. In some places it has also been referred to as the 'contingency theory' of organizational design (e.g. Lawrence and Lorsch, 1967). It includes, in addition, the work of March and Simon (1958), Bell (1967), Thompson (1967) and Perrow (1967, 1971).

The strength of the 'task' approach is that it does attempt to provide the organizational analyst with the intellectual framework for tackling a particular problem and developing a range of alternative solutions which 'fit'. It thus postulates a 'fit' between 'task' and 'organization'.

The 'task analysis' approach is not without its critics. It is therefore pertinent to note its objectives and the criteria which we may apply to evaluate them. First, we would argue that its objectives have in some instances been misunderstood. In general, the aim of theorists is prescriptive, and deliberately so, though its main contributors are not necessarily those most involved in its application to ongoing practical problems. The theory is based upon certain kinds of descriptive research investigation, abstracting from these propositions which relate to specified objectives. For example, a major concern is the degree of flexibility of an organizational system. Thus Bell (1967) has extracted propositions based on a variety of investigations and used them to indicate possible connections between task-characteristics and professionalization. Second, the task-perspective does not seek to refer to all behaviour in organizations. This is a crucial point. It is made quite explicitly by Woodward (1970), but seemingly ignored by some critics. Elsewhere it is implicit (e.g. Perrow 1967). For this reason the contention that the task analysis approach is a form of 'technological determinism' is misplaced. The approach does not currently seek to predict such facets as 'workers' orientation' to colleagues, or to the job (Goldthorpe, 1968).

The criteria for evaluating such a prescriptive theory must be in terms of its own internal logic as applied to the relationship between the objective (e.g. flexibility of structure) and the propositions delimiting its occurrence and non-occurrence.

A feature of the task and organization perspective is that it has been developed in western industrialized societies largely, but not solely, with reference to industrial enterprises. This raises a number of fairly immediate problems. For example, it is plausible—if not empirically demonstrable—to assert that there are sufficient common aspects of the norms governing work within industrial enterprises for this aspect to be assumed to be standardized. We may note that Etzioni (1961) argues that industrial enterprises 'are more pervaded than pervasive', and Goldthorpe (1968) provides tentative evidence supporting the contention. In this cultural context it may be valid to explore the 'task-control system-structure' dimension in the way adopted by Woodward (1970). Whether it would be relevant in a cultural system in which the separation of the community and the household from the place of work is less sharp than in advanced industrial societies (Stinchcombe, 1965) is more questionable. Here we are in effect pointing to the existence of certain assumptions about 'rationality' which pervade the task perspective.

We may therefore have in mind at least two possible limitations of this perspective for organizational design outside the industrial context. First, the range of variables covered, which is recognized as being restricted (see later) may be so narrow that significant aspects of non-industrial enterprises (e.g. the church) are omitted. Second, the assumptions built into the perspective in certain formulations may not apply to, for example, the military. Before going on to examine these two questions in more detail, we briefly summarize the main points of Perrow's schema. We take this as an example because we felt it would be of value in the study of the military (Cherns, 1967).

Perrow has made a number of relevant contributions to discussion of the 'fit' between task and organization. In an early paper Perrow (1961) distinguished between the professed goals of a social unit and its operating goals. Later he examined the 'technology' of a hospital (Perrow, 1965) and explored differences in organization among three institutions catering for delinquents (Street and coworkers, 1966). That study suggested that the senior executive's choice of the form of treatment for delinquents strongly influenced the institution's organizational form. The keynote paper came in 1967. In less than fifteen pages Perrow both set out a framework for examining organizations as entities and making systematic comparisons between them, and also managed to subsume within his theory a very wide range of existing empirical studies undertaken in welfare agencies, the military, tobacco factories and education. He made a strong suggestion that a number of existing perspectives on organizational analysis were in practice relevant only to specific situations and these could be identified from the schema (e.g. the work of March and Simon (1958)).

Perrow's proposed scheme starts by characterizing the activities undertaken by the first line operators in an organizational unit when 'transforming' the raw material on which they work. The raw material can be a 'thing', people or symbols. The thrust of the characterization is to identify the extent of uncertainty which the 'raw material' creates for those working upon it. Uncertainty can arise from the operators' knowledge of the raw material and its stability on the one hand, and from the kinds of 'exception' and the 'search process' adopted to resolve exceptions on the other. The 'exception' and 'search process' elements respresent the influence of March and Simon (1958) and their inclusion in the scheme provides important connections with thinking on socio-technical analysis (e.g. the concept of variance) and with the focus of Burns and Stalker on decision-making. 'Exceptions' can be located on a continuum from high to low. The next element to be tackled is what happens

156

when there is an 'exception'. The 'search process' for a solution may be simple and logical at one end of the continuum and complex and judgemental at the other end. If we now place the two dichotomized dimensions in a two by two table we have the starting point of the schema. From here on Perrow suggests that there are systematic influences from the location of a particular unit on the schema to the extent of formality of the structure.

The crucial point in this approach is the hypothesis that two characteristics of the interaction between the individual and the 'object' influence the organizational design. These two dimensions are the number of exceptional cases which occur during the interaction and the search process which has to be undertaken when an exception occurs. These two dimensions may be set out as shown in Figure 1. Perrow argues that organizations which are located in box 'C' will have different organizational designs from those in box 'B'. The differences will be found in terms of the formality/flexibility of the organization structure; the areas of discretion available to the members of the organizational unit; the nature and content of horizontal and vertical communications; the method of co-ordination of activities; relationships between the organizational unit and its headquarters. An example is given in Table 1.

In the preceding paragraphs we have outlined a number of schemata which can be useful to the process of organizational design. Their common characteristic is that they begin the analysis from a characterization of the task of the organizational unit and then postulate that some forms 'fit' between task and organization, and are appropriate for given objectives. The discussion of such schemata in the classroom situation and in research seminars has pointed to a number of theoretical problems, but we are here concerned with the problems of using them in practical situations. It must be said that the major problem facing novices in using them, especially that of Perrow, is that the definitions of concepts are so general that their application in a particular unit becomes

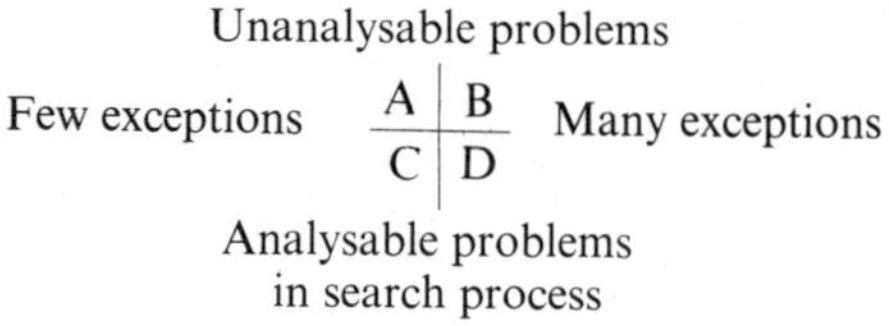

Unanalysable problems

Few exceptions $\dfrac{A \mid B}{C \mid D}$ Many exceptions

Analysable problems
in search process

Figure 1. A scheme showing the two dimensions of the interaction between the individual and 'object'

Table 1. An example of Perrow's Scheme

		Box 'C'	Box 'B'
1.	Formality/flexibility	Formal	Flexible
2.	Area of discretion	Low	High
3.	Communications	Hierarchical	Network
4.	Co-ordination	Programmed	Negotiated
5.	Relations with H.Q.	Prescribed and defined	Two-way relationship

problematic. Few analysts have the experience of tackling a wide range of organizational units. A. K. Rice was a notable exception, and a man who wrote with great urgency and clarity.

We had found the Perrow schema useful in two projects on organizational design in civilian locations. Its value was in helping us to organize our thinking about the existing organization and some of its important determinants. Our emphasis upon this aspect rests on the assumption/theory that the members of enterprises learn a particular pattern of social activities and interactions. It should be noted that we are not referring to values/orientations in the sense that Goldthorpe (1968) defined these. However, we do anticipate that members become attached to particular configurations of activities and interactions and that their expectations of others with regard to areas of autonomy and control are important when dealing with situations in which technological change occurs. Touraine observes that the crucial feature of technological change is its impact upon the existing structure of relationships (Touraine and coworkers, 1965). In our thinking we would anticipate that the members of organizations develop concepts (very limited) to express this dimension, and behave in terms of it. Clark (1965) observed in a study of the organization of supermarkets that each of the separate departments was organized in different ways. For example, the organization of the department handling prepackaged goods was similar to the 'mechanistic' as depicted by Burns and Stalker (1961) whilst that for fruit and vegetables approximated more to 'organic'. These differences could be explained by reference to the task. It was noticeable that the store managers always emerged from the departments in which the task was most predictable (e.g. packaged provisions). Clark noted that in the weekend peak period of operating, when the manager was most to be seen in the store, he concentrated his attention upon the departments which were least predictable, especially fruit and vegetables. He focused upon what he regarded as deviances from the orderly conducting of operations and attempted to control these. The postulate is that the manager's conception of the appropriate 'fit' of task and organization was significantly influenced by his own experience and this influenced his idea of what was the adequate 'fit' for the supermarket as a whole.

These postulates can be applied to the area of organizational design. In instances where there is technological, administrative and market innovation then it is important to focus upon the structure of relationships.

In practice the application of the task analysis perspective requires that the enterprise is not only conceived as a whole, but is also conceptualized as a differentiated entity. It is not sufficient to achieve a 'fit' for one part of an enterprise in isolation from other parts. Consideration has to be given to the requirements for integration (Lawrence and Lorsch, 1967) and the 'mechanics of segregation' (Litwak, 1961), that is the need to separate some departments. It may be prudent to decrease their visibility to one another in instances where there are radical differences in task and organization. The point is made sharply by Burns in his comments upon the position of scientists (Burns and

Stalker, 1961). Similarly Rice and Miller have pointed to the problems of the extent of coincidence between 'task boundaries' and 'sentient boundaries' (Miller and Rice, 1967).[1] As we noted at the start, all discussion of the task perspective must recognize that it refers to only a limited facet of the social system. We have outlined the catchment area of the perspective, but are there important aspects which that catchment area neglects? It might be argued that the neglect of cultural definitions by the members of enterprises is crucial.

We have so far proceeded without directly explicating why we consider organizational design to be so significant, though we have hinted at this. Our argument is that the conceptual frameworks which the experienced administrator brings to bear when exploring the organizational consequences of major changes are typically restricted (Cherns and coworkers, 1971). Hence they expect the social scientist to contribute *only* to the introduction of change, not to advising on what forms of change may be considered appropriate. Typically the social scientist is perceived as the specialist who smooths the introduction of a new system, that is planned change. We contend that this is too limited a role. The nature of the social system is too important to be left as an unanticipated consequence of technological designs. Hence we argue the case for social scientists' being involved at the design stage.

In our experience of this, the task organization perspective has been fruitful— for our analysis. It has been necessary also to undertake studies of the cultural system. This was because the task perspective does not sufficiently predict, or claim to predict, such aspects as the orientations of members to one another and their work; yet this is crucial to identifying the existing 'sentient boundaries' (Miller and Rice, 1967). The existing cultural system has considerable implications for the choice of control system and for the allocation of people within it. It was our experiences of needing to account for the cultural system that led us specifically to include its consideration in a project undertaken in the military.

We now turn to examine that study. Later we shall return to a discussion of the task perspective, and particularly to the problems of making its central postulates relevant to those who are unwittingly involved in organizational design.

The Military

We have referred to Cherns' paper, 'Organization and Primary Task', contributed to the NATO Symposium on Manpower Research in the Defence Context in London in 1967. This paper aroused the interests of the Ministry of Defence and we were invited to submit to the Ministry a proposal for research to follow up the suggestions made in the paper. The proposal we submitted followed closely those ideas and went on to suggest that an appropriate site for the study would be Training Command of the Royal Air Force. There were special reasons for this choice: Cherns had previous experience of work in the Command, and the Command's Research Branch was willing to cooperate.

But there were theoretical reasons also: training is one of the activities which are performed by both civilian and military organizations, and in both cases in special purpose institutions. The implicit comparison of military and civilian organizations involved in a study of this kind have more validity than a comparison of, say, a manufacturing firm's organization with that of an operational service unit.

Training, furthermore, is one of the activities for which the military developed a specialized organization in advance of similar civilian models. Civilian organizations setting up special training departments tended to look to two models: military training establishments such as apprentice schools, and civil educational establishments such as technical colleges. Industrial training officers are often drawn from the military ranks. Although we did not set out to draw specific comparisons between service and civilian organizational frameworks for training, the differences, as well as the similarities, were in our minds.

The history of management theory and practice began with borrowing from military models. Concepts such as 'line' and 'staff', span of control, supporting chains and so on were derived from military practice. In the early days of management consultancy a profitable recipe was to see how the military did it and advise accordingly. Modern management theory and practice, however, have developed away from these models and we now know more and take into account our knowledge concerning the relationship between 'task' and organization. Nor have developments passed the military by. While civilian industry has given birth to the 'matrix organization' (Kingdon, 1973), military 'task forces' of all sizes and shapes have been developed to cope with turbulent environments. Nevertheless, the military training establishments adhere more closely to traditional military patterns of organization structure than do their civilian counterparts. We advanced the hypothesis (Cherns, 1967) that the secondary task of internal control was a dominating factor in the organizational design of military establishments and that this was one reason why military units, serving vastly different functions, nevertheless possessed strikingly similar structures.

The function of internal control is of major importance both because of the necessity for instant preparedness and because of the 'total' nature of military institutions. The latter is, of course, partly a consequence of the former. Military values emphasize separateness from civilians because local community ties would hinder mobility and readiness for action. The inculcation of distinct military values means that the military unit itself must serve as its own community; i.e. as a 'total' institution. Because of the less obvious nature of the organizational requirements deriving from the total nature of the institution as compared with those imposed by the primary task these are in danger of being squeezed by attempts to apply to them techniques of cost-effectiveness.

One further attraction of the training establishment as the focus for this study is just that it comes into Perrow's category of 'people-processing' organizations. Now as we shall see later, the ambiguities both of Perrow's approach and of other task analysis approaches are emphasized when the 'raw material' is people and when the basic unit of raw material is sometimes the individual, sometimes the group.

In consultation with the Service we selected for our field sites three RAF training stations, one concerned with recruit training, one with trade training, one with flying training. The basis for this selection was as follows. In the first place these three functions represent as wide a range of tasks as could be found in training. Secondly, the stations selected were as far as possible typical, but uncomplicated examples; i.e. they did not house other activities. The organization of all three was basically similar, the differences being small compared with the differences in tasks. And this, of course, is the nub. We were interested to see why this was so and what were the consequences.

In our research we were able to test for ourselves the value both of the approach derived from task analysis and of the concept of sentient group boundaries. It is, of course, true that the value of an approach depends upon the objectives of the study. And in this particular study we had multiple objectives. First we aimed at understanding, explaining to ourselves the behaviour of men under training and the people responsible for their training in the RAF. Here our perspective was limited by an interest in organization: we were more likely to be interested in, to observe and to draw conclusions from people's behaviour in relation to the Service's objectives than their behaviour in relation to private objectives of their own unless these were in direct conflict. Our second aim was description, the development of concepts (and the language in which to express these concepts) which would enable us to generalize from the behaviour we observed. Here again our perspective was limited by our concern that these concepts should enable us to generalize in a way that would be recognized by people whose aims were the official Service objectives. Our third aim was communication—communication of our description to the Service. Once again our perspective was limited by our understanding that the Service's interest would be in prescription, however much we insisted that prescription was not our purpose. We expressed our own intentions as to develop with the Service a language which would enable us to express our descriptive concepts in terms which could be handled in their action frame of reference.

Two consequences flow from these terms of reference. First, for our own understanding we would tend to use a grounded theory approach, but one in which sociological rather than psychological categories would predominate. Secondly, for description we would isolate categories on which we could compare and contrast the field situations we had chosen to observe. Thirdly, for communication we would enter the frame of reference of the Service training organization and evaluate the behaviour we observed and described in terms of official goals.

It seemed to us that the insights derived from task analysis were of greatest value in relation to communication, while those derived from the consideration of sentient group boundaries were of most use in relation to description. Neither helped us to any great extent in understanding.

In our individual field studies we were observing situations each possessing its own special characteristics and each dictating its own framework of understanding. In each, behaviour is constrained by the existence of relationships based on a formal organization structure. But the whole flavour of the experience is unique and differing greatly from one situation to another. Our first field site was a recruit training station. This station is the basic organization concerned with 'people-processing', the process by which the civilian becomes an airman. During his six weeks' training the recruit receives an induction into service life and procedures and a basic military training: in the modern service this is viewed as essential but still only a very small part of the journey towards a man being fully trained. However, recruit training with its associations of drill and 'bull' is the traditional form of military training from the viewpoint of a wider public, especially with ex-service and national service reminiscence. More, recruit training is usually carried out against the potentially traumatic break from civilian life, home, family and 'outside' values. The station is organized to 'process' efficiently the throughput of recruits. Its organizational chart shows an adaptation of basic RAF pattern with a straightforward 'two-prong' system of two wings, a training wing and an administrative wing. Within the two squadrons of training wing, the basic training unit is the flight, comprising flight commander (Flying Officer/Flight Lieutenant), a Senior NCO and two Junior NCOs—each flight being responsible for up to 65 recruits during the period of training.

The behaviour of recruits at their training school can be described in terms of their adaptation to the formal demands of the organization and is largely evaluated in such terms. It is, however, unlikely that this description would have meaning for the recruit as an account of his experience. For him recruit training is a *rite de passage*, a transition from one status to another. His new status as fully fledged airman is given him by the Service, but its personal validity is warranted by his peers' acceptance of him in that status. His experience is better described as a continuous re-evaluation of self and identity in response to his ability to meet the expectations of his fellow recruits. The NCO, the principal immediate representative of organizational demands, is experienced more as the vehicle for the constraints within which this experience has to be played out than as the role model for the recruit. For purposes of description this understanding can well be translated into the insight that the sentient group for the recruit excludes the NCO; the task group sometimes includes him, as when the squad and NCO are together on trial on parade. When finally we aim at communication we observe that the variances the squad generates are of three kinds, intra-individual, interindividual and intergroup, and that the control only of the last is within the scope of the NCO. The first requires self-control; the second control generated within the group itself. The organizational response to this is to provide some sort of informal authority figure, a senior recruit without formal power but hopefully with charismatic influence. This appointment is one which is liable to create considerable misunderstanding. He is appointed, not elected, yet the sanctions he has at his command are informal rather than formal. He is therefore an appointed leader expected to behave as would an emergent one.

When we talk of 'exceptions' as previously in this paper we discussed Perrow's use of this term, we imply that there is a norm to which exceptions occur, that this norm is defined by the person controlling that particular situation and that this norm is shared by others in similar controlling situations. But when we substitute the concept of 'variance' as used by Emery we have less obvious rules for deciding what aspects or elements are to be taken as variable. As Perrow and Emery use these terms, exceptions appear to have objective status, whereas the concept of variance implies an experiential element. Thus what is experienced as varying will depend upon where the control is located. As it is also used to indicate the most appropriate location for such control, there is an inherent circularity which does not, of course, necessarily invalidate but does complicate its usage. The problem is most acute in the context of 'people-processing'. Here, as we go on to show, the control may be placed at several levels. When located as low in the hierarchy as possible, i.e. at the level of the *individual under training*, what is experienced as variance may differ profoundly from the overt differences among individual behaviours which would constitute variance for the superior officer or which would throw up 'exceptions' for him.

There are some variances relevant to task performance whose very nature differs from one individual to another. It is true that from the organization's point of view the task to be performed can be specified without consideration of the special characteristics of the individual, but the meaning of these tasks differ for different individuals and their salience for the individual's own goals differ too. For one recruit his ability to obtain acceptance by his mates is the very essence of his identification with the service; for another it may be almost irrelevant. Individuals in industry also possess different goals and at some level the meaning for them of the tasks they perform may differ; the significance in the service situation is that the recruit is the raw material as well as the operator. The traditional choice of 'technology' is based on assumptions about the nature of the 'raw material'. The assumptions that are made then determine both the nature of the control to be applied and the interpretation of the response of the individual — the raw material. Because the task and the technology are defined in this way, in attempting to understand the world of the recruit formal organizational categories, task analysis and all are barely relevant. For descriptive purposes the concept of sentient boundaries takes on value. The recruit is a member of one smaller and one larger sentient group: the barrack room and the flight. The first is a subsection of the second. The principal group tasks are based likewise on these units. The boundaries here are clearly drawn in the right place. At a higher level of organization, however, questions do arise. The change in legal status of the recruit occurs at attestation, i.e. before he enters the recruit-training station. The change in his perceived status takes place on graduation from recruit training. The Service's organization design links recruit training with subsequent trade training; it allocates recruiting and attestation to a separate organization. This means that there is a contrived contradiction between the perceptions of the staff and those of the recruit or trainee. Does this matter? It may mean that certain objectives are harder to achieve than they might be. But on the whole it is doubtful where the contradiction is a significant hindrance to Services' immediate goals of socializing the recruit. For the recruit the experience of self-development may be less satisfactory but his short- and long-term performances are unlikely to be significantly affected.

That the organization of recruit training appears to be adequately designed for its purpose should occasion little surprise. The classic organization of a military unit is especially adapted to the task of internal control (Cherns, 1967).

The simple skills and behaviours that are taught at recruit school, all within the compass of virtually all recruits, together with the acquisition by the recruit of certain habits of punctuality, turn-out and so on, lend themselves to face-to-face leadership and control without the mediation of machine or specialism. The line system of command is perfectly suited to this purpose. Furthermore, the interchangeability of one squad, section or flight of recruits with another presents no difficulty for the system of postings which moves officers and NCOs in and out of the organization. A station whose concern is solely recruit training performs what we should describe as a 'pure' task: see later.

Having considered the initial 'socialization process', our next choice of site was a station where the airman's technical training begins for trades in the field of ground radar and ground communications. The organizational picture is complicated. Like a large technical college the station copes with a range of students at different stages in technical training. As well as recent recruits, apprentices receive training in a combined recruit and trade training course. The station also provides 'further education', i.e. for airmen improving their skill and knowledge within a trade group, and also 'conversion' and 'assimilation' training to allow for changing demands within the trade structure.

The organization is somewhat more complex than that of the recruit training station: a basic studies wing, a trade training wing and an apprentice wing take the place of the single training wing of the recruit station. A senior Wing Commander has the role of senior training officer, providing an intermediary level of authority between the Group Captain (Station Commander or Commandant) and the other Wing Commanders. The Senior Training Officer controls a wide range of training activity, bewildering on first consideration by the outside observer. This training ranges from general education in basic studies wing through to very specific instruction on equipment and techniques in trade training wing. Within the training function are two basic types of trainers: the first we might describe as the 'professional educators' and the second, technically trained personnel involved in the instructional function. However, within the second category will be a number of officers with a lot of training experience within their particular field. Also, there exists a tradition of engineer officers returning to the station on an instructional tour of duty.

Unlike other trainees apprentices have a mixed course, i.e. it involves the military socialization process as well as technical training. In their case responsibility is split between the basic studies and training wings — similar to subject teachers in a school or college — and the trainers within apprentice wing who are responsible for the apprentice as a person, and for his general and basic military training. Another feature of this 'mixed' training program for apprentices is the separation in all general respects of apprentices from airmen, though in practice they may be similar in age if not status. For them the service has responsibilities different from those applying to airmen.

In technical, trade, training the station's task is immeasurably more complex. Not only are there many trades, many levels of training, many types of equipment on which men have to be trained, but the differences among the capacities of different trainees is highly important. Competence is less easily acquired than in recruit training: few fail the latter; containing wastage in the former is a continuous problem and effort. The 'task' of the station and of its subunits can be expressed in terms of numbers of men to be trained in various skills. For convenience men must be assigned to classes but the class as such cannot be said to have a task. The class members are only to a very small extent dependent upon each other's performance for their own success. But the shared experience, the shared work situation and stress makes the class a sentient group. Insofar as this results in the stronger helping the weaker, in equitable sharing of facilities, task performance is thereby aided. But treating the class as if it were a task group obscures certain realities of the task. The individual trainee, the equipment he is trying to master, and his instructor constitute the immediate task group. The variances set by the differential capacitities of individuals can only be partially controlled by the instructor in the class situation. He can control the pace of instruction and allocate his time and that of the equipment to fit the capacities of the broad middle section of his class. The price of this is that few proceed at their ideal pace; almost automatically some are irretrievably behind the rest and a few fail. The ideal of self-paced instruction, whereby the control of variance is delegated to the individual himself, is consonant with an organization structure and style in which the instructor is a resource to, not commander of, the trainee.

But the technical trainee in the Service has other tasks besides the acquisition of skill. They include playing a part in the station's activities, as a continuous affirmation of Service membership, and maintaining a standard of turn-out, deportment and domestic order adequate for the Service's self-presentation.

One can very quickly become engulfed in complexities here; there are many different kinds of training at different career levels, all conducted within one technical training station. Some courses are provided at advanced level for NCOs and men who are senior enough to live off the station while under training if their homes are near. At the other extreme are wings for apprentices who are receiving their basic service training and undergoing socialization as well as trade training. Because of the apprentices' prestige their socialization is of an elite character; the apprentice is taught to regard his future as a cut above that of the adult airman trainee. Apprentices are organized primarily into flights based on their 'domestic' wing organization. The wing is divided into squadrons, each containing elements of each 'entry' and each trade. Squadrons, in turn, are divided into flights. Traditionally the sentient group is the 'entry'. But the entry has no organizational counterpart. Its existence is recognized by its number so that an apprentice will be identified as of No. 'X' entry and by its graduation as an entry. For all other activities, however, it is divided among flights and squadrons in which it is mixed with other entries. In technical, educational instruction, classes will be made up of members of the same entry who are learning the same trade; but trade is not the basis of the flight and squadron structure. Sentient and task boundaries do not coincide for apprentices and this is recognized by everybody concerned with apprentice training.

The 'elite' aspect of the apprentice training demands a different structure of organization from that required by their technical training. Special *esprit* needs to be fostered. Identification of the apprentice with an appropriate role model is also needed, and the senior technical NCO, preferably an ex-apprentice who would symbolize the apprentice's future role, would ideally provide this. But an organizational design which made this possible, i.e. one in which the apprentice's immediate commander for all purposes was a senior technical man in his own trade, is one which conflicts with the Service's solution of segregating Service and technical training. It would also make combining the technical training of apprentices and airmen on the same station extremely difficult; the alternative being a costly duplication of expensive equipment. The nature, too, of such a relationship of apprentice with role model combines with difficulty with postings policy. A rapid cycle of postings conflicts both with the establishment of organizational subunits according to a special design, and with the establishment of close ties of sentiment between a group and its commander.

The task of a technical trade training station is mixed in more than one sense. It has several groups of trainees which differ substantially from one another: apprentices from airmen ex-recruits; ex-recruit airmen from technically trained and experienced men on advanced or refresher courses. The goals of training also differ and in the case of the apprentice an elite socialization has to be combined with trade training. The more mixed the task in this way, the more the station organization tends towards the exercise of management functions—managing the facilities with the main training tasks delegated to separate subunits. These separate subunits do not differ from one another so obviously as to obtain the kind of functional independence granted to 'lodger units'. There are thus considerable strains towards similarity of design. Yet a design ideally suited to providing familiarization with advanced technical equipment is very different from that tailored to elite socialization. Further, the location of the managerial and caretaker functions at the highest, most prestigious level endows them with an undesired priority over the separate training functions. Here again our understanding of the experience of apprentice and adult trainees, which alerts us to the points of strain in the system, is derived from fieldwork far removed from consideration of variances. For purposes of description the sentient group analysis evokes immediate recognition by the Service; the task analysis of variances enables the organizational design problems to be communicated.

The third station selected was a station where the straight flying training task is performed. The training organization here is an *epitome of basic RAF organization*. In terms of its organizational chart, the station shows the three-prong organizational structure with the flying wing of the operational station replaced here by the flying training wing. Flying stations tend to be geographically isolated and to have a day and night commitment in terms of flying training, and of 24-hour Master Diversion Airfield facilities at all times. This necessitates the provision of amenities for officers (instructors and trainees) and airmen. Flying training is also part of the officer-training process; the student is being evaluated all the time in terms of personal and officer qualities, as well as on his ability to fly an aircraft.

Thus flying training is not simply the inculcation of a technical skill.

The flying training school in RAF Training Command has on the face of it a pure task. In the main, one homogeneous population undergoes training as pilots. In fact, as we have pointed out, the task is mixed in that officer training has to be combined with aircrew training. We shall see, however, why this does not raise the same complications as in the case of apprentice training.

The experience of the trainee is one which approximates most closely to the popular stereotype of Service life in the Air Force. It includes the constant sight and sound of aircraft, the presence of instructors and students in flying gear (as in the recruiting advertisements), and the camaraderie of the crew room and the mess, the swapping of flying experiences. To relate to and understand this world of experience, the outsider must learn a new language and technology. The dangerous aspect of flying is a constant theme in the background and conduces to the students seeking support from one another, their instructors and commanders who are all flying men. This supportive community has its intense side, and the student experiences strain from the constant surveillance under which he feels placed as part of his training as an officer. He is able, however, to identify with his instructor who represents for him a true role model — flyer and officer — and with whom he shares a series of potentially dangerous experiences whose successful outcome depends on their mutual trust. Against them both, and against the organization as a whole, is a constant enemy, the weather, whose vagaries call for periods of maximum effort and stretching of resources. The shared experience of a successful all-out effort to make good time lost through adverse weather conditions is expressed in a state of high morale in which mutual respect permits, without danger to discipline, a relaxation of normal rules and constraints.

We can abstract from this lightly sketched picture an analysis of the sentient groupings. The members of one entry or intake share the same battle with the weather, the same dangers and hazards, are under surveillance together. In their officer-training exercises they are allocated from time to time group tasks, but for the most part the task interdependencies are low. From the point of view of the instructors each has a handful of pupils for whom he is responsible and the task group is always the pair, instructor–pupil. In the battle with the weather and with the aircraft state of readiness he is allied with other instructors, technical staff, his squadron commander and so on. His principal sentient group is the group of instructors in his flight and squadron, responsible jointly for taking an intake through training. Less salient is the group which includes the technical and support staff responsible for the state of readiness of the aircraft and equipment with which the task must be performed. In all these cases the sentient group and task group coincide reasonably well. For example, for the student pilot the peer group is in a sense a task group where the task is mutual support under conditions of stress. But we are all the time conscious of the many different nuances with which we are using terms like task, task group, sentient group. A constant difficulty is introduced by the dual role of participant and raw material-for-processing which we have to attribute to our trainees, students, recruits.

When we try to draw the implications from this analysis for organization design to communicate them we once again employ a task analysis approach. The variances among individual students and the exigencies of flying together promote the need for a close student-instructor relationship in which the student is teamed with one instructor. The requirements of elite socialization equally argue for a close association of student with role model. Thus, in this case, the components of the task mix have the same implications for organizational design.

One special characteristic of the Service situation which has a bearing on organizational design is the postings cycle. In civilian industry organization structures are not only frameworks representing communication, reporting, task allocation, they are also career ladders. But it is in the military and in the Civil Service that we are confronted most acutely with the implications of careers for organization design. In the first place the regular and frequent posting of officers means that there are few jobs of the kind which have edges of responsibility blurred by the comfortable chafing of the incumbent in the chair, the jobs which are 'made' by an individual and are unlikely to be filled in the same way again. Secondly, as roles must be learned quickly, positions at the same rank level cannot differ more widely than the differences in the tasks make inevitable. The incoming officer must be able to learn his way about the structure without difficulty. Thirdly, the equation of position with rank provides a further constraint. All three constraints exert pressure to make all Service structures look alike. All Air Force stations, regardless of function, have a 'three-prong' or modified three-prong structure of 'wings'— flying, engineering/technical and administrative. On a training station the 'flying' wing may be replaced by a flying training or a training wing. Thus the structure is essentially an operational wing, technical wing, administrative wing. All wings are subdivided into squadrons, squadrons into flights and commanded by officers of the appropriate rank. Also because promotions are within branches (general duties (flying), secretarial, technical, etc.), the officer is obliged to keep an eye on what is happening within his branch of the Service. His career structure is not closely bound up with the station on which he is serving.

What might be the most effective organization design for the particular tasks a station is performing may cut across these other important considerations. Again, there is always a secondary role which Service units must be prepared to perform—its emergency role, aid to the civil power. Too task-specific an organization structure could be a hindrance here. And yet again each station has the functions of providing a military presence, of maintaining the military and civilian boundary. Finally, and perhaps most important of all, the station's organization has to cater for the whole-life needs of the airman. A whole underground of secondary tasks have to be performable within the structure adopted for the primary tasks. Activities which a civilian discharges in his own time must be programmed into Service time; the organization takes the strain which falls on the individual civilian. This is not to say that approaches to organizational analysis and design appropriate to civilian organizations cannot be appropriate to military units; it is to say that factors which can safely be ignored in the one situation must be taken into account in the other.

In the course of our study we were impressed time and time again by the mixed nature of the task that stations are required to perform. Tasks which look homogeneous from an administrative point of view—e.g. a single source of intake of standard size and duration—may contain mixtures which have conflicting requirements for organizational design. Woodward (1965) showed the consequences for industrial organizations of the attempts to combine different technologies within one unit. There is not necessarily an easy solution to problems of this kind. One avoidable danger, however, is that they may not be recognized. RAF training establishments require developed airfields and their associated buildings as well as the other buildings needed to house training and administrative staff and their families, trainees and complex equipment. They are thus relatively permanent compared with changes in the training task brought by changes in equipment and manning requirements which are, in turn, dependent upon changes in defence policy or changes in the role of the RAF dictated by developments in the technology of warfare. The Service has always to be prepared to redeploy existing training or accommodate new training requirements and this implies that mixed tasks are likely to increase rather than decrease. Under these circumstances there is a need for knowledge of which kinds of training are organizationally compatible and which less so. Faced with accommodating a mix of tasks the Services sometimes resort to the 'lodger unit' device. This is effective in protecting the special task of the lodger. As the number of such units grows a new danger appears. The task of the dependent station organization becomes that of administration and the preservation of internal order. These essentially secondary tasks now have greater weight in terms of rank and authority and the administrator's tail begins to wag the functional dog.

Increasing specialization has as its aim the induction of mixed to pure tasks. But the costs of specialization are, as we know, loss of flexibility. In turbulent environments more and more civilian organizations seek the flexibility that comes from diversification. They, too, are faced with the organizational consequences of task mixes. This would justify a good deal more study than it has hitherto received. A change in task mix can occur unrecognized as the elements may remain the same, but their salience alters.

Conclusion

In our study of the problems of applying a task analysis approach to the design of service organization we found ourselves confronting from a different standpoint some of the issues which Rice and his colleagues had been facing during his latter years. The task analysis approach which owed its origins to the study of manufacturing and extracting industries has acquired a great deal of sophistication as its practitioners have tackled other organizations, commercial, service and educational. The concept of the sentient group became more prominent in these latter organizations when their boundaries could not be made to coincide with task boundaries and had to be organized differentially. We have seen the kind of problem this raises for apprentice training. And Miller and Rice (1967) described the problems this raised for airline organizations. 'An effective sentient system relates the members of an enterprise to each other and to the enterprise in ways that are relevant to the skills and experience required for task performance'. The sentient groups of airline pilots and aircraft apprentices relate them together all right, but *against* rather than *to* the enterprise. The problems set by the need to relate organization to task *and* to sentient groups increase as we move away from production organizations. Does this *reduce* the relevance of task analysis?

We return again to Rice (1970 p. 4) and his last publication in which he studied the problems of university government. A central concept used in the analysis is that of the *primary task*. This is the task that treats any institution or subinstitution as an open system: '. . . universities are multiple-task institutions; and each task, though interdependent with other tasks, requires its own characteristic organization which differs from the organization required for other tasks and for the whole'. What then? Rice analyses separately the main functions of the university and traces out the appropriate 'operating systems' for each. Thus he describes a model 'first-order managing system' for undergraduate education. This has to contain 'task-oriented sentient groups for both faculty and students'. 'Each member of the faculty and each student should have more than one role, and more than one route, through which he can make his voice heard'. Rice admits that all this could result in 'a Babel of "voices"', but looks to mechanisms for simplifying procedures for making views known.

When to all this are added managing systems for post-graduate education, professional training and for research, the result is formidable. Rice is his own critic:

'... The model makes provision for members of the faculty to take multiple roles in different systems of activity and to belong to sentient groups, so that they have several roles and several routes through which they can make their voice heard. In so doing, however, it also provides almost endless opportunities for the confusion of task-system boundaries and of the authorities and responsibilities attached to different roles.' (Rice, 1970, p. 102)

In fact, Rice effectively reaches a *reductio ad absurdum*: a 'model' organization which accommodates task groups and sentient groups but whose probable result would be that hard decisions about priorities would be even less easy to make than they are now.

Universities face, as do the services, the task of culture transmission, with its associated problem of the maintenance of discipline. Rice's solution has echoes of the college system which is the model which has inspired the solution of this problem in the services. We are thrown back on a dual organization which exemplifies the point that each task requires its own characteristic organization which differs from that required for other tasks. In plain facts, the tasks of internal control and of cultural transmission require one kind of organization which differs from that required, say, for the acquisition of technical and administrative skills.

In a word, the task analysis approach emphasizes the linkage task → role and the subsequent building of organization structure to relate these roles in an integrative fashion. Different analysts—the socio-technical school of Rice, Trist, Emery, Miller et al; Perrow, Woodward—have grounded their systems on different aspects or dimensions of task and technology and each has contributed valuable perspectives. Each, as we have found, has something to offer to the description and communication of organizational problems to managements. The concept of sentient group has added another dimension, allowing us to explore the relevance of the shared values of professional and skill groups and their divergence from those of other groups within the enterprise. But this again does more to describe the differences which have to be organized for than the qualities they represent. When the business to be organized is as mixed as the preservation of internal order (as an overriding goal) combined with the transmission of values and a culture, as well as technical skills, the weaknesses of these approaches become apparent. Again Rice (1970) was thinking along these lines: '...the (supervisory) system will not achieve an integrative function merely by putting it into the organizational model. It will work effectively only... if the culture of the school is congruent with the definition and method of performance of its primary task'; (Rice, 1970, p. 78) and, 'Each specific task requires specific skills, an appropriate organization, and a congruent culture' (Rice, 1970, p. 82). The concept of culture, which belongs to a different domain of discourse from task, technology and sentient groups, can become the joker in the pack.

An organization whose overriding value is that of internal control has to hold to a minimum transaction across the system's boundaries. Modernization of weapon systems and their associated skills requires constant and increasing transactions across the boundaries or the continuous enlargement of the system. The university is, as Rice shows, a striking example of the weakening of internal control as a result. The more that transactions across the system boundary grow in number and in salience for the organization's goals and the more that these transactions consist of intake and output of people, the more permeable becomes the organization to the society to which it belongs. What goes on inside the organization can less and less be described in terms of the organization's own characteristics. The more the description of the organization is couched in terms and concepts which would offer prescriptive advice to management, the more it leaves out. The more the study of organizational behaviour becomes another of the management sciences, the less valuable it will become to management. But if it is to be a social science, then social scientists, especially sociologists, will have to make it so. Wanted: a micro-sociology.

Notes

1. Etzioni (1961) makes a useful discussion of this facet when examining the 'division of compliance'.
2. The fieldwork upon which much of this section is based was carried out by our colleague, Mr. Stephen Parrott, whose help we gratefully acknowledge.

References

Bell, G. D. (1967), Formality versus flexibility in complex organizations, *in* Bell G. D., Ed., *Organizations and Human Behaviour*, Prentice-Hall, Englewood Cliffs, N. J.

Burns, T. and Stalker G. M. (1961), *The Management of Innovation*, Tavistock Publications, London.

Cherns, A. B. (1967), Organization for change, *in* Manpower research: the proceedings of a conference held under the aegis of the NATO Scientific Affairs Com. in London, 14–18 Aug. 1967, Ed. by A. N. B. Wilson, London, E. U. P., 1969, pp. 460–463.

Cherns, A. B. Clark, P. A. Sinclair, R. and Harries, T. W. (1971), Aggregates and structures: two complementary paradigms in manpower studies, *in* Bartholomew, D. J. and Smith, A. R., Eds., *Manpower and Management Science*, London, E. U. P., 1971, pp. 31–40.

Clark, P. A. (1965), The effects of peak periods of working on the management system and intra-organizational relations, mimeographed.

Clark, P. A. and Cherns, A. B. (1970), A role for social scientists in organizational design, *in* Heald, G., Ed., *Approaches to the Study of Organizational Behaviour*, Tavistock Publications, London, pp. 72–86.

Clark P. A. and Ford, J. R. (1970), Methodological and theoretical problems in the investigation of planned organizational change, *Sociological Review*, **18**, 29–52.

Clark, P. A. (1972), *Organizational Design: Theory and Practice*, Tavistock Publications, London.

Crozier, M. (1964), *The Bureaucratic Phenomenon*, Tavistock Publications, London.

Dill, W. R. (1962), The impact of environment on organizational development, *in* Mailick, S. and Van Ness, E. H., Eds., *Concepts and Issues in Administrative Behaviour*, Prentice-Hall, Englewood Cliffs, N. J., 1962, pp. 94–109.

Eldridge, J. E. T. (1968), *Industrial Disputes: Essays in the Sociology of Industrial Relations*, Routledge and Kegan Paul, London.

Emery, F. E. (1959), *Characteristics of Socio-technical Systems*, Tavistock Institute of Human Relations, Document No. 527, mimeographed.

172

Etzioni, A. (1961), *A Comparative Analysis of Complex Organizations: on Power, Involvement and their Correlates*, Free Press, New York.

Goldthorpe, J. H., Lockwood, D. Bechhofer, F. and Platt, J. (1968), *The Affluent Worker: Industrial Attitudes and Behaviour*, Cambridge University Press, Cambridge.

Kingdon, D. R. (1973) *Matrix Organization: Managing Technological Complexity*, Tavistock Publications, London.

Lawrence, P. R. and Lorsch, J. W. (1967), *Organization and Environment: Managing Differentiation and Integration*, Harvard University Division of Research, Boston, Mass.

Litwak, E. (1961), Models of bureaucracy which permit conflict, *American Journal of Sociology*, **61**, 177–184.

March, J. G. and Simon, H. A. (1958), *Organizations*, Wiley, New York.

Miller, E. J. and Rice, A. K. (1967), *Systems of Organization: the Control of Task and Sentient Boundaries*, Tavistock Publications, London.

Mumford, E. and Banks, O. (1967), *Computer and the Clerk*, Fernhill House Ltd., Atlantic Highland, N. J.

Perrow, C. (1961), Analysis of goals in complex organizations, *American Sociological Review*, **26**, 854–866.

Perrow, C. (1965), Hospitals: technology, structure and goals, *in* March, J. G., Ed., *Handbook of Organizations*, Rand McNally, Chicago, 910–971.

Perrow, C. (1967), A framework for the comparative analysis of organizations, *American Sociological Review*, **32**, 194–208.

Perrow, C. (1971), *Organizational Analysis: a Sociological View*, Tavistock Publications, London.

Rice, A. K. (1970), *The Modern University: a Model Organization*, Tavistock Publications, London.

Silverman, D. (1970), *The Theory of Organisations*, Heinemann, London.

Stinchcombe, A. L. (1965), Social structure and organizations: a sociological framework, *in* March, J. G., Ed., *Handbook of Organizations*, Rand McNally, Chicago, pp. 142–193.

Street, D., Vinter, R. D. and Perrow, C. (1966), *Organizations for Treatment: a Comparative Study of Institutions for Delinquents*, Free Press, New York.

Thompson, J. D. (1967), *Organizations in Action: Social Science Bases of Administrative Theory*, McGraw-Hill, New York.

Touraine, A., Durand, C. Recant, D. and Willimer, A. (1965), *Workers' Attitudes to Technical Change: an Integrated Survey of Research*, O.E.C.D. Paris.

Trist, E. L., Higgin, G. W., Murray, H. and Pollock, A. B. (1963), *Organizational Choice. Capabilities of Groups at the Coal Face under Changing Technologies*, Tavistock Publications, London.

Woodward, J. (1958), *Management and Technology*, H.M.S.O., London.

Woodward, J. (1965), *Industrial Organization: Theory and Practice*, Oxford University Press, London.

Woodward, J., Ed., (1970), *Industrial Organization: Behaviour and Control*, Oxford University Press, London.

Task and Organization Structure in Marketing

Philip Sadler

Most studies of the relationships between tasks and forms of organization structure have focused on production systems,[1] although there have been some noteworthy excursions into other fields.[2] Relatively little attention has been paid to organizations or organizational units which have marketing as their primary task.[3] 'There remains a tendency, however, among theorists and practitioners alike to look upon the organization of production operations as central and typical, and to assume that the principles of delegation and control that have emerged constitute general laws of organization. The organization charts of sales or research departments with their traditional chains of command often appear to be designed more on aesthetic grounds to harmonize with the corresponding chart for the manufacturing department than to facilitate task performance' (Miller and Rice, 1967, p. 45). It is the purpose of this paper to analyse the characteristics of marketing operations, to attempt to isolate the main factors which differentiate between different types of task in marketing, and to identify at least some of the major constraints which different marketing tasks impose on decisions about organization. It is written with the hopeful intention of putting forward some ideas which will be helpful to practising marketing managers while at the same time suggesting some fruitful lines of research for academic workers in this field.

The Determinants of Organization Structure

The formal organization structures which enterprises adopt, not only in marketing but in any field of activity, will reflect a number of influences other than constraints arising from the nature of the task. Some of these influences may operate against effectiveness, but nevertheless they must be taken into account as very real forces helping to shape the structure of organizations. They include the factors given under the following headings.

Values, Beliefs, Attitudes, etc. which Members of the Organization Share in Common

These may be derived from the general cultural and social environment of the enterprise or they may be inherited as traditions or customs from the organization's own past history.

They will include certain beliefs and values which will partially determine the way the organization as a whole is structured—for example, beliefs about the appropriateness of hierarchical authority, attitudes towards the question of status differences, and values such as the extent to which loyalty to the concern is regarded as a major virtue.

There will also exist a range of attitudes which have a particular influence on the way the marketing function is organized. Foremost among these will be attitudes to the importance of marketing relative to other business functions, i.e. the extent to which the enterprise is marketing oriented. There will be other relevant attitudes and beliefs—for example, beliefs about the ways in which marketing activities are best carried out ('there is no substitute for the personal call by a company representative'), and values which determine the range of activities in marketing which are seen as legitimate (in some organizations such practices as door-to-door selling or the sending of unsolicited material through the post might be regarded as unethical).

Values and beliefs of this kind may, of course, operate against the effective performance of tasks. For example, where, for reasons of tradition, low status is accorded to sales personnel, it is unlikely that the organization will be able to recruit personnel of high ability into its sales organization, nor is it likely that senior sales appointments will carry sufficient authority to ensure that the sales viewpoint is given adequate weight in top-level decisions.

Systems of values, however, are none the less real and influential for being dysfunctional. In practice, they may well exercise greater influence on the design of the marketing organization than constraints stemming from the task, and any attempt to install a theoretically more appropriate structure based on task analysis may well founder on the resistance to change associated with well-established attitudes, beliefs and values.

The Size of the Organization

Size creates its own special constraints which may outweigh those stemming from the task in determining some aspects of organization structure. Pugh (1970) has shown, for example, how specialization within the marketing function tends to increase with increasing size of company. According to his data, of 24 organizations employing 1000 people or less, only 4 per cent (i.e. one company) had specialized public relations and advertising departments compared with 57 per cent of 28 organizations employing over 1000 people. Similarly, among the smaller firms only 8 per cent had specialized marketing research compared with 32 per cent among the larger enterprises.

Weinshall (1971) has discussed the effects of size in relation to a theory of stages in organizational growth and development. He argues that as companies grow in size (measured by the increase in the number of managers) management has continually to reorganize itself into new structures appropriate to an increasingly complex decision-making process. Figure 1 shows his conceptual scheme of the stages in the development of organization structures which are associated with the growth of the enterprise. He suggests that the first

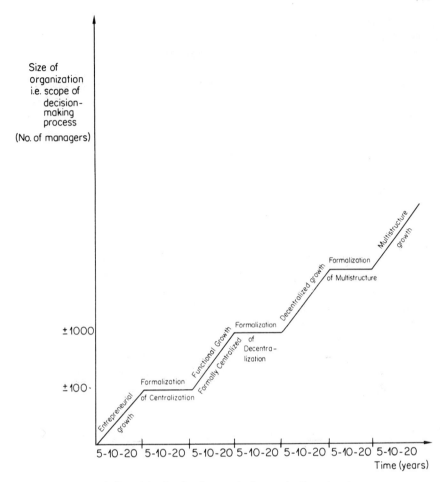

Figure 1. Stages in the development of organization structure

stage in the development of the company is characterized by rapid growth and an entrepreneurial type of organization structure, in which control is highly centralized in the hands of the chief executive but at the same time there is a marked absence of formality. When the complexity of the decision-making process increases so as to render this structure ineffective, the company enters a period of consolidation during which time it develops a new structure which will enable rapid growth to be resumed. This new structure, Weinshall suggests, is typically a functional one with a high degree of formality as well as a high degree of centralized control. In turn, this structure proves inadequate to deal with even further complexity in decision-making, and growth once again slows down until the company successfully develops a third type of structure which is still formal but which involves decentralization on the basis of products, markets or areas. Finally, Weinshall suggests that this decentralized type of structure will ultimately be superseded by what he calls the multi-structure type of organization which combines in one extremely complex structure elements of all three previous stages.

Thus, if one accepts the Weinshall thesis, the key to good organization design lies in management's ability to diagnose correctly the stage of development which the enterprise has reached or is about to enter at any given time. In his analysis Weinshall gives little attention to task influences, although he does acknowledge that different rates of development are to be observed in different industries, implying some degree of relationship between the tasks facing organizations and their developmental patterns.

Specific Theories Concerning the Relationship between Organization Structure and Effectiveness

Such theories are frequently developed by senior executives as a result of experience, or they may be acquired by attending courses of management education or by reading textbooks. Quite often they are imported into the enterprise by management consultants. Sometimes such theories appear to go in waves of fashion so that at a particular point in time it is 'the done thing' for companies to appoint brand managers, regardless of whether the nature of the marketing task makes such roles necessary or even desirable.

It is possible to discern all the above influences at work in any given organization structure. There will, however, remain important differences between organization structures which can only be explained by reference to differences in tasks. However, before proceeding to an analysis of the influence of task on structures in marketing organizations it is necessary first to define the nature of the marketing task in general terms and secondly to examine the observable variations in organization structures and tasks in marketing.

The Primary Task of a Marketing Organization

The primary task of a marketing organization is to manage the relationship between the enterprise as a whole and the market in such a way that the long-term profitability of the enterprise is conserved.

This definition calls for some qualification and, at the same time, for some elaboration. First, it assumes that the total organization of which the marketing organization is a department or subsidiary has long-term profitability as one of its major objectives. In situations where this is not so—for example a hospital or a university—it can be argued that a marketing function is still required even though it is most unlikely to be described as such. To fit such situations the definition would need to be stated in a more general way—as follows: 'The primary task of a marketing organization is to manage the relationship between the organization as a whole and the actual and potential users of its outputs in such a way that over the long term the primary task of the organization as a whole is achieved'.

Secondly, some explanation is called for of what is meant by managing the relationship with the market. This process will certainly involve, in a commercial enterprise, selling goods or services to customers at prices which will ensure an adequate return on investment. It will, however, involve much more than this, especially when viewed as a dynamic process which is carried on in the face of environmental change. Perhaps the most useful way of describing the essential nature of the activity which has come to be known as 'marketing' is to say that it involves matching competence of some kind possessed by the enterprise (or capable of being developed by it) with needs both manifest and latent which are present in the market. What this means in practice, in terms of the tasks to be performed by marketing personnel, will be discussed in greater detail in the following sections.

Sources of Variation in Marketing Organization Structures

Organization structures in the marketing functions of business enterprises appear to vary in five main respects:

(1) The extent to which marketing functions are clearly differentiated from other functions of the business enterprise.

(2) The extent to which there is task specialization within the marketing function, together with the form this specialization takes.

(3) The way in which the marketing activities are grouped into organizational units.

(4) Configuration. This includes such factors as the span of control of the chief marketing executive, average span of control in the sales force, number of levels in the hierarchy etc.

(5) The organizational arrangements for managing the interface with the market.

Each of these will be discussed in turn.

Differentiation of the Marketing Function

In smaller enterprises marketing often forms part of the responsibilities of the chief executive or managing director and in such cases no clearly defined marketing function exists as part of the formal organization structure. The chief executive may personally carry out the whole range of activities involved in marketing the firm's goods and services or these may be delegated in varying degrees to other executives. Larger organizations normally do have a separate marketing function defined as a division or department of the company on the organization chart, the senior manager at the head of this department normally being designated sales or marketing director or manager, though in some cases the term 'commercial' is preferred to either marketing or sales (British Institute of Management, 1970, p. 6). This is the most common form of organization in single product companies.

178

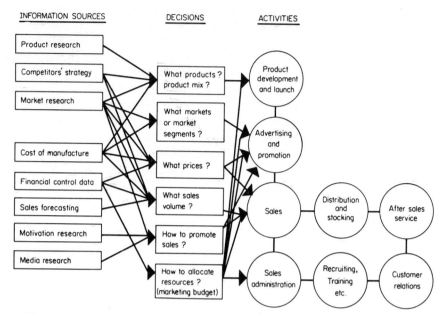

Figure 2. The marketing task as a system of decisions, activities and information

However, where a company is concerned with more than one product it may be organized into product divisions with each division having its own manufacturing and marketing activities. Normally in such cases the head of the product division has the overall responsibility for marketing, but in practice this would usually be delegated to a marketing manager enjoying equal status with a production manager. In the case of some large enterprises entirely separate marketing companies may exist as subsidiaries of a manufacturing parent or as joint subsidiaries with manufacturing companies of a parent holding company. In such instances the chief executive of the marketing subsidiary is usually also the chief marketing executive of the company as a whole.

Degree of Specialization within the Marketing Function

The primary task of a marketing organization is to manage the relationship between the enterprise and the market in such a way that the long-term profitability of the enterprise is ensured.

To achieve this task decisions of various kinds will have to be taken and activities of various kinds will have to be carried out. The marketing process as a system of decisions and activities is represented in Figure 2. Not all these decisions and activities will be required in every case. For example, where prices are fixed by governmental regulation or by international agreement as in air transport, pricing decisions are not called for. Similarly, not all organizations will see the necessity for sales training as an activity. In special cases other activities will be included within the marketing process which are not shown in Figure 1 as being typically present. An example is the activity of site acquisition in a company marketing petroleum spirit (gasolene). Some activities such as distribution can be subcontracted to other organizations. However, this general description of the process will serve adequately enough for the purposes of the argument.

In the simplest possible case a unified sales or marketing department will carry out the whole range of decisions and tasks involved in supplying a particular market. At the other extreme, in a large multiproduct organization there may be separate departments, sections or individual specialized roles associated with each decision area of activity. In between the two extremes will be found organizations which have gone some way towards task specialization. The most common form of specialization in such cases is for sales activities to be distinguished from other marketing activities while the various marketing decisions are grouped together and included in the role specification of the marketing manager. Sales activities are usually further differentiated into selling and sales administration, while the remainder of the marketing organization may be differentiated into research and advertising. However, the precise form of specialization adopted varies considerably from one marketing situation to another.

The Basis for Differentiation of the Marketing Organization

Marketing organizations may be internally differentiated in a variety of ways in addition to the differentiations by marketing specialisms discussed above (British Institute of Management, 1970, p. 10). For example, internal organizational boundaries may be drawn on the basis of the products being marketed where the enterprise produces more than one main product. Secondly, they may be differentiated organizationally on the basis of customers or markets served where there are major differences between particular groups of customers which affect the execution of marketing activities. Thirdly, they may be structured on a geographical basis where customers or markets are spread over a wide area. Large complex organizations are, of course, simultaneously differentiated on the basis of two, three or even four criteria.

Because of the very large number of possible combinations which exist, it is probably useful and practical to distinguish between organizations in terms of the differentiation which takes place immediately below the level of the senior marketing executive. For example, if the most senior managers in the company below the top marketing executive are concerned with functions such as sales, market research and advertising, then it can be said that the company is primarily organized on a functional basis. Similarly, if the managers immediately reporting to the top marketing executive are in charge of products or brands, then the company is primarily differentiated on a product basis. In the case of some particularly complex organization structures, the basis of primary differentiation is a mixed one in that, for example, both managers of

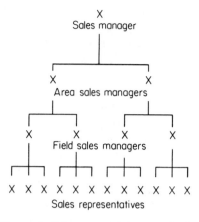

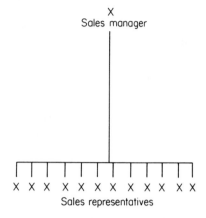

Figure 3. Sales organization employing 12 sales representatives (steep hierarchical configuration)

Figure 4. Sales organization employing 12 Sales representatives ('flat' structure)

products and managers concerned with particular customers or particular geographical areas occupy the same level in the organization structure and report to the top marketing executive.

Configuration

The configuration or 'shape' of an organization structure is mainly a function of two interrelated factors—whether spans of control are narrow or wide, and the number of levels in the hierarchy of decision taking. To some extent the shape of the structure for an organization of a given size can be determined by management decision regardless of constraints arising from the task or from other sources. For example, a sales organization employing 12 sales representatives could be organized as in Figure 3 so as to give a steep hierarchical configuration or as in Figure 4 so as to produce a 'flat' structure. Such decisions are most likely to be influenced by specific theories held by management concerning what makes for effectiveness in organization structures.

Nature of the Interface with the Market

Here organizations can be grouped in a rough and ready way into two categories. On the one hand there are those which deal directly with the customers for their products by direct personal selling by the company's own sales force, by direct mail order selling or by use of the company's own retail outlets. Secondly, there are those organizations which use third parties, i.e. wholesalers, retailers, agents, etc., to mediate the relationship between the marketing organization and the customer. (The term 'customer' is used here to refer to the person or corporate entity buying the product for the purpose of consuming it or transforming it into some other product of service. A mediator, i.e. wholesaler, retailer or agent, neither consumes nor alters a product, he merely assumes responsibility for its transfer between parties.)

Some organizations, of course, use both direct and indirect forms of interface in their marketing operations and may be regarded as a third category.

The thesis being developed is that certain characteristics of the marketing task will act as constraints which tend to determine the particular solutions which companies adopt under each of the above five headings, but before the nature of these constraints can be discussed, it is necessary to examine the ways in which marketing tasks themselves vary.

Sources of Variation in Marketing Tasks

The tasks facing marketing organizations vary in three principal respects:

(1) What is being sold
(2) To whom it is being sold
(3) The nature of the market in which transactions take place.

These three sources of variation interact with each other to form systems of decisions and related activities. For example, selling paint to householders in a highly competitive market involves a different system of activities and decisions from selling paint to industrial users in the same conditions of competition. Similarly, selling steel to industrial users involves a different system of activities and decisions from those involved in selling computers to the same organizations, or selling steel in a sellers' market is different as a task from selling steel in a buyers' market.

What is Being Sold

Differences betwen products which affect the nature of the marketing task are many. Some of the most obvious are:

Durability/perishability
Technical complexity
Degree of standardization
Price
Goods versus services
Mass produced versus custom built
Cost of transportation and storage
New products versus established products
Cost of initial investment

To Whom it is Being Sold

Similarly, customers differ in such respects as the following:

Corporate entities versus individuals
Socio-economic class, sex and age differences
Many customers–few customers

Geographically dispersed versus geographically
concentrated customers

The Nature of the Market

Finally, market conditions can vary, for example, in:

Balance of supply and demand
Elasticity of demand
State of competition
Longer-term stability of demand
Seasonal stability of demand

Variations in these three sets of factors, in interaction, result in the overall characteristics of marketing tasks as systems of activities and related decisions. In terms of the general model of the marketing task shown in Figure 2, what this means in practice is that in relation to variations in products, customers and markets there will be differences in:

(1) The range of decisions, activities and information flows involved in each particular marketing task.
(2) The relative importance of each of these.
(3) The relationships between them.

The most complex marketing tasks will be ones which involve all the decisions, activities and sources of information shown in Figure 2 and which are of such a nature that almost all the factors in the task are equally important and critical for success. Such highly complex tasks are typically found in the marketing of mass-produced, high-volume, low-priced consumer durable goods such as domestic electrical appliances, and in fast moving branded consumer goods such as foods, toiletries and confectionery.

On the other hand there are certain types of marketing task which are typically much less complex. These include ones in which there is a single product being produced to the specific requirements of a known customer (e.g. ship building), ones in which there is no tangible product to be packaged, stored, distributed or serviced (e.g. most 'service' industries) and ones carried out under conditions of monopoly or fixed prices or where demand chronically exceeds supply.

In general, the marketing of consumer goods will involve more complex tasks than the marketing of industrial goods which in turn will involve more complex tasks than the marketing of services. However, there will be many exceptions to the general rule and the traditional breakdown of marketing tasks into these three categories is likely to be extremely misleading if used as the basis for decisions about organization.

Task Constraints and Marketing Organization Structure

The effect of various task constrains will now be discussed in relation to each of the principal types of variation in organization structures outlined earlier.

Task Constraints and Differentiation of the Marketing Function

Undoubtedly the extent to which the marketing function is differentiated in the organization will be more a function of the size of the enterprise (particularly as measured by number of employees) than a reflection of particular task constraints. However, for enterprises of similar size there may be certain differences in the extent to which the marketing function forms a separate part of the organization which are explicable in terms of differences in the nature of the marketing task. For example, where goods are produced to the special requirements of known customers and where these customers are few in number, there will be a tendency for the production function to embrace many of the specialisms which normally fall within a differentiated marketing function. In such cases the sales specialism is often rudimentary while general managers or production managers tend to be responsible for such things as product development, pricing decisions, customer relations, distribution, after-sales service and a great deal of sales administration.

Another task characteristic which results in a tendency for the marketing function to remain undifferentiated is where goods or services are being supplied under monopolist conditions or in a strong sellers' market. Under such conditions few of the marketing activities or decisions in Figure 2 are of critical importance to the commercial success of the company, and the ones which remain such as sales administration, distribution and after-sales service (where these are involved at all) are often subsumed within the production function.

Degree of Specialization within the Marketing Function

As was pointed out earlier, this feature of organization structure is likely to reflect differences in size to a greater extent than differences in the nature of the marketing task, the tendency being for larger organizations to carry a wider range of specialist activities. Here again, however, one can expect to find important differences in the degree of specialization between firms of comparable size and be able to account at least for some of these differences by reference to differences in the nature of the task. Fairly obviously, the more activities, decisions and information flows involved in the task, the greater the tendency towards specialization. Table 1 shows the extent to which different marketing situations conform to the general model of the marketing task contained in Figure 2. In the general model there are six areas of decision, eight distinct sets of activities and eight principal information flows into the system. As can be seen from Table 1, there is considerable variation from one marketing task to another in the extent to which these factors are likely to be involved. However, there is a world of difference between the question of

Table 1. Task characteristics of different marketing situations

Selected marketing tasks in order of complexity	Information								Decisions						Activities							
	Product research	Competitor's strategy	Market research	Cost of manufacture	Financial control	Sales forecasting	Motivation research	Media research	Products	Markets	Pricing	Sales volume	How to promote sales	Allocation of resources	Product development	Advertising/promotion	Selling	Sales administration	Recruiting, training	Distribution	After sales service	Customer relations
Mass produced consumer durable/intense competition	**	**	**	**	**	**	**	**	**	**	**	**	**	**	**	**	**	*	**	*	**	*
Branded, fast moving consumer goods (e.g. packaged foods)	**	**	**	**	**	**	**	**	**	**	**	**	**	**	**	**	*	*	*	**		*
Computer systems to industrial users/strong competition	**	**	**	**	**	**			**	*	**	**	**	**	**	*	**	*	**	*	**	**
Jobbing printing to industry/strong competition	**	*	*	**	**	**			*	**	**	**	**	**	*	*	**	*	*	*	**	**
Consumable stores (e.g. office stationery) to industrial users		*	*	**	**	**			**	*	**	**	**	**	*	*	**	*	*	*		*
Service to general public in face of strong competition (hotels)	*	*	*	**	*	**	*	*			**	**	**	**	*	**	**	*	*	*		**
Monopoly service to general public (commuter transport)	*		*	**	**	**			**	*	**	*	**	**	*	**		*	*			**
Services to industrial users, e.g. management consultancy	*	*	*	*	**	*			*	*	**	*	**	**	*	*	*	*	*		**	**
Large scale building works for government, by tender	*	**	*	**	**	*			*	*	**	*		**	*	*	*	**			*	**

* = Functions normally of sufficient importance to be specialized in medium sized and large organizations.
** = Functions of vital importance to commercial success

whether or not a particular activity is a necessary part of the marketing process and the question of its critical significance in relation to the commercial success of the company. In some marketing operations decisions about prices may be absolutely vital to the success of the operation, whereas in others, although pricing decisions may be called for, their effect on success is marginal. In Table 1 the factors which are probably most critical for success in each marketing situation are given double asterisks.

The implication for organization structure of the critical significance of a decision, activity or information flow is likely to vary according to each type of factor—decision, activity or information flow. Thus where *decisions* are of critical significance they are likely to form part of the role specification of the chief marketing executive rather than to be delegated to lower levels and allocated to specialists.

However, in very large organizations with complex marketing operations where the chief marketing executive is responsible for many important decisions, much of the preparatory work to assist him in reaching decisions on such issues as prices may be carried out by specialized staff. As far as *activities* are concerned, the greater their importance in relation to commercial success the more likely they are to be carried out by specialized subdivisions of the marketing organization, and one crude index of the relative importance of activities is the level in the organization hierarchy occupied by the managers responsible for carrying them out.

Finally, where particular types of *information* are critical to the success of marketing, it is again likely that specialist sections will be set up to ensure an adequate flow of such information and that the managers responsible for these information flows will be located very close to the chief marketing executive in the organization structure.

Task Constraints and the International Differentiation of the Marketing Organization

Three task factors have a fairly obvious bearing on this aspect of the organization structure. The first is the range of products with which the marketing organization is concerned and the extent to which there are important differences between the products which call for separate marketing arrangements. Differences between the products of a single enterprise can take various forms of which the following may serve as examples:

(1) Differences in quality or finish of what is essentially the same product (e.g. standard or de luxe model automobiles).
(2) A range of closely similar products in which each one in the range has distinctive attributes in the eyes of the consumer. These attributes may involve differences in flavour, design, packaging, etc. They are intended to appeal differentially to consumers of different tastes and income groups (e.g. the various brands of cigarette produced by one manufacturer).
(3) A range of products in which each product differs from the others in

important respects but has in common with the others a particular end use such that one product can be substituted for another where the consumer is seeking variety (e.g. packaged or canned convenience foods).

(4) A range of products in which each product differs from the others in important respects but the range as a whole forms a complementary series such that sales of one product tend to reinforce sales of the others (e.g. a range of stationery or a range of car accessories).

Differences between products of the kinds exemplified in (1) to (4) above are unlikely to create a requirement for an organization structure differentiated chiefly by product because in each case there is little variation in either the product knowledge or in the knowledge of customer requirements required of the marketing organization. On the other hand, the product differences listed below are frequently associated with a product-based marketing organization.

(5) A range of products in which there are considerable differences in the technological complexity of each. (For example, a range of office equipment from typewriters to computers. The ability to acquire adequate product knowledge of computers will normally involve much higher educational attainment and longer periods of training than in the case of typewriters—thus suggesting a need for specialization of personnel in each field. At the same time those responsible for purchasing a company's typewriters will seldom be the same people as those responsible for deciding which computers to install.)

(6) A range of products stemming from the same basic raw materials but having different end uses (e.g. gasolene and petro-chemicals).

(7) A range of products sharing a common manufacturing technology but having different end uses (e.g. automobiles, trucks and buses).

Clearly, the kinds of differences between products which are likely to call for separate marketing arrangements are ones which call on the one hand for a wide range of types of knowledge about products and their characteristics or on the other hand for a range of knowledge about markets and their needs such that real advantages come from specialization.

Secondly, there is the extent to which the company is directing its marketing efforts towards different categories of customer or 'marketing segments', such that different types of relationship will need to be established with different groups of customers. Assuming the situation is such that the marketing organization is concerned with a single product or a reasonably homogeneous product range with regard to manufacturing technology or end use, the requirement for organizational differentiation based on markets will possibly arise under the following sets of conditions:

(1) Some customers (usually a small proportion of the total) purchase a high proportion of the firm's sales turnover while other customers (the majority of total customers) purchase a relatively small proportion of turnover. This situation is frequently encountered in industrial marketing, particularly in the

components field. It also occurs in the consumer goods market where the increasing concentration of retail outlets results in a high proportion of turnover of a food product being purchased by two or three supermarket chains.

(2) Some customers are private individuals, others are corporate entities. The main results of this difference will lie in the fields of purchasing methods, credit arrangements and customers' criteria of choice. Examples of products used to a considerable extent by both private and industrial consumers are automobiles, telephone services, fuel, hotel accommodation, air travel, etc.

(3) Different types of customer may use the product in different ways. For example, different types of expertise may be called for in selling a computer to a bank on the one hand and to a manufacturing organization on the other.

All the above sets of conditions have in common a need to deal with different groups of customers in different ways, either because of varying needs on the part of the customer or differences in the relative bargaining strength of customer and supplier.

Finally, there is the extent to which the market is geographically dispersed and calls for a geographically structured marketing organization to meet its requirements. Most marketing organizations of any size include within the organization structure some breakdown of responsibilities on a geographical basis. In relatively simple marketing situations involving a single product or a homogeneous product range and a single market, this may be the only form of internal differentiation apart from functional specialization. In more complex cases geographical differentiation seldom emerges as the principal method of structuring the organization. Where it does so, it is usually in the form of a home sales division and an export division.

The foregoing argument has in general tended to assume a certain simplicity in the marketing situation facing the enterprise which is not much in evidence in the typical large modern business enterprise. In effect the argument runs: 'Given more than one product, the marketing organization will probably need to be differentiated by product under certain conditions; given that a product is being sold to more than one type of customer, under certain conditions the marketing organization will need to be differentiated on the basis of markets served; given the existence of distinct geographical markets, the marketing organization will need to be differentiated geographically; in addition, functional specialization will be necessary'. The problem facing many large organizations in their marketing is, of course, that they face all four problems simultaneously. They have to provide for adequate specialization in knowledge of both products and markets, for adequate local concentration on regional markets and for adequate specialization in the marketing functions. In the face of such complex tasks, decisions have to be made about which are the most vital and most productive forms of organizational specialization. Organizations faced with complexity of this kind tend to undergo an almost continuous process of searching for the right solution, involving successive reorganizations. Walker and Lorsch (1968) in a review of the criteria affecting the choice between a product-based organization and one based primarily on function, point out that in some situations conflicting requirements are extremely finely balanced with the result that some kind of organizational compromise is called for. They list as examples of such compromises adopted in practice:

(1) The use of cross-functional teams to facilitate integration. In marketing this approach would be exemplified by the creation of a team to launch a new product, drawing its members for the duration of the project from various centres of functional expertise such as market research, advertising, promotion and distribution.

(2) The appointment of full-time integrators or co-ordinators. In marketing this is exemplified by the appointment of brand managers who are normally expected to co-ordinate all the marketing activities associated with a particular product brand in an organization which is otherwise structured in terms of the marketing functions and geographical areas.

(3) The 'matrix' or grid organization which combines the product and functional forms by overlaying them. This solution, in which everyone has 'two bosses'—his functional boss and the boss concerned with a particular product—appears to find less favour, perhaps because it violates the classical organizational principle of unity of command. The matrix can, of course, cover products and markets, or markets and functions as well as products and functions, and it is probably in this approach to dealing with complexity that the most interesting future developments will occur.

Task Constraints and the Configuration of the Marketing Organization

This factor is also more likely to show the influence of size than to reflect constraints stemming from the nature of the task. Generally, the larger the organization the more likely it is to develop the type of configuration associated with bureaucratic structures, i.e. a hierarchical pyramid divided into clearly defined levels of authority and status. Configuration will also be influenced by factors associated with the social system—for example, the extent to which the traditional hierarchical form of authority is regarded as acceptable and appropriate. Finally, it is this area that particular theories about the design of organization structures can be expected to make an impact—particularly theories about the optimum span of control. [4]

In view of the many sources of influence on the configuration of the organization, it is difficult when analysing actual cases to discern what constraints, if any, stem from the particular nature of the task. If the theorists are right (see, for example, Burns and Stalker (1961) and Perrow (1970) among others), traditional bureaucratic structures lend themselves most readily to tasks which are stable and capable of being routinized or where the processes being managed are subject to more or less certain knowledge. On the other hand, more 'organic' less rigidly hierarchical structures are associated with tasks characterized by rapid environmental change, considerable uncertainty as to the processes being managed and a requirement for creative (non-programmed) rather than routinized (programmed) decisions.

Applying these theories to the organization of marketing activities, one would expect to find departures from the traditional hierarchical pattern of authority in the following task situations:

(1) A high frequency of product obsolescence with an associated need for frequent development and launching of new products (for example, the fashion industry).

(2) Considerable uncertainty surrounding such questions as the factors making for consumer acceptance or rejection of a product (for example, brands of cigarette, toothpaste, other toiletries, etc.).

(3) A 'turbulent' marketing environment (Emery and Trist, 1965) in which rapid, interacting changes in such factors as the level of demand, intensity of competition, emergence of new products and effects of government intervention render forward planning and routinization of activities extremely difficult.

Task Constraints and the Nature of the Interface with the Market

This factor is likely to be particularly closely associated with the nature of the marketing task. The task conditions which will call for a direct face-to-face relationship between members of the supplier's organization and the customer (or members of the customer's organization) will include:

(1) The manufacturing of goods or the provision of services tailored to the specific requirements of the customer. In such cases the interposition of a 'middleman' would add considerably to communication problems while offering few compensating advantages. Examples include, in the manufacturing field, custom built machine tools and other capital goods, and in the service field, advertising and management consultancy. Much of the activity of the building and printing industries also falls into this category.

(2) Situations in which the use of the product or service involves a continuing interaction between the marketing organization and its customers (for example, computing systems calling for intensive, highly specialized maintenance and updating of software systems; the telephone service).

(3) Situations in which the location of the retail outlet is critical for the success of the marketing effort (for example, the marketing of beer and gasolene).

Mass-produced goods intended for individual domestic consumption (e.g. food, clothing, furnishings) and with little or no maintenance requirement or other after-sales service will tend to be placed on the market via independent wholesale and retail outlets.

In between the two extremes are products such as electrical appliances and automobiles where the relationship with the market may be mediated through licensed dealers or agents rather than through wholly independent retailers.

Implications for Marketing Management

The approach to organizational analysis and design which has been outlined in this chapter is based on the assumption that 'for any primary task a model can be constructed that gives a best organizational fit to task performance' (Rice, 1963, p. 197). In other words, the best way of organizing a business function is to start with a careful analysis of the work that has to be done.

It is not, however, the intention to suggest that organizational design can ever be reduced to the application of some kind of formula derived from task analysis. It will remain an activity calling for a very special blend of judgement and experience on the part of management and because of the many conflicting pressures in any complex modern organization, it will remain an activity in which reasonable compromise must be accepted and attempts to find theoretically perfect solutions abandoned. Most important, it should always be seen as a continuing activity in which there are no final solutions. As the constraints, both internal and environmental, change so there will arise a need to take another look at the structure and develop it further.

It should also be stressed that although analysis of the task should be the starting point when designing or re-designing an organization structure, there will be other factors which need to be taken into account before decisions are reached. Not least in importance, of course, will be the availability and quality of human resources. It is no use developing a theoretically ideal structure if people capable of carrying out the roles in that structure are simply not available. It is always necessary when designing a new structure or changing an existing one to keep one eye on the human beings who will man the structure. This includes not only taking account of their abilities and aptitudes, but also the personality factors likely to be relevant to task performance.

A further problem which will need to be faced is the need to design an organization structure which will not only provide an adequate framework for the various decisions and activities involved in the primary task, but which will at the same time comprise a system of organization capable of motivating people and giving opportunities for satisfaction of needs. It is in this field that some of the most finely balanced compromises will be necessary in order to cope with the very real conflicts between the organizational requirements for effective and economic task performance on the one hand and the needs of human beings for satisfying and secure working environments on the other. There is by now a great deal of literature (Schein, 1965; Tannenbaum, 1966) concerned with the relationship between forms of organization and employee motivation and satisfaction, and it is important to take account of ideas of this kind when making decisions about organizational structures. It is equally important, however, that those who are going to be most affected by organizational decisions should be consulted about them and given opportunities to contribute to the design process.

Perhaps the least useful source of inspiration will be the conventional type of management text book with its well-worn principles of organization. Such attempts to provide a formula without reference to the nature of the primary task, the capacities and personalities of the available human resources, and the more general social and psychological needs of people may initially inject a false sense of confidence in that their statements are reassuringly precise. They can, however, offer no real substitute for the keys to managerial success in organization—a grasp of the essential nature of the primary task, a sensitive awareness of the needs and aspirations of the people who are to carry it out, and a willingness to search continuously for new solutions as the pattern of constraints shifts.

Notes

1. See, for example, Rice (1958) and Woodward (1965).
2. For example, the work of Charles Perrow in corrective institutions and hospitals (Perrow, 1970).
3. Notable exceptions include: Emery and Trist (1965) and Miller and Rice (1967), Chapters 5–8.
4. A. K. Rice has described in an amusing and very pointed manner the tendency in sales organizations in particular to develop hierarchical pyramids of authority and status, regardless of the relevance of such structures to effective task performance. 'The introduction of extra levels in the management hierarchy is perhaps best illustrated in the control of large consumer sales forces in which representatives report to field supervisors, field supervisors to branch managers, branch to district managers, district to regional managers, regional to divisional managers and divisional managers to a general sales manager who himself reports to the sales director. This may be extreme, but six-tier hierarchies are not uncommon, and five-tier are usual. On the criteria I have outlined such a differentiation would imply that each field force under a field supervisor has a discrete task that differentiates it from other field forces and from branches; that each branch has a discrete task that is different from all other branches, and so on. Certainly at the levels of regions or divisions there may be differences—selling in the north of England, for example, may be different from selling in the south and may require special techniques and marketing services—but it is often doubtful if a true difference extends any further down. With national marketing compaigns that extend to the whole country even this differentiation is doubtful. In discussing the differentiation of tasks at various levels in sales force organizations, I can frequently find no definition of the task of a manager on one level other than that he supervises his subordinates. I cannot avoid the ridiculous picture of the representative in his Anglia being followed by the field supervisor in his Consul, who in turn is followed by the branch manager in his Zephyr, and so up the hierarchy of cars and managers until the procession finally ends with the sales director in his Bentley—each one supervising his immediate subordinate carrying out his job of supervising his immediate subordinate and so on. Ridiculous—of course—but with no adequate discrete primary task to differentiate levels, not outrageous. Certainly one is often unable to escape the impression that the burden on representatives' backs comes more from their own towering hierarchies than from their customers' preferences for competitors' products. Also intermediate managers close to the representatives often find it difficult to discover just what their operating responsibility is—they have personnel and training tasks, merchandizing responsibilities, and

192

sometimes even inspection functions, but these are, or should be, differentiated control and service functions, not operating or "line" management' (Rice, 1963, pp. 226–227).

References

British Institute of Management (1970), Marketing organization in British industry, Information Summary No. 8, April.

Burns, T. and Stalker, G. M. (1961), *The Management of Innovation*, Tavistock Publications, London.

Emery, F. E. and Trist, E. L. (1965), The causal texture of organizational environments, *Human Relations*, **18**, 21–32.

Miller, E. J. and Rice, A. K. (1967), *Systems of Organization: the Control of Task and Sentient Boundaries*, Tavistock Publications, London.

Perrow, C. (1970), *Organizational Analysis: a Sociological View*, Tavistock Publications, London.

Pugh, D. S. (1970), The structure of the marketing specialisms in their context, *British Journal of Marketing*, **4**, 98–105.

Rice, A. K. (1958), *Productivity and Social Organization: the Ahmedabad Experiment*, Tavistock Publications, London.

Rice, A. K. (1963), *The Enterprise and its Environment: a System Theory of Management Organization*, Tavistock Publications, London.

Schein, E. H. (1965), *Organizational Psychology*, Prentice-Hall, Englewood Cliffs, N. J.

Tannenbaum, A. S. (1966), *Social Psychology of Work Organization*, Tavistock Publications, London.

Walker, A. H. and Lorsch, J. W. (1968), Organizational choice: product versus function, *Harvard Business Review*, **46**, No. 6, 129–138.

Weinshall, T. D. (1971), Application of two conceptual schemes of organizational behaviour in case study and general organization research, Ashridge Management College Papers in Management Studies.

Woodward, J. (1965), *Industrial Organization: Theory and Practice*, Oxford University Press, London.

Environment, Cohesion and Differentiation in a Secondary School

Geoffrey Hutton

Introduction

The occasion of the publication of this book has, to me, been a welcome opportunity to contribute to Ken Rice's memory, to display my indebtedness to some of his thinking and to publish an account of a particular research study from the point of view which gave rise to it. I was, at the time of the study, directing the Social Environment Research Unit of the University of Edinburgh, which was conducting research into family and neighbourhood questions. The work was financed by the Joseph Rowntree Memorial Trust. This study of the organization of a Scottish secondary school in its local environment was conducted by myself and my colleagues in collaboration with the headmaster of that school, which I shall call Lauriston School, during the period 1962–1964. The original working papers and conference papers from which much of the material for this study is drawn were written by myself and my colleagues, in particular, Molly Harrington, many of whose ideas have found their way into the paper.

One of my own declared aims at the time was to see to what extent the organizational models generated by my former colleagues at the Tavistock Institute and in particular Ken Rice could be applied to the analysis of a school. I had already attempted to apply them to the analysis of a mental hospital (Hutton, 1962). I had developed a particular interest in the problems of reflexive organization, that is to say, the organization of enterprises some of whose members constitute the material on which the enterprise operates. I wanted to see how far asking questions about primary task, environmental demands and constraints, import, conversion and export procedures, and differentiation and cohesion would produce sensible answers and helpful analyses in a school. The headmaster's interest lay in seeing to what extent his policies for the school had found concrete expression. This meant looking at the demands and constraints surrounding his role, his conception of the purposes of the school, to what extent these were shared by other members of the staff and by the pupils, and to what extent the organization and operations of the school expressed these purposes.

The paper attempts to analyse some of the relations between the organization of the school and its environmental demands and constraints. The school relates to a number of subenvironments, differing in their demands and constraints. The analysis presented here gives perhaps a disproportionate emphasis to those arising from the local environment of the school. This is for two reasons:

first, that I and my colleagues made some empirical studies of local reactions to the school and therefore have more first-hand evidence to offer, and second, that the policies of the school and the constraints acting upon their execution of these policies relate very closely to the local situation.

The events forming the subject of the analysis occurred in the early 1960's. The situation in the school and in the locality has of course changed since this time. The headmaster of the school has retired and many of the staff and all the pupils are now different. I visited the school early in 1971, to discuss current policy and organization. A brief account of the current situation is included as a postscript. While the original research was in process, we attempted to make analyses of current situations and to play them back to the people involved. I am now, however, reviewing these events from a distance in an essay in the relation between policy, organization and environment.

The School in the British Educational System

The school was what is known in Scotland as a junior secondary school, in the process of becoming what is known in Britain as a comprehensive school. It is now known as 'Lauriston' Comprehensive School. Its position was, at the time of the study, transitional, and to some extent, anomalous. Its relation to the somewhat complex educational system in Edinburgh was important, and as the Edinburgh system varied from the general Scottish system, and that from the system in England and Wales, some explication is appropriate.

Most schools in Britain are run mostly by local authorities on finance derived partly from local rating revenue but mainly from Central Government funds. Each local education system is determined within a framework of law and as the outcome of the interplay between local intentions and Government persuasion, pressure and guidance. Other schools are owned and managed by private foundations, which may be churches or educational trusts owning a chain of schools, or the foundation of the school itself. These include the wholly independent and self-financed 'public' schools, and a number of schools (178 in 1962) which receive a direct grant from the State in return for the admission of pupils from the neighbouring local education authorities.

The last major Education Acts were in 1944 for England and Wales and in 1945 for Scotland. The 1944 Act established the tripartite principle of education under which there were grammar schools, taking a selective intake of academically and intellectually able pupils, technical schools and secondary modern schools. Secondary education extended from the age of 11 to the age of 18, grammar schools keeping pupils until the age of 18 and secondary modern schools at least until the school leaving age of 15. This replaced the parallel system of elementary education for children of parents who did not pay fees and of secondary education, including the grammar schools whose pupils either paid fees or won free places through scholarship. The 1944 Act did not preclude other forms of organization including other arrangements of ages. The 1960's saw a variety of alternative patterns being evolved, including the great tendency towards comprehensive or all-ability schools promoted and backed by the Labour Government. In 1973, the minimum school leaving age was raised to 16.

The Scottish system has always been different. Local schools which were, in effect, comprehensive schools, were the order of the day in most towns and country districts. There were also, and are still, academic or senior secondary schools which are academically selective and which since 1945 have not been fee-paying except for certain schools in Edinburgh and Glasgow. Edinburgh, in 1962, had an unusually large proportion of independent schools, of direct grant schools, of corporation schools which were selective and charged fees (which had been abolished in England and Wales in 1944) and also of corporation schools which were selective and did not charge fees. Secondary education in Scotland begins at age 12, many of the independent schools and some of the corporation schools providing their own preparatory and primary departments.

The school which we are examining was nominally a junior secondary school, that is a corporation school which did not charge fees, which took a non-selective local entry and did not keep children beyond the school leaving age to the point where they took public examinations. In fact, this school had already begun to keep children beyond school leaving age to take 'O' level examinations at the age of 16. It was also taking in academically brighter children who would otherwise have gone direct to one of the selective senior secondary schools or academies. The arrangement with these children was that they stayed two years in the school and then left to join a local Academy. It was also, at the time of the study, keeping an increasing proportion of children beyond the statutory leaving age without necessarily preparing them for public examinations.

It was a large school. It began in 1948 with 275 children and 15 teachers and grew over the succeeding 14 years to 1962 on what is basically a straight line curve. The numbers reached a peak in 1961 and 1962 and they were, at the maximum, 1,930 pupils and, a year later, 113 teachers. The numbers fell in the spring of 1963 as a new secondary school was opened in the same district which had the effect of reducing its intake. At its peak, it was one of the eight largest comprehensive schools in Britain, though the number of schools of this order and size has subsequently increased.

The comprehensiveness of the school's intake was limited firstly by bias in its catchment area, which consisted predominantly of housing estates owned by the corporation and included relatively few housing areas likely to contain people with higher incomes and better education. It was also limited by the competition which faced it from fee charging corporation secondary schools and from the fee charging independent schools. That effect was that although the range of scholastic aptitudes of the incoming children was wide, the distribution was bottom-heavy. For instance, in autumn 1962, the total intake was 637 children, of whom 129 were for the academically selective stream eventually intended to leave after two years and go on to the local Academy. As the courses which these children took included languages, they were known as the 'language course'. The language or senior secondary stream should, on average in the city as a whole, have contained 30 per cent of the intake, which in this case would have been 191 children against the actual 129. The discrepancy was even greater than the figures would show, because in this school the benefit of the doubt was often given to the child when questions of entry into the language course were considered.

It will be seen that the school was streamed. In fact, the streaming of entrants into classes was done precisely on the basis of classification test results. These were given to all primary school children and tested scholastic aptitude and intellectual ability. The full entry was divided into consecutive bands of test scores and these bands constituted the classes. The streaming was not maintained rigidly throughout the years of the school. In the third year, there was a certain overlap between streams on some of the special vocationally biased courses. In the fourth year, that is, beyond school leaving age, the streaming was done separately for each subject—the practice known as 'setting'. There was, furthermore, an experiment going on at the time in the first year, with the whole of the intake from one of the feeder primary schools being kept together as a non-streamed class. Nevertheless, at the time of the study, the main practice in the school was teaching in classes which were streamed on averaged measures of academic performance.

Most of what we have to say about the management of the school arises from the demands placed on its structure and organization of work by its very rapid growth in size, by the extension in its educational services and by the complication of the pressures arising from its local environment. The increase in numbers of pupils had already slowed down, but its curriculum was becoming increasingly diversified in a complex and changing environment.

Before looking at the internal management and organization of the school, I will describe what we discovered about the reputation and image of the school held by local residents.

Local Reactions to Education and the School

During the spring of 1962, the headmaster of the school and the Director of Education of the city expressed an interest in such information as the research unit might be able to gather within a few months about the local reputation, appreciation and expectations of the school, and any observation or information we might be able to offer on general reactions to education and factors influencing these reactions.

We drew upon interview material collected from residents throughout the research district which included the catchment area of the school but extended some way beyond it in each direction. Most of the information came from interviews which had already been conducted about the locality and family life, but some interviews and group discussions were conducted especially on the question of education for the purposes of this school study. In all, a little over 100 interviews and group discussions contributed to the findings. They included people in every life stage from early adolescence to pre-senility and in occupational grades from unskilled manual to professional and managerial. About one third of the families interviewed had, or expected soon to have, children at this school. The picture which emerged, although complex, was sufficiently consistent and clear in the opinion of the research unit for considerable reliance to be placed on the major points.

Initial discussions with the headmaster and Director of Education clarified some starting assumptions. It was thought likely that the school would not be well understood by parents and that parents would be ill-informed in their choices, preferences and opinions, and would be as much influenced by perceived or assumed social class distinctions as by observed educational criteria. Local protest was current in one part of the district about the increasing selectivity of a fee-paying corporation academy nearby which children from this district had beed attending. This had increased the probability of their going to Lauriston School. The presence of a relatively large number of fee-paying secondary education places was likely to prove a critical feature in any consideration of parental expectation and choice as these places (a) carried prestige, (b) extended lower in the social prestige scale than fee-paying schools in many parts of the country, (c) offered an apparently greater degree of parental choice in primary and secondary education compared with the non-fee-paying schools and (d) gave greater opportunity than in many parts of the country for parents to 'avoid the pot-holes in the State system' as one parent put it. These factors were thought to combine to put such a school as Lauriston at multiple disadvantages in developing senior or advanced secondary education facilities and in attracting suitable pupils. In its work with academically less apt pupils it was also likely to suffer through the lack of commonly recognized criteria of success in the absence of academic examination successes. We began from the point that the dice were loaded against the school in its attempt to provide a comprehensive educational service of high repute.

We found in the field work that school and schooling were topics of direct interest which excited feeling and disputation. Parents were deeply interested in the contrast between what they saw now and what they remembered from their own days. There was a great deal of myth, fantasy and strong feeling in the beliefs and opinions which many people expressed. In relation to the school, we found that it had two distinct simple images in the locality—positive and negative—and that of these the negative image did not occur when people had direct personal knowledge of the school. People also held a number of more complex and discriminating images.

Feelings, beliefs and attitudes about schooling in general form a background against which particular beliefs and attitudes about Lauriston School were imposed. Perhaps to us the most striking thing about the interviews was the high degree of emotional involvement expressed. It is certainly true to say that schools and schooling was a topic on which it was easy to get people to talk and on which it was easy to get people to talk with feeling. It was not, however, easy to discover balanced judgements based on information. If the interviewer was to place himself in the position of a parent seeking information about local schools or the Edinburgh system, we would have been forced to say that the picture available from parents we have met would, apart from certain general trends, be full of contradiction and inaccuracy.

For some parents, school was seen as a feared and punishing place. It was quite possible for people to hold this view simultaneously with the view that present-day schools, that is the schools to which their children were going, were not like this. In a way they were tending to see schools from the child's point of view and to contrast the badness of what they remembered of their own school days with the goodness of what they saw now through their children. There was a very frequent undercurrent of feeling that love played a part in school life nowadays. They welcomed this for their children and felt some envy.

There was a deep degree of contrast between old and new. People felt that nowadays children enjoyed their schooling, learnt more and were less afraid and less socially distant from their teachers. This was so for people who themselves liked their own schooling and for those, a few in number, who produced recollections of school days which made them sound as though they had been spent in the lifetime of Dickens, rather than in the 1930's. Some of the strongest feelings were associated with recollections of physical punishment, which in Scottish schools is usually administered with a leather strap. Parents who had come into the city from England were surprised and offended to find that strapping took place in the classrooms of local schools. The Scottish parents had mixed feelings, but by and large, they disapproved of strapping for faults in work and were divided in their opinions about the benefit of it for disciplinary use. They all agreed that it was a declining practice. The generally perceived trend towards permissiveness in schools was not universally approved.

Schools sometimes expect to be seen as devices for teaching a fairly limited range of useful skills. While this view was expressed by some people, it was, on the whole, remarkable for its absence or low priority. People did, however, commonly see the schools as devices for insuring social mobility. On this point, the peculiarities of the Edinburgh system were particularly pertinent.

Schools were commonly seen as being ranked in a hierarchy of esteem. We attempted to construct the rank order from various comparisons and contrasts which people had made in interview. This was rather an unsystematic process but in broad terms it became clear that the independent fee-paying public schools stood at the top with the main residential public school not figuring in the local scheme of things. Lower down came the fee-paying day schools, the corporation selective schools and the rest which tended to be graded on roughness. There was a very widespread feeling that the advantages of the fee-paying schools were hardly to be questioned and if one had ambitions for one's child then such a school should be sought. People tended to set their sights a certain way up the scale of esteem which is, of course, correlated with the scale of cost. Schools higher up the scale would be rejected not only because they were expensive but because they were felt to be socially out of reach. Schools lower in the scale from the point of choice were felt to be of a poorer social standing or of a poorer academic standing.

Widespread agreement that the system had to be used was not accompanied by such a widespread agreement that it was a good system. The fee-paying system was seen as representing an elite, membership of which was eligible to those who could pay. Disquiet was occasionally expressed at the incompatibility of this notion with the ethic of equal opportunity for all and sometimes flatly contradictory statements were made by the same people in support of both of these propositions. The general assumption seemed to be that however desirable equality of opportunity might be, it did not exist.

Information of a sort about schools circulated easily, especially information about the social grading system and myths about particular schools. Professional and managerial parents coming into Edinburgh, particularly if they worked for a large organization, would very quickly be told by their colleagues what the social grading system implied for their own choices. Among other people and among wives in a locality, stories about particular schools circulated freely. They were indeed proffered to parents whose child was about to go to a particular school. The myths were not usually of a reassuring kind.

It is against a background of a lack of information, of the prevalence of myth, of concern for social grading and of the importance of individual ambition in educational choice that we must examine the particular reactions expressed towards Lauriston School.

It is, perhaps, not surprising in view of the foregoing, that the aspect of the school most frequently discussed was its ethos and social climate. Reactions to its scholastic aims and methods were less frequently expressed. People were concerned about standards of behaviour, values, social class, emotional climate and social control. It was about the expectations that people had of the ways in which children and adults ought to behave towards each other—whether one's child would mix with 'people like us' and whether Lauriston School was civilized.

The image which people held about the school varied according to the kind of information they had and according to the way in which the school appeared in their own spectrum of ideas about ambition and educational opportunity. I have already mentioned some general reactions towards schools in which schools are seen as uncontrolled or punishing places. These kinds of antipathy are those which we might regard as primarily determined by personality. There were some parents who saw this school specifically as a den of hooligans and libertines, staffed by well-intentioned but ineffective teachers. Some of those who thought that immorality was rampant in the school attributed its existence to the teaching of sex which they saw as a direct invitation and encouragement to adolescents to go ahead and experiment. Free rein to the grosser fantasies was only for people who did not have children at the school. Even those most troubled by anxieties about safety and control were reassured when their own children finally went to the school. One mother said that she nearly went out of her mind when her daughter had to go to Lauriston. Within six months, the school had been added to the home in her mind as a safe area, leaving the journey between school and home as the dangerous bit.

Less driven by personal need and also susceptible to erosion through exposure to information were the views of the school that were mixed up with the views about the district which formed its catchment area and about adolescents. The district, particularly in its earlier years, was widely regarded in the city as being one of the poorer and rougher areas of the city, characterized by rowdyism, gang fights and noise. Some people described the school in almost exactly the same terms; other descriptions appeared to correspond to the stereotype of working-class adolescents—cheeky, noisy, rowdy, badly dressed, slovenly and promiscuous. Views of this sort, although widespread, were never held in our experience by people who had children at the school. These were views circulated about the school by people with no direct experience of it. Those who did know the school were ready enough to admit that there were some rough children at it but they were careful to make distinctions among pupils and to distinguish between the pupils and the school, exonerating the school from responsibility for street fighting. The school tended to pick up, not the reputation of its catchment area as a whole, but the reputation of the least reputable part of that catchment area. Primary schools had smaller catchment areas and got caught up in the process by which people tended never to regard their own area as quite the worst in the district. The local secondary school, however, with its wider catchment area, took in pupils from those parts of the district that one had placed lower in the order of respectability and tended to pick up the worst available reputation.

Again, it was clear how direct experience was important in modifying the process. There was one part of the district which had recently been made part of this school's catchment area and parents were no longer able to send their children to one of the corporation selective schools. Most of the vocal opposition to the school was met from parents in this district. A body of local myths had developed of a terrifying nature as far as small children were concerned. We observed the process of mutual reinforcement of prejudice and anxiety among parents and their children. The effect of concrete personal experience was a most dramatic one in these instances. None of the vehement antipathy was expressed by any parent in this district who had a child at the school.

Among people who had direct personal experience of the school through having their children at it more positive appreciation was universally expressed. This is not to say that all parents had a wholly positive image of the school. For greater discrimination necessarily produced a mixture of adverse and positive criticism. The simplest positive images related particularly to the ethos of the school.

'Oh, that's a good school. Nobody will ever get me to run down Lauriston. I have seen how our Betty has changed since she was there. She is much more grown up and responsible.'

'There is nothing wrong with the children there. Anyway, it doesn't hurt them to mix with all sorts.'

'My son goes back there regularly in the evenings, sometimes four evenings a week, and if it hadn't a good influence he would never have gone back.'

'Everyone said: "Send her to Hamilton Street, the element is not so rough. She'll get in with nice girls", but the senior secondary girls at Lauriston *are* nice.'

One ex-pupil said to a professional worker in the district that it was only while she was at this school that she felt herself to be of use to anybody. It was the only time in her life when she ever considered she mattered.

These are strong statements but were very widely expressed. The idea is that the school is well-ordered, that children are considered to be individually important and that there is a rich variety of activities to capture their interest and to give them room to develop. Such a situation would clearly be in line with the headmaster's intention for the school and if these characteristics were wholly to describe the school's situation it might be considered to be an administrative and educational triumph. We have, however, to notice the rosy tinge in the simple positive image.

When we turn to educational aim and method we found that there was much more discrimination expressed and a greater level of sophistication in discussion. It was here that the most complex and discriminating images were held. Clearly, each family had its own expectations and requirements for the school and the school of necessity would fail to provide all that all parents wanted.

Educational activities and educational facilities were very closely connected in people's minds. The school tended to be appreciated as an amalgam of buildings and people. We encountered no resentment of opposition to the main permanent buildings of the school or to their location. The facilities provided were widely approved. Criticisms of courses tended to be specific to the relevance of a particular course as seen by a particular child and his parents or about issues of the availability or non-availability of particular courses to particular children. One issue on which there appeared to be considerable discrepancy between the perceptions of parents and the intentions of the school related to the work done with the least intelligent children. On this there were striking differences of opinion. Some people felt that the method of approach adopted by the school was over-permissive and neglectful. Others thought that the effect of the work on the least able children was strikingly successful. These children were taught in smaller classes by special teachers with free and flexible timetables designed to capture the interest and the span of attention of children and using special activities, visits, camping at weekends and so on.

On the whole, the people we met clearly regarded the education offered at the school as satisfactory and as having become so by the efforts of the staff and particularly the headmaster. There was, however, an interesting discrepancy between the way in which people regarded this secondary school and the way in which they regarded the local primary schools. The primary schools were regarded more warmly and in a more personalized way. Parents tended to know the headmaster and the class teachers better. Lauriston School tended to be seen as a somewhat remote institution which parents found difficult to comprehend or to learn very much about. This was in spite of the manifest attempts of the headmaster and staff to communicate to parents, to invite them along to meetings and to consult with them about decisions affecting their children's education. Parents of children on academic courses tended to use the children's homework as a means of communication to judge what the children were doing and how they were getting on. Parents of other children who had less homework and who were working in a classroom situation strikingly different from what the parents themselves had known, found it difficult to feel that they were in touch or understood what was happening. Many of them did go along to the school, usually to see the headmaster about some specific complaint or anxiety, a change of course, a disciplinary difficulty. Many others did not. People still, however, felt themselves remote from the classroom situation.

On the whole, the school can be seen as existing in an environment of hostile and unwelcoming attitudes, readily converted by exposure and first-hand information into more positive and discriminating attitudes but with little development of sophisticated educational and cultural discriminations. The school was seen as one which had fine buildings and facilities and which was improving. Children were seen as exhibiting many degrees of rectitude outside the school. Inside the school, their standards of behaviour were thought to be high, and the control exerted over children to be secure and sometimes even strict. Relations between teachers and pupils were seen to be easy and friendly, on the whole, though tending to be variable. The school was seen as paying good attention to children of all kinds. Its educational services were thought to be good as far as they went, which was quite far enough for most parents, but not far enough for some.

Policy and Organization within the School

The work of analysis began with a long series of interviews with the head-master about his aims for the school, its history and organization. I am not analysing in this paper much of the work we did over many hours on his own aims and role. Other information comes from interviews, most of them repeated, with the deputy headmaster, the principal teachers and other members of the managing system; interviews with a sample of teachers; observations and visits to several of the school activities; a full week's visit on my part to the school which contained many observations and interviews with pupils and staff; an analysis of critical incident returns about expectations of ideal and rejected pupil behaviour and of gratifying and disturbing incidents in the teacher's life, which were filled in by about half the staff; interviews and group discussions with past and present pupils in their homes or in the Unit's offices; and a good deal of analysis of school records, staff turnover and so on.

Analysis of policy and organization in a large and expanding enterprise like this may appropriately begin by asking what are the tasks around which it is organized and what are the principles on which the allocation of responsibility and the grouping of activities are made. At the beginning, we must say that it is difficult to state what the task of a school actually is. I will take for the sake of argument here the conception of the task of the school held by the leadership, particularly the headmaster. From this point of view there were three tasks. Firstly, there was the development of individual skill and ability in the children with respect both to conventionally defined academic performance and to potential vocational skills. The second task was the development of individual norms of behaviour, which is usually put in some such terms as preparing the children to play a part as discriminating citizens. Thirdly, there was the attempt to exert a direct social influence on the school's environment. This third task is not usually recognized as part of a school's function and would not have been recognized by many of the staff of Lauriston, but the headmaster himself was quite explicit in his aim to provide services such as accommodation and technical assistance to organizations and individuals in the district. It was, in fact, his involvement in neighbourhood affairs that brought us into contact.

We have then to consider to what extent the activities and the organization of the activities in the school may rest upon these stated aims and in what way these aims are interpreted in more detail. In looking at the relation between aim and actuality we may attempt to see in what way the external pressures on the school had an effect.

Differentiations in Task Organization

A salient feature of the work organization of the school was the division into subject departments under principal teachers. These teachers were below the headmaster in rank, but their salaries were higher than those of other teachers. They met regularly with the headmaster to discuss the direction of certain of the school's activities—staff deployment, special events, examination arrangements, changes in organization, academic standards and methods and current operational decisions. They had separate relations with similarly placed people in other schools and some of them with central supervisors for their subject in the local authority's headquarters. All staff were allocated to one or other department, sometimes to a couple, particularly in the case of English, history and geography. Teachers specialized in the subject which they taught. They were nominally responsible to the head of their department for their teaching. All this constitutes a *departmental* principle of organization.

A second principle of organization was that of *course* organization. Children took one of several courses and even though there were exchanges between courses, the principle remains. Children were either on an academic course or a course leading to the local School's Certificates, or courses leading to commercial qualifications, or courses leading to certain other vocationally inclined specialities like the nautical course, the engineering course, the home-craft course, the art course and so on. Not all these courses were basically attached to one department. The engineering course was attached to the technical department, and the art courses to the art department and the commercial courses to the commercial department. This was not so for the academic courses and the general courses. Questions then arise about how the allocation of children to these courses was determined, how the progress of children on these courses was assessed and how the courses themselves were composed and integrated.

So far we have been talking about what goes on in classrooms, but in view of what was said about the tasks of the school it is clear that many activities derived from the stated tasks of the school went on outside classrooms and outside school hours. The school was by Scottish standards, though not so much by English standards, highly active in the field of extra-mural clubs. These were mostly run by members of staff and the headmaster himself was much concerned with this field of activities though not necessarily in detail with each club. There was thus a distinction between curricular activities on the 'day shift' and voluntary, extra-curricular activities on the 'night shift'. There we have what I would think of as another principle of organization, the *temporal*.

There were differentiations or cleavages in the school corresponding to each of these principles, that is between departments, between courses and between curricular and extra-curricular activities. The question now arises about when these cleavages operated, and how they related to each other. Let us take the relation between the course and departmental cleavages.

The organization of the school by departments clearly corresponded with the salary and career structure, and was the vehicle through which deployment to particular teaching assignments was arranged. There were, however, four specific ways in which the course cleavage opposed the departmental.

Firstly, however clearly the teachers saw themselves as organized in departments, and as belonging to departmental groups, the children saw things differently. Their daily programs were organized in courses. The children with whom they spent most of their working day were on the same courses. They belonged to courses. When I pointed this out in a passing sentence in one working note, one of the principal teachers found it something of a revelation.

The second major opposing tendency to departmental specialization was the special arrangements made for children in the slowest of the streams. These were called the 'less ables' or sometimes the 'modifieds' because they were following a modified general course. In this school, responsibility for one class was given for as much of the week as could be managed, which might amount to a good deal more than half of the week, to a single teacher who was specially interested, skilled, and more recently, trained and paid for this work. The special classes usually lasted for the first two years and there was an attempt to feed the classes back into the main stream by integrating them into some of the third-year specialized courses which overlap the streams. The existence of this special group of teachers, the special interest of the headmaster in this work and the breakdown in departmental boundaries and teaching specialisms in the work of the teachers of this group, collectively constitute a breakdown of departmental cleavages.

A third opposing tendency arose from geographical accident. Between September 1961 and March 1963, when the size of the school was at its peak, it could not be accommodated within its permanent buildings or in the temporary huts erected in its grounds. Provision was made to accommodate a sizeable number of pupils and staff in two small schools some distance from the main building. The headmaster decided that the pupils to be sent to these outlying annexes should be neither new pupils nor pupils in their last year, and that they should therefore be second-year pupils, as there were only three years in the course at that time. Further, because of the difficulty of splitting the departments for academic subjects, especially the language department, between the main school and the annexes, and because the second-year academic classes were in their last year, it was decided to send only the general and modified classes. Furthermore, the two schools used had been built and designed as a boys' school and a girls' school and because of the difficulty of duplicating laboratories, workshops and needlework and cookery rooms, one of the annexes was used exclusively for boys and the other exclusively for girls. Thus there were two small split-off fragments of the total organization which consisted exclusively of boys or girls of the non-academic streams in their second year. That is to say, what distinguished them from the rest of the school was in each case a course cleavage. These annexes functioned to a certain extent as small schools, within which boundaries between departments were much less rigid than in the main school.

The fourth tendency opposing departmental cleavage was provided by what is called a register teacher arrangement. Each class had a teacher who kept its register, and who was expected to know more about the children in his or her class than did other people in the school. It was the register teacher who ascertained the reasons for absence, and initiated truancy proceedings if these were indicated. The register teacher made up at the end of the year what is called the profile of the child which gave his examination results and reported on his general adjustment and progress. There was no formal grouping of register teachers in years or courses and the amount of direct reporting and supervision between them and the headmaster was not very great. What might be considered the key principle and the key channel in the whole school according to its stated task was in fact placed in a very subordinate position because it was staffed by people of lower status and pay than the principal teachers.

The cleavage between the day-shift and the night-shift did not present the same sort of organizational problem as did the opposition of departmental and course cleavages. There were, however, differences in the kind of relations required between teachers and pupils on the night-shift from those required on the day-shift. The clubs were mostly for fun and the atmosphere was more libertarian and permissive. Some of the staff felt that the effect in the classroom situation was adverse for some pupils and some staff. I have described something of the pressure of opinion in the district relating to such issues. I am not arguing whether the school should or should not have had clubs, but quoting this to show that there was a meaningful cleavage. The night-shift tended to act as a series of devices cross-cutting the course and departmental specialization. To some extent, clubs were based on departments: for instance, the farming club was run by the geography master, and the literary and debating society by the senior history mistress. Others were not, like the general boys' and girls' clubs. To some extent, clubs were specialized as far as the scholastic aptitude of the children went. This was more marked in the case of more explicitly intellectual clubs like the literary and debating society than in the farmers' club or the film club.

The question now arises as to the relative appropriateness of these cleavages in relation to the tasks of the school. It might be argued that if the school was seriously to concern itself with the position of the child in society when he left, and to develop in him a range of useful skills and capacities for judgement relevant to this position, then it would be missing the boat if it concentrated on the departmental organization. The departmental organization implicitly assumes that the child consists of a number of specific deficiencies in classroom subjects which are independent of each other and can be remedied in courses specially adapted to each deficiency. A departmental organization as such does not take care of what I have come to call the pilotage activities. On the other hand, it is difficult to see how some of the subjects in the school could be taught other than by teachers who specialize in them. If the school moreover was to concern itself with other than curricular kinds of deficiency and academic aptitudes and successes then it can be clearly argued that all these extra-curricular activities are relevant and are a part of the organization.

Activities in the school may be regarded as being basically of three kinds, operational (O), pilotage (P) and extension (Q). The O activities are the instructional or teaching activities, fairly rigidly defined as being concerned between the teacher and the pupil with the pupil's learning of the subject matter in hand. They could in principle be carried out by machines.

The pilotage or P activities are concerned with the position of the child as a whole in the social system of the school. In some educational circles the idea of 'pastoral' activities is similar, provided this is taken to carry no necessary moral or religious connotation. Activities range through choice of course, detection of differential progress between subjects, seeing to cross-subject relevancies, taking up problems of morale and personal development and the career orientation of children. Subject teachers are apt to claim that their work with children includes a great deal of P activity even though they are nominally for instance teaching French, and this may well be so.

The extension or Q activities are the extra-mural and non-curricular. The concept of 'social education' corresponds to some extent, although it may also include P activity.

If one distinguishes between them it is possible to ask of a school to what extent these activities are differentiated and how they are organized. The school in 1963 instituted a series of evening coaching sessions as a supplement to day-time teaching, particularly to help the fourth-year pupils who were going to go in for public examinations, without having followed preparatory courses in the preceeding years. This can be seen as carrying O and P activities into the night-shift which hitherto had been primarily concerned with explicit Q activities, and presumably, implicit P activities. There is a change in the principle of organization around them. Similarly, in the courses for the modified or the less able pupils, there is a large component of P activities in the relations between the teacher and the pupils whom he has for so much of the week and to whom he teaches so much of the total range of subject matter. In fact, this is the whole idea, to build in pilotage with instruction.

In this respect an innovation in the fourth year in 1963 should be mentioned. For various reasons to do with instruction and staffiing, it was proposed to adopt a complete setting parallel timetable. Such a timetable arrangement means composing teaching groups or classes separately for each subject, and holding the classes in parallel, at the same time. The groups are graded, and the membership of pupils in a group is independent between subjects, so that a pupil may be in the most advanced group in one subject, and in a less advanced group for another. The adoption of this system meant that with 100 boys and girls in the year the register teacher system could do nothing to help in understanding and handling the position of the whole child in the social system of the school. The need for this was, however, especially acute. A resolution proposed for an experimental trial was to take groups of children and place them under tutors whose job would be to integrate all the pilotage activities with respect to this child. This broke new ground in the organization and stimulated some demand for the principle of setting plus tutorial 'pilots' to be extended to lower years.

Problems of Cohesion and Control

I would conceptualize the position in the school, with the possible exception of the fourth year, as being one in which there was a common assumption among staff that the school was organized in departments, but that in fact it was organized at different times and for different purposes according to departmental, course, territorial and temporal (that is day- and night-shift) principles. The course-based emphases emerged not because they were willed to be that way but simply from the pressure of the work and because of the limitation on the degree to which the leadership interpretation of policy was spread through the organization. It might be postulated that if the departmental principle was held to be the proper one, and if most of the formal decisions were made using it, yet if in fact it did not extend over the whole range of activities over the school, then signs of strain must appear somewhere. Further, if the school should appear to be functioning effectively in terms of cohesion, then some force or process making for cohesion should be identifiable other than the prescribed procedures.

We should then look at what did emerge in the course of the field work in the way of felt diseases or complaints and see how they relate to this organizational difficulty. It should be borne in mind that the main point of the study was to see how the school was in fact working and in what ways the organization could be described. We were not seeking in the field work to bring out sore spots or hunt down problem areas, even though I am picking these out for the moment. There were two points around which complaint seemed to condense.

One had to do with communication. There were complaints about the amount of time taken in writing up notes and in having children interrupt classes to bring in notes, and about the unevenness in communication, in that teachers for instance found out about afternoons off from their classes, rather than from other staff. I have also grouped under the heading of communication complaints those related to a pressure of ancillary or managerial or clerical activities on principal and other teachers.

The second main point around which complaints or difficulties seemed to cluster was the issue of group affiliation and intergroup relations. Part of this relates to a discrepancy between the core staff and the peripheral staff, so I need here to discuss briefly staff turnover and the informal group structures.

I made detailed analyses of the staff turnover and individual length of stay over the school's history and I was able to draw up a composite decline curve showing the probable length of stay of teachers. These probabilities have varied from year to year throughout the school, but in total they more or less cancel out. The teacher had a 60 per cent chance of staying on beyond the end of his first year. In following years there is an almost consistent loss of 5 per cent per annum and after nine years the rate of loss levels out. The three phrases of the decline curve which have been analysed in Rice and Hill's earlier work on labour turnover figures (Rice and coworkers, 1950) emerge clearly here. The first is the phase of induction crisis which lasted in this school one year. The second phase of differential transit lasted for eight years and the third phase of settled connection of the core staff extended from then on. The interesting thing about this curve is that the cycle of work in the school is as long as the length of stay of the children. The probability of a teacher staying on for more that two and a half years is just over 0·5. In a school basically working on a three-year course, the oldest children of the school have mostly been there for two and a half years. The pupils very considerably outstay the teachers. This is of course a national problem, but judging from what some of these younger teachers said in interview, the induction of young teachers and the cutting down of this peripheral loss and lack of attachment is one of the challenges to the school and the existence of the problem is a symptom of all not being well with the management.

I have made a distinction between the core staff and other groups of staff. There were in fact a number of informal groupings to which teachers attached. The importance of these informal groupings for cohesive functions was borne in on me at the time. I was thus predisposed to find helpful the notion of sentient group boundaries (Miller and Rice, 1967). I have not adopted their term myself, referring in preference to commitment or identification groups.

The group of core staff were mostly but not all principal teachers. They were the long-stay people, several of them surviving from the early or more cohesive and heroic days and they were to be seen in the evening at a parents' meeting or a club meeting. There were certain faces which were around more. Judging from some of the interview material, the status of old-guard or core staff could to some extent override formal status differences in the way of reserving little privileges or getting away with things that other teachers could not. There were two points I made at the time about the informal groupings. In the first place, inasmuch as these groupings were cohesive and exclusive, they hindered communication and co-operation on principles appropriate to the work organization and their existence could be taken as an indication that such co-operation was deficient in this school. On the other hand, the teacher, especially the new teacher, in a school of this size, is faced with problems of attachment and getting to know just what is going on. Attachment to these groupings had in my judgment a cohesive effect in the school as a whole.

This school started as a small school with a strong ideology and a small close-knit group of teachers. In a small school, department cleavages cannot become of very great importance because there is only one teacher per subject, or two at the most, and they would not be able to talk to anybody unless they talked to people in other departments. A strong leader can assist this, especially when the group as a whole is faced with a new and challenging situation and is in the heroic or pioneering phase of the enterprise's life. Given, however, 2000 pupils and 110 teachers, many of whom are new and not likely to stay very long, it is impossible for the headmaster to reach them directly with his indoctrination, for reasonable fear of boring the old hands with repetition. Yet if it is left to the intermediate people, that is the departmental heads, to induce teachers to an awareness of the task of the school as a whole, there is likely to be some distortion by the very fact that the teacher doing the induction is a subject specialist talking to subject specialists who never have any direct contact with the work of the school as a whole. What we had in fact was a difference between the cohesive and loyal core group and shifting peripheral staff. It was not the formally prescribed authority structure which maintained the fairly smooth operation of the organization of this school over the whole growth crisis phase, but the operation of these informal commitment groupings and in particular the loyalty and toleration shown by the core staff. But this loyalty and co-operation surrounding the headmaster's office as it were does not extend rapidly and completely to new teachers coming in. There is not very much to take hold of a new teacher and to induce him into the culture of the school. It is rather a sink or swim procedure, and many of them sink, or rather climb out of the bath. One cannot tell whether the organizational difficulty arises from rapid changes in staff or whether the organizational difficulties exacerbate or even have produced the high turnover. It is clear, however, that they are dynamically interrelated.

Organizational Adaptation and Environmental Pressure

These two problem areas of the peripheral staff and the informal groups on the one hand and the communication complaints and difficulties on the other, together seem to be related to lack of cohesion in the intermediate levels of management. This is one of the three main organizational problems which I saw facing this school and possibly other schools in the same sort of position, of which there may be an increasing number in the future. The two other areas of organizational problem are not developed fully in this paper, but I will mention them here and take up the first again later.

One is the whole question of the determination of the task of a school in a situation where there are conflicting demands on it and an uneven distribution of the extent to which the school itself has initiative. Lawrence and Lorsch's work (1967) has drawn our attention to problems of cohesion, or integration in their terms, arising from the differential pulls of differentiated subenvironments. Schools have peculiarly difficult situations to face, in that their different subenvironments, local, official and professional, imply not only different styles or time scale of performance, but different goals, tasks and criteria for judging success without any secure measure of organizational effectiveness which could be used to evaluate policy decisions.

The second area is the problem of the support of the teacher in developing his pupils. This was connected in this school with the problem of the peripheral staff, but it has mainly to do with variability and the kind of attitude which teachers have to pupils and in the dominance of discipline problems in certain teachers.

We cannot understand or deal with the problem of intermediate management if we confine our analysis to structural or task consideration. Already we have seen that the question of staff attachment or commitment enters in. The problem is also interconnected with the other two—uncertainty and ambiguity in goals, and the support of teachers. It is particularly with the latter two that the impact of local environmental pressures is most directly evident.

In thinking about goals, there were important differences in emphasis between teachers as between a concern for academic standards, a concern for what might be called humanity and caring and a concern for control and rectitude in the behaviour of pupils. The last point connects with the bother of some teachers over discipline. To some extent the headmaster's manifest concern about individual pupils was seen by some staff as lack of support for them. Local pressures, as we have seen, were strong in the direction of requiring control, supporting the 'humanity' ethos, but weak in demand for scholarship.

Organizational adaptation is therefore not simply a question of task definition and task differentiation. There were constraining pressures in the school derived from the need to maintain or to strengthen the level of social control in the school.

Four key areas for attention in organizational analysis were, in this case, linked through the organizational problems described:

(1) Environmental pressures
(2) Policy and task formulation
(3) Internal culture
(4) Task organization.

Environmental pressures made for uncertainty and ambiguity in policy and task formulation, and for pressure to attend to the ethos, in particular, in the internal culture. The difficulties in task formulation and emphasis, and the constraint on staffing structures made for problems in intermediate management levels, which in turn made for difficulties in cohesion and support. Adaptations in task emphasis (for instance in scholastic emphasis or in more flexible task organization) were constrained by conceptions about environmental pressures.

Alternative forms of task organization were discussed and examined during the project. In understanding alternative forms of management differentiation, we may contrast two forms, neither of which would necessarily be capable of operation in concrete circumstances. The first of these ideal forms is the 'confederation of village schools' characterized by:

(1) Continuity of pupil group within week and year.
(2) Continuity of teacher contact with it.
(3) Small teacher-set or group of teachers to which each child is exposed.
(4) Wide range of subjects or problems in teacher–pupil relations.

The opposite forms we may call the 'confederation of special schools' characterized by:

(1) Variation in pupil groups within week and year.
(2) Variations in teacher contact.
(3) Large teacher-set.
(4) Special narrow range of subjects or problems in teacher–pupil relations.

The first is well adapted to conduct P-type activities, that is to pay attention to the whole child. Its differentiation into operating units is neither by department principles nor by course specialization but by territory. Primary schools operating a series of family-grouped classes would be an approximation to this model.

The second model is well adapted to pursue O-type activities of a specialized nature. Its principles of differentiation would be departmental or technical. A university to some extent approximates to this model.

Difficulties in operation for the first model lie in the area of the development of sufficient expertise to handle special subject matter. For the second model they lie in the area of paying sufficient attention to the total activities of each pupil or student to be able to help him make his way through the community.

The study of Lauriston School suggests that no single form of organization would be suitable for all kinds or all ages of pupils and that a considerable degree of organizational complexity is required. No single organizational principle can be so supra-ordinate over others that it can provide the basis for a single and unequivocal set of work differentiations. Essentially, the operation of cross-cutting principles is required. I have come to call such organization 'dual' or 'multiple'. It is in some usages referred to as matrix organization (e.g. Mee, 1964). This term is in my view better reserved for the more flexible and open forms of contractual or trading relations between departments with special tasks. It may be that matrix organization in this sense is appropriate for a secondary school operation, but I would not wish to advocate this point systematically.

Dual organization on the principles of course specialization and departmental or professional specialization has been attempted in some technical colleges and polytechnics. Difficulties have arisen according to my understanding because of the difficulty in aligning the two kinds of hierarchy with a single career structure (which are the more senior jobs, course or departmental directors?), and with territorial differentiations (which rooms do you put together, course or departmental?). Dual organization on operational and pilotage principles appears in the house system in residential schools, and subsequently in day schools; and also in the collegiate system in certain universities such as Oxford, Cambridge, York and Kent.

In this and presumably other secondary schools, one has not only these problems but also that of the flexibility of altered emphasis on course and departmental specialization according to the varying ages and individual needs of pupils. Conceptualizing the problems and solutions in each case is not an easy job. In many ways schools and other educational institutions represent more difficulties in conceptualization and in management than do industrial enterprises.

Structure Representation, Task and Group

One of the key problems of looking at organization from the managerial point of view is that of assessing the efficiency of the functioning of social systems. The social system in this case is an enterprise, which can be defined as an organization of people and materials about some common task. It should therefore in principle be possible to define what that task is and to establish criteria against which the efficacy of its performance can be assessed, and then to assess current functioning in these terms. There are, however, conceptual difficulties, both general and specific in this case.

The general conceptual difficulty is that of attempting to match ideal situations with real life organizational processes (Etzioni, 1960). The specific difficulties of attempting even to define objectives in a school are enormous, once we move beyond such goals as maximizing successes in public examinations or minimizing cost per pupil place, neither of which matches closely educational criteria that thinking teachers would wish to advance. They might well, however, be adopted as objectives by certain parents and by certain factions within the official environment. Criteria to assess the attainment of other objectives like those set by the leadership of this school as constituting its task mix are very difficult to establish in quantifiable terms. One is concerned with establishing policy in an area of ambiguity, uncertainty and conflict. Both at the time of the study and now we tended to lower our sights from these problems and to concern ourselves with the analytical account of what was actually happening in the school.

The definition of an enterprise as an organization of people and materials about a common task raises a number of issues immediately. I believe it to be helpful to adopt the idea of organization as distinct from the ideas of structure and function. This distinction has been made quite clearly by Burns (1963), who proposed to relate them in such a way that it would be possible to say of some particular set-up or enterprise that its activities were organized so as to maintain the structure or alternatively that its activities were organized so as to alter the structure.

In thinking about the specific problems of this school, I reached a slightly different standpoint from that produced by Burns. I see structure arising out of, or as one way of saying something about, the organization. Classically, one can say in any case that social structure is a patterning of social behaviour, typically defined in terms of a constellation of social roles or positions. I would see the relation between structure in this sense and organization as simply that behaviour is organized and that structure is a statement about the design of this organization or about its programme. A statement about structure is, as it were, a momentary freezing of the pattern of organization from the particular point of view. It seems clear that structure as seen by one person need not necessarily be the structure as seen by another person, and that the best we can say about the 'structure' is that it would represent the best consensus available. Design of task organization, seen technically, is not necessarily free to adapt to operational demands, because of the way in which tasks are organized into roles and are linked thereby with the concerns and objectives which people carrying the roles have with issues of authority, status, power and personal needs. These can bind and constrain the change of task structure. (This point is argued in a little more detail in Hutton (1971)).

So far so good, but if one uses terms this way, then how is it possible for an organization to change or to alter a structure when the structure is merely a set of abstract statements about the organization itself. I was struck here by an analogy with personality theory where we can have a model for a structure of personality and where this model can include as a part a particular organization which we can call the self-image or the self-representation. This is not the same thing as the whole structure or the whole organization of personality but is a sub-region of the total organization. It makes perfect sense to talk about behaviour so being organized as to maintain the integrity of self-representation. I was led then to think by analogy that there might be operating in an enterprise, that is to say, in the actual thinking of members of it, something which we might call a structure representation and that this was not necessarily consonant with the best consensus of the structure which we might get, taking all the available factors into account the best we are able to. The discrepancy might be due to only part of the information being taken into account. It might be due to a persistence of a well-fitting idea beyond the time when it fitted any longer. If the organization changes, the structure changes inevitably, but a structure representation might persist. This is perhaps only saying that things might have changed without people noticing it, but the representation might be so discrepant as actually to disguise from people the nature of the current role structure. Inasmuch as role structure is in any case not defined solely with respect to work or task organization but is constrained by authority, status, power and personal needs, so structure representation can act as a further constraint.

It seemed to me that there were three core ideas in understanding the situation in this school. The first is that there was a current structure representation which was discrepant from the actual structure and that the organization to some extent was concerned with maintaining the structure representation as well as getting on with the effectual prosecution of the task. The structure representation had persisted from the days when the school was smaller and was in its heroic phase and the feeling associated with it matched some of the concerns and bothers expressed by people in the district. To some extent the school was behaving as though it had not achieved the degree of positive reputation among people who knew it which our evidence showed that it had. The second core idea is that of discrepant and ambiguous goals which was discussed above. The third was the way in which commitment goups had acted as a cohesive force in the face of demands for organizational complexity which had not been systematically appreciated or met.

This was a successful school judged by the esteem which its work had gained in certain local educational and parental circles, at least in respect of its humanities and order. It was perhaps working in an unusually unfavourable general climate of local opinion but it was not this alone which produced the organizational complexities and ambiguities which characterized this school and, most likely, many others.

Postscript

The Position in 1971

During the drafting of this paper, I revisited the school, both to seek agreement to publication, and to check on development subsequent to the period of the study.

The school had now become a comprehensive school, with a sixth form. The headmaster had retired, and his successor had been in role for just over two years. His appraisal of the situation was that there was an atmosphere of humanity and a well-developed way of looking at individual children, but there were three major points for attention. These were the relatively weak academic standard, the existence of single-sex classes in a mixed-sex school and the alienation of older children in lower streams. His initial policies for organizational development comprised the introduction of a house system (which he had had experience of introducing in his last school), coupled with the unstreaming and mixing of classes. He spent a year working with the staff in preparing for the changes.

The house system separated fifth- and sixth-year pupils to allow for a distinct treatment and working climate. Other houses were mixed for sex and age, and divided into 'groups' which replaced forms and which were mixed for sex and ability within a single year. Register teachers were replaced by group tutors, and the new posts of house directors were recognized, and paid, as equivalent to heads of department—the first school in the City to establish the principle.

The school had thus established a full dual work organization, the departments dealing essentially with O activities, and the houses with P and Q activities. Two new deputy headmasters were beginning to develop functional specializations approximating to this same split.

In terms of the analysis of the situation existing a few years before, the headmaster and staff had innovated organizational forms to cope with the lack of cohesion at middle level managing systems. I did not attempt to evaluate the effectiveness of the changes, and the staff I met were not willing yet to do so. There had been substantial difficulties in coping with the changes, and people were cautious at claiming success. Some did agree that the pupils liked the new arrangements.

References

Burns, T. (1963), Organization, A paper read to the British Sociological Association, Scottish Branch, Edinburgh, February 1963.

Etzioni, A. (1960), Two approaches to organizational analysis: a critique and a suggestion, *Admin. Sci. Qtly.*, **5**, 257–278.

Hutton, G. (1962), Managing systems in hospitals—the implications of a case study, *Human Relations* **15**, 311–333.

Hutton, G. (1971), *Thinking about Organization*, 2nd ed., Tavistock Publications, London.

Lawrence, P. R. and Lorsch, J. W. (1967), *Organization and Environment: Managing Differentiation and Integration*, Harvard Graduate School of Business Administration, Boston.

Mee, J. F. (1964), Matrix organization, *Business Horizons*, and *in:* Cleland, D. I. and King, W. R. (1969), *Systems, Organizations, Management*, McGraw-Hill, New York.

Miller, E. J. and Rice, A. K. (1967), *Systems of Organization*, Tavistock Publications, London.

Rice, A. K., Hill, J. M. M. and Trist, E. L. (1950), The representation of labour turnover as a social process, *Human Relations* **3**, 349–372.

Entry into the Mental Health Centre: a Problem in Organizational Boundary-Regulation

Daniel Levinson and Boris Astrachan[1]

The problem of *entry* is a fundamental and pervasive one in individual and organizational life. For the individual, the problem is one of *getting in*: gaining admission to school, union, professional society, neighbourhood, social network and the like. Getting a job means, in effect, achieving entry into a work organization. To obtain the services of a health organization, one must initially go through an 'intake' procedure by which applicants are screened and selectively admitted. Indeed, the term *'applicant'* can be used generically to refer to a social position at the boundary gate of a social system; applicant and system examine each other with an eye to his possible admission into the system and access to its resources. Similarly, the term 'applicanthood' refers to the condition of being an applicant. It is a common condition and one that merits further study.[2]

From the vantage point of the organization, entry involves the problems of *bringing in* and *letting in* members (employees, students, patients, clients, customers). Our chief concern here is with the entry of clients into an organization for which the primary task is to bring about important changes in its clients. The example to be used is the community mental health centre, though similar issues are found across the broad spectrum of health–education–welfare organizations. By various means, direct and indirect, every mental health centre recruits an applicant population and, through its screening ('admissions' or 'intake') procedures, selectively allows some applicants to enter as patients while rejecting other applicants or referring them elsewhere.

The entry system serves crucial functions for the organization. It is a major element in the relation of the organization to its environment (in the local community and the wider society). It determines the character and composition of the client population that will receive the organization's services (treatment, education, rehabilitation, etc.). If the entry system operates ineffectively, the organization will be faced with an overabundance or a scarcity of clients, or with a client population inappropriate for the services offered. Also if, as so often happens, it operates in ways that humiliate, intimidate or degrade the applicants, this has serious consequences: the 'rejected' applicants often have a damaging experience without receiving direct service or a referral to a more appropriate source; and the 'successful' applicants often form a conception of the organization (as impersonal, insensitive, oppressive or the like) that runs counter to its educational or therapeutic philosophy and interferes with the work to be done.

Given the importance of the entry system, it is remarkable how little attention has been paid to problems of its design, functioning and evaluation.[3] Especially in psychiatric facilities, authority over the entry system is usually located in a position of limited organizational authority (or is diffused to such a degree that no one quite knows *who* is responsible), and the entry system is rarely subject to systematic evaluation and redesign. There is a growing recognition that health organizations are not sufficiently aware of, nor responsive to, actual community needs. If progress is to be made in this direction, it is essential to develop a more systematic view of entry both as an intra-organizational task and as a link between organization and community.

In this paper we present a conception of the entry system (ES) as a major component of the client-serving organization. Our primary aims are as follows:

(1) To describe the place of the ES within the overall organizational structure. The ES exists at the boundary between the organization and its environment; it thus has crucial consequences both for the internal workings of the organization and for the relationship between organization and environment.

(2) To specify the major tasks of the ES. These are: (*a*) receiving and dealing with the applicant population; (*b*) providing a link between the newly admitted patient and the treatment system; (*c*) providing a link between the mental health centre and the community. Clear definition of a system's tasks is an important precondition for the design, operation and evaluation of the system.

(3) For each task, to identify some of the major problems involved, to consider some of the ways in which it is now handled in different clinical facilities and to offer suggestions for the design of better ES's. In particular, we shall focus on the various linkages which mental health organizations develop with their communities (task *c*) and the relationship of the ES and organizational management.

Throughout, we shall be taking a combined *clinical-organizational* approach. Clinical considerations are of primary importance in understanding, evaluating and improving the ways in which a mental health centre deals with the entry of patients. At the same time, designing and managing an entry *system*, and relating it both to other parts of the organization and to the external environment, requires a perspective beyond the purely clinical. This broader perspective involves a conception of organizational structure and functioning, and a broader framework that places the organization in the immediate community and the larger society. Clinicians often find organizational theory excessively impersonal and mechanistic (Levinson and Klerman, 1967). Organizational scientists often find the more 'human' aspects of organizational life uninteresting, irrelevant or too difficult to include within their more behaviouristic models. This paper is an attempt to define a middle ground—a conception of the organization that takes into account its psychological aspects as well as others.

The Place of the Entry System within the Organizational Structure

We conceive of the organization as an open system that engages in continuing transactions with its environment (Miller and Rice, 1967; Rice, 1963; Sheldon and coworkers, 1970). It must obtain selectively from the environment diverse *inputs* (persons, ideas, material resources, etc.) that are essential for its survival and growth. It must also have the capability of giving selectively to the environment diverse *outputs* that are direct or indirect products of its work. The primary work of the organization is on the *throughput*—the 'raw material' that it imports, converts into a product having greater value in certain important respects, and then exports. In the case of a production industry, the throughput is physical raw materials that are converted into presumably useful commodities such as cars or furniture which are then sold at a profit through which new inputs can be obtained. In the case of a health organization, the major throughput is the patient or client population—persons who are 'imported' in a state of illness, suffering or impaired functioning, who receive services that presumably bring them to a higher level of health, competence, or capacity for living, and who are then discharged (exported).[4]

We shall use the term 'entry system' to identify that part of the organization which is concerned with the admission and screening of patients, and which serves as one of several elements linking the centre to the communities served. Organizational management has the major responsibility for regulating the interaction of centre and communities and through that process identifying priorities for service. An important issue for human service organizations is the degree to which structures can be established, staffed and developed to carry out institution–community interaction, as well as the degree to which entry systems serve as the interface between organization and communities.

Conceptually, the ES may be said to form a *boundary region* between the organization and its environment. A boundary serves two major functions for an open system. First, it has a *separating* function: it draws a line, so to speak, that distinguishes what is within the organization (or organism or other open system) from what is external to it. Reasonably clear definition of its boundaries is crucially important for any organization. The establishing of boundaries is an essential part of the process by which a system develops its own character and becomes capable of initiative and action in relation to its environment.

In addition to the separating or demarcating function, the boundary has a *transactional* function: it exists not to encapsulate the organization but to enable useful intercourse between system and environment (Boulding, 1968; Hall and Fagen, 1968; Danielli, 1973). The regulation of external boundary transactions is essential for the survival and growth of the organization. This means that a boundary is to be conceived of not simply as a line marking the outer limits of the system but as a multi-dimensional *region* created at the margin—a region within which subsystems are generated to regulate transactions with the environment. In principle, a boundary should be regarded not as a static divider or barrier or encapsulating device (though in some cases it may take this form) but rather as a highly functional, active region in which vital regulating functions occur; it must therefore be subject to change in accord with changing internal and external requirements. A boundary region exists only to the extent that the organization has created a structure which regulates its exchange with the environment. That is, boundary *structures* are needed to create the *space* within which selective transactions can occur.

The ES of a mental health centre has both of the boundary functions noted above. It defines the boundary between patient and non-patient, and makes the determining judgment in each case. Needy persons outside the centre can 'get in'—can gain membership as patient and access to its services—only by getting across the boundary defined by the ES. For the organization, the ES has the *primary task of regulating the patient-input boundary so as to import an appropriate patient population at a manageable rate.*

If patients are admitted at too fast a rate the treatment system may be flooded and the therapeutic work impaired. If patients are admitted too slowly, the private institution may be forced out of business or the public institution may lose its budget and its mandate. If the ES admits patients who do not need or cannot use the available services, the provision of service becomes pointless. In this case, it becomes necessary: (*a*) to change the ES so it recruits more 'appropriate' patients, or (*b*) to change the treatment system so it offers services that are more appropriate to the population seeking help. The classic example of this dilemma is the out-patient clinic that offers primarily long-term psychotherapy (after a long waiting period) in a predominantly lower-middle or lower class community (Levinson and coworkers, 1967; Schneiderman, 1965). The staff spend most of their time screening out applicants who desperately need help—but not the kind being offered. As we shall see shortly when we examine the major tasks of the ES, the definition of what constitutes an 'appropriate' patient population has to be considered in relation to the kinds of service offered. This involves basic issues of policy and is problematic for every clinical facility. The key question: To what extent can services be modified so that they are relevant to the needs of the populations to be served?

From the point of view of open-system theory, the management sector of an organization has two crucial tasks.

(1) It must ensure that the 'conversion' work—manufacturing, educating, providing treatment and the like—is effectively carried out.

(2) It must ensure that the external boundaries are regulated in ways that foster the survival and continued growth (or, at some point, the appropriate demise) of the organization. Both of these are essential for organizational well-being. Responsibility for the first can be delegated largely to second and third levels of management. If top management centres its efforts primarily upon the internal subsystems, the organization will become encapsulated and out of touch with its environment; it will then inevitably be weakened in its capacity for growth and for creative adaptation to changes in the environment. The regulation of external boundaries must be the first priority of top management,

through their own direct involvement and through the creation of effective boundary systems. Top management must also develop mechanisms for facilitating information transmission, interaction and resource allocation with managers responsible for internal task accomplishment. The effective management of external boundaries is only a continuing pre-condition for high level task performance. Management of the boundaries and management of the internal work of the organization require differing but equally competent leadership (Hodgson and coworkers, 1965).

The ES, regulating as it does one of the major external boundaries, thus requires a direct tie to top management. The head of the ES should be a member of the executive group of the mental health centre or should report to a member of this group. There are at least two important reasons for this. First, the ES feeds the treatment system. In admitting patients the ES has in effect the power to commit the resources of the treatment system. The boundary between these two systems requires high-level review and regulation. Second, the ES is a vital link between mental health centre and community. It is a potentially valuable (though typically underdeveloped) means by which the organization can influence. and be influenced by, the community.

We have briefly identified the ES as a component of organizational structure and have traced its connections to other components as well as to the external environment. We turn now to a consideration of the major tasks of the ES and the various structural arrangements by which these tasks may be carried out.

Major Tasks of the Entry System

As we have noted above, the central or underlying function of the ES is to regulate the patient-input boundary so as to import an appropriate patient population at a manageable rate. At a more operational level, this involves two major tasks:

Task 1. *To receive and deal with the applicant population* (the admission, gatekeeping, referring function).

Task 2. *To provide a link between the newly admitted patient and the treatment system.*

The first two tasks involve the ES in boundary-regulating activities related to the internal needs of the organization. In addition, the entry system participates in other organizational boundary-regulating activities that are part of the larger management's responsibilities. In these activities the organization interacts with, is modified by and attempts to influence its environments. We must take into account, therefore, an additional task of the ES that is often neglected:

Task 3. *To serve, along with other boundary structures, as a link between the mental health centre and the community.*

We shall consider the three tasks in turn.

Task 1: To Receive and Deal with the Applicant Population

The 'processing' of prospective patients is the most obvious function of the entry system. Every clinical facility has an intake or admission unit that serves this task, but such units vary widely in their stated purposes, structure and modes of functioning.

We conceive of the admission work as a process of exploration and negotiation between various parties (including the patient, one or more staff members and one or more third parties), with the aim of deciding whether the applicant will become a patient in this facility or will do something else. For present purposes, we may group the possible outcomes of this process as follows:

(1) The applicant *enters a treatment programme* in this organization.

(2) The applicant *receives limited service by the admission unit*; he is seen several times and given some assistance in handling a current crisis.

(3) He is *referred* elsewhere. The referral may be a form of 'dumping' in which the facility irresponsibly gets rid of unwelcome applicants; or it may be done in a responsible manner, when the facility cannot offer appropriate help but works with the applicant to obtain such help from another source.

(4) After a brief initial contact, the *applicancy is terminated*.[5] The termination may be decided unilaterally by the applicant, who is then defined as a 'dropout' —often with the collusion of the organization through its indifference or rejection. Ideally, the decision to terminate the application will be based on joint discussion and negotiation between applicant and staff, and the applicant will leave with a better understanding of the kind of help he wants (if any) and the kind of help that is available should he someday want it.

In the ideal of the helping professions, the admission process will be carried out on a basis of mutual respect and dignity among the various parties involved. The task is to determine what the applicant needs and wants, what this facility can offer, and, if there is a disparity, what alternative options might be available. Coercive elements in this process will be minimized; that is, the facility will not be under pressure to offer inappropriate treatment and the applicant will not be forced to enter treatment against his will.

This ideal is difficult to sustain; by and large, it is honoured more in the breach than in the practice. If the admission process is to be made more humane and collaborative, if the elements of coercion and degradation (for both the applicant and the staff) are to be minimized, much greater attention must be given to admission as an organizational problem (one that includes, but goes beyond, individual staff attitudes and skills). An essential element in the humanizing of the admission process is exploration and forthright identification of the differential power and authority of the various parties in this process.

Many clinical facilities are legally required to accept for treatment every applicant who meets certain eligibility requirements (e.g. residence, income, court order) whether or not the services it offers are indeed appropriate. In these cases the admission unit cannot adequately control its boundary. It is likely to admit patients indiscriminately, in too large numbers, and thus to flood the treatment units. When the treatment staff regard the admission unit as a leaky sieve, they find their own (often illicit) ways of generating protective boundaries so that unwelcomed patients are neglected, transferred or discharged early through a 'revolving door'.

On the other hand, the admission unit may 'overcontrol' the boundary, admitting only a very special group of applicants and turning away large numbers who are considered unsuitable. This has been a striking phenomenon in out-patient clinics offering primarily longer-term psychotherapy; typically, about 20–30 per cent of the applicants have received more than minimal service, while most of the others drop out or get lost on the waiting list (Brill and Storrow, 1960; Harrison and coworkers, 1965). In facilities of this kind the primary organizational task is defined very narrowly as the provision of an extremely limited range of services to a small number of patients who meet the staff's criteria of suitability. Large numbers of actual or potential applicants are neglected and major community needs are unmet.

No mental health centre can cover the full spectrum of direct and indirect services: nor can it expect to offer treatment to every applicant in need. In other words, it is not necessary that the outcome of applicancy always be the first of the four options noted above (treatment). The admission unit can be said to have done a good job when it offers its own limited service (such as crisis intervention) where this is indicated, when it negotiates and carries through an appropriate referral, or when as a result of its work with the applicant he gets a clearer idea of the kinds of help available and decides against trying any of them at this time (termination).

The entry system should be much more than a sieve or gatekeeper allowing some applicants in and excluding the rest. It can do useful work in helping the applicant consider and evaluate alternative sources of assistance and, when he so chooses, in facilitating his efforts to gain assistance elsewhere. This means that the entry system must constitute a boundary structure that links the organization not only to the applicant population but also to numerous other systems (health, education, welfare, employment) in the community. *An admission unit that is highly encapsulated within its own facility is severely handicapped in its work.* An encapsulated unit may function as a loose sieve that admits virtually all applicants indiscriminately; or it may follow a highly restrictive policy of admitting only the most 'suitable' patients; but it will have great difficulty in making alternative resources available and in working bilaterally with applicants toward a negotiated outcome.

Finally, we must take note of the fact that there are often multiple parties to the admission process. Various persons, groups and institutions have a stake, and may wish to have a voice, in the outcome of the applicancy. Family members (spouse, parents, children), referring professional or agency, employer, school, insurance company, police, courts and the like are frequently involved in the applicant's difficulties and in the search to obtain—or to avoid—some form of treatment. They play an important part in arguing or opposing treatment and in defining the terms on which treatment will take place.

The presence of the various 'third parties' creates many potential hazards. They may sabotage every effort to bring about a sustained course of treatment. They may intrude so strongly that it is they, rather than the patient, who arrange for admission and define the treatment contract. When the patient is not a responsible party to the initial decisions and planning, he is not likely to become a responsible participant with a strong internal commitment to the therapeutic enterprise.

Along with the considerable risks, however, there are also great advantages to the inclusion of relevant others. It is essential that the admission staff take into account the major systems (family, work, etc.) in which the applicant is currently involved and, where this seems in the applicant's interest, that it include them in the admission process and beyond (Astrachan and coworkers, 1968; Detre and coworkers, 1961; Fleck, 1963). The staff have a special responsibility, of course, not to get caught up in the frequently destructive struggles between the patient and significant others. The ambivalent efforts of a severely disturbed young adult to extricate himself from his family, and to make a place for himself within the adult world, may be doomed unless other family members join the therapeutic endeavour, learning to facilitate his change and to change themselves as well. Also, especially when a person is being hospitalized, he is crossing various group boundaries—entering a new system and giving up or modifying his membership in existing systems. In this process, his own boundaries as a person are threatened. The stresses of entering treatment are added to those that brought him to seek treatment. The admission unit should recognize and help deal with these, serving as a social–clinical link between applicant and treatment programme. Entry into patienthood is a crucial period in the patient's career. The admission unit provides a context that shapes his course through this period and thus has a major impact upon his subsequent career as a patient.

These considerations bring us to the second task of the entry system.

Task 2: To Provide a Link between the Entering Patient and the Treatment System

The focus in Task 1, above, was on the mental health centre's reception, through its admission unit, of the applicant population as a whole. We use the term 'applicant' to point out the fact that not all persons who seek help are taken into the organization's treatment system. The admission unit can provide extremely useful services of various kinds to applicants, whatever the outcome of applicancy.

This second task involves the work of the entry system with the applicants whom it admits into one or another of the centre's treatment units (in-patient ward, day hospital, out-patient psychotherapy, family therapy, extended medication programme and the like). The admission unit serves as a link between the newly admitted patients and the treatment units, and it has important functions for both.

For the entering patient, the admission unit is the place where he establishes his membership as a patient in the mental health centre. In it he begins to form an impression of the organization as a whole, of the staff, of the gross and subtle character of staff–staff and staff–patient relationships, of the ways in which his personal dignity will be respected or demeaned. It is a source of learning and a taste of things to come. For many patients, the admission process yields a first, and lasting, sense of what it means to be a patient in this organization. It may be said that treatment begins in the treatment unit; but the course of admission has crucial effects that hinder or facilitate the patient's subsequent participation in the therapeutic work.

A major function of the admission process is to establish a therapeutic contract between the clinical facility, the patient, and any other parties involved. The contract may be solely between patient and clinical facility, but in many cases others are directly or indirectly involved. A referring physician may make the basic arrangements for admission and define the treatment goals, to such a degree that the patient becomes a relatively passive object of the admission procedures rather than an active agent in his own behalf. Other parties, such as the court, the school or the patient's family may also take an active part in defining the terms of admission and the goals of treatment.

Ideally, the patient will be reasonably satisfied with the negotiations relating to his admission. He will feel that he (rather than some third party) is the primary client, that his admission is primarily to help him rather than to serve the needs of others, that he has had a major voice in defining what the mental health centre will offer him and what are his responsibilities and goals as a patient. This ideal is rarely fully realized. To some degree (and often with more justification than staff care to admit) he is likely to feel that his admission is forced rather than voluntary, that the staff are agents of societal or familial control rather than of his health and well being, that the therapeutic contract is dishonest, oppressive, fraudulent.

The admission staff must identify these anti-therapeutic elements, attempt to minimize or eliminate those that are present, and then define ways of working clearly and explicitly within the context of those that remain. Entry is an initial, formative period in the person's evolving career as a patient. As in all developmental sequences, the unresolved problems of the earliest periods become obstacles to development in subsequent periods. If the patient initially feels oppressed, manipulated, deceived by those who brought about his admission, his relationship to the mental health centre and its clinical staff is seriously impaired. Until these difficulties are confronted and resolved, they will hamper all efforts of patient and staff to deal with the problems for which he is receiving treatment.

In principle, most clinicians would probably agree with this notion. On the basis of our experience and observation in many clinical facilities, however, we offer the following testable proposition: In every clinical facility, *the problems most frequently encountered in the process of termination* (including pre-discharge transitional period) will be directly related to *problems in the entry process that went unresolved at entry and were neglected during the course of treatment.*

Analytically, the admission process can be divided into two stages: (*a*) the decision that the applicant shall receive treatment of some kind in this organization; and (*b*) the decision that he shall be admitted to a particular treatment unit (ward, clinic, programme) or seen by a particular clinician. In some facilities, the treatment unit is almost entirely responsible for its own admissions, so that it in effect makes both decisions. This arrangement is most feasible in a small hospital containing several roughly equivalent wards. It is not possible in a mental health centre or other multipurpose organization. Here, a central admission unit is needed for the initial reception of all applicants. The admission unit decides whether an applicant shall be admitted and, if so, to which treatment unit.

The management of the boundary between the central admission unit and the treatment unit is of crucial importance. If the admission unit feeds in too few patients, the treatment unit will be deprived and underemployed. If, as is more often the case, the treatment unit is sent too many patients, or too many difficult patients at a time when tensions are already great, the entire treatment programme may be threatened. The adequacy of the arrangements enabling communication and negotiation between the admission unit and each of the treatment units is thus a basic condition of effective treatment.

In our view, it is necessary that the admission unit have the authority to commit the treatment resources of the organization; such authority is a corollary of its responsibility to receive and deal with the applicant population. It is wasteful of organizational energy, and hurtful to entering patients, for the treatment unit to conduct a duplicate admission procedure in order to decide whether it will accept the patient. There are times when a treatment unit must be required to accept a patient despite the strains this will create. For this to work, the treatment units have to be identified with, and regard themselves as an integral part of, the organization as a whole. This requires effective leadership internal to the organization which is committed to the goals of both the organization and the individual subunits.

The authority of the admission unit will be effective only if it is seen by the treatment unit as legitimate and reasonably just. When a technology for clear assignment to treatment does not exist, assignments by the entry system will appear arbitrary. If clear distinctions can be made, as for example between in-patient and out-patient treatment, the entry unit should be able to insist upon locus of treatment. The treatment unit should, however, have wide latitude in the choice of treatment modality; for example, the choice as to individual, group or family out-patient therapy should be made by staff and patient within the out-patient unit. If the admission unit operates in a highly autocratic, unilateral manner, allowing the treatment unit insufficient voice in the allocation process, the costs will be great for both the unwelcome patient and the organization. The gap between the two units will be experienced by the patient as a void; he will be unprepared for his entry into the treatment unit, and it will be unreceptive to him. Every group has its ways of disposing of unwelcome newcomers.

As we have said, this is primarily a matter of boundary management between interdependent units within an organization. Adequate linkage of the units depends upon at least the following conditions: (a) that a managerial structure exist, with its members drawn from the leadership of admission as well as treatment units, and with authority to establish, review and modify policy (Lynton, 1969); (b) that the admission unit be regarded (as it often is not) as performing an essential and valued function and its head as a first-class professional capable of exercising high-level authority; (c) that collaborative relationships develop between the staffs of the linked units so that joint consultation and the negotiation of disagreements can regularly occur; and (d) where feasible, that staff of one unit work part-time in the other, thus contributing both to staff collaboration and to the ease with which patients move from admission to treatment unit.

The two tasks above are the primary responsibility of the entry system, which manages the major input into the mental health centre—the individuals who receive service. There are, of course, numerous other boundary transactions between the organization and its communities. It acquires a variety of inputs (staff, supplies, etc.); it exports a variety of outputs (community members with enhanced job skills, research reports, etc.); and it maintains relationships to a number of groups and organizations (community groups, professional societies, family service agencies, health delivery organizations, etc.) through which productive transactions can occur. The mental health centre must create multiple boundary structures for the management of these relationships. We turn next to a consideration of what we have already identified as the primary task of organizational management, namely, regulating the linkages between organization and community. We shall consider the place of the ES in this process.

Task 3: To Serve, along with other Boundary Structures, as a Link between the Mental Health Centre and its Communities

The primary task of an organization will importantly influence the goals and the structure of its relationship to its communities. The primary task of a *private psychiatric hospital* is to make a profit through providing good treatment. It may (by custom rather than by charter) draw its patients from a local community or from a referring network covering many parts of the country. Its communities will include the physicians who refer, the voluntary sector (most often people with prestige and power) who help raise funds and speak well of its services, the pool of potential patients from which it draws and to a greater or lesser extent its immediate neighbours. It will endeavour to keep all of these communities pleased with its services. Viewing its community relations as educative tasks, it will seek to educate physicians about psychiatric referral, to destigmatize mental illness and particularly its own services and to be part of the city or town (lecturing at P.T.A.'s about mental health, etc.). The ES staff will have only a small part in these tasks, but their work will be significantly influenced by management's success in managing hospital–community boundaries.

The primary task of *state psychiatric hospitals* is to care for those who are identified as sufficiently ill to require in-hospital, relatively intense attention. The population receiving such 'service' is defined by society, family and/or self as meeting the appropriate criteria for hospitalization. Statutory definitions in regard to hospitalization will seek to maintain societal tranquillity while protecting individual rights. This primary task has significant implications in regard to the nature of service offered and the communities to which the hospital will relate. One such population is, of course, the patients served, or those who seek to protect their rights. The 'right to psychiatric treatment' currently being debated in various states is now identified not as an unlimited right but as a right only for those who are shown, through commitment procedures, to require hospitalization. If hospitalization is required, treatment must be available.

State hospital management relates to numerous sectors of the community: to legislative groups, which provide funding, define tasks—although often only implicitly—and review functions; to voluntary groups, which speak for quality of care and help educate the public; to referral sources such as physicians and clergy; and to the area where the hospital is located, and in which it is often the major employer, the major purchaser of services and consumer of utilities, and the major source of local controversy. In regard to such boundary relationships the ES has few tasks. In state hospitals criteria for admissions are to a large extent externally defined (e.g. commitment processes; service to diagnostic groups such as the alcoholic or drug addict, etc.). In these circumstances the ES participates little in relating hospital to environments. Even when the hospital has responsibility for a defined geographic area, as long as its primary task is in-patient care and treatment the ES need have only minimal ties to the geographical area served. Small wonder that the state hospital has been so distant and encapsulated from its environs; the barriers (rather than exchange-promoting boundaries) created between hospital and community help to limit the numbers of patients and to increase the autonomy of the hospital—but at a great cost in terms of the therapeutic effectiveness and the humaneness of hospital life. As the state hospital attempts to develop a more diverse and flexible service system, and to be more responsive to community needs, it must develop a more effective entry system with links to many segments of the community.

The main case to be considered here, however, is the community mental health centre that is committed to provide a comprehensive range of services to a defined, bounded community. Implicit in the conception of 'comprehensive services' is the idea that the particular services offered at any given time will be *geared to the needs of the community* at that time; and that there will be changes in the services offered and in the segments of the community that are given special priority on the basis of *changing community needs and therapeutic capabilities.*

The primary task of such a centre is much more difficult to define because its potential mandate for service is so broad. A 'comprehensive' service system should include in- and out-patient treatment programs, emergency services, partial hospitalization, preventive and educative programs, consultation and intervention in other organizations and communities (Community Mental Health Centers Act, 1963). Is the task to treat the severely ill, to be available to those in pain, to work for community change in directions that foster mental health? With a vaguely defined, broad mandate the potential for action is relatively great. Resources are never unlimited, however, and the mental health centre cannot provide an unlimited range of service. It therefore establishes *priorities* for service, e.g. emphasis on direct versus indirect services; work with the severely ill versus work with those manifesting early symptoms of dysfunction; choice of specific population areas. In planning for direct services, it identifies target populations. Information from an ES is often critically important in this work. Also, staff behaviour in the ES will give dramatic evidence of the centre's relationship to the community.

In establishing and modifying its service priorities, the mental health centre needs to be knowledgeable of and responsibe to community needs. Considerable effort must be devoted to the boundary between centre and community (Sheldon and coworkers, 1970; Astrachan, 1973; Baker and O'Brien, 1971). The centre needs active ties with other health agencies, private practitioner networks, referral sources and therapeutic resources of all kinds. Beyond these, it has to develop working relationships with numerous other groups and institutions: schools, courts, employment resources, welfare agencies, government programmes and groups representing various ethnic, religious, class and other sectors of the community. The ES requires input into such interaction because these centre-environment transactions may serve to increase the potential applicant pool or may be utilized as referral resources for the centre.

Management of these boundaries is, however, primarily the task of centre management. Such interaction between centre and community provides information about the incidence of persons-in-need who are not receiving mental health services. This information can play an important part in the development of extra-mural services of various kinds: field stations in the community, home services, consultation to schools and other organizations, and preventive programmes oriented less toward clinical service than toward change in pathogenic institutional and community conditions.

The establishing of service priorities is not a purely intraorganizational matter. Multiple external groups and forces are involved. These include the following:

Local Political Pressures from local agencies, planning groups, community organizations and even at times partisan political groups. These groups may wish to participate in defining which population groups should have highest priority for service (e.g. inner city minority and poor versus affluent white suburban; those already being served in agencies versus the relatively unserved—alcoholics or geriatric patients, etc.). Although the pressures will be directed at centre management, the ES will be directly involved; for example, in their attempts to modify a centre's admission policies an agency or community group may present unserved patients for service to the entry system. Additionally, members of the ES will have useful sources of input about community resources (because of the ES's needs to refer back out to community) and community need.

Larger Scale Political Pressures from regional, state and federal agencies and 'sponsoring' groups, which often impose legal and financial constraints upon the nature of the area and population to be served. A mental health centre may serve a rather amorphous region containing multiple cities or towns or it may provide comprehensive service to a well-defined locality with relatively simple and identifiable political structures. The 'sponsoring' groups will participate actively in decision-making about allocation of funds and will have a critical influence in setting priorities. For example, the state may provide mandated funding for direct services and, without officially opposing indirect services, may simply fail to provide funds for them! The ES will generally not be significantly involved in this area.

Market Research. The centre can, in collaboration with other agencies and funding sources, develop planning and data analysis mechanisms to identify need and demand for service and even to identify what can be done, at what cost and to what benefit. This work requires an analysis of the centre's resources and skills and an ability to modify function as conditions change.

The centre must develop boundary structures in addition to an ES by which it carries out these complex explorations. The structures are monitored at the most senior managerial level. Input from community groups is organized and assimilated by the ES or by a separate community-focused unit.[6] Input from patient groups seeking service is collated and processed (by the ES alone or in conjunction with a programme evaluation section). Data from the unserved community are developed (particularly when no group is speaking for the unserved) and brought into conjunction with the other collected information. Information about preferred priorities from funders is then tied together with locally identified needs and demands.

In transactions occurring at the boundaries between two or more systems, none of the parties involved is in a position to exercise a high degree of authority over the outcome. One party may successfully impose its will in the short run, but in time the boundary arrangement will break down if it does not permit collaborative problem-solving, negotiation of disagreements, and a structure within which unresolved differences can be settled by an orderly due process. It is very difficult, however, to create boundary arrangements within which fruitful collaboration and negotiation can take place. Inadequate boundary structures have increasingly hindered the relationships of professional organizations (such as hospitals and universities) with each other and with the community. Greater progress has been made in the realm of labour-management relations, particularly through the use of government (third party) mediation and arbitration. Perhaps these models will in time be used in the health field. They are relevant to the formation of community boards and the vexing question of 'community control' or 'community participation' in the design and use of health facilities (Tischler, 1971; Tischler and coworkers, 1972).

The task of relating centre to community has immediate implications for the ES and the admission of patients to the centre, as well as larger implications about the very direction of the centre. Most mental health centres, like other health organizations, are severely lacking in the structures, staffing and resources needed to deal effectively with this task. The director, and perhaps the administrator, are frequently the only ones in senior management positions who spend a considerable part of their time on the external boundaries. There may be a number of individual staff members—such as a public relations officer, or a clerical staff for filing (but not seriously using) records, or some clinicians who do informal liaison work with other agencies—who occasionally leave their intramural labours, but these efforts are generally sporadic and unintegrated. They have limited impact upon organizational policy and limited utility in achieving organizational goals.

The managerial outlook reflected in this system of organization–community relationships may be called *proactive pluralism*. A major effort is made to involve the centre with diverse pressure groups on a local and wider level, each identifying service needs. The centre continually identifies its own purposes, capabilities and resources, as well as the capacity that other groups have for utilizing resources. It actively exchanges information with these groups. The centre uses its own willingness to modify its structures and programmes as a wedge to insist that other agencies and pressure groups modify their programmes and enhance their service capability. It is prepared to accommodate within a turbulent environment but it also defines its own values and goals and seeks actively to realize them.

If the mental health centre is to take seriously its responsibility to the community, it has to deal more effectively with the questions: What is our community? What are its health problems and needs? What part can we best play in meeting them? To do this, it must create structures capable of managing the various boundaries with external systems. These boundary structures must be integrated within the centre so that they can influence, and be influenced by, other parts of the organization.

The ES is one of the most important of the centre's boundary mechanisms. In its relationship with patients and community representatives, it serves as a visible model of centre-community relationships, a model which all too often underscores the inadequacy of those relationships. The ES provides data on service need and utilization and, by relating centre to other agencies for purposes of interagency referral, provides linkages that are beneficial to collaborating institutions. When the functions of an ES are neglected, and when the management of external boundaries is not made a major organizational task, the mental health centre cannot help but be split off from its community and be unable to engage in self-initiated change. The centre may continue on its long-established course, blissfully (or more often, painfully) ignorant of its deficiencies; or it may change capriciously, buffeted about by powerful external forces that it cannot understand or control. However, effective entry and management systems which continually interact with the centre's communities are essential if the centre is to take a proactive stance toward its environment, changing in accord with both external realities and its own values.

Notes

1. There is no adequate way of indicating, in the listing of authors' names, that two authors are equally responsible for their collaborative work. The order of names in this case has been determined by the flip of a coin. We wish to emphasize, however, that we are conjointly and equally responsible for the conception, content and writing of this paper.
2. For the successful applicant, the next step in the entry sequence is the position of *newcomer*, which is situated just inside the boundary of the system. The newcomer is formally a member but he must go through a process of *establishing his membership*: getting oriented in the system, achieving an identity within it, forming relationships, etc. The individual's further career in the system is initially (and often irrevocably) shaped during the periods of applicanthood and newcomerhood (Goffman, 1961; Levinson and coworkers, 1967).
3. With regard to the entry of personnel into industrial firms, there is a body of research on interviewing and other recruitment–selection procedures (Guion, 1967; Alderfer and McCord, 1970), but very little on the overall structure and functioning of the entry system.
4. In this paradigm the client is identified as the patient receiving direct clinical care. There are other paradigms as well. Thus, in the custodial mental hospital the primary client is often the family or a segment of society that finds the patient dangerous or noxious; the task of the hospital is not to treat the patient but to make life better for others by removing him from their midst. A very different paradigm is represented by the tasks of community organizing and organizational consulting as performed by certain mental health centres. In this case the client is an organization, group or total community, and the output involved is a reduction in social pathology or an increase in the health-promoting character of the community. Since the focus of the present paper is on the entry of patients receiving direct clinical service, we shall limit our consideration to the paradigm given in the text.
5. When resources for service are limited and the potential client population is large, entry systems develop structures and procedures to discourage or even prevent entry. This phenomenon has been amply described for mental health facilities. It has also been well documented by Piven and Cloward (1971) for Public Welfare Services. They cite admissions policies which are established to degrade applicants so as to exact a high cost from those requiring service. 'Secrecy, intimidation and red tape are adaptive patterns designed to inhibit completion of the application process and facilitate arbitrary rejections and terminations. Agency procedures are designed to make it easy and safe to reject or terminate cases but complicated and risky to accept them.' They identify the function of waiting periods and other 'rituals of degradation' as being to discourage utilization and make potential clients feel powerless.
6. In our experience, the task of relating organization to community is often devalued by clinicians and these tasks receive limited priority. In our organization negotiations with

community groups are initially developed by a Community Consultation Unit which has resources for community consultation and education and which can commit the resources of the admission unit to back up community-organized services.

References

Alderfer, C. P. and McCord, C. G. (1970), Personal and situational factors in the recruitment interview, *Journal of Applied Psychology*, **54**, 377–385.

Astrachan, B. M., Harrow, M. and Flynn, H. R. (1968), Influence of the value system of a psychiatric setting on behaviour in group therapy meetings, *Social Psychiatry*, **3**, 165–172.

Astrachan, B. M. (1973), Many modest goals: the pragmatics of health delivery, *Connecticut Medicine*, **37**, pp. 174–180.

Baker, F. and O'Brien, G. (1971), Intersystems relations and coordination of human service organizations, *American Journal of Public Health*, **61**, 130–137.

Boulding, K. E. (1968), General systems theory: the skeleton of science, *in*: Buckley, W., Ed., *Modern Systems Research for the Behavioral Scientist*, Aldine Publishing Company, Chicago.

Brill, N. Q. and Storrow, H. A. (1960), Social class and psychiatric treatment, *Arch. Gen. Psychiatry*, **3**, 340–344.

Community Mental Health Centers Act of 1963, Public Act 88–164, *Federal Register*, May 6th, 1964.

Danielli, J. F. (1973), The bilayer hypothesis of membrane structure, *Hospital Practice*, 63 71, January.

Detre, T., Sayres, J. Norton, N. M. and Lewis, H. C. (1961), An experimental approach to the treatment of the acutely ill psychiatric patient in the general hospital, *Connecticut Medicine*, **25**, 613–615.

Fleck, S. (1963), Psychiatric hospitalization as a family experience, *Acta Psychiat. Scand.*, **39**, Suppl. 169.

Goffman, E., (1961), *Asylums*, Doubleday, New York.

Guion, R. M. (1967), Personnel selection, *Annual Review of Psychology*, **18**, 105–216.

Hall, A. D. and Fagen, R. E. (1968), Definition of system. *in*: Buckley, W., Ed., *Modern Systems Research for the Behavioral Scientist*, Aldine Publishing Company, Chicago.

Harrison, S. I., McDermoff, J. F., Wilson, P. T. and Schrager, J. (1965), Social class and mental illness in children, *Arch. Gen. Psychiatry*, **13**, 411–417.

Hodgson, R. C., Levinson, D. J. and Zaleznik, A. (1965), *The Executive Role Constellation: an Analysis of Personality and Role Relations in Management*, Harvard Business School, Cambridge, Mass.

Levinson, D. J., Merrifield, J. and Berg, K. (1967), Becoming a patient, *Arch. Gen. Psychiatry*, **17**, 385–406.

Levinson, D. J. and Klerman, G. L. (1967), The clinician-executive, *Psychiatry*, **30**, 3–15.

Lynton, R. P. (1969), Linking an innovative subsystem into the system, *Admin. Science Quarterly*, **14**, 398–416.

Miller, E. J. and Rice, A. K. (1967), *Systems of Organization*, Tavistock Publications, London.

Piven, F. F. and Cloward, R. A. (1971), *Regulating the Poor: the Function of Public Welfare*, Pantheon, New York.

Rice, A. K. (1963), *The Enterprise and its Environment: a System Theory of Management Organization*, Tavistock Publications, London.

Schneiderman, L. (1965), Social class, diagnosis and treatment, *American Journal of Orthopsychiatry*, **35**, 99–105.

Sheldon, A., Baker, F. and McLaughlin, C. (1970), *Systems and Medical Care*, Massachusetts Institute of Technology, Cambridge, Mass.

Tischler, G. L. (1971), The effects of consumer control on the delivery of services, *American Journal of Orthopsychiatry*, **41**, 501–505.

Tischler, G. L., Henisz, J., Myers, J. and Garrison, V., (1972), The impact of catchmenting, *Administration in Mental Health*, **1**, 22–29, Winter.

Organizational Design and Therapeutic Effect

Lars B. Lofgren

Investigation of therapeutic efficiency suffers often from lack of criteria of adequate personality functioning. Thus it becomes difficult to know what exactly to treat, or how to evaluate the result of treatment. Freud's dictum that to love and to work well is a criterion for psychological health remains probably one of the most useful ones but in a specific situation it remains too vague to provide a guideline for action. This paper will first try to introduce a relatively simple concept against which to judge adequate functioning and then try to discuss certain problems of organizational design against this background.

The concept of boundaries has been discussed as far as personality organization goes by Federn (1952) in a contribution that has not influenced psychoanalysis to any great degree and in a more generalized way by Rice (1963) and Miller and Rice (1967). In the most general sense everything that can be defined as set apart from the background in time and space must be bounded in some way. In so far as we are dealing with an open system there must be an influx and outflux across this boundary, which must remain functionable under this stress. An amoeba must be able to take in substances and process them internally and still retain its cell-membrane intact. If the cell-membrane is destroyed during the process the organism will soon die and becomes indiscernible from the background. Reversible damage will cause reversible malfunctioning. What is a physical reality as a cell-membrane can be used as a concept when it comes to the psychological apparatus. When the infant is already a separate bodily entity its personality system is not clearly bounded from the mother. Such a symbiosis is postulated as a necessary step in development (Mahler, 1963). Later on the child needs the support of the adult to handle certain processes (A. Freud, 1937). The general movement in development is, however, to establish the personality system as a separate entity with a well functioning boundary across which intake and output is possible. Erikson's (1959) concept of ego identity fits well into this view, especially Erikson's consideration of the impossibility of intimacy before identity is firmly established. Personality boundaries are threatened in the intense interchange with another person that intimacy involves.

The concept of personality system boundaries is applicable to a great many points of view of psychology. So is reality testing, basically the ability to discern the outside from the inside, obviously closely related to this concept. Adequate perception and the ability to deal with incoming material by logical thinking requires a well-functioning boundary. When adequate perception becomes impossible, the personality boundary becomes disturbed and thinking becomes more animistic (when dusk falls tree stumps become menacing figures). For a fuller discussion of this see Potzl's experiment on central and peripheral perception (Fisher, 1960). Encountering a complex and perplexing situation probably involves a temptation to regression. From the point of view of personality boundaries, regression means a move in the direction of malfunctioning boundaries, and on the other hand progression means reestablishment and reinforcement of boundaries. This becomes especially apparent when regression leads to projection, maybe of a paranoid nature, or projective identification, that is an attempt to locate a personal quality in another person. A child confronted with a difficult situation may recourse to a temper tantrum, on the other hand by acquiring certain skills a person can retain boundaries even in difficult situations. Here the concept of personality boundaries touches on learning theory in general. Some of these processes are clearly demonstrated in the Tavistock groups as described by Bion (1959). In this unfamiliar situation there is a universal tendency among the members to regressive behaviour. In the dependency group the members merge together before a leader that is going to take care of the difficulties. By projective identification all skills are located in him and members become progressively deskilled (Rice, 1965). By judicious interventions the consultants to the group may reverse the process. Projections are recovered, personality boundaries reestablished and learning takes place. Members emerge with increased abilities to function in small groups, and there might also be a carry over to other difficult situations, i.e. a general therapeutic effect.

The psychoanalytical situation may also be treated as one where boundaries fluctuate. The difficulty of perceiving the analyst, the reclining position and the use of non-directed free association enhance regression. During this the boundaries of the personality system of the analysand become partly inoperative. The analyst is included in the boundaries of the analysand and qualities belonging to the inner world of the analysand are ascribed to the analyst: transference. Through the use of genetical interpretation the analyst helps the analysand to reestablish his boundaries. This work forms a crucial part of a psychoanalysis together with similar work on intrapsychic boundaries between ego, id and superego. The analysand emerges from a successful psychoanalysis with a kind of mastery of the psychoanalytical situation: regressions are shorter in duration, only partial, and can be terminated by the analysand himself. However, the gains are much more than this. Due to the non-specificity of the analytical situation, the skills may be applied to a wide range of social situations. Where before regression, projection and other non-serviceable reactions had taken place, learning and mastery now appear instead. The boundary disturbance is temporary and skills to deal with the new situation develop rapidly. The lifespace of the individual increases markedly, choice replaces anxious non-coping mechanisms.

It is easy to see that confusions, psychotic decompensations and similar states may be defined in terms of non-functioning personality boundaries, and that recompensation means reestablishing such boundaries.

Generally speaking, it becomes increasingly clear that the concept of boundaries can be used in order to discuss mental health. In this context there is some definite limitation to the term. A quite undeveloped and a very well developed personality system may at a given time both have adequately functioning boundaries. Thus the concept has more to do with defining optimal functioning of a given personality. In addition, the better developed a certain system is, the better are probably the possibilities that boundaries will remain intact under stress. Thus maturity and the ability to retain personality system boundaries are related.

Up to this point we have mostly dealt with rather gross disturbance of boundaries that are easily discernible in an isolated personality system. Certain boundary difficulties appear only in interactional systems. There are families where the husband is responsible for all punishment, hostility and aggression, while the wife remains calm and tender. By projective identification she has got rid of a particular part of her personality and deposited it in her husband. The chances are that he has done the same and transferred many of his tender feelings on to her. In such a way a situation is created where the personality boundaries between man and wife are incomplete with a resulting impoverishment of both. The situation is often reversible. Suitable therapeutic measures may reestablish the boundaries. The husband will discover tender feelings that he was unaware of and the wife may be conscious of a new asperity.

This last example leads us to discuss therapy in general. I will define the general therapeutic task as reestablishing boundaries or creating conditions where they can remain functionable. If there was a minimal intervention that could establish a boundary between the personality systems of man and wife in the last example this would seem to be the therapy of choice. Maybe one could enter into the family life in their home at a given moment, ready to interpret the malfunctioning, and remain until the situation seems to have changed definitely. This would be the paradigm of home visiting used for crisis resolution.

The situation is not that simple however. Some people may say the observed boundary disturbance is just a specific sign that something is generally wrong: merely the tip of the iceberg. According to this view both contrahents in the marriage should be studied very carefully and helped to remedy the situation with the greatest possible amount of free choice. This would be the paradigm of psychoanalysis, ideally of both parties, and maybe their children too.

Of these two therapies one may call the first one *highly socially specific* and the psychoanalysis *highly socially non-specific*. The first one may provide the parties with adaptive skills sufficient to settle the business between them and nothing else. The psychoanalysis will enrich their personality and provide maximal opportunity for a free choice not tied to any particular social situation.

Between these extremes fall a whole range of possible interventions, group therapies, conjoint therapy, institutionalization and others that can be ranged on this scale from social specificity to non-specificity. Each of them may at least theoretically be quite effective in remedying the breakdown in personality boundaries in the given example. How to choose? The important thing may be to see that the indications for certain methods are not dependent on the situation they are supposed to deal with. The choice must be made because of other criteria: the wishes of the couple, the skills and tastes of the therapist, ethical or financial considerations. In this sense psychiatric indication for therapy is very different from the rest of medicine.

Institutional Treatment

The rest of this paper will be devoted to a discussion of therapeutic institutions, mainly of the in-patient psychiatric type. If institutional treatment were to be considered in the given example the most specific way would be to admit the whole family to the institution and there study their interaction and intervene appropriately. In this way one could improve functioning in the family but little else. A few additional strains might have to be dealt with because of the presence of other persons in the institution but apart from that the treatment would be highly specific. Certain institutions function in such a way. In general, however, institutions do not operate in such a way. Instead one person, the one designated sick, is removed from a certain social situation and admitted to the institution. Very often his plight is considered not to be the result of social interaction in his particular locus, but a result of some overwhelming internal process. From another point of view, hospitalization can often be better understood as a collusive acting out between the doctor and the environment with or without the active participation of the sick person. Be that as it may, it can be stated that in order for the sick person to agree to hospitalization his personality system boundaries must be quite shaky. In my opinion, only psychotics, ambulatory psychotics and borderline cases agree to become hospitalized.

The expectation is now that during the hospitalization something should happen to the patient. The sickness should be cured, he should be discharged and he should be able to deal better with the reality to which he must return. Our task will now be to examine certain conditions that make this goal possible. In a certain sense most in-patients are the same. They feel sick, they are ready to be taken care of, they agree to relegate decision-making, they have no commitment to change. Values clustering around *dependency* are highly cathected regardless of the psychiatric diagnosis that may be attached to the particular patient. Every person who agrees to psychiatric in-patient treatment is ready to delegate many important personality functions to the staff. In other words, his personality system boundary is largely non-functioning.

It is evident that an important task will be to deal with this boundary disturbance. Let us first consider some ways in which this should not or cannot be done. One temptation is for the staff to go along with this request on the part of the patient. This endangers staff personality boundaries. A situation is created whereby everything sick is delegated to the patient and everything healthy to the staff. Old state hospitals functioned in this way. This is an essentially stable social situation, an excellent medium in which to grow chronic cases. Attempts on the part of patients to get well were very often greeted with intense anxiety on the part of the staff, and the patients were forced back into sickness. Anyone who has tried to deal with such symbiotic wards can bear witness to such processes.

Individual psychotherapy is also to little avail. As S. Freud (1919) has pointed out, the cure must take place in an atmosphere of frustration. When the patient's dependency needs are met and the therapist has a factual authority relation vis-à-vis the patient, individual psychotherapy becomes only an acting out of dependency needs on the part of the patient. A seeming exception to this takes place in certain institutions of unusually complex design. Due to the many complicated interrelations that face the patient, relevant psychotherapeutic material is produced. Since this material stems from the institutional situation the tendency is for the psychotherapeutic process to create perfect patients. This may sometimes be a condition for discharge as will be discussed later.

Once again the reason why psychotherapy usually does not work in an in-patient setting is because personality system boundaries are not intact. The doctor is *really* responsible for much of the patient's life in the institution and this is an ideal situation for projective identification. This is a parameter that cannot be analysed away (cf. Eissler, 1953) because it is a reality factor operating during the entire stay in the institution. Therefore it is my firm conviction that ordinary psychotherapy is of little avail in the in-patient setting. Once again, this is also perfectly compatible with psychoanalytic theory. The reason for its remaining popularity is probably a devotion that focuses mainly on the one-to-one contact, i.e. a *method* rather than on adequate theory.

The therapeutic work in the institution must instead be centred around work with the patient's non-functional personality boundaries, rather than as psychotherapy would do on intrapersonal boundaries. The staff must be trained to observe signs of personality boundary collapse such as the tendency to projective identification, whether it is directed against staff or other patients, and to intervene with explanatory comments. Staff must consistently behave in relation to the patient in such a way as to recathect remaining independency values. This means assuming an attitude that may be perceived at least superficially as uncaring. This goes against the grain of medical personnel in general and constant staff education is necessary until the necessity of such an attitude is deeply understood.

An old view of an in-patient ward is that it is a kind of container where the patient is kept until some therapeutic agent has exercised its effect. The design of the ward becomes important only in so far that it increases the patient's safety and comfort. It seems unlikely that the patient's encounters with environment and objects while he is in a highly regressed state should not be of crucial importance. Therefore great care must be given to the general design of a ward.

The encounter with the ward culture will further enhance dissolution of the personality boundaries and by projective identification assigning many personality functions to the WARD or the STAFF. In so far as the staff is conscious of these processes and deals with them constantly, the patient will be able to deal with, or adapt to the ward, without damage to his personality boundaries. This is another way of saying that he is learning certain adaptive skills appropriate to the ward situation. If these skills have no outside relevance the patient is so much the worse for the experience. The adaptive requirements in a classical prison are of this kind, i.e. the outside relevance is absent. The inmate is changed in such a way that he either becomes a recidivist or becomes a member of a criminal subculture *extra muros*.

In order to be productive the adaptive work required by the institution should be maximally directed to the outside and minimally to the inside. The adaptive skills should paradoxically have little relevance to remaining in the institution but instead further discharge. As indicated before, some institutions are able to further discharge in the face of adaptational requirements of high internal relevance. I worked for many years in such a small therapeutic institution devoted to psychoanalytically oriented psychotherapy. Not because of active design this institution had many similarities with a small college. It was, therefore, logical that the institution would do well with young college dropouts: once they had mastered the institution they could also return to college. It seemed at times as if the institution was doing less well the more removed from this paradigm the patient was. With this in mind it might be possible to design treatment institutions specifically designed for anxious bankers, sick poets, etc., but the practical problems would be considerable. The religious retreats may partly be effective in this way.

The average institution has, however, obligations to serve a population of more or less diverse nature. This becomes especially the case when the institution must serve a catchment area instead of selecting patients to its liking. The director of such an institution controls the boundary between the institution and the catchment area and has to decide which policies would best serve the incoming patients. There seems to be a growing conviction that the stay in the institution should be short. The reintegrated patient should also hopefully be in better shape to deal with his life situation either by himself, by continued therapy of some sort, or by at least knowing where to turn for help before the situation deteriorates completely. The director has to institute a design that reflects current values in the catchment area as a least common denominator. The greater the heterogeneity of the environment, the more generally applicable must be the values of the institution. Stressing an honest day's work would probably be adequate in an institution serving the Pennsylvania Dutch, but would make little sense in an area riddled with poverty, crime and drug abuse. Through study of the situation in a very heterogenous part slum, part ghetto, part drug and street-people area, I have formed a tentative conclusion that at least in our Western culture there are certain minimal skills necessary in order to continue to live in any social niche. They are: (*a*) a certain measure of independence, (*b*) some ability to make decisions and (*c*) some ability for interpersonal exchange in simple situations. These skills must be reflected in the values of any institution that attempts to perform a reintegrative function for any community.

They also serve the criterion established above of having high external relevance and little meaning for continued institutionalization. As stated before, the patient culture values are derived from dependency. Staff, of course, centres around independence. Therefore, when the patient under pressure from the adaptational requirements of the institution recathects his own previous independence values he no longer fits into the patient culture. As a rule he cannot become staff. Continued stay in the institution, therefore, becomes impossible and he will move to discharge.

The Mount Zion Hospital Psychiatric In-patient Unit in San Francisco, California has been designed according to these principles. The incoming patients are usually grossly psychotic, confused, suicidal, depressed or show some other signs of grave mental disturbance. All of them have opened their personality boundaries and are ready for an extensive projective identification, assigning such functions as responsibility, decision-making, health and so-forth to the staff. Thus patients form a uniform culture centred around dependency values. Partly by indoctrination and partly by inclination, the staff culture is centred around independence and values derived from this concept. Thus, there is constant tension in the organization between two cultures and the main therapeutic task takes place along this axis. We feel it is important that the independence values are demonstrated in action, in efficient encounters between patients and staff. These encounters are of two kinds: mainly cognitive, and mainly expressive-emotional. The cognitive encounters consist of small groups and a community meeting (cf. Edelson, 1970a and 1970b). The small group has two consultants concentrating their work around personality boundaries, thus listening more to the quality of the interchange in the group than to content, and they intervene accordingly. The community meeting also has two consultants dealing with process in general and members of the nursing and O.T. staff who serve as resource personnel and stay in role. Each patient also has an individual nursing consultant who consults with the patient around up-coming issues deriving from the stay on the ward and the return to their society. The use of the word 'consultant' in this context indicates the delineation of this role as different from the classical psychotherapeutic one.

In spite of these anti-regressive measures, there is always a tendency for patients on the ward to revert to the simplest form of emotional expression: the temper tantrum. We have thus isolated the components in the temper tantrum and dealt with them in separate patient/staff encounters where once again staff is stressing independence values. The kicking in the temper tantrum is absorbed through movement and dance sessions, the screaming through music sessions, the possible smearing and weeping through art sessions and the general tendency to dramatic display in sociodrama. In addition, we try to channel the patients' creative potential through O.T. work of a more complex nature.

It is very difficult in an interwoven design like this to evaluate the efficiency of each particular part. However, together they form a highly efficient organization for reconstituting a psychotic patient. A grossly psychotic patient usually reconstitutes to precrisis functioning in eight to ten days. It is not yet possible to give exact figures for rehospitalization but comparison with other hospitals who receive a randomly assigned proportionate part of the same patient material shows that our rehospitalization frequency is about one-third that of a conventional unit.

The details of the structure and a fuller evaluation of the results will be published elsewhere.

References

Bion, W. (1959), *Experience in Groups*, Basic Books, New York.

Edelson, M. (1970a), *The Practice of Sociotherapy*, Yale University Press, New Haven, Conn.

Edelson, M. (1970b), *Sociotherapy and Psychotherapy*, University of Chicago Press, Chicago.

Eissler, K. R. (1953), The effect of the structure of the ego on psychoanalytic technique, *in Journal of the American Psychoanalytic Association*, L, 104–143.

Erikson, E. H. (1959), Identity and the life cycle, *in Psychological Issues*, Vol. 1., International Universities Press, New York.

Federn, P. (1953), *Ego Psychology and the Psychoses*, Imago Publishing Co. Ltd., London. (Reprinted 1961, Basic Books, New York).

Fisher, C. (1960), Preconscious stimulation in dreams, associations and images, *in Psychological Issues*, Vol II, No. 3, Monograph 7, International Universities Press, New York.

Freud, A. (1937), The ego and the mechanisms of defence, The International Psycho-Analytical Library No. 30, Hogarth Press, London, (fifth impression 1969).

Freud, S. (1919), *Lines of Advance in Psycho-analytic Therapy*, Hogarth Press (Standard Edition 1955), London.

Mahler, M. S. (1963), Thoughts about development and individuation, *The Psychoanalytic Study of the Child*, Vol. XVIII, International Universities Press, New York.

Miller, E. J. and Rice, A. K. (1967), *Systems of Organization: the Control of Task and Sentient Boundaries*, Tavistock Publications, London.

Rice, A. K. (1963), *The Enterprise and its Environment: a System Theory of Management Organization*, Tavistock Publications, London.

Rice, A. K. (1965), *Learning for Leadership: Interpersonal and Intergroup Relations*, Tavistock Publications, London.

Organization and Training for the Task of Treatment in the Prison Service*

J. H. Fitch and D. G. Hewlings†

Introduction

Society no longer believes that those who offend against its laws must be treated as incorrigible to be pushed out of sight, forgotten or got rid of as quickly as possible. The hope is that the offender has the possibility of change within him and that with the appropriate encouragements or constraints, legal sanctions can be used to produce such change. At the same time, a developing humaneness in the regulation of all forms of social interaction has affected the thinking about the ways in which offenders should be treated in penal institutions. Of recent years, prisons have made considerable efforts to improve the conditions available for inmates; despite the severe problems presented by overcrowding, attempts have been made to have living standards raised, amenities increased and elements of deterrence restricted or abolished in favour of procedures designed to encourage rehabilitation. The modern prison service is faced with an overall complex task; while being perceived as containing elements of punishment and retribution, it has at the same time hopefully to perceive those committed to its custody as possessing attitudes amenable to influence and change. The official position is well stated in the 1969 Government White Paper, 'People in Prison' (page 7): 'It is the task of the service, under the law, to hold those committed to custody and to provide conditions for their detention which are currently acceptable to society. Secondly, in dealing with convicted offenders, there is an obligation on the service to do all that may be possible within the sentence to encourage and assist them to lead a good and useful life'. This statement suggests that there is an ostensible treatment task for the Prison Service even if the means of carrying out such a task are left to the service itself to determine. Treatment may be defined as being any deliberate attempt to modify behaviour or change attitudes towards some previously decided end. In a penal context, the end must be behaviour that is socially desirable so that the ultimate aim of treatment for the offender must be to enable him to become law-abiding and not revert to crime. In this respect, treatment methods within a prison service may be open to the criticism that they are

* Throughout this paper the word 'prison' is used as a convenient shorthand to denote any penal establishment, prison, borstal, remand centre, detention centre or allied institution.

† Respectively Principal Psychologist and Assistant Controller in the Prison Department; the authors' wish to acknowledge the help given by those colleagues whose views and experience are represented in this article. The views expressed do not necessarily represent those of the Prison Department of the Home Office.

designed to produce social conformity in offenders rather than to pursue individualistic ends such as personal happiness.

The thinking behind 19th and early 20th century penal policies seems to have been that, if socially acceptable behaviour could be obtained by influencing the prisoner, then it must be done through the concept of training, that is to say the acquisition of social competence through the learning of individual skills. This thinking dominated the decisions of those prison administrators who first attempted to set up rehabilitative elements in prison regimes. Whether it was the moral precepts behind the single-celled, radial prison, that change could arise from exhortation and individual penance; or whether it was from the concepts of the early borstal system, with its ideas of education for the under-privileged, training implied a massing of what were considered to be therapeutic agencies in successive or simultaneous assaults upon the individual. So that, within prisons, time and space began to be found for chaplains to take services and practise their ministry; for educators to teach the basic skills of literacy; for doctors to relieve bodily, and possibly mental, ills; for industrialists to proclaim the benefits of regular and repeated physical labour.

The infiltration of these 'treatment' agents was a slow process but it was aided by the general favourable change in social attitudes towards prisons with its desire for their humanizing and betterment. It was flattering for prison staff to be seen as rehabilitators as much as custodians and made them feel that they were employed in socially constructive work. As the pressure groups for penal reform in society became more vehement and more respectable, so the pressures on prisons to move more and more towards training and treatment goals increased. It was a collusive process, presenting the prisons with attractive, if unrealistic, aims and objectives while enabling society to avoid facing the real responsibilities in its use of imprisonment. The escape of George Blake from Wormwood Scrubs in 1966 showed on what insecure foundations had been built the whole edifice of prison training that had arisen during the previous 40 years.

Historically, the treatment agencies had become accretions to the basically simple, quasi-military management structure by which any prison was adminis-tered and run. The primary task of any institution was still considered to be security and containment; even within the borstal system, any training task was, in theory at any rate, secondary to that. However, the introduction of treatment agencies had presented the management of any institution with the recurrent problem of deciding whether and how to subordinate the demands of security to those of training. Social pressures in the community at large were not in-frequently brought into play to erode the concept of security as the primary task in order to allow more freedom to the rehabilitators and the growing extension of the 'open' and 'semi-closed' institution had favoured the process. Staff became confused as to function and role; the prison officer saw himself first turned into a custodian by the introduction of increasing numbers of specialists with 'treatment' functions and then deprived of any real specialism of his own as a custodian by the apparent devaluing of his security and custodial skills. The inquiry led by Lord Mountbatten following Blake's escape revealed both to the

Prison Service and to society the confusion that reigned over security and treatment objectives and the incoherent patterns of management which evolved as a result (Report of the Inquiry into Prison Escapes and Security, 1966).

The lesson was quickly learnt: two years later a senior prison administrator could describe the management needs to relate the necessary treatment and security objectives in any system of corrections as follows:

'Management studies and management training have particular value in relation to systems of correction. It is increasingly the tendency to recruit into the managerial grades and to a lesser extent the basic staff grades, persons who have particular aptitude and training for social work and especially social case work. This is an important element in the total functioning of any system of corrections but it is not the sole element and, particularly in the middle levels of management, there is scope for the application of management training. Some of this will need to be directed towards the specific problems of the particular part of the system, but there is also room for the extensive use of generic management training. This training will be of particular value in enabling the manager of a particular institution or group of staff to weld together, organise and harmonise the contributions of an increasing number of specialists who are employed in or in connection with systems of correction. In addition to social case workers, there are contributions from the fields of medicine (including psychiatry), education (including physical education), industrial managers concerned with the employment of prisoners, psychologists, and priests or ministers of religion. This list is by no means exhaustive but it does indicate the complexity of the managerial problems facing the individual in charge of a particular establishment. There are also valuable techniques from other fields of management, particularly industrial, concerned with the problems of staff relations. Even if a correctional system is mainly hierarchical in structure, the staff nowadays cannot be effectively managed in an old-fashioned military manner and it will be part of any effective system of corrections that the roles and duties of the staff are clearly defined, understood and accepted.' (Woodfield, 1968, p. 5).

But the appropriate ways of organizing and training custodial staff for a treatment task have still to be found and currently preoccupy the prison service today. It is with the search for organizational models in prisons within which to attempt the treatment task that this paper will concern itself.

The Problem

In their study of social forces operating within prisons, American sociologists have commented that it is amazing that prisons should work at all. The conflict between custodial and treatment goals is potentially more likely to produce a chaotic mess of social relations than any coherent, interdisciplinary approach to the problem (Cressy, 1961). The two chief protagonists in a penal institution are obviously likely to adopt quite different *a priori* conceptions as to its task and function. To inmates, committed unwillingly, sceptical as to staff values, uncertain as to their own needs, the prison is something to be got through, or got out of, as painlessly as possible. Their chief desire is to avoid institutional sanctions and to win full remission. Even if they have any belief in the institution's being able to help them, they are more concerned to adapt to its regime than to change their own social attitudes. Overt conformity is seen to be a quicker passport to release and to establishing acceptable relations with staff than is any desire for help or conversion. Staff tend to see inmates primarily as offenders, those who have broken the laws they themselves must strive to maintain, and only secondarily as individuals in need or distress. Staff may have only limited belief in the capacity of prisons to act in any therapeutic or 'people-changing' way. They may prefer unambiguous objectives for the institution, simple, direct, short-term ones of custody and control, rather than doubtful, confused, long-term ones of therapy. The goals of the institution must affect both the staff's perception of its purpose and their belief about inmates, the sort of security they need, the quality of control, the type of discipline If custodial goals are seen as all-important, this will govern the staff's beliefs about the inmates' needs: if treatment goals are stressed, problems of control and discipline are seen as less relevant. Different types of organization, arising from different concepts about the task and function of the penal system, produce different responses in both the inmates and the staff of the institutions concerned.

It would not be appropriate here to enter into a discussion of the many theories of the psychology of delinquency but, in general, people convicted of persistent anti-social behaviour appear to have two major characteristics in common. Firstly, they display in their behaviour their difficulties in relating to other people; they seem unable to appreciate the effects of their own actions upon others and thus may have a disturbed sense of their own identity. Secondly, they have obvious difficulties in relating to authority figures and frequently try to play off one person in authority against another by seeking to display different aspects of themselves according to whether they see the authority figures as 'good' or 'bad', one which they want something from or one that they want to avoid. These mechanisms of splitting and of projection make it important for those social agencies who work with delinquents to be in good communication among themselves if they are to present and maintain a coherent line of action in response to delinquent behaviour. It is of even more importance to do this if the different agencies are all represented within one institutional staff. Thus the management of delinquents has to demonstrate not only that authority represents both control and concern but that control and concern are indivisible attributes of any management. Similar mechanisms of splitting and projection can of course occur in authority's attitude to the delinquent. Too often, the offender is expected to display anti-social attitudes to all authority figures and to be resistant to any imposed authority, or alternatively, if he responds in one direction, he will then be judged to be capable of conformity in others. As has been pointed out, in institutions, staff and inmates share perceptual distortions and see the differences between their assigned roles in greatly exaggerated ways (Wheeler, 1958). If unchecked, these distortions increase the possibility of staff–inmate conflict and reinforce negativistic attitudes to each other. In fact, the behaviour of any individual inmate in a prison results from compromise; the compromise he has to make between adjusting to the values of the total inmate group or to the values of the staff group. The less conflict there is between the value systems of these two groups, the easier will the individual find it to accept them both. The more treatment-oriented the institution, the more likely it is that inmates will show positive and cooperative attitudes to staff. But in any security institution, it is highly unlikely that there will not be conflict over the way in which staff and inmates perceive the custodial restraints. Similarly, treatment may be perceived very differently by staff and by inmates. It must not be presumed that there is necessarily uniformity of attitude prevailing among either the staff or the inmate group. There will be obvious problems in an institution where the attitudes and values felt and shown by the staff may not correspond with, or may even be in conflict with, the ostensible goals of the institution. A staff which perceives inmates as basically in need of discipline and control in order to promote obedience and conformity will not further the aims of an institution whose goal of individual therapy for inmates must allow for some degree of independence, questioning of authority and self-expression. It has been demonstrated that conflict among staff is likely to increase as the institution moves along a continuum from the more simplistic custodial goals to the more complex treatment-oriented ones (Street and coworkers, 1966). This conflict seems to be not so much a function of lack of agreement or of the degree of departmentalization among the staff as of the interdependence between departments. Where interdependence is high between those in the staff who represent custodial goals and those who represent treatment goals, tension and conflict are reduced by the promotion of mutual understanding.

The problem seems therefore to be an organizational one. Neither custodial nor treatment goals can be seen as mutually exclusive since they are both presumed to be subsumed by the total task of the institution and thus their relative effectiveness must depend on how they relate to each other. Whatever the inmate learns while undergoing his sentence that may produce any change in his subsequent behaviour is clearly a result of his total institutional experience, his experience of both custody and treatment. The term 'treatment' in this context can be extended to cover anything that happens to the inmate during his period in custody. This has been well put by Dr. Peter Scott:

'Treatment is best regarded not as a passive process applied only by a doctor but as any approved measure used by anyone or any group (staff member, inmate, relative) to change a person in a desired direction. It is hoped that it will be the person himself who desires the change, otherwise the change must extend only to the abandonment of unlawful or manifestly self-damaging behaviour. This definition of treatment clearly includes that variety of punishment (perhaps better called conditioning) which is rationally applied according to the rules of learning and must sometimes include solitary confinement'. (Scott, 1970, p. 167)

The Counselling Model

One attempt to bring together security and treatment goals in the English penal system was the early experiment with group counselling, adapted from the Californian model (Fenton, 1957, 1965), that was initiated in the late 1950's and early 1960's. Drawing its concepts and practice from the fields of education, psychiatry and social psychology, group counselling had the threefold aim of reducing the social distance between inmates and staff; of introducing treatment goals to staff who saw their task as primarily custodial; and of introducing inmates to ideas of self-help. It can now be appreciated that this was the first fundamental change in treatment practice to challenge the appropriateness of the organization and management structures in the conventional prison. With its underlying premise that all offenders must have difficulties with their concepts of themselves, and thus problems in their relationships with others, it pointed to the need to examine the social context within which treatment must be carried out and, in particular, the relationship of the individual, staff member or inmate, to the authority of the institution.

The original hope behind the introduction of group counselling seems to have been that, by simply sitting down and talking together in a reasonably relaxed and permissive atmosphere, staff and inmates would get to know each other better, that fantasies of 'we' and 'they' would be dispelled and that inmates would become more accepting of staff goals. The group situation was thus seen as an extrapolation from the individual counselling situation. It was expected too that this was a reasonably self-contained activity that could take place alongside the traditional activities of work and education and one that would provide a safe area in which the inmate could discuss his 'problems'. What quickly became apparent was that the individual staff member could be faced with problems of role-conflict if he operated a counselling relationship in the small-group situation but a disciplinary relationship to inmates elsewhere; and that the individual inmate could be faced with the problem of exposing himself to fellow-inmates in the counselling group at the risk of their using what they learnt of him to exploit him elsewhere. Being unable to see adequate safeguards against these possibilities, the tendency was for both staff and inmates to go into collusion to turn the counselling sessions into meaningless discussions where only 'safe' topics were talked about; or for enough organizational difficulties to be found from the conflicting task priorities in the institution to make it impossible for staff to be found to be able to act regularly as counsellors with their groups or for inmates to be spared to attend them.

What was learnt from the introduction of counselling was that if the disciplinary officer is to see himself as a potential treatment agent, he must not be split off from other possible treatment agencies in the institution. Similarly, other staff, whether doctors, priests or teachers, who identify with a treatment role, must accept a responsibility as authority-figures within a framework of enforced containment. This necessitates a system by which all staff can be trained in the understanding of the total tasks of the institution and the setting-up of an organizational structure in which there are proper communication channels from management to the counselling, or any other, treatment situation and vice versa. As the staff need management to prevent them from being split among themselves, so the inmates need management to protect themselves from being fused together. The intentions for personal change stimulated in the individual inmate from the counselling situation may not sustain the concerted accusations of 'grassing' or 'crawling' voiced from the larger inmate group outside it. To make and sustain a change of attitude in both staff member and inmates, counselling cannot be contained within a part of their institutional lives. By bringing together inmates in counselling groups and staff in training groups, forces and feelings are liberated which cannot be contained within the limited communication system of a traditional prison. The realization at last came that group counselling was far from a self-contained activity; it was in fact an ethos, which once introduced must pervade and affect the whole philosophy and organization of the institution or perish (Morrison, 1961).

The Community Model

From the counselling model wherein every staff member is a potential treatment agent, it is a logical extension to a community model wherein everything that happens in the institution is potentially a treatment force. This model is a familiar one in the mental health field and has been described in its application to mental hospitals in a number of publications by psychiatrists and sociologists (Rapoport, 1960). The use of this model frees the institution from thinking that treatment is something that is only done by certain people in certain places and at certain times, but instead poses the problem of the correct role specification and diversification among grades of staff. Its relevance to the treatment of the mentally ill and the socially deviant is that since both mental illness and delinquency are social problems, then treatment for them needs to be socially based. The study of the individual's behaviour in a variety of group settings within a hospital or prison is thus a relevant way of helping both that individual and others to understand and deal with the problem of social malfunction. It also suggests that the basic working tool in the institutional treatment must be the relationship between those in authority, the staff, and those under authority, the inmates. A group process, whether in the small, intimate counselling situation or the larger community one, can provide the individual with the opportunity to develop greater self-awareness through an increased awareness of others. Awareness of personal relationships and the effects of behaviour on a relationship can be experienced as the individual acquires more insight into how his behaviour affects that of others. As the group or community must include both staff and inmates, the possibility of looking at relationships across the 'we–they' boundary can be examined. Inmates can look at their feelings for staff and seek to examine how relations with authority figures may be used positively. Staff members can look at their feelings for inmates and seek to examine how they come to terms with the problem of exercising authority. However, before a community model can be applied to the prison situation, the realities of the relationship between inmate and staff in a penal institution need to be examined as do the nature of the constraints within which any penal institutional treatment must take place.

Of particular concern to the penal community is the problem of control.

This has two aspects: in the first place, there is the control that the staff feel called upon to exert over the inmates in order to carry out the custodial and security tasks imposed on them by society in a way acceptable to society and, secondly, there is that internal, regulatory control through which the tasks of the institution have to be done and by which any individual inmate or staff member can be protected from exploitation by any other. Enough has been said about control within what have been called 'total institutions' (Goffman, 1961) to show that this can be used as a means of devaluing the inmates in order to protect staff but it is equally true that, in a prison situation, the staff can never hope to achieve complete control and that the inmates can organize their own defences against staff penetration (Sykes, 1958; Mathiesen, 1966). To see control in prisons as an 'either–or' situation, with on the one hand staff claiming to be 'winning the battle' and on the other inmates saying 'we've got a quiet nick here and we want to keep it that way', produces just those extremes. As most prison staff realize, the inmates can, in the end, only be controlled by their own co-operation and it is in the creating of a staff–inmate relationship within the penal community through which that co-operation is given willingly on the one hand and received with respect on the other that the skill of governing a prison lies. Some examination of the realities involved in this relationship, and of the internal boundaries between task and sentient systems within an institution, needs to be made in order to understand what a community model approach must require for a treatment task in a prison.

The Prison as an Intergroup Situation

Because of the diversity and heterogeneity of the staff it employs and the inmates it has to control, a prison is constantly faced with the problem of relations between different groups of people, the boundaries differentiating those groups and the controls over transactions across those boundaries. Inmates can be diversified into a number of different categories, some of which need to be segregated from each other. Staff are employed in a number of different roles, many of which need to be functionally distinct and distinctive. The differences and distinctions between staff and inmates, between inmates and inmates, and between staff and staff have to be recognized and delineated so that an effective administration of the institution to fulfil its tasks can take place. The working context within the institution is one of seeking to define boundaries between groups and to set up relations between groups.

The most obvious intergroup situation is that between the inmates and the staff. For an individual staff member, a personal awareness of how he is operating in this situation is crucial for his professional survival. A lack of awareness can lead either to manipulation by the inmates, disastrous not only for the security task but also for any treatment one, or to total incorporation within a staff culture that is so far out of communication with the realities of the inmates' needs as to be equally unable to mobilize effective control. The need to understand the intergroup relationship between staff and inmates, to know what this is based on, what governs interaction between the two groups, what feelings each develops for the other, what fantasies are projected by both sides and how these are revealed in their mutual behaviour is necessary, at the lowest level for self-protection but above that for any effective working relationship, on both sides. The potentiality for conflict between the two groups, if understood, can then become a major treatment resource and both staff and inmates can be helped to learn about how to cope with stress. Too often conflict is seen as only negative, and too often displayed in purely negative behaviour, but conflict can be a positive element in treatment if its origins are understood and its expression can be used as an agent for learning. For this to be done in a prison situation necessitates an understanding of the intergroup relationship to see if the conflict originates from that or is being projected onto it by the individuals involved. The individual staff member who seeks to use his relationship with inmates as a treatment agency, must examine what he is projecting into the situation from his group membership and allegiances and, similarly, what is being projected onto him.

A further set of intergroup relations which can affect how an institution's staff perform their custodial and treatment functions, are those among the staff themselves. Within the staff of a prison or borstal, there are differences of rank between individuals in different levels of a hierarchy; differences of role between specialists and non-specialists; differences of task between staff with different training and experience. Such differences are legitimate boundaries, set up to define groups and subgroups so that function, task and responsiblity can be appropriately decided and designated. Too often the institutions and the individuals they comprise look at such boundaries and seek to turn them into barriers for fear of the anxiety that might arise if such boundaries were crossed. At times the recognition that boundaries are being used as barriers gives rise to guilt and much time is spent in deploring them and in seeking to break them down. Most prisons have experienced situations where staff have come together to deplore their difficulties in communicating with and understanding one another. There is no point in trying to break down barriers without first examining the initial need to erect them and to discover whether or not they are being used as institutional defences against anxiety (Menzies, 1961).

The anxiety which so often arises in a prison context stems from fears of contamination, from fantasies of the damage that might be done to oneself in having to deal with 'bad' people. The management of a prison should be concerned to examine the appropriate boundaries among its staff which are relevant to the given task, and which in fact may have nothing to do with grades or hierarchies, and then to set about devising the necessary controls over the transactions across those boundaries so as to make positive use of them. In a treatment situation, the staff–inmate relationship must be a boundary and not a barrier.

Treatment as an Intergroup Task

In this situation, therefore, it can be seen that treatment of inmates by staff must be an intergroup task, a quality of that relationship operating between them. In the three main areas of prison administration, security, control and treatment, decision-making in the latter two areas can involve inmates. If they are allowed to share in decision-making about the quality of their life in prison, they are that much more accessible to management. It is not enough that staff in a prison need to be involved in policy-making if any policy within the institution is to succeed; if the quality of life for inmates is to be maintained in a progressive way, inmates too must have some part in decision-making as it affects their lives. Obviously, security considerations must be given their due weight here; equally obviously, if the Governor is to be held legally responsible for all that happens in the prison, he must retain a power of veto. But if the concept 'freedom in containment', which has been recently put forward as a penal aim (Report of the Advisory Council on the Penal System, 1968), is to mean anything, it must necessitate a constant dialogue or series of dialogues, staff to inmates, inmates to inmates, staff to staff, so that insight can develop and communication can take place. Such a dialogue is the essential requirement if the inmate is to learn from his social relationships within the prison environment and if his learning is to motivate a desire for self-help.

The situation is as true whether the prison is an 'open' one, with little physical constraint upon inmates and easy staff-inmate contacts, or a 'closed' one where staff and inmates are frequently physically separated by the technical methods of modern security. The on-going task for any prison should be the preparation for release of inmates within it and this should begin for the individual the moment he is received into the institution. It has been said that treatment cannot occur in prison as prison is an unreal situation which cannot be generalized from to the outside world. In fact, the staff are the eyes and ears of that outside world, the bridges to it, and thus treatment is essentially a shared situation, between staff themselves and thus with the inmates. The degree of authoritarianism or permissiveness which staff display will control the freedom with which inmates feel able to relate to them. Offenders are usually people who feel isolated in society at large and the first task of prison treatment must be to reduce that isolation by helping the offender to relate to the staff.

As has been pointed out this relation can be affected by the inmate's earliest experiences with staff. At the start of a lengthy sentence, a prisoner tends to look to staff for help but to move progressively away towards contacts with other prisoners as his sentence goes on. Towards the point of release, he again moves towards relationships with staff as his anxiety about the outside world increases (Wheeler, 1958). Since there is now a formidable literature on the sociology of prisons which suggests that a culture can exist to produce institutionalization and prisonization in a milieu where guards and captives are in collusion to resist change and maintain a status quo, the need to understand the ways in which inmates and staff are made to relate by the pressures of the institution itself is that much greater. The treatment problem for any prison management is how to utilize the social forces within the institution so that any personal change that takes place is to the standards acceptable within a free society and not simply an accommodation to the values of a captive one.

In an on-going dialogue between staff and inmates, feelings about dependence and about authority can be explored. At the reality level, imprisonment is a dependency-creating situation and the realities of the necessary dependence of inmates upon staff for physical needs to be met can be carried into a fantasy level where inmates can feel psychologically dependent upon staff for their very existence. Dependency of this kind in an individual causes a with-drawal behind the defences within the personality, the setting up of barriers to communication with others, with concomitant feelings of aggression for those in authority who have apparently brought about this state of affairs. Such feelings about authority can block the mutual treatment task with staff and render the inmate inaccessible to staff help. Similarly, dependency feelings in staff can be equally destructive. Staff need to feel realistically dependent upon their management in order to feel supported and to be provided with the necessary resources for their tasks. If such dependency goes beyond the realistic level or if staff are deprived of resources and made to feel powerless, it can lead to a passive dependence on management with the concomitant anger towards an authority which demands things of them while apparently making them impotent. In this case, the aggression felt towards those colleagues and superiors who are seen to be deskilling them, is displaced onto inmates who are thus rendered inaccessible to a real relationship. Treatment, to be effective, must essentially take place in a relationship of interdependence, where the realities of mutual dependency can be explored and the nature of the authority which both sides bring to the relationship can be examined and worked with. In the prison situation there is a particular need for the testing of fact and fantasy since often the psychopathology of the delinquent suggests that he lives in a fantasy world and a prison, whether closed or open but particularly the former, offers the possibility for the creation of further fantasy worlds. Such testing needs to be done in a management situation where the reality of individual and group relations can be examined.

Institutional Organization for an Intergroup Task

There is a well-known phenomenon of institutional relationships which likens them to a mirror-image: each level desires to treat the level below it in a way which it sees itself to be treated by the level above. Another way of putting it is to point out that the presentation of a model to one group by another usually brings about the use of that model by the first group in its dealings with any other. Any management of a prison which seeks to enter into dialogue with inmates must first talk to its own staff. Communications do not happen by themselves and the involvement of staff in policy-making through, for example, management councils and committees, gives them a model which they can then transmit to inmates. The problem for a prison which seeks to implement any treatment task is that of the management of change, the setting up of a structure and design by which the basic needs for treatment can be recognized and handled. An additional complication for prison organization in this country is that the top management of institutions changes frequently and regularly and this, coupled with an inmate population which is also rapidly coming and going, leaves the main body of staff, who frequently serve long periods in one place, sandwiched as the stable element between two unstable ones. Since too, the main body of this staff, the prison officers, are in constant face-to-face situations with inmates and are thus those on whom the greatest emotional demands are being made, management itself must provide an organization which can sustain change within it while providing consistent ongoing staff support. As has been pointed out: 'It is the needs and activities of existing role incumbents that determine the attitudes of working groups toward change, and hence may generate resistance to change. The painful consequences for future incumbents are too familiar to need elaboration' (Miller and Rice, 1967, p. xii). A prison therefore has a special need for understanding the form of organization needed, firstly, to control task performance; secondly, to secure the commitment of staff members to those tasks in an environment where changes of role incumbents must be expected; and thirdly, to regulate relations between task and sentient systems, where the latter may be seen as the only refuge and protection from the anxieties and insecurities of the task performance itself.

In institutions organized on a traditional basis, it is frequently impossible to avoid tension among the different categories of staff because conflict between the formal tasks of the institution and staff who are identified with them, e.g. 'therapists' versus 'custodians', can lead to the forming, for sentient needs, of groups with norms of behaviour and value-systems that can be contrary both to one another and to one or other of the institution's tasks. This, in itself, facilitates the development among inmates of informal groups with their own norms and value-systems and to the growth of an inmate 'culture' that can be strongly opposed to the patterns of values and behaviour put forward by the management of the prison. Differentiation in the methods of control and treatment used by staff will cause essential differences in the way the inmates react and behave, leading to splitting and the forming of subgroups, to tension, rivalries and opportunities to project and act out aggression and mutual distrust. The need is for a clear statement of aim throughout the institution, a definite organization and task system and a stable ethos such that the proper security for the class of inmate is ensured; the regulations to reduce accusations of prejudice or favouritism in the attitude to individuals; an avoidance of the inappropriate use of personal force; constant awareness of and control over internal procedures; and the ability by the staff to act quickly and consistently in the face of inmate pressures.

Such an organization requires a style of management within the prison that is not so preoccupied with communications up and down its own hierarchical ladder as to be unaware of the social context within which those communications have to operate. This necessitates an acceptance by management of the inevitability of group processes. As has been indicated already in this paper, inmates and staff are forced into groups in prison, groups whose force and influence are complex and can be both negative and positive. An effective mobilization of staff resources for both custodial and treatment tasks necessitates a perceptive understanding and use of group processes. As has been said:

'Authority cannot be successfully exercised when those in command positions rely solely on the one-to-one superior–subordinate relationship. Many administrative decisions must be generated within and evolve from interactions which take place in primary groups even though such "groups" are rarely provided for in the formal structure or organization. When the groups function effectively, they become more than an additional mechanism of efficient communication. They serve a support and reinforcement function for the individual vis-à-vis subordinates and superiors. At an even deeper level, identification with a primary group serves to counteract the feelings of alienation and "anomie" so characteristic of life in large bureaucratic organisations'. (Guest, 1968, p. 133)

The application of this can be seen to be relevant to the general management development of the prison itself. In any prison the broad tasks of security and treatment need to be broken down into subtasks with detailed job-descriptions in order that roles can be clearly defined and staff resources allocated. A programme of staff training in the security and treatment techniques necessary for the tasks of that particular prison can then be drawn up. Levels of decision-making within the prison, central, unitary, departmental, can then be defined so that tasks of units and departments can be broadly identified and accepted. This is necessary before any degree of accountability or autonomy can be accepted by the units or any criteria decided on for assessing the relevance to those tasks of activities within the prison. Decisions must be seen to be made appropriately and at the right level, whether such decisions are entirely personal to the Governor, unit manager or departmental head, as for example in crisis situations or confidential staff matters, or whether they are those taken within a group with the maximum consultation. The role of specialists within the institution, and within any unit or department, must be defined so that the contributions they make to decisions, whether on treatment or security, can be seen to be properly advisory to management. All this entails a structure which provides opportunities for staff at all levels to discuss with management the professional implications for them of the policy decisions taken in executive meetings. For this purpose both communication meetings, where views are expressed and where staff can seek and receive support and where management can test the validity of its decisions, as well as representative meetings, where staff associations can discuss with management the working conditions of staff and the personal and domestic implications for staff of policy decisions, are necessary. One can only repeat that such a structure and organization require an appropriate understanding of boundary control within an intergroup situation, and of the boundary role, for which an appropriate staff training is demanded.

Staff Training Implications

We have defined the treatment task as the setting up in an intergroup situation of a relationship between staff and inmates so that the former may facilitate the learning of the latter and encourage within them a desire for self-help. To do so, the staff must be sure of their roles in relation to the inmates and of the boundaries between staff roles and between staff and inmate roles. The acceptance of a role establishes what and where that person is in social terms and calls forth reciprocal behaviour in others. The staff role in treatment is to offer a relationship with the inmate through which it is hoped that the latter will learn about himself and thus generalize from that relationship to relationships in the larger world outside. If staff are to help inmates to come to terms with and examine the behavioural implications of concepts such as responsibility, co-operation, authority and others pertaining to satisfactory social and personal relationships, they need to understand how these are demonstrated through their own behaviour in an institutional environment. The task of management in the prison is to support and aid the staff in doing this and to increase their awareness by providing them with such training as will help towards an understanding of behaviour, their own and others, in an intergroup context.

The training of basic grade discipline staff in the Prison Service has a generic basis which is the necessary drilling in the 'tools of the craft'. The general emphasis is on the custodial skills, training in control, the supervision of inmates, so that the prison officer comes to understand the role he occupies as the embodiment of the containment inherent in the prison function. This is not to say that he is not encouraged to look at and examine his use of such authority and in fact the initial selection process for such staff seeks to insure that individuals who are attracted to an authority role for personal reasons which they seem not to understand are not recruited into the Service. After such generic training at a central training school, specific training in the treatment tasks is more usually given at the institution to which the individual staff member is posted. The experience of the treatment role can thus be given in the actual context of the institution and the needs of the inmates it contains and can be examined in conjunction with the disciplinary relationship which the officer is simultaneously experiencing.

The problem of the treatment role for basic grade staff is frequently that of coming to terms with the dual function of authority, that of control and that of care. The fantasy is that one function can impair or destroy the other, while the reality is that authority can only be effective if both are operative. Many prison staff come from a similar social and cultural background to the inmates and can, on entry into the Service, experience the anxiety of realizing how very close, behaviourally and psychologically, they are to their charges (Morris and Morris, 1963). In order to protect what they are experiencing as new-found authority roles, they may seek to deny this and to distance themselves unduly from the inmates. The institution management's task is to help the staff understand delinquent behaviour and yet not to condone it. There must be an empathic relationship and yet the staff member must not become swallowed up and destroyed by the intensity of the inmate's need for understanding and support.

In his everyday working relations with inmates, the individual prison officer may move naturally in and out of a number of sets of behavioural responses which are relevant to his composite role as the containing and caring authority. His behaviour to the distressed inmate in his cell may be very different to that of the unruly inmate in the workshop. He may permit an informality in his relationship to a small working party that he would not find appropriate when marshalling large numbers of men. A large part of training in personal relationships necessitates making explicit to the staff member that which he normally does implicitly so he may look at and come to understand the social pressures that affect behaviour in his role accordingly. Thus all training which seeks to look at the way people interact needs to have both didactic and experiential content. There needs to be a theory against which experience can be tested and there needs to be a felt appreciation of behaviour in order to provide a basis of reality.

What has been said of training for basic grade staff is equally applicable to the training of staff in managerial and sub-managerial roles. For the senior management of the individual prison or borstal establishment, the staff is the major resource it has for carrying out those tasks of inmate containment and treatment with which the establishment is charged. The proper use and deployment of this resource, its adequate support and development, its constant scrutiny and review, should be of prime concern to management. Thus for anyone in a management position, there would seem to be a number of factors to be considered if his management is to be effective. He must have a clear understanding of those tasks with which he is charged and a knowledge of those resources with which he is provided to carry out those tasks. He must be aware of how to organize and deploy those resources in the social field within which the tasks have to be performed and he must have constant feedback from the field situation as to the effects of the use of his resources and whether he has deployed them appropriately to the task.

Where senior management is in a leadership position in what is essentially a number of intergroup relations, the problem is to decide the type of management training for Governors and Assistant Governors to enable them to be effective in task performance. As has been indicated previously, the designated leadership function is essentially that of controlling transactions across a boundary (Rice, 1965). The Governor controls the boundary between the institution and its environment; his submanagers, Assistant Governors, unit and departmental heads, control transactions across their boundaries within the institution. The nature of the authority that leadership holds is that which is vested in the individuals who control those internal and external boundaries. This is what the staff seek to demonstrate to the inmate, although the latter may frequently initially need help in how to control the boundary between his inner world, his impulses and feelings, and his environment.

Managerial training for an institutional task, whether of containment, of treatment or of both, should be based on a relevant theoretical model of organization and on a first-hand experience of the problems of leading and of being led and of the problems of interpersonal and intergroup relations. The nature of the organization that a prison management must set up to perform its tasks must be based on an understanding of how to set up and control boundaries, 'boundaries between the individual's inner world and the environment, between person and role, institution and environment'[1]. Staff and inmates need to distinguish that which is real in their behaviour from that which they project on to one another. Staff members need to discriminate between that behaviour which is appropriate to their role from that which is a personal need in that role. Staff groups with differing theoretical standpoints or professional values need to examine whether their relationships should be of conflict or co-operation. These are all boundary control problems that management must seek to make clear at the risk of loss of task performance through the distortion of boundaries into barriers. Within the Prison Service Staff College, use has been made of this type of managerial training for both Assistant Governors and other management and specialist grades.

Conclusion

The premise behind this paper is that a concept of penal treatment is developing which implies that everything that happens in an institution is an agent for treatment. This is to weld together the previously considered antagonists of 'security' and 'treatment' into the working partnership of 'treatment within security'. The approach is towards the concept of the total community as the treatment agency and, within this concept, it is management that must exercise both care and control. It can be seen then, that treatment can only take place if the institutional management is appropriate for the task and effective in deploying its staff resources to carry out that task.

The thinking that this paper embodies is that no longer can delinquent and anti-social behaviour be treated institutionally in an individualistic piece-meal fashion. The offender must be treated 'in the round', not as an assemblage of parts. This is not to deny that individual offenders may not need individual treatment to remedy specific defects, nor that the individual remedial skills of, say, psychiatrist, educationalist and chaplain are not required in prisons. The offender is a product of his interaction with his social environment and his delinquency symptomatizes his particular problem in that environment. He must be treated in an environment which affords him learning models appropriate to the one in which he must function when in freedom. The social environment of most offenders is one where problems of inter-personal relations and feelings for authority are paramount. The treatment task for those who deal with imprisoned offenders should be that of the provision of learning situations about social organization and authority.

Treatment can only be attempted through a relationship, although in a security situation the relationship may of course be mediated and distanced through mechanical means. The relationship between staff and inmates in a penal institution is the basic treatment modality and this relationship is one of authority. It is a *sine qua non* that delinquents hold feelings for, and fantasies about, authority that can hinder and prevent effective treatment. Equally, the staff have problems about the appropriate use of authority and about how to establish effective work relations between diverse grades of staff so as to work within a recognized responsible authority. It is the task of management to provide appropriate structures and training by which the staff can understand and utilize their own feelings for authority in a way that can help the inmates to examine theirs.

It is to be hoped that, if prison staff recognize and accept the possibilities of a treatment role and its implications for institutional organization, then they will be in a position to enter into a dialogue with society as to the appropriate tasks that should be given to a penal system. Currently, it seems that society is ambivalent as to the part that it wants prisons to play. Despite a current concern about overcrowding and the physical conditions under which men are kept in prison, it does not seem that there is any real desire to change the nature of the penal task. Prisons are still required to symbolize the archaic, repressive aspects of civilized society, those primitive, punitive parts of it that can then be split off and derided. One would not expect to find a popular gaoler in myth or literature, but need the preferred image of penal authority be that of an authoritarian, pompous, vicious and corrupt institutional staff as displayed in, for example, the film 'The Loneliness of the Long-distance Runner'? Popular media identify with the social protester and need the prison as a scapegoat. There is much resistance to the necessary change that is needed to substitute a proper correctional service in society for the current penal system.

Notes

1. This is quoted from the brochure of a working conference on 'Authority and Organisation' (December, 1969) sponsored by the Grubb Institute of Behavioural Studies and the Tavistock Institute of Human Relations.

References

Cressy, D., Ed., (1961), *The Prison: Studies in Institutional Organization and Change*, Holt Rinehart, New York.
Fenton, N. (1957), *What Will be Your Life?*, American Correctional Association, New York.
Fenton, N. (1965), *Handbook on the Use of Group Counselling in Correctional Institutions*, Institute for Study of Crime and Delinquency, Sacramento, California.
Goffman, E. (1961), *Asylums*, Doubleday, New York.
Guest, R. H. (1968), *Organizational Change*, Tavistock Publications, London.
Home Office (1966), Report of the Inquiry into Prison Escapes and Security (by Earl Mountbatten). (Cmnd. 3175). HMSO, London.

Home Office (1968), The regime for long term prisoners in conditions of maximum security, Report of the Advisory Council on the Penal System (Chairman: The Rt. Hon. K. Younger). HMSO, London.

Home Office (1969), People in prison: England and Wales, HMSO, London.

Mathiesen, T. L. (1966), *The Defences of the Weak: a sociological study of a Norwegian correctional institution*, Tavistock Publications, London.

Menzies, I. E. P. (1961), The functioning of social systems as a defence against anxiety, (Tavistock Pamphlet No. 3) Tavistock Institute of Human Relations, Centre for Applied Social Research, London.

Miller, E. J. and Rice, A. K. (1967), *Systems of Organization*, Tavistock Publications, London.

Morris, T. and Morris, P. (1963), *Pentonville*, Routledge and Kegan Paul, London.

Morrison, R. L. (1961), Group counselling in penal institutions, *Howard Journal*, **10**, 279–297.

Rapoport, R. N. (1960), *Community as Doctor*, Tavistock Publications, London.

Rice, A. K. (1965), *Learning for Leadership*, Tavistock Publications, London.

Scott, P. D. (1970), Punishment or treatment; prison or hospital? *British Medical Journal*, No. 5702, 18th April, pp. 167–169.

Street, D., Vinter, R. D. and Perrow, C. (1966), *Organization for Treatment*, Free Press, New York.

Sykes, G. H. (1958), *The Society of Captives*, Princeton University Press, Princeton.

Wheeler, S. (1958), Social organization in a correctional community. University of Washington (Ph.D. Dissertation).

Woodfield, P. J. (1968), Organization of a system of corrections. A report presented to the European Committee on Crime Problems, Sixth European Conference of Directors of Criminological Research Institutes, Strasbourg.

The Local Church and Its Environment

Bruce Reed and Barry Palmer

In this paper we endeavour to construct a model of the local church as a social institution, and of the dynamic relationship between the church and its environment.

We have been concerned primarily with churches which are local in a sense similar to that in which a public house may be referred to as 'the local'; that is, with churches which have a special relationship to, and significance within, the locality in which they are situated. We have taken as examples of local churches those which are most familiar to us, namely churches in England affiliated to the Church of England. We decided against using the more restrictive term 'parish church', since the model which we put forward is with certain modifications applicable to churches of other denominations, which have no parish, but which come to be regarded as the local church by those living nearby.

The local church is also to be distinguished from the national and inter-national bodies referred to in titles like the Methodist Church or the World Council of Churches, and from the metaphysical concept of the Church as the total company of the faithful, living and dead. In this paper we have used the word 'Church', with a capital C, for these bodies.

This study develops ideas put forward in a previously published lecture (Reed, 1970). They have emerged in the course of consultancy and training with clergy and laity, and have provided working hypotheses for research on the task of the church sponsored by the Grubb Institute and carried out by D.M.K. Durston. In a fuller study we hope to explore the role of the priest or minister in the local church, and to compare these concepts of the church and the ministry with those contained in, or inferable from, the Old and New Testaments and the liturgical and doctrinal statements of different traditions. While the model presented here calls into question many current assumptions about the church and the ministry, we believe that it is compatible with theology that is orthodox in the major Christian denominations.

The Object of Study

A church is, according to one's viewpoint at any particular moment, a building, a group of people or a distinctive pattern of activities. Looked upon simply as a building upon a site, a church may be an object of architectural interest, or an obstacle to a new motorway; what happens inside it may be of no interest. Or it may be regarded as a container and resource for religious activities, for which it is designed and adapted, and from which it derives symbolic and emotional overtones. The relationship between container and contents may be felt to be compatible or incompatible; in the latter case the building may be seen as a 'steeple-house' which impiously limits the worship of God to a prescribed form and location.

Alternatively a church may be thought of as a group of people, periodically gathered together for worship, at other times dispersed throughout the community. In the New Testament the word 'church' frequently refers to the group of faithful who meet in a particular place: 'Give my greetings...to Nympha and the church in her house' (Epistle to the Colossians, 4, 15). Conceived in this way, a church only becomes manifest when its members come together, and in particular when they come together to perform the distinctive activities through which they express their Christian beliefs and commitment.

Building and group of people both acquire their distinctive character as 'church' through their association with a distinctive pattern of activities, that is with religious rites or acts of worship. Thus the Church of England, in its Articles, declares that the Church of Christ is manifested, not simply in the gathering of the group, but in the gathering of the group for specific activities:

'The visible Church of Christ is a congregation of faithful men, in which the pure Word of God is preached, and the Sacraments be duly administered according to Christ's ordinance ...' (Book of Common Prayer, Articles of Religion, xix)

In his ordination the priest receives authority to perform these distinctive acts:

'Take thou Authority to preach the Word of God, and to minister the holy Sacraments in the Congregation, where thou shalt be lawfully appointed thereunto ...' (Book of Common Prayer, The Form and Manner of Ordering of Priests)

Any examination of the local church must take account of the building and location, the men, women and children who take part in church events, and the pattern of activities which recurs through all changes of venue and clientele. In the following analysis we have focused upon the pattern of activities as the constant factor, and have regarded persons and material resources, including buildings, as variable factors which are assembled to perform the activities. It will be apparent, therefore, that, while many of the activities of the typical Anglican church take place in the church building, this analysis is not restricted to these activities, but must also include activities taking place in private homes (such as house communions and visits by the clergy), in public places (like open-air services) and in other settings like hospitals and schools, which may be visited by clergy or laity in the name of the local institution.

By the same token we have excluded from our analysis activities which may be inspired by the individual's involvement with a church, but which are not carried out with the specific authority of the church, and cannot therefore be regarded as activities of the local institution. The behaviour of a church-goer in his office on Monday morning is significant when we come to consider the 'outputs' of the local church institution, but is not in our terms an activity of his church, although it might be regarded as such within a theological frame of reference.

The Open-system Model

We shall thus look upon a church as a *system* of interdependent, purposive activities. The system finds embodiment in the persons and material resources, assembled in a particular location at a particular time, through which these activities are performed. The use of the word 'system' implies that the activities we are concerned with are in some respect linked to one another or dependent upon one another, and that the institution as a whole is identifiable as being independent of other institutions, if only to a limited extent (cf. Miller and Rice, 1967, pp. 6f). Thus, while attendances at a church's services may depend upon the weather, other public events in the locality, and what is on television, the activities that take place in these services—the hymns, lessons, sermon and so on—are not, or need not be, influenced by these factors. On the other hand, the activities that take place in different services of the same church are intimately related to one another, by common theological assumptions, liturgical practices and cultural traditions, by the conventions of the particular church, and by the planning of the church's programme by the leadership of the church.

While a church is identifiable as an institution which has a boundary separating it from its environment, it is not a *closed* system, independent of its environment. Some studies of organizations have employed, at least tacitly, a closed-system model. They have assumed that interchanges between the organization and its environment do not take place or may be ignored. This may be a workable assumption when environmental conditions are constant. One of the first organizational studies ever carried out, upon the Roman Catholic Church, employed a closed-system model (Mooney and Reiley, 1931). This may have been satisfactory when the study was published; it is doubtful whether the interdependence between the Roman Catholic Church and its environment could be ignored today.

A church is more appropriately looked upon as an *open* system; that is, as a system which survives and develops through interchanges of persons, materials, money, energy, ideas and other things with its environment. Through its activities it performs a large number of processes, through which its 'inputs' are converted into 'outputs', and from which it receives benefits which enable it to continue. At the same time the environment, and in particular the human environment, receives certain benefits or satisfactions which stimulate the supply of further inputs to the system. Unless the activities of the church generate further inputs, the system runs down and eventually undergoes radical change or disintegrates. In more concrete terms, the survival and continuing vitality of any local church depends, amongst other things, upon the satisfactions derived, on the one hand by its clergy, and on the other hand by its worshippers, from its activities. If the clergy find that its activities do not approximate sufficiently closely to their idea of what a church should be, they will eventually become apathetic, resign, or not be replaced when they move on. If the congregation do not derive the satisfactions they expect from the services and other events, they will not continue to attend its services. In either case the institution will not continue in its present form indefinitely, even if the crisis point is a long time coming.

We have adopted the open-system model for our analysis of the local church because of its proved usefulness in representing other institutions. It is also evident that there have been major changes in church and society in recent years, and that only an open-system model can take these effects into account. The model is also congruent with theological concepts of the church, which represent every local manifestation of the Church as in relationship with, and existing for, 'the world'.

Distinctive Activities of Churches

The activities of any institution contribute to the tasks or processes which it carries out. Every institution performs many tasks, each of which may be thought of as a process by which an input is transformed into an output through one or more activities (Miller and Rice, 1967, pp. 5ff.).

This language may be felt to be more appropriate to a factory than a church. It proves, however, to be helpful in enabling us to distance ourselves from behaviour in churches, and to distinguish what actually happens from the interpretations which are put upon what happens. Through its public events, like services of worship and meetings of groups and committees, and through the activities of individual clergy and lay men and women, a Church performs a number of tasks. These include:

Conducting acts of worship, including Holy Communion and Morning and Evening Prayer

Providing ceremonies or rites for the baptism of children and adults, marriage and the burial of the dead

Instructing children and adults in Christian doctrine, participation in worship, and other subjects

Providing pastoral and practical care for the sick, the elderly, the lonely, the dying and others in need in the locality

Persuading those professing no attachment to the Church to accept its beliefs and discipline

Raising money

Providing opportunities for cultural activities like choral singing and bell-ringing

Providing a meeting-point where people can enjoy social intercourse

Each of these, and other tasks, may be represented as an input-conversion-output process (using the word 'conversion' in a strictly non-theological sense).

In order to construct a model of the local church it is necessary to identify and examine the distinctive task or tasks which it performs. We regard as distinctive those tasks through which opportunities for worship are provided. These include the provision of regular services of worship, and of occasional rites and ceremonies as required, and that aspect of pastoral care which includes fostering an attitude of worship. We have therefore chosen to focus attention upon those events in the life of a church which provide opportunities for worship. This also accords with the standpoint represented by the Book of Common Prayer, which as we have seen singles out preaching and the administration of the sacraments as the distinctive activities of the priest and of the local congregation.

If this is taken as the central task performed by the local church, the other tasks listed are seen as facilitating this task, or as results or by-products of it.

Behaviour in Worship

As we have said it is difficult for those who are familiar with services of Christian worship to examine what takes place without investing the behaviour of the participants with the meanings which it has for them. In what follows we have endeavoured to retain a sense of the mysteriousness, or even oddity, of this behaviour, when viewed without these preconceptions. We have taken a service of Holy Communion as an example of an act of worship. Our description is based upon a visit by the writers to a north London parish church. We have selected a traditional form of Holy Communion service, not because we regard it as typical of, or normative for, Christian worship, but because it will be familiar to many readers. We use this particular example to illustrate elements in an act of worship which may also be identified in forms of service which are very different in style, mood and conception.

The most obvious 'inputs' into this event are men, women and children, attending singly and in families and groups. They arrive at the church over a period of about ten minutes before, to a few minutes after, the time when the service is due to start. The imminence of the service is signalled by the ringing of bells. As they arrive, some participants greet each other, but there appears to be a certain reserve, suggesting that they are already adjusting their demeanour to that which they regard as appropriate for worship. They are received by officers of the church known as sidesmen, who provide them with a prayer book and hymn book and show them to a seat. The seats are arranged facing the focal furnishings of the church, which include the altar or communion table, the stand or lectern from which the Bible is read, the pulpit and the seats for the choir and officiating clergy. On arrival, most worshippers kneel for a few moments and then remain seated without talking.

The act of worship consists of a planned sequence of activities, some of them indicated in the prayer book, and others announced at a suitable moment. Most of these activities include explicit or implicit references to an unseen person addressed as 'God', 'Father', 'Lord', 'Jesus Christ' or 'Holy Spirit'. They include prayers addressed to this unseen person from a kneeling or standing position, recited either by the priest or by the whole congregation; readings from the Bible by one of the officiating clergy or a layman; singing of hymns and portions of the liturgy, in a standing position; recitation, in unison, of a creed; the presentation of money given by the worshippers and its formal reception at the communion table; a recitation by the priest of the events of the

Last Supper, with a formalized dramatization of certain actions of Christ during that Supper; a ritual act by which some of the worshippers walk forward to the communion table, eat and drink small portions of bread and wine, which they receive kneeling from the officiating clergy, and return to their places; and, at the conclusion of the service, prayers of thanksgiving and blessing, and dismissal by the priest. The worshippers do not leave immediately. There is a formal procession of the clergy and choir from the church. Some worshippers kneel briefly before leaving. Some greet each other as they leave the church, or remain talking outside. The clergy take up a position at the door and speak to, or shake hands with, worshippers as they go out.

The Object of Worship

We should notice first that every act of worship is structured as a formalized series of interactions with the unseen person addressed as 'God'. The service is a kind of drama in which roles are allocated to priest and congregation. For some sections of the drama their parts are written out for them. During other sections they have the freedom to improvise within certain conventions. The drama in which they take part is one of approach to, communion with and commissioning by, God. This comparison with drama draws attention to the distinctive behaviour of the participants, which is very different from their behaviour in other spheres of their lives. It is not intended to imply that the worshippers are deliberately acting a part, although they have the opportunity to do this.

The role of the worshipper includes participation in hymns, prayers and other acts in which God is addressed directly, and in acts in which the attributes of God, and doctrinal ideas about God, are rehearsed without addressing him directly.

The officiating priest has two roles. He has the task of managing the act of worship, through instructions and more elaborate exhortations. He also has the traditional priestly role of representing the congregation to God and God to the congregation. On certain occasions he addresses God on behalf of the congregation. On others he speaks in the name of God and with his authority. On no occasion does he unequivocally take the part of God, although in the Holy Communion service he in effect takes the part of Christ at the Last Supper. His role is a subtle one, in that it constitutes both a series of acts by which God confronts, instructs, feeds, absolves and blesses the congregation, and also a screen between God and the congregation, in that God's initiatives are always mediated through the priest.

Symbolic and Imagined Actions

Behaviour in worship is not solely verbal. While Anglican worship is generally less demonstrative than that of some other traditions, the relationship of the worshipper to God and to his fellow members of the congregation is given expression in various symbolic actions. Baptism, Holy Communion, confirmation, matrimony and the burial of the dead all include symbolic acts at the climax of the service. The worshipper kneels, to pray and to receive sacramental blessing, as a means of self-abasement. At every stage in an act of worship, the participants' thoughts and attitudes have a counterpart in the way they move, sit, stand, kneel, speak and sing.

In imagination the worshipper participates in a much wider range of acts. He is a soldier, marching to war; he is casting down a crown before the throne of God; he is weeping beside the waters of Babylon. Looked at from the outside, the discrepancy between the imagined activity and the personal attributes of the congregation can be laughable. Yet they are seldom felt to be laughable by those engaged in worship. There are clearly points of similarity between this form of activity and the part played by fantasy in children's play and in certain psycho-therapeutic techniques.

It is also noteworthy that the worshipper adopts a remarkable variety of identifications. He speaks as an individual and as the assembled congregation; in singing psalms he identifies himself with the Hebrews of the Old Testament; on other occasions he identifies himself with the disciples of Christ, with angels and archangels, and with 'all sorts and conditions of men'. The liturgy thus assists a loss of individuality on the part of the worshipper.

The Place of Feeling in Worship

An act of worship is thus a drama in which the individual, in his role as worshipper, expresses a series of attitudes and responses to God, through words and actions. Just as the words and actions of a play, and the words, action and music of an opera, convey the feelings of the characters towards one another and about their circumstances, so these components of the act of worship give expression to feelings associated with the present relationship between the worshipper and God, at different phases in the service. The congregation expresses, in succession, awe, guilt, gratitude, hope and a whole spectrum of emotions. The hymns and readings selected for the service may reinforce this pattern, if skilfully chosen, or may break it up.

Instrumental music, choral music and congregational singing play a large part in creating the emotional climate of the service. For example, many acts of worship are preceded and followed by organ music, often soft and unobtrusive at the beginning, louder and more bracing at the end. Those who are accustomed to this, and have attended a service preceded or followed by silence, may have become aware of the effect which the music is normally having. The singing of hymns and psalms also contributes to the loss of individuality already referred to, as the congregation are caught up in shared feelings and aspirations.

Words are used in a distinctive way in worship. It is clear from the volume of words which are used, and the rich succession of ideas which is evoked, that their effect does not rely upon intellectual comprehension. They are used rather to create a mood and evoke an emotional response. In the same way architecture, furnishings and decorations, special dress and ritual movements are employed to arouse in the worshipper feelings and images congruent with the purpose and movement of the liturgy.

An act of worship thus makes use of a wide range of media to create a setting in which the worshipper may experience feelings explicit or implicit in the words and actions of the liturgy. There is, however, often a discrepancy between the worshipper's public words and behaviour and his private thoughts and feelings. In fact it would be impossible for any individual's feelings to resonate with every sentiment and belief expressed in the liturgy. He may sometimes feel guilty when he takes part in a corporate confession of sin, but often he has no such feeling, though he may not wish to deny that he is guilty. We may accept it as usual that the worshipper is at times internally dissociated from the behaviour in which he is engaging. This does not necessarily imply pretence or hypocrisy on the part of the worshipper, as Wilson (1971, p. 50) points out. The role which the individual takes up in worship thus has an interesting dual function. It awakens in him emotions and images which were previously absent or dormant. It also constitutes a defence against emotions and images which might be powerful and alarming, by allowing him to dissociate himself from what he is doing and saying.

Dependence

A service of worship thus provides an environment and a role in which individuals can behave in a way which expresses a modulating relationship with an unseen person referred to as 'God'. We have endeavoured to find a satisfactory word with which to name this pattern of behaviour, so that we are able to investigate further what it means. We have concluded that the word 'dependence' is the most useful word for this purpose, in spite of its pejorative associations.

We thus describe the role of the worshipper as that of one who is in a *dependent condition*, expressing and experiencing dependence upon an invisible person referred to as 'God'. This description carries no assertion about the character of this person, or indeed whether such a person has any reality outside the mental world of the worshipper. As will be evident from our exposition, we differ from those, including Schleiermacher (1928, Chapter 1), who regard dependence as a feeling. In order to make clearer the meaning which we attach to the word 'dependence' we shall outline the context in which this term is used by W. R. Bion.

As a result of his study of small therapeutic groups, Bion concluded that behaviour in any group is attributable to two different kinds of mental activity. He referred to these as 'sophisticated' activity and 'basic assumption' activity (he also uses the term 'work group' activity to refer to the former).[1] Sophisticated activity is that activity which is consciously directed towards the performance of the task for which the group has met together. It is rational activity directed towards discovering facts, deciding upon appropriate responses, and evaluating results. Bion also describes other activities which generally obstruct sophisticated activity, and appear chaotic to an observer who is not immersed in the feelings and fantasies of the group. Bion's contribution was to recognize that 'these activities, at first sight chaotic, are given a certain cohesion if it is assumed that they spring from basic assumptions common to all the group' (Bion, 1961, p. 46).

Bion described patterns of behaviour in small groups which are attributable to different basic assumptions. One of these suggests the assumption that the group is met 'in order to be sustained by a leader on whom it depends for nourishment, material and spiritual, and protection'. This he referred to as basic assumption *dependence* (*baD*). More colloquially, whenever people meet together, and for whatever overt purpose, part of their activity is directed towards the construction of their own group religion. This is something distinct from the process of establishing group norms identified by other writers (e.g. Whitman, 1964); it is that activity through which a sense of security is built up, based on a shared but unexpressed trust in some idealized person, institution or idea.

It appears that every individual is able to produce from his inner world an image or fantasy of a magic, all-providing leader, parent, or god, and another image of an empty, vulnerable infant or organism. In a group these individual images as it were coalesce into shared fantasies of one who is depended upon and one who depends. The group then sets about creating these persons or objects in its midst, that is making these fantasies concrete. This is the activity described above as constructing its own religion. The group may thus select one member to be the omnipotent leader; any designated leader is the obvious choice. This selection is made instinctively, intuitively and instantaneously. The individual selected for this role is then tempted to accept it, by being offered problems to solve, questions to answer or people to help. Alternatively, the group may corporately take on the role of the omnipotent leader, and feel itself to be full of power to heal and solve problems. Or alternatively again, the magic qualities may be invested in a book, which becomes a group bible, or in an external group or institution.

In the same way the group seeks to create a concrete embodiment of its fantasy of a weak and fragile infant. This role also may be taken by the group corporately, by one individual, who may be the designated leader, or by some external body.

Every feature of the group dominated by *baD*, as described by Bion, can be observed in church life, not merely as an occasional diversion or aberration, but as an aspect of the prevailing culture. When we compare behaviour in the two settings, we notice first of all that there is in each case a shared image of an omnipotent leader or god. In small groups this is an unconscious fantasy, inferred from members' behaviour. Individuals behave as if they had identified such a leader but they would in most cases deny any such belief. A member of a group described by Bion said: 'I do not need to talk because I know that I only have to come here long enough and all my questions will be answered without my having to do anything' (Bion, 1961, p. 147). It may be assumed that he did not believe that Bion was in fact a god or possessed superhuman powers.

In church events participants also speak and behave as though they had access to a God who is described as almighty, all-knowing, eternal and invisible. The worshipping congregation therefore undertakes deliberately what the ordinary small group becomes diverted into through the pressure of fantasies seeking expression. The significant difference is that in the church the fantasy of the omnipotent leader is conscious and actively affirmed. It is, moreover, not simply the product of the internal worlds of those present, but is institutionalized and given expression in various components of the liturgy, which are 'given' as far as the worshipper is concerned. We have also said that, in the small group, members seek to find concrete embodiment for their fantasies of the omnipotent leader and the impotent infant. This also takes place in churches, not only in services of worship but in other meetings and encounters, and in attitudes towards the church building itself. Articles such as the altar, and the area around it, the Bible, and to a lesser extent other objects are treated with veneration and fear. The most obvious tendency is for the priest to be made into the omnipotent leader, and for the lay participants to become passive, de-skilled and lacking in initiative. Clergy frequently bewail the fact that men and women who are in responsible positions in business, local government, education or social work in their ordinary lives, show no capacity to draw upon their skill and knowledge in furthering the organization, teaching or pastoral care of their church. This is usually deplored; it is seldom recognized that this phenomenon at least indicates that the church remains a distinctive institution within the community, with a function different from other kinds of working organization.

What Bion calls the 'dual', or mirror image, of this pattern also occurs. The parish priest and the institution are regarded as weak and fragile, requiring the support and protection of a powerful laity. For example, there is frequently a reluctance to criticize the clergy to their faces, or to speak about criminal or sordid aspects of human life in front of them, as though they were innocent children who would be shattered by these disclosures. The laity are urged to 'support' their church, and to 'support' particular ventures. They are manipulated to attend meetings by being made to feel that, if they do not, they will be guilty of leaving the church, the vicar or God, to loneliness and disillusionment.

Regression to Dependence

The act of going to church is thus accompanied by a change in the individual's state of mind. He adopts attitudes and behaviour expressing a condition of dependence. As we have seen, these tend to permeate all the activities of the church, which can be inconvenient for those who are responsible for managing a church's temporal affairs.

We have had difficulty in finding a suitable term to refer to the transition made by the individual, between the state of mind in which he faces the demands of everyday life, and the state of mind in which he engages in worship. We now prefer the expression *regression to dependence*. This is used by Winnicott in describing the behaviour of patients in psychoanalysis. He also regards it as 'a normal phenomenon that can properly be studied in the healthy person'. In the paper from which this quotation is taken (Winnicott, 1958, p. 278 ff.), he refers to friendships, nursing during physical illness, and poetry, as means by which normal people find restoration and a sense of being real. In conversation with one of the writers he commented on a similar use of the Church and music.

The word 'regression' is used here in a purely descriptive sense: no negative judgment is implied. Both Winnicott and the psychologist Ernst Kris have used the expression 'regression in the service of the ego', to distinguish this process from the uncontrolled process in which the ego is overwhelmed by regression (Winnicott, 1965, p. 254; Kris, 1952). In a similar way Balint (1968) distinguishes between benign and malignant regression. From birth onwards the individual moves from a state of dependence which was total in the womb towards a state of independence. As he moves towards independence he encounters situations which threaten him, as well as others which he is able to master and learn from. When he feels he has adventured too far, he needs an opportunity to recuperate, to regroup his forces or recover his health, and in order to do this he regresses to dependence. This condition of dependence is a 'resting state out of which a creative reaching-out can take place' (Winnicott, 1971, p. 55). From this state he is able to move towards independence once more. This repeating sequence of events is characteristic of normal human behaviour. In illness and times of severe crisis there may be a less controlled regression to dependence, out of which the individual is reluctant or unable to return.

The word 'independence', and also Bowlby's word 'autonomy' (see later) are not altogether satisfactory, since they imply a state in which the individual has no relationship to the object or 'attachment figure' to which he was manifestly related in the state of dependence. It gives no indication that there is something 'inside' him, which enables him to identify objects of dependence on future occasions. A word is required which suggests that he internalizes the object of dependence, making it part of himself. We have coined the term 'intra-dependence' for this state, and the corresponding term 'extra-dependence' for the state of the individual, in worship, when he believes or experiences the dependable object as external to himself. The transition to intradependence is dramatized in the communion service, in the eating and drinking of the sacramental bread and wine. In the 1662 rite the bread is given to the worshipper by the priest, with words which conclude: '... Feed on him in thy heart by faith with thanksgiving'. The symbolic eating and drinking of the body and blood of Christ represents the internalization of Christ, not as an alien object invading and controlling the recipient, but as a presence which is assimilated and incorporated into his personality.

Marion Milner has described the transition to intradependence in her interpretation of William Blake's sequence of paintings illustrating the book of Job. Of one of the later pictures in the sequence she writes:

'It seems that Job no longer needs the omnipotent Father God commanding from above-within and identified with the "wrought image" of himself, for he has found a kind of control that is inherent, part of what is controlled, not separated and split off. He has found a power that transcends the duality of controller and controlled. "And that day ye shall know that I am in my Father and you in me and I in you" says the text. Thus the psyche is surely no longer split into a part which orders and a part which obeys—or rebels. The resulting control of instinct is based on love rather than fear.' (Milner, 1956)

Other Accounts of Religious Behaviour

Other writers have discussed the function of churches in comparable terms. The ideas of Erik Erikson and John Bowlby are of particular interest.

Erikson uses the expression 'basic trust' to refer to the foundation of confidence in a dependable parent upon which the identity of the child is built. The basic trust of the child becomes in adulthood, in his view, a capacity for faith which requires periodic confirmation through some institution, just as the trust of the child is confirmed by occasional return to the mother.

'Religion, it seems, is the oldest and has been the most lasting institution to serve the ritual restoration of a sense of trust in the form of faith while offering a tangible formula for a sense of evil against which it promises to arm and defend man. Childlike strength as well as a potential for infantilization are suggested in the fact that all religious practice includes periodic childlike surrender to the Power that creates and re-creates, dispensing earthly fortune as well as spiritual well-being; the demonstration of smallness and dependence by reduced posture and humble gesture; the confession in prayer and song of misdeeds, misthoughts, and evil intentions and the fervent appeal for inner reunification by divine guidance'. (Erikson, 1968, p. 106)

A key concept in the recent work of John Bowlby (1969) is that of 'attachment behaviour'. Bowlby's concern is with the nature of the child's tie to its mother. In Bowlby's view this bond manifests itself in attachment behaviour. This is behaviour, on the part of the young child, directed towards gaining proximity to certain specific people referred to as 'attachment figures'. The infant's first attachment figure is usually his mother. Bowlby identifies a number of patterns of attachment behaviour: sucking, clinging, following (bodily or with the eyes), crying, calling, smiling. Complementary to these are various forms of 'care-taking' behaviour on the part of the mother: she checks that he is safe, responds to his crying and so on. Attachment behaviour alternates with autonomous behaviour. The child plays by himself, intent on what he is doing. Periodically he checks where his mother is and may follow her from room to room. If he is suddenly frightened, or hurts himself, he may run back to her and cling to her. In general attachment behaviour is activated by unfamiliar and alarming situations. It is also more frequent when the child is tired, hungry or sick.

Bowlby regards attachment and autonomy as normal aspects of adult human behaviour, and suggests that 'a school or college, a work group, a religious group or political group, can come to constitute for many people a subordinate attachment-"figure", and for some people a principal attachment-"figure"'. (Bowlby, 1969, p. 207).

An institution is, of course, an idea held in the mind, to use P. M. Turquet's expression (Turquet, 1969). It is experienced in many partial manifestations: the sight of the church building, externally and internally, the internal furnishings, sacred objects, the sound of choral singing and of the organ, the language of the Authorised Version, the voice of the priest, the smell of incense (or damp, or dry rot), the feel of cool air after the sunshine outside, the bodily sensation of kneeling, the taste of the communion elements.

Most of the patterns of attachment behaviour identified by Bowlby find their counterpart in religious behaviour and religious language. The verbal content of worship is frequently concerned with proximity to a specific attachment-figure, usually God or Christ. An obvious example is the well-known hymn beginning 'Jesu, lover of my soul/Let me to Thy bosom fly'. Nearness to God often includes feeding upon Him, drinking, following Him, finding pasture. Crying and calling are also typical attachment behaviour, and find a close parallel in supplicatory prayer. The emphasis upon prayer in most religions is perhaps the most striking point of contact with Bowlby's observations.

The Environment of the Church

Up to this point we have been concerned with the activities which take place within the local church, and in particular with acts of worship. In order to understand the significance of these activities it is necessary to construct a model of the environment of the church, the environment to which worshippers return. For the activities of an open system are only intelligible when related to the source of the inputs into the system, and the destination to which outputs are returned.

This environment we may refer to as the *profane world*, as contrasted with the *sacred world* which is created in worship. We prefer the world 'profane' (literally, 'before (i.e. outside) the temple') to the less accurate word 'secular'.

We have already begun to delineate this environment. It is an environment of intradependent or autonomous activities. It is furthermore an environment in which the individual is required to venture into the unknown, into situations of uncertainty and danger in which he experiences anxiety which may be overwhelming. His sense of the basic trustworthiness of his environment is threatened. It is thus an environment which gives rise to a periodic wish to find a setting in which regression to dependence is possible and permissible.

In more concrete terms, the profane world is a world of activities directed towards securing the survival and welfare of individuals and the groupings to which they belong, and towards achieving objectives which have practical and symbolic importance for them. We may think of it as the world of work, if work is seen not only as a direct or indirect means of securing survival and protection from discomfort, but also as a means of achieving ends which have personal, emotional significance. These activities demand sophisticated forms of social organization, in which roles, authority, rights and obligations are precisely designated. They may be broadly classified into two categories. There are those which contribute to the 'operative' systems which support life directly, obtaining and processing food and drink, and providing clothing, shelter, transport and other commodities. There are also those which contribute to the 'regulative' systems. These preserve order and facilitate co-operative activity, by reinforcing a shared value-system, maintaining law and providing information and education (for this concept of operative and regulative systems, see Nadel, 1951, p. 136). The activities of industry, agriculture, medicine, recreation and defence are primarily, though not exclusively, operative. Those of government, education and the legal and penal systems are primarily, though not exclusively, regulative. Religious activities are most readily seen as regulative, but our argument here emphasizes their distinctive function.

The state of mind, or type of mental functioning, which is demanded in the profane world may be compared with Bion's concept of sophisticated or work-group activity, in that it is directed towards understanding, modifying and adapting to the realities of the physical and social environment.

As he engages in the activities of the profane world the individual is exposed to anxieties which may be personal or may be shared with groups and communities. There are those which arise in the course of identifying, understanding and overcoming threats to life and welfare—in facing physical and social danger, or the threat of being unable to earn a living. There are also anxieties about the potential or experienced breakdown of the regulative systems. While some of these may arise from unfounded fantasies, some are an irreducible element in human experience, since human beings are subject to injury, disease, ageing and death.

The stability of the systems of the profane world is thus inherently precarious. The world is built upon chaos. Peter Berger points out that, while at one level the opposite of sacred is profane, at a deeper level the opposite is chaos. 'The sacred cosmos emerges out of chaos and continues to confront the latter as its terrible contrary' (Berger, 1969, p. 27). The anxiety we are speaking about is not a fear of identifiable threats, but 'the experience of the threat of imminent non-being' (May, 1958, p. 50), the obliteration of identity. If a group, or larger social system, has no mechanism for controlling this anxiety, constructive and adaptive behaviour is progressively impeded by behaviour springing from primitive fantasies of destruction and chaos. Groups and communities are dominated by behaviour characterized by Bion (1961, p. 152) in his description of the 'fight–flight' basic assumption by ruthless conflict and impetuous flight.

If sophisticated activity is to be maintained, it is therefore necessary for these anxieties to be dispelled or contained. Unfounded fears may be progressively dispelled through the advance of knowledge and education. In the Western world, for example, we may be awed by an eclipse of the Sun, but we no longer need to employ special rituals to allay our terror. But even Western man's knowledgeability is only skin-deep. Faced with the strange and the unexpected, he falls back on responses which he was not taught in school. Some other means of containing these primitive anxieties is required.

The Function of Religion

The individual gains relief from the anxieties of the profane world through regression to extra-dependence. He seeks a setting in which he can adopt a dependent attitude, in which he can believe that he is free to relinquish his responsibilities, at least temporarily, and rely on someone or something else to deal with the sources of his anxiety. In some degree every individual uses the groups and institutions to which he belongs in this way. His home, his employing organization, his leisure associations, his local community, become important sentient systems[2] for him, in which he seeks security, care and love. If he goes to church, this also provides him with a sentient system of this kind, though this is not its distinctive function.

The dependability of all these groups and institutions is limited and derivative. An individual may invest his home or his firm with superhuman qualities of trustworthiness and concern for his welfare, but sooner or later their human limitations are bound to become apparent. The profane world cannot derive its sense of stability and value from these institutions. Integral to our model is the hypothesis that the profane world requires a sacred world, manifested in local institutions, the object of whose worship is believed to transcend the profane world, endorsing its structures and values. This object may be a god, goddess or pantheon, an ideology, or an ideal such as freedom. In the United Kingdom this sacred world has been provided by the Christian churches, though we may now be in a time of transition to a condition in which a plurality of religions endorses a plurality of value-systems.

The function of worship within the local church is therefore to provide a mechanism for the containment of anxiety within its neighbourhood, and in particular those anxieties which arise through confrontation with death and the hazards of human life.

We shall now examine in more detail the model we have broadly sketched in.

Oscillation

One of the first influences upon our thinking about the function of churches in society was Bion's speculative idea of the Church as a 'specialized work group'. Bion (1961, pp. 156 f.), following Freud (1922, p. 41), suggested that the Church is budded off by society to neutralize or cope with manifestations of the dependent basic assumption. In this way sophisticated activity is enabled to proceed in society as a whole, unimpeded. The shape of this idea persists in our present model. Bion speaks of the Church as though it were a permanent group within society—the priesthood perhaps. He does not record any consideration of the behaviour of those who move between the activities of the profane world and those of the specialized work group.

The nature of this *oscillation* is illuminated by the work of Victor Turner. Turner's study of the use of ritual and symbol among primitive African tribes led him to draw a distinction between the everyday behaviour of the tribe in food-gathering, family life and political activity, and behaviour during ceremonies for such occasions as marriage, the birth of a child, rainmaking and the installation of a new chief. He concluded:

'All human societies implicitly or explicitly refer to two contrasting social models ... The first model is of a differentiated, culturally structured, segmented, and often hierarchical system of institutionalized positions. The second presents society as an undifferentiated, homogeneous whole, in which individuals confront one another integrally, and not as "segmentalised" into statuses and roles.' (Turner 1969. p. 177)

Turner sees society, not as a static pattern of structured relationships, but as a process, a constantly changing pattern:

'Society seems to be a process rather than a thing—a dialectical process with successive phases of structure and communitas. There would seem to be—if one can 'use such a controversial term—a human need to participate in both modalities.' (Turner, 1969, p. 177)

Every society is thus the scene of continual oscillation between two states, as individuals, groups, communities or the total population move between the structured relationships of everyday working and social life, and the undifferentiated relationships of religious activity (communitas). This religious activity provides a vehicle by which the society can give expression to fantasies and emotions which, if expressed in the structured area of life, would threaten chaos by disrupting co-operative relationships. In a country the size of the United Kingdom it would be very difficult for the whole population to engage in religious activity simultaneously, as is possible in a small tribe. How then do the activities of a minority within the sacred world protect the activities of the profane world from the dislocation of disruptive anxieties? We have concluded that those who do not go to church participate vicariously in the church-going of those who do. Work with many churches has convinced us that the existence of a functioning church has great emotional significance to those who live in its neighbourhood, irrespective of whether they ever attend its services. For some it is a focus of idealized images of worship which would be shattered if they ever went to church. For others it is an object of 'negative dependence': it is necessary for them that it should exist, so that they can hate and stay away from it.

More precisely, it seems necessary to distinguish between three types of people. There are those who participate regularly in acts of worship. There are those who seldom or never attend worship, but for whom it is important that a member of their family, or an acquaintance, goes to church, as it were on their behalf. Thirdly there are those who do not identify themselves with any particular church-goer, but for whom it is important that church buildings should continue to exist and be used for worship. The existence of this third group may not become manifest until a church is threatened with closure.

The Primary Task of the Church

Our most important conceptual tool in examining the function of churches in society has been Rice's concept of *primary task*. This he defines in his later writings as that task which, at any given time, an enterprise must perform if it is to survive. Trist and his colleagues speak of the primary task as being 'the key transaction which relates an operating group to its environment and allows it to maintain the steady state' (Trist and coworkers, 1963, quoted in Smith, 1970, p. 46). It appears to us that the meaning of the concept 'wanders', in the work of Rice and others, so that it also sometimes denotes the task which defines the identity of an enterprise, and sometimes, reverting to an earlier definition, the task which the enterprise was created to perform. The statement by Trist helps to pin the concept to what we regard as its basic meaning in Rice's later thought, the meaning which we shall adopt here.

The primary task of an enterprise, as thus defined, is a function of its environment as well as of its internal structuring. It is a task which provides both enterprise and environment with a pay-off. As such it is to be distinguished from the aims or purposes entertained by members of an enterprise, which need not necessarily be realized, and cannot be realized if a complementary environment cannot be found. The aims of individuals can only be realized through activities which relate institutions to reciprocating environments. The tasks which they are in reality able to perform are therefore in part determined by the 'bargain' which the environment strikes with the institution. Enterprise and environment each seek to shape the transactions between them to fit the goals which they seek to achieve.

The distinction between aim and task is important in any consideration of the activities of churches. Clergy and laity have hopes and ideals for the Church which are often entertained with great passion. They find it correspondingly difficult to acknowledge that what actually happens in their churches is an expression not only of these aims, but also of the aims of the individuals and groups which make up its environment.

The foregoing discussion leads us to the following definition of the primary task of a church, in England, affiliated to the Church of England:

to contain, or render manageable, anxieties associated with the activities of the profane world, so that individuals and institutions are able to carry out the tasks on which the survival and well-being of their society depends.

The process by which this task is performed may be represented in this way:

Individuals and groups, representative of society, expressing the anxieties of the profane world	Activities facilitating regression to extra-dependence, worship of dependable objects, and transition to intradependence	Individuals and groups, representative of society, expressing trust in the survival of the profane world

This is a general model, which provides a basis for the examination of the activities of any church. For a particular church the corresponding model would need to be more specific about the identity of the community served by the church. Only in rural areas does this approximate to the parish.

There is the major complication that, while some churches thrive and others decline, for reasons which may be discernible, all are interdependent. All draw upon, and contribute to, the same capital fund, which is the vitality and credibility of its essential images and doctrines within the population as a whole. This fund is also partially shared with other denominations and sects, and with churches in other parts of the world. Our statement also takes no account of judgements which are made about what constitutes an authentic Christian, or an authentic Anglican, institution. So far we have been concerned solely with churches as centres of the dominant religion or 'folk belief' (Mensching, 1964) of this country.

Inadequate Primary Task Performance

According to our model it would be expected that, if the churches ceased to provide a vehicle by which the society (or societies) they served oscillated between extra- and intra-dependence, co-operative work and social order would progressively break down. Putting this the other way round, if such breakdown was judged to be taking place, this would imply that religious institutions were ceasing to fulfil this function. The correlation between these two factors would be very difficult to demonstrate on a national scale; nevertheless the state of affairs in our society today seems open to this interpretation. At the local level the hypothesis could be tested more readily. An unpublished pilot study, by our Institute, of an urban community where the parish church had been closed down seven years before, gave indications that this had led to a deterioration in the morale of the community. Beliefs in the locality about the effect of this closure were typified by one woman, who said: 'Re-open the church and bring back the neighbourhood, the closeness. People just pass you by on the street. It's not so close-knit'. A sound research study would of course need to draw upon other evidence besides the conscious beliefs and feelings of residents; it would also be necessary to investigate whether any apparently linked declines in church attendance and community morale were attributable to some prior factor affecting both.

Our pilot study suggested that the loss of the parish church as a symbol caused individuals and families to, as one person put it, 'withdraw into their shells'. In general we might expect that if this defence failed, or was not available, communal life would progressively disintegrate through delinquency, violence, mental illness, suicide, decline in productive work and other such effects.

We might also expect to observe a search for alternative religions which could be invested with the vitality which the declining religion was no longer felt to possess.

The Nature of the Regression Fostered

We have already referred to the fact that psychoanalytic writers have identified two types of regression, a controlled or benign regression (regression in the service of the ego), and an uncontrolled or malign regression (the ego overwhelmed by regression). Our model of the local church has so far taken no account of these two possibilities. The distinction is an important one.

The uncontrolled type of regression is also referred to by Winnicott as 'withdrawal'. He describes occasions in which the patient withdraws into what appears to be a brief waking sleep or reverie; he 'switches off'. Patients have subsequently described fantasies which they had during these periods. They have momentarily felt themselves curled up in the womb, or lying in a mother's lap. It appears that this behaviour is associated with a fantasy of reversion to a state in which no attention need be given to maintaining relations with other persons or with the environment. Usually 'the withdrawn state is not profitable, and when the patient recovers...he or she is not changed' (Winnicott, 1958, p. 225).

There is a form of religious behaviour which might also be called withdrawal. Participation in worship is used as a respite from the demands of everyday life. The worshipper entertains imprecise hopes of divine care and of a life after death. He does not question or bring into focus the nature of the being on whom he is depending for this. He makes no distinction between the emotions he experiences, which are immediate and therefore certain, and the god which is their object, who is not perceived by his senses, and whose existence is therefore uncertain. This inhibition of sophisticated ego function is also apparent in the partial loss of distinctions in task between one type of meeting and another. Educational meetings, church council meetings and community service activities are all used as further opportunities for regression to dependence (see above).

If the parallels which we have drawn with psychoanalytic experience are sound, the use of the activities of the church for withdrawal or uncontrolled regression does not lead to enhanced intradependence. The individual returns home with a renewed willingness to fulfil the tasks allotted to him, but nothing more. If this pattern of religious behaviour predominates in a society, it must be expected merely to reinforce the *status quo*. Fears of death and disorder are not only contained but suppressed. Within the static social framework thus reinforced, existing forms of work, social relationship and cultural activity have freedom to continue. But the society has little capacity to respond to new challenges, from new knowledge and technologies, for example; nor to question its own value-system and social order.

We conclude that if the predominant behaviour of clergy and worshippers in a society implies a definition of task which permits uncontrolled regression, then the churches will survive and maintain a stable form only as long as other challenges do not bring about major changes in the society. Church and society are symbiotic; they nourish each other in stable conditions but, when conditions change, unless one can throw the other off, they perish together.

Controlled Regression to Dependence

By contrast, worship in which controlled regression predominates may be expected to lead to enhanced intradependence. It is characteristic of such worship that the worshipper retains the knowledge that his god is not an object of the senses. In religious terms, he walks by faith, not by sight. He also uses his intellect to endeavour to understand the character of the god whose existence he is affirming. Because the ego is not overwhelmed by regression he also continues to recognize the painful realities of everyday experience, such as failure, pain, loss and death. Worship is used as a means of facing them, not of denying them. Their attendant anxieties are not suppressed, but rather contained by being transformed into manageable fears (cf. Bion, 1962).

If the predominant form of worship in a church is one of controlled regression to dependence, we would expect that there would be an enhanced capacity to meet new challenges and adapt to change in the surrounding community. The threat of chaos which is present in change would be less severe, because members of the community would have an idea of a dependable god which survived the loss of feelings of security.

The sense of basic trust which is restored in such worship would lead to enhanced confidence in the reliability of organizational structures, laws, contracts and customs. The individual would therefore know where he stood, with a consequent sense of freedom to exercise his capabilities and discretion within this framework. This concept of freedom is to be distinguished from the negative concept which envisages only freedom *from* something—freedom from constraint, from encroachment, from demands. This is a form of extra-dependence upon a bad, limiting object. Intradependence is characterized by freedom *for* creative work and constructive relationships.

In groups and communities in which there is a high level of anxiety, people's capacity to perceive and acknowledge the reality of situations and events is reduced. Reassuring fantasies are preferred to facts which may threaten the individual's position. There is a corresponding tendency to see and use others as objects, rather than to recognize them as persons and enter imaginatively into their experience. Where anxiety is made manageable through the activities of churches, it is to be expected that there would be an increased respect for truth and capacity to perceive it, and also an enhanced valuation of the individual. The latter would find expression in just laws and contracts, and in altruistic behaviour.

Where the churches foster worship characterized by controlled regression to dependence, the possibilities for freedom, truth and justice within the profane world are thus increased. The churches do not bring about these conditions; they are created or prevented by the activities of men and women within the operative and regulative systems of the profane world.

In view of the increasing involvement of the Christian churches in direct social action, it is worth pointing out that, according to our model, the basic function of the churches in this country is not to feed the hungry or secure the rights of the oppressed. Christians may undertake to do this, individually or in groups, as an expression of the beliefs they have professed in worship. The Old and New Testaments both affirm that the test of true worship is that it leads to compassion and just dealing. But the distinctive task of the churches as institutions is to provide the occasions for true worship, without which Christians and unbelievers alike lose the inner freedom from which true compassion and realistic social action spring.

The churches abandon their distinctive task when they confuse the realms of the sacred and the profane. In the sacred world the normative behaviour is the worship of God; in the profane world the normative behaviour is the service of man. Our assertion that the Church's institutional task is confined to the sacred world does not, if accepted, commit the Christian to the belief that God is so restricted. Theologically, it implies only that God's relation to the profane world is different.

Notes

1. We now prefer other terms for these two types of activity, but have retained Bion's terms here since they are more familiar.
2. 'Sentient system': a system to which the individual gives loyalty, and from which he derives a sense of identity and belonging (Miller and Rice, 1967, p. xiii).

References

Balint, M. (1968), *The Basic Fault*, Tavistock Publications, London.
Berger, P. L. (1969), *The Social Reality of Religion*, Faber, London.
Bion, W. R. (1961), *Experiences in Groups*, Tavistock Publications, London.
Bion, W. R. (1962), A theory of thinking, in *International Journal of Psychoanalysis*, **43**, 308.
Bowlby, J. (1969), *Attachment and Loss. Vol. 1: Attachment*, Hogarth Press and Institute of Psycho-Analysis, London.
Erikson, E. H. (1968), *Identity—Youth and Crisis*, Faber, London.
Freud, S. (1922), *Group Psychology and the Analysis of the Ego*, Complete Works, Vol. 18, Hogarth Press and Institute of Psycho-Analysis, London.
Kris, E. (1952), *Psychoanalytic Exploration in Art*, International University Press, New York.
May, R., in May, R., Angel, E. and Ellenberger, H. F. (1958), *Existence*, Basic Books, New York.
Mensching, G. (1964), The masses, folk belief and universal religion, in Schneider, L., *Religion, Culture and Society*, Wiley, New York.
Miller, E. J. and Rice, A. K. (1967), *Systems of Organization: the Control of Task and Sentient Boundaries*, Tavistock Publications, London.
Milner, M. (1956), The sense in non-sense, in *New Era*, January.
Mooney, J. D. and Reiley, A. C. (1931), *Onward Industry*, Harper, New York.
Nadel, S. F. (1951), *The Foundations of Social Anthropology*, Cohen and West, London.
Reed, B. D. (1970), *Going to Church*, Grubb Institute of Behavioural Studies, London.
Schleiermacher, F. (1928), *The Christian Faith*, T. and T. Clark, Edinburgh.
Smith, P. B., Ed. (1970), *Group Processes*, Penguin, London.
Trist, E. L., Higgin, G. W., Pollock, A. B. and Murray, H. A. (1963), *Organizational Choice*, Tavistock Publications, London.

Turner, V. W. (1969), *The Ritual Process—Structure and Anti-structure*, Routledge and Kegan Paul, London.

Turquet, P. M. (1969), *Aspects of Primary Task*, unpublished paper.

Whitman, R. M. (1964), Psychodynamic principles underlying T-group processes, *in* Bradford, L. P., Gibb, J. R. and Benne, K., Eds., *T-group Theory and Laboratory Methods*, Wiley, New York, pp. 310–335.

Wilson, J. B. (1971), *Education in Religion and the Emotions*, Heinemann, London.

Winnicott, D. W. (1958), *Collected Papers*, Tavistock Publications, London.

Winnicott. D. W. (1965), *The Maturational Process and the Facilitating Environment*, Hogarth Press and Institute of Psycho-Analysis, London.

Winnicott, D. W. (1971), *Playing and Reality*, Tavistock Publications, London.

PART III

Approaching Organizational Change

Introduction to Part III

The writers in Part II were by no means unconcerned with change. As they teased out the characteristics of tasks, explored the implications of defining tasks in different ways and discussed the design of organizational models to fit these alternatives, all of them were looking towards capability for organizational change. If the contributors to Part III differ at all, it is in a greater preoccupation with processes of change and innovation as such and with the issues these raise.

They examine these processes and issues in a variety of systems—families, university departments, hospitals—and from a variety of perspectives. Shapiro and Zinner are psychiatrists engaged in treatment and research with disturbed adolescents and their families; Hausman is attempting to transform a department of psychiatry in a medical school from his position as department head; Colman is implementing a new approach to treatment in a psychiatric ward and putting to practical test an organizational model for innovation; and finally Rogers (who was himself first a successful businessman and second a university student before engaging in consultancy, teaching and research in organization) describes the educational model that he has developed to help his own students become effective initiators of institutional and social change.

A psychiatrist's case-study of a disturbed adolescent may at first sight seem incongruous in a volume on organization. Shapiro and Zinner, however, as their title implies—'Family Organization and Adolescent Development'—view the family as an organization performing tasks. They propose that the primary task of a family with adolescents may be formulated as:

'The promotion of relative autonomy and identity formation in its adolescent members leading to their individuation and eventual separation.'

Using such a definition enables them to infer criteria for effective task performance and to identify constraints that may interfere with it. In particular they postulate the operation of unconscious assumptions, and associated anxieties and defences, which affect performance.

A central concept they advance for the study of family interaction is 'delineation', which is the behaviour by which one family member communicates his mental representation of another, either explicitly or implicitly. Three levels of inference are made through the use of the delineation concept. First, specified behaviour in one person implies a particular delineation of another. Second, the delineation by one person of another is either reality based, or based on the mobilization of dynamic conflict and defence already present in the delineator. Thirdly, from family interaction containing defensive delineations, evidence can be built up of the shared characteristics of the family as a group, and of the unconscious determinants of these. This evidence of unconscious fantasy and defence in the family, the authors conclude, is analagous to Bion's concept of 'basic assumption' behaviour in small groups (Bion, 1961). The authors present case material to exemplify these processes and show how the child, by internalizing his parents' defensive delineations, moves into a complementary role to fit their defensive requirements. These defensive delineations and the unconscious assumptions on which the family operates as a group can hold the adolescent in a fixed role and so interfere with the primary task of the family.

Apart from giving insights into the family and adolescent development, the paper demonstrates the importance of unconscious assumptions as part of group life. The concept of delineation helps to explicate how individuals lodge images of themselves in a system of interaction which sustains and reinforces their delineations to create a shared reality. The concept is a bridge between the inner world of the individual, his actions and systems of interaction. Exploration of the family's delineations may then be a fulcrum for therapeutic intervention, in much the same way as a consultant may work with members of a larger organization to explicate what Hutton called their 'structure representations'.

Thus the Shapiro-Zinner paper illustrates within one type of very small-scale organization the kinds of forces that administrators and consultants may have to contend with in trying to bring about changes in larger enterprises. The papers by Hausman and Colman offer other illustrations.

Hausman's paper, entitled 'The Reorganization of a University Department of Psychiatry: A Blueprint for Change', describes his experience, as the head of a department with clinical, research and teaching responsibilities, of working with his colleagues to initiate change and innovation. He drew heavily on Rice's concepts both to analyse the prevailing organization and to formulate directions of change and approaches to it.

Briefly, when Hausman took over his position the department was divided into four areas of work: adult psychiatry, child psychiatry, clinical psychology and research. The primary task of the department appeared to be serving the clinical activities alone. In view of the range of throughputs of the department—patients, students and knowledge—Hausman reformulated the primary task in the direction of a broadly based educational programme with particular emphasis on the social aspects of the mental health field.

Embedded in Hausman's descriptions of the actual changes achieved, there is examination of the difficulties of a leader who wants to use a theoretical frame of reference to understand the system he is managing, but who, at the same time, is also working within it and has ongoing responsibility for the outputs of the system. He has to be aware not only of the constraints operating on the system from outside, but also of those that are present within it: for example, existing alignments and conflicts in the department. Hausman discusses the nature of authority and sanction necessary to support creative innovation and change in the face of the potentially neutralizing effects of such constraints.

Colman's paper, 'Operant Conditioning and Organizational Design', is also an account of an attempt to introduce change from a position of administrative leadership. He begins with a provocative comparison of operant conditioning and organizational theory. Each has its own distinctive perspective on human behaviour, uses its own language and deals in its own sets of data; yet both are concerned with the analysis and design of task-oriented human environments. Colman describes how he has used the two frameworks in his work of designing and running psychiatric wards. He argues that development of the therapeutic community concept has been hampered by vaguely specified design models which fail to take into account the total social milieu in which the hospital ward is set, and the social processes generated by both staff and patients. The evidence is that operant conditioning has proved valuable as a behaviour therapy, particularly the use of a 'token economy' whereby patients are paid in artificial currency for specific behaviours. When token economies were first introduced to therapeutic institutions, it was found that there were considerable organizational constraints. Colman puts this down to the fact that no attention was given to the inevitable impact that technological innovation has on task performance and organizational structure. In the last part of his paper he describes how, using the concepts of Miller and Rice (1967), he designed and introduced a new operant treatment system for delinquent men at the Walter Reed General Hospital in Washington.

The paper by Rogers, 'Teaching and Learning for Responsibility', addresses the problem of relevant teaching of organizational behaviour. He starts from the premise that universities have to take realistically into account the turbulent environment of rapid and unpredicted change, within which there is widespread protest against the conduct of established institutions. Students are specifically angry at what the educational system is teaching them about society: they want an education that will develop the system of values that they hold, enhance their capacity for self-respect and enable them to engage with the social realities they live in, as opposed to having their concerns defused or 'cooled out'. To respond effectively places a formidable load on educators who, like Rogers, take their responsibilities seriously.

He describes the educational model that he himself has devised and uses. He perceives his own task as to develop his students' competence to understand and engage with social institutions. They have to be able to grapple with contemporary and future institutions in all their complexity—their internal contradictions, conflicts, dislocations, inequities. The starting-point is in the design of the organization of his educational institution itself, and in the way it is operated. It is a method of helping students to become aware of their own experiences, first among themselves and then outside, so that they can not only identify changes and adapt to them but, over and above this, bring about changes in their environment.

Thus Rogers, like many of the writers in Part II, is describing an organization for performance of a task; and indeed there are parallels with the model Lofgren has developed for psychotic patients. Lofgren, however, has the limited objective of producing an output of patients who can operate with some degree of independence in their external social situations. On the other hand, the student outputs of the Rogers system—and this is my reason for making it the last paper in the volume—are themselves to become agents of change. They will have had an opportunity to consider and conceptualize their responsibility for inventing the future of their society.

References

Bion, W. R. (1961), *Experiences in Groups*, Tavistock Publications, London.
Miller, E. J. and Rice, A. K. (1967), *Systems of Organization*, Tavistock Publications, London.

Family Organization and Adolescent Development*

Roger L. Shapiro and John Zinner

Introduction

This paper is concerned with the area of experience comprising the boundary between the individual adolescent and his family group. Exploration of transactions across this boundary area entails two levels of observation, that of individual behaviour and that of family group behaviour. The goal of such exploration is to clarify the relation of adolescent personality functioning to family functioning and the consequences of family functioning for the individual adolescent.

The understanding of adolescence is enhanced by study of the adolescent in the context of his family group (Shapiro, 1969a). During adolescence a marked alteration occurs in the individual's relationship to his family, to his peer group and to other groups in society (Erikson, 1956, 1962; Shapiro, 1963). This alteration is in part determined by maturation in the ego and the id during puberty resulting in important changes in cognitive and affective capacities (Freud, 1936, 1958; Inhelder and Piaget, 1958). It is codetermined by the nature of the internalizations of family relationships which have occurred through infancy and childhood (Jacobson, 1964; Schafer, 1968). Adolescent development brings about a reorganization of these internalizations in relation to ego–id maturation and new experience (Blos, 1962; Erikson, 1956). One consequence of this reorganization is an increase in the relative autonomy of the ego of the adolescent, which leads to the establishment of ego identity (Shapiro, 1966, 1969b).

The adolescent's relation to his family group is his central experience of continuity in relationships from earliest childhood through late adolescence. Family experience establishes a core of internalizations derived not only from characteristics of the parents as persons, but also from the quality of their perceptions of and attitudes toward the child and adolescent (Loewald, 1960). These perceptions and attitudes may be ascertained through direct observation of family interaction.

Our study of the family is facilitated through application of Rice's concept of primary task to the family group (Rice, 1969). From the point of view of adolescent development, we consider the primary task of the family group to be the

* Presented at the 58th Annual Meeting of The American Psychoanalytic Association, Group Studies in Progress, Panel on Adolescent Development from the Perspective of Family Studies, Washington, D. C. April 29th-May 3rd, 1971.

This paper comes from work done in association with Carmen Cabrera, M. A., Doris Droke, Winfield Scott, Ph.D., John Strauss, M. D.

promotion of relative ego autonomy and identity formation in its adolescent members leading to their individuation and eventual separation. This task may be interfered with by unconscious assumptions in the family which militate against the development of ego autonomy and individuation in the adolescent. In this paper we will consider evidence in family interaction from which we infer the existence of such unconscious assumptions within the family, and discuss the consequences of these assumptions for the accomplishment of the task we have defined.

In order to study the family as a group distinguished from the individual members who comprise it, our research with 45 disturbed adolescents and their families includes weekly sessions of conjoint family therapy, as well as weekly marital therapy for the parents, and three sessions per week of individual psychotherapy for the adolescent. The weekly conjoint family therapy sessions are the source of the research observations of family interaction.

A central concept in our study of family interaction is delineation, a concept closely linked to observable behaviour (Shapiro, 1968, 1969a). Delineations are behaviours through which one family member communicates explicitly or implicitly his perceptions and attitudes—in fact, his mental representation of another family member—to that other person. Through use of the concept of delineation we make formulations involving three levels of inference from observations of family interaction. A first level of inference is that specified behaviours in one person imply a particular delineation of the other person.

A second level of inference is about the determinants of delineation. Delineations may communicate a view of the other person which appears to be predominantly determined by his reality characteristics. Or delineations may communicate a view of the other person which appears to be predominantly determined by the mobilization of dynamic conflict and defence in the delineator. We call the latter category defensive delineations. We pay particular attention to parental defensive delineations of the adolescent. When parental delineations are observed to be distorted, stereotyped and over-specific, contradictory, or otherwise incongruent with the range of behaviours manifested by the adolescent, we make the inference that these delineations serve defensive aspects of parental personality functioning. That is, they are not simply realistic responses to the current characteristics of the adolescent. Also we further hypothesize that the parents through their defensive delineations seek to hold the child and adolescent in relatively fixed roles throughout development.

In addition, we make a third level of inference, that of characteristics of the family group as a whole. From excerpts of family interaction containing defensive delineations, we accrue evidence of shared or complementary characteristics of the family as a group and of the unconscious determinants of these characteristics. We conclude that this evidence of coordinated, shared, complementary behaviour in the family relates to a level of unconscious fantasy and defence in the family group analogous to Wilfred Bion's concept of small-group behaviour organized around particular unconscious assumptions

(Bion, 1961). The group theory of Bion derives from psychoanalysis and is a way of conceptualizing conscious and unconscious systems of motivation and defence in the group as a whole. Bion's small group theory characterizes the basic assumption group as one in which for defensive reasons the group appears to be dominated and often united by covert assumptions based on unconscious fantasies. The work of the group, its functioning and task performance, is impaired with deterioration of the ego functioning of the members. The realities of the situation and the task are lost sight of, reality testing is poor, secondary process thinking deteriorates and more primitive forms of thinking emerge. There is new organization of behaviour which seems to be determined by fantasies and assumptions which are unrealistic and represent a failed struggle to cope with the current reality situation. Thereby the group survives as such, though its essential functioning and primary task are now altered in the service of a different task (Turquet, 1971).

When the family is in a situation of anxiety leading to predominance of defensive delineations, there are interesting analogies to small group basic assumption behaviour. When defensive delineations predominate in family interaction, conflicting motivations, anxiety and defence are seen with accompanying ego regression and behaviour determined more by fantasy than by reality. Work failure is evident in the family situation, similar to basic assumption functioning: there is emergence of confused, distorted thinking; failure of understanding and adequate communication; breakdown in the ability of the family to work co-operatively or creatively on a task, to maintain a progressive discussion in which family members understand each other, or to deal realistically with the problems under discussion. In short, the family is in a situation in which unconscious assumptions are mobilized with associated anxiety, a variety of defensive behaviours are seen, and there is disturbance in the family's reality functioning. In contrast, in the absence of anxiety related to unconscious assumptions, the family does not manifest predominantly defensive behaviour, is clearly reality oriented, and is well related to the family primary task.

We now turn to consideration of the individual child and adolescent maturing within the framework of family group assumptions. We consider identification processes to be internalizations which are central determinants of structure formation in the child (Schafer, 1968). In addition, we believe that the child internalizes aspects of family relationships in which the parents attribute particular characteristics to him and communicate attitudes towards him. These delineations also modify the child's self representation and are determinants of structure formation. Delineations of the child and adolescent which serve a defensive function for the parent are particularly coercive in that behaviour in the child which counters these parental delineations leads to anxiety in the parent. The child is then motivated to behave so as to mitigate this parental anxiety. Internalization by the child of the parent's defensive delineations of him moves the developing child and adolescent into a role which is complementary to parental defensive requirements (Wynne and

Singer, 1963; Singer and Wynne, 1965). Defensive delineations are consequently dynamic determinants of role allocation in the family. The role allocated is necessary to maintain parental defence and mitigate parental anxiety.
The dynamics of role allocation operate in a broader framework of unconscious
assumptions of the family as a group and modify the internalizations of the
self representation. These influences are important in the reorganization of
internalizations which leads to increased ego autonomy and identity formation
in adolescence.

Example of a Situation in a Family Group

We will now present material from one of the families we have studied to
exemplify the methods of observation and inference we have discussed. First
the identity crisis of the adolescent is described and then observations of family
interactions containing defensive delineations are reported in the form of
excerpts from tape recordings of conjoint family therapy sessions. First-level
inferences from family interactions are formulations of the delineations
they contain. Second-level inferences concern evidence that the delineations
are defensive, and are statements of the dynamics of delineations in these
interactions. Finally we make formulations about the unconscious assumptions
of the family as a group, a third level of inference from these observations. The
excerpts are selected as examples of defensive delineations in which unconscious
assumptions of the family group are central dynamics of interaction. Shifts
are seen over time in the roles played by the various family members in relation
to shared assumptions. These assumptions are clearly operative in all members
of the family group. We will consider in particular the importance of the family's
unconscious assumptions for the identity crisis of the adolescent.

In this family a dramatic personality change occurred in the adolescent, a
boy of 18, during his first two years of college. This reached a crisis with feelings
of confusion, of merging with others, being controlled by others, withdrawal,
extreme shifts in mood and rage episodes which finally resulted in his hospitalization. In the patient's freshman year at college he followed the pattern he had
established in high school of compliance, obsessive studying and constricted
social relationships. He initially dealt with the transition from living at home
to living in a large university in another city by attempting to maintain continuity with the pattern of life he had previously known. He did well academically,
wrote frequent and lengthy letters to his parents, and established no close new
relationships with boys or girls. His identity as compliant student and relative
social isolate was familiar but ungratifying. He became more aware of other
choices and other possibilities in observing the lives of other students. He
envied their greater freedom to enjoy life and wanted to emulate them; but he
could not, and felt inadequacy and confusion in any other than his familiar
pattern of living. However, his old equilibrium was disturbed, and when he
returned home for the summer, he felt estranged there as well. In the presence of
his parents, particularly his mother, he felt pressures against change. He felt

the dilemma that in order to remain related to his parents as a son he could not be the person he wanted to be in college. He felt ashamed of his family and felt alienated from them because of wishes to grow beyond the identity he had established with them. During the summer he was solitary and spent much time reading, particularly in the areas of Zen, Yoga and psychoanalysis. Upon his return to college he determined to follow a new direction to avoid the identity of grind and to dedicate himself to some cause larger than himself, to develop his human relationships, and to relate his mind to 'real life'. He became active in a campus political organization, became involved in a Yoga study group, and neglected his academic work. He pursued this course with a clear feeling that he had found the life of a grind unrewarding and with a determination to find something more gratifying. Within a few weeks he was feeling agitated and confused. He felt that he was over-involved in extracurricular activity, felt concern over his academic commitments and felt unsure about the choices he had made. Intense feelings of unworthiness and guilt tormented him, and he sought refuge in Yoga exercises and meditation. He wrote to his parents about his new interests, hoping to obtain his mother's approval and under-standing. His mood shifted frequently from feelings of unworthiness and despair to periods of euphoria and excitement. These latter eventuated on several occasions in mystical experiences characterized by feelings that there was a central unity in the universe, that all consciousness was identical to his individual consciousness, and that his individual identity was only a temporary and artificial separation from a larger identity. He attended few classes and after several months his adviser recommended that he see a student health psychiatrist. Because of preoccupation and withdrawal, unusual behaviour such as long periods of meditation and poor academic performance, it was finally determined that he should leave college and return home.

Throughout this period of turmoil, the patient felt an agonizing diffusion in self definition. In personal relationships this was manifested in disturbing feelings of merging, of being controlled by and becoming the other person. The loss of a sense of himself was confusing and frightening and resulted in feelings of great weakness and vulnerability. He originally felt a danger of loss of himself in relation to his parents, and his original repudiation of the identity of student grind was a reaction against this. His actual separation from his parents facilitated this reaction. Similar feelings of vulnerability at college led to wariness in new relationships and defensive isolation. His attraction to Eastern philosophy and particularly to meditation techniques was part of an effort to augment his independence in new relationships. However, the shift in identity from grind to mystic resulted in disorganization of obsessional defences. Ego regression ensued in which Yoga exercises and meditation seemed to have dynamic consequences analogous to sensory deprivation experiences. They did promote a new degree of ego autonomy from the environment; but they left the ego's autonomy from the id impaired. This led to further withdrawal, to mystical experiences, to bizarre affective states and to rage episodes which eventually resulted in the patient's hospitalization.

Discussion of the Example

In conceptualizing the identity crisis described, ego regression is assumed to be a consequence of pre-existing impairment in adolescent ego development. Instead of an adolescent development characterized by gradual achievement of relative ego autonomy, a disturbance in the ego's autonomy from objects in reality is manifested by persisting feelings of vulnerability in relationships. In the investigation of determinants of this ego disturbance, we turn to examples of family interaction for analysis of content and dynamics of parental delineations of the adolescent.

Since it is in the area of independent functioning that the adolescent manifests his greatest disturbance, we select for investigation characteristics of delineations in family interactions where concrete independent behaviours of family members are discussed. In this family a striking and characteristic pattern of behaviour is seen when issues of independent functioning are under discussion. These behaviours are initially most apparent in delineations of the adolescent. Later they are seen to be present in reaction to independent behaviour and thinking in other family members also.

An aspect of delineation of particular importance to independent functioning is the response of family members to differences and disagreements. In family observations we focus upon the degree of tolerance of family members for differences; for separate, distinct and disparate ideas and feelings within the family group. In this family the adolescent's feeling of being controlled by his parents' disapproval is clearly illustrated in the first two excerpts. In the third and fourth excerpts a similar sensitivity and similar feeling of being controlled is expressed by the mother in response to disagreement and disapproval from the adolescent, and it is clear that it is not only the adolescent who feels controlled by differences and disagreements. This is further exemplified in the fifth and sixth excerpts where the father's response to criticism and feeling of vulnerability to control by the adolescent and by the mother is seen. It is apparent that intolerance of disagreement and the feeling that disagreement is equivalent to the exercise of control is a shared feeling in this family. This is important with respect to the models for identification available to the adolescent and the relation of these models to the identity problems he manifests.

It is assumed that in the adolescent, identification with important aspects of the personality functioning of each parent is found. In this case the adolescent's striking intolerance to criticism and disagreement is a characteristic shared with his parents which is evidence of identification. However, these parents appear to reinforce identification through their delineations of the adolescent. They are impaired in their capacity to differentiate themselves from the adolescent and tend to project their own characteristics into him. Under these circumstances we find identification and delineation to be related in a specific way. The bridge between them is projection (Zinner and Shapiro, 1971). Through identification, images of the parents are internalized by the adolescent which determine characteristics of his personality functioning. Through delineation, projection into the adolescent of aspects of the parents' personality characteristics results in an active definition of him by the parents systematically related to what the parents are themselves. Thus certain characteristics which have been learned by the adolescent in identifications are also actively imposed by the parents in defensive delineations.

In the following excerpts of family interaction, we will attempt to elucidate the interplay of adolescent identification and parental delineations determined by projective identification.

The first excerpt is taken from a family session which occurred ten months after the patient's admission to the hospital. The patient has been talking in recent family sessions about returning to college in several months. He has been working successfully for two months in the community at a part-time job. He raises the issue of college again in this session, but this time it is coupled with a new and more immediate project. He states that he wants to leave the hospital as soon as possible but to move into an apartment of his own rather than live again with his parents.

Excerpt 1

ALLEN: *...I'm thinking of leaving here and getting an apartment on the outside...and I think I've found that...for my OWN good, the approval I want is the absence of disapproval.*

FATHER: *That I don't understand. I don't know what the absence of disapproval means.*

MOTHER: *Either you approve or you disapprove.*

ALLEN: *Well, you don't disapprove or don't approve. You can...*

MOTHER: *In other words, you're going to do this regardless of how we feel? Is that it?*

FATHER: *No, no, no, no—that isn't what he's trying to say ...*

MOTHER: *The absence of disapproval...*

ALLEN: *That's probably true, though, anyway. But that's not what I said. It's your interpretation.*

MOTHER: *Well, I'm interested in hearing what your plans are.*

THERAPIST: *I wonder how you arrived at that conclusion, though...*

MOTHER: *At WHAT?*

THERAPIST: *...from what Allen said.*

MOTHER: *That it means whether we approve or disapprove, he's going to go ahead anyway—with his own plans? Is that what you're referring to?*

THERAPIST: *Well, what Allen said originally I thought was that he—merely hoped for the absence of disapproval. That it meant something to him, more than approval. I wonder how you made the move—from THAT—which to me, at least, implied he was very sensitive to disapproval—to your statement, which was that he's going to do what he wants to do whether you approve or not.*

MOTHER: *Well, that's what I got from the fact of...*[short laugh]*from the*

> *absence of approval. Of DISapproval...I mean, if we don't say anything about...not wanting to, not approving of the fact of his going into the apartment—he's going to do it* anyway. *That's the way it sounded to ME.*

FATHER: *I mean getting to the point of absence of disapproval—I mean I just don't—get it! He—even if we sat and didn't say a word about it, you would KNOW whether we approved or disapproved.*

ALLEN: *How?...How?*

FATHER: *I think you lived with us long enough and know our thoughts and our ways and...*

ALLEN: [Quickly] *And you—you haven't changed any of them.*

FATHER: *Huh? Basically, I don't think so.*

ALLEN: *I was afraid of that.*

FATHER: *I don't think you've changed any eith—...basically either.*

MOTHER: [Brief silence] *But in order to give you our approval or disapproval, we have to know what it is you're planning.*

THERAPIST: *It doesn't matter—that he doesn't want it...he'll get it anyway?*

MOTHER: *You mean he doesn't want our disapproval? If I disapprove I'll let him know anyway! If I approve I'll...I'll also let him know.*

This interaction exemplifies the mother's delineation of Allen as someone she has the unquestioned right to control. She defends her definition of him with great energy, insisting that she know Allen's plans in order to register her approval or disapproval. It is clear that she fears and disapproves his independent actions. A related and characteristic delineation is the mother's view that unless she exerts great force her son may not acquiesce to her wishes. Her need to operate as a constraint upon him appears automatic and unyielding, and the inference of defensive delineation is based upon this and upon evidence of anxiety and great need for control in her response to him.

The interaction further exemplifies the father's delineation of Allen as someone who knows what his parents think without asking and who must be controlled by this. He communicates an extremely pessimistic attitude about the possibility for increased independence and for change. The formulation of defensive delineation is based upon the inference of projection in this interaction. The father attributes to Allen feelings of the inevitability of compliance which are his own, at a time when Allen is actively attempting a different kind of behaviour.

Excerpt 2

MOTHER: *If you go into an apartment...*

ALLEN: *...it's a way of defending myself.*

THERAPIST: *Against what?*

FATHER: *What are you defending against?*

ALLEN: *Against both of you.*

MOTHER: [Rather vehemently] *I want to know that if you go into an apart-ment that you're going to live like a human being.*

THERAPIST: *Which is. . .?*

MOTHER: *Which is—knowing that he's going to have three meals a day, because I know how negligent he has been about his meals, even being here. . .*

ALLEN: [Low voice] *I don't get three meals a day here either.*

MOTHER: *Well, that's your own fault! I know that he gets up late and he hasn't been eating breakfast—and he has his lunch, may be 3 o'clock, may be not. Then he has no supper!. . .and THAT's under proper supervision. Now what's he going to do if he's in an apartment by himself???*

THERAPIST: *He'll need a supervisor, won't he?*

MOTHER: [Brief pause] *Well, that's what I mean! Those things concern me. He's—unless he realizes that these things are important—to his health, and his maintenance—he has to know that he's—that he has to sleep on time, if he doesn't get enough sleep, which he feels isn't important, at least he didn't—and I had hoped already that he had thought that eating was important.* (This speech spoken with much feeling.)

ALLEN: *I'm surprised you haven't brought this up earlier. It's the first time you've mentioned this since. . .*

MOTHER: *And if he goes into an apartment. . .I mean, when you say 'apart-ment', you can get a one-room apartment, you can get a two-room, three-room apartment. . .I want to know that he's with somebody!*

The mother's delineation of Allen as unable to care for even his basic physical needs, as well as her insistence that he needs supervision, is contradicted by current evidence known to the mother that he can in many ways care for him-self. This evidence is ignored in her delineations of him, and the inference of defence is made because of the incomplete and strikingly limited view of Allen she communicates. The view is derogatory of his ability to maintain himself independently and, in its emphasis upon his need for supervision, supports the view that he is still in fact very much in need of her. Her repeated expressions of mistrust of Allen and insistence upon his need for supervision do not reflect his current demonstrated ability to work and to behave appropriately in the community. These attitudes seem to be determined more by the mother's need to remain necessary to Allen then by realistic evaluation of him.

Underlying these delineations of Allen was a continuing struggle for control within the family. This struggle became more explicit following Allen's dis-charge from the hospital as he, with increasing clarity, questioned the basis of his parents' authority. His attacks upon them were similar to attacks he had experienced from them. He repeatedly questioned their competence.

The following excerpt is a discussion of the argument which ensued. It is taken from a family treatment session three months after Allen's discharge from the hospital.

298

Excerpt 3

MOTHER: [Very accusing voice] *And you feel that I'm so—ignorant—that I'm so MORONIC—and he told me last night...he informed me that I should go to COLLEGE.*

ALLEN: [Quickly] *I didn't say that.*

MOTHER: *Well, that I should educate myself more...*

ALLEN: *You're not getting along with me very well either. You don't know how to get along with ME...[?] your knowledge...*

MOTHER: *No, I don't know how to get along with you at all—you're the only person I can't get along with! Evidently.* [pause] *And I'd like to know the reason WHY! Because no matter—how much education I would get, if I told you you would still be—education-wise, you would be above my level anyway. And I have no intentions of—uh getting more education just for your sake!*

ALLEN: (Starts to speak but Father intervenes.)

FATHER: *This, I think, is a basic...*

MOTHER: [Louder] *I don't know WHAT it is...*

FATHER: *I think your—I think your basic thing is—to understand each other better...and to try—try to make a point of understanding each other better and do it different ways. Not ONE way.*

MOTHER: *Well, I think I TRY to understand Allen and I—I know that I— what he expects of me and what he doesn't want me to say and— when I ask him something and if he feels I'm trespassing on his privacy, well, he's very wrong.* [Hurt tone]

ALLEN: *Perhaps I feel you should get more education for your OWN sake.*

(10-second silence)

FATHER: *Now see when I mentioned the point of trying to understand each other better—uh...you gave me, you came up with the answer that you were trying to understand. Allen is—did NOT come up with an answer; but HE—is trying to understand YOU. And it's not a—one-way uh track. Things have to work both ways.*

MOTHER: (sounds offended) *But I'm not a mind-reader and I can't uh react in the way he expects me to react, on the spur of the moment. Uh he thinks I should give him a serious answer possibly—the answer—not particularly just an answer or uh if I want to act in a spontaneous way...*

FATHER: *Well, here I can't understand—is—I don't talk the same language that Allen does...uh...possibly I am as far off course as you are—in the—when we talk to Allen, who is a brilliant person, has a vast uh knowledge in his head. And when I talk I try to talk under- standably in MY own fashion...he has learned to accept—MY way, but why he is trying to fight to accept YOUR way, I don't know. Maybe YOU can come up with an answer.*

(Brief omission)

FATHER: *But I don't condemn mother's way of thinking. I don't think she's—*

as far as her—her herself—this is the way she thinks, this is the way she feels...this is the way she thinks and feels, then this is her way of living her life...

MOTHER: And not only that but when I say something I don't sit and think, 'Well, am I hurting somebody or I'm not hurting someone', I say what I want to say at the time.

ALLEN: Not caring whether you hurt someone or not.

MOTHER: Have you seen or heard me hurt someone intentionally???

ALLEN: No, you do it UNintentionally.

THERAPIST: Apparently Allen has hurt YOU quite a bit.

MOTHER: Yes, he has!...because uh for the greater part of the day I mean he's—just like his old self (ALLEN: Old) but then it seemed as though all of a sudden a screw turns—and it's the other side of the record!

The delineations in this excerpt reflect the mother's view of Allen as controlling her or attempting to control her through his hostility and criticism. They communicate a view of Allen as a persecutor and an accusor when he is critical of and hostile to her. The issue of control is central. The mother sees her son's anger and criticism as implying a demand that she should change. She describes two views of Allen in this excerpt, one in which he is his old self (presumably compliant and non-attacking) and another in which he is angry, critical and controlling. It is clear in this interaction that Allen also experiences his mother as hurtful and by implication coercive and controlling. Although there has in fact been an unpleasant argument in the family and Allen has been angry at his mother, it is less evident that he has as a central motivation the wish to control his mother. His argument with her seems rather an effort to defend against her attempts to control him. His interest seems more to preserve the new increment of independence he has attained than to change his parents.

In her delineation of Allen, his mother emphasizes a view of Allen as attempting to change her. She attributes to her son a wish to tell her what to do, which is characteristic of her behaviour with him. Her view of the angry, critical Allen as a persecutor who is trying to control her seems to refer more to the mother's mode of operating than to Allen's behaviour as it has been described and as it is seen in the interaction. Thus projection appears to be an important determinant of the mother's view of Allen as attempting to control her. It is significant that Allen's view of her is clearly that she is trying to invade and control him in this excerpt. His reactions to feelings of being criticized, pried into and trespassed upon are to fight and to insult his mother. Her view of this behaviour is that it is unjustified and motivated by a wish to change her, and she denies any basis in her own actions which might have caused Allen to be angry.

The father expresses a view of Allen as superior to him intellectually, defining Allen as a brilliant person with vast knowledge. The father claims that Allen is tolerant of him despite the fact that they think differently. Here the father does not see Allen as critical and controlling as the mother does, but seems more identified with Allen in his struggle with the mother.

The dilemma that there are not identifiable bases for negotiation in the relationship other than submission and control continues to be the dominant dynamic in the family. These issues are further exemplified in the following interaction.

Excerpt 4

MOTHER: *Disagreement is one thing. Disagreements I can understand. It's—after all uh nobody agrees with uh with ME or I don't agree with Daddy all the time or with you or with anyone. Disagreement is one thing, but the way you vented your anger—or whatever you want to call it—on ME—I mean for no reason at all!*

ALLEN: *Perhaps I was angry at you!*

MOTHER: *Well, WHY??*

ALLEN: *Because you weren't trying hard enough . . .*

MOTHER: [Sounds very puzzled] *Trying hard enough to do what. What do I have to try uh so hard to do?? I was being myself, that's all! I accept YOU for what you are. Can't you accept me for what I am? For what I say?*

ALLEN: *You DON'T accept me for what I am. You know you don't accept me for what I am. Do we have to go through that again?*

MOTHER: *I think I accept you—uh—the same way that DADDY does . . .* (Allen: *No—Just as much. But you don't—you don't—feel the same way. YOU don't perceive it the same way. Perhaps.*

ALLEN: *I don't think you accept me . . . uh looks like I'm going to mention the dirty word again . . .* [slight laugh] *Yoga—you don't accept me as a Yogi. Or as a student of Yoga.*

MOTHER: [Louder] *I don't accept Yoga. NO. But that doesn't mean that I don't accept YOU for what you are. I don't like the idea of your getting so involved in Yoga . . . I thought that was something of the past. But I was surprised . . .*

ALLEN: *You surely didn't accept me as a chela.*

MOTHER: *A WHAT?*

ALLEN: *Chela. Means a student—a Yoga student.*

MOTHER: *If I showed surprise—when you told me how involved you are in Yoga, yes. I was surprised.*

ALLEN: *No—but you don't accept me for that . . .*

MOTHER: *That wasn't something that you have to get so angry about . . .*

ALLEN: *We're not getting anywhere with this—along this line . . . I'm just pointing out disagreements.*

MOTHER: [louder] *But that's what makes you ANGRY—when I disagree with YOU you get—completely off—and you really let me have it!*

THERAPIST: [Brief pause] *How did Allen 'let you have it'?*

MOTHER: [As if therapist should know] *Well, I mean he becomes so insulting—as though I was the most stupid person in this world—and I don't understand him and I'm prying, and uh—I'm not uh if I don't ask him questions then I'm not interested. If I ask him questions I'm spying—I'm being critical. And uh I don't know, he was just very insulting and very obnoxious towards me.*

ALLEN: *I guess I was.*

This excerpt contains further delineations of Allen by his mother as someone who becomes enraged and insulting any time she disagrees with him. She insists that there is no reason for his anger. However, when the discussion focuses upon an interest of Allen's of which the mother explicitly disapproves— his interest in Yoga—there is contradiction in her delineation of Allen as someone she accepts. It is apparent that her acceptance is conditional upon her control of Allen and her approval of his behaviour, although she denies this. It further appears that his anger at her reflects a continuing feeling of vulnerability to her. She is unable to see this and continues to define him as someone who is rude and who tries to control her with his insults. She does not perceive his attachment to her and his sensitivity to her disapproval.

The issue of Allen's involvement in Yoga, which is unacceptable to the mother, becomes the focus of this discussion. Allen's definition of himself as a chela arouses anxiety in the mother, who considers Yoga not only an unconventional interest which she does not understand, but also a symptom of his illness. She criticizes her son while insisting that the problem is his attempt to change her. She does not see his anger at her as an evidence of his vulnerability to her, although this is interpreted frequently in this phase of therapy. She insists upon her right to criticize Allen, but remains indignant when he becomes angry with her.

The struggle over issues of controlling and being controlled continued to be the focus of discussion in the family sessions. The mother was generally the protagonist for the parents in these discussions with the father tacitly agreeing with her. If he presented a view other than the mother's it was with such unclarity as to render it ineffective. When the struggle between Allen and his mother was overt, the father retreated to an alliance with her. When Allen was critical of both parents, the father reacted with sensitivity and defensiveness.

Excerpt 5

ALLEN: *...When I said I was embarrassed by you* [omission] *this was an indication of my feelings—and my feelings about YOU. Uh...I wish you would appreciate it more as something that's going on within me rather than something which is about you. And—I don't mean to say when I'm embarrassed by I—I don't mean to say your, you lack as a human being...or that uh...or that uh—there are things that cause me embarrassment or the standard against which, in comparison, you embarrass me. That those standards are right rather than you are right. I don't mean that at all. When I said I was embarrassed, this was a feeling I had. In me. And it had to do* *with ME. As well as with you. And to some extent I feel that even though I am embarrassed, what this means to me is not so much that I have to throw YOU over and take up—whatever it is, the great intellectual standard...but uh to some extent I have to find out what it is about YOU that's good and there ARE good things about you.*

(omission)

FATHER: *Let's look at it from THIS point. It's not every student that can say their father is a genius!*

ALLEN: (Brief pause, then thoughtfully) *No...but...*

FATHER: *Then how can you uh—your mother be inadequate if she married a genius?*

ALLEN: *Are you saying you're a genius?*

FATHER: [?] *I AM.*

MOTHER: [facetiously] *Oh, and am I a genius too?*

FATHER: *I didn't say that.* [laughs]

ALLEN: [sounds amused] *This...this...this...*

MOTHER: *You said uh if—if I married you I have to be a genius too...*

FATHER: *No. I said uh How can you be inadequate if you uh—if you married a genius.*

ALLEN: *I'm rather reluctant to—using such superlatives. But—*

FATHER: *I'm not. I feel that I AM. In MY field, I think I AM.*

THERAPIST: *That's the first time you've told Allen.*

FATHER: *No...*

THERAPIST: *You reacted, I thought, as if it were the first time you had ever heard your father tell you that.*

ALLEN: *In public. Where other people could—gets embarrassing! For you to say that.*

(Omission)

FATHER: *What, does it embarrass you?*

ALLEN: *It sounds vain.*

FATHER: *I don't think so. I think if a person develops himself—or is at that point where—they feel that they surpass other people in a certain field—that they can take credit of being—a genius.*

The delineations of Allen in this excerpt grow from his assertion that he is embarrassed by his parents because of their lack of sophistication and education. His father reacts sensitively to this discussion and proceeds to define himself as a genius which embarrasses Allen further. Allen has stated that his embarrassment by his parents is a problem which is his own. His parents do not understand or accept this. His father is clearly extremely hurt despite Allen's contention that his feelings about his parents are a problem for him, not for them.

The parents are extremely vulnerable to Allen's criticism. Differences between family members and critical attitudes continue to stimulate anxiety and defensive responses. The father is moved to define himself as a genius, a definition mobilized by his son's criticism. This is a striking interaction because it contains the overt expression of a fantasy of superiority which the father uses here defensively in self definition. In a previous excerpt, delineation of Allen as brilliant contained elements of the father's fantasy of superiority projected into his son. In this session he takes these qualities back into himself and defines himself as a genius. The argument over where the superiority and genius resides continues to be related in this family to a right to criticize and control others. In other discussions authority was seen to require a fantasy of absolute morality and knowledge which was a burden both to the parents and to the adolescent. Many of the struggles in the family were over this issue. Freedom to act independently in a state of uncertainty was sharply inhibited in all family members.

In ensuing family sessions and in relation to discussion of these issues in therapy, the father revealed more of his own thinking. This resulted in a clear differentiation between the father and the mother for the first time. A shift ensued away from the old alignment of the father joining the mother in argument against the adolescent. Now a new alignment between the father and the adolescent against the authority of the mother was seen. An excerpt from a family session two months later exemplifies this change. Early in this session the father says that he missed Allen when he did not visit home last week. He goes on to amplify his reasons for this.

Excerpt 6

FATHER: *...I actually think it was uh—probably I use him for somebody to lean on.*

THERAPIST: *How do you mean?*

FATHER: *Well, maybe as somebody that can understand me...a lot of times we get into—discussions—and...reasoning and things—he hears me out...I think this is important.* [low voice, slight laugh] *Nobody understands me anymore!*

THERAPIST: *'Nobody' being...*

FATHER: (low voice) *Well, in our family...people in our family—that I'm more, so intimate with—you know, the family group* (THERAPIST: *Like?)...like my wife, like my sister-in-law, like my brother-in-law...I guess that's part of it.*

THERAPIST: *Mrs. N isn't looking very understanding at this moment.* (slight laugh)

MOTHER: (irritated voice)—*So I suppose that every time you disagree with ME. I'm suppose to say that you don't understand ME! Is this the idea??*

FATHER: *Well, if I disagree with you, I don't UNDERSTAND you...*

MOTHER: *Well...*

THERAPIST: *So you've been having disagreements all week?*

FATHER: *I guess we've been having them, but I guess this past week was the uh*

*no more than usual, but the fact that uh—I feel like I'm—sort of
lost.* (short laugh)

Here we find delineation of Allen by the father as similar to him and as the
only one in the family who understands some aspects of what he says and thinks.
The father makes its explicit that he feels lost without the support and agreement
of the mother, a feeling which has been expressed most frequently by Allen.
As the discussion continues both parents describe how the father is different
from the mother and her family. The similarity between the father and Allen
is implicitly in their opposition to the mother. The father seems to equate the
mother's ideas with the standards of society. However, he really has many
ideas contrary to hers. Allen is seen as similar to the father in this.

The discussion continues with the father asserting that the mother wants
him to change his views. It is similar to discussions the mother and Allen have
in which Allen protests that the mother wants him to change and the mother
insists he wants her to. In this struggle Allen is important in that being anti-
society himself he is seen by the father as someone who can understand his
ideas and sympathize with them, which the mother and her family will not do.

Excerpt 6—Continued

FATHER: *...and don't you say—haven't you said that, 'You're talking just
like Allen!'...doesn't THIS involve him?*

MOTHER: *Well, the fact that people don't agree with you, or they give their
OWN point of view, doesn't mean that you're not accepted. If you
don't agree with them, does that show that WE'RE not accepted??*

FATHER: *I would like people, to whom I'm closer, to...*

MOTHER: [louder, interrupting] *Well, you can't change other people!*

FATHER: [continuing]...*accept my point of view as my point of view. I'm not
asking ANYbody to change their way of thinking and change their
way of thinking to think the way I think...I don't ask anybody to do
that. What—if somebody wants me to express my point of view,
I express it. (*In background, MOTHER: *Well, nobody asked you to
change your point of view either.) When I ask somebody else to
express their point of view, I accept it. But whether they CHANGE
me or not, that's up to ME. But I accept their point of view.*

MOTHER: *Nobody's trying to change you! Because you know they think a great
deal of you! Even though you THINK that they don't! (pause) Well,
ELABORATE.*

There is great tension over the father's disagreement with the mother. Her
assertion of acceptance of disagreement is no more believed by the father than
it was believed by Allen when she told him she accepted him in a previous
excerpt. It is as difficult for the parents to agree to disagree as it is for them to
allow disagreement in Allen; in a disagreement it seems one family member or
the other must change.

It is not clear from what has been discussed in the family session that the father's definition of Allen as like him in his deviant thinking is accurate. He assumes Allen's support saying that Allen understands him and implying that he and Allen think the same way about things. In fact, they seem to share primarily their opposition to the mother. The father seems more to use Allen in phantasy for support in a struggle with his wife than to share with him a common point of view. This delineation of Allen seems to be a defensive projection into him by the father of qualities similar to his which have little to do with any agreement with Allen about what he actually feels about the matters which have been under discussion.

To recapitulate for a moment, these excerpts have been selected to illustrate aspects of parent–adolescent interaction relevant to independent functioning. Delineations of the adolescent by both parents contain no clear or consistent view of the adolescent as capable of effective independent actions. Independence in thinking is almost as great a problem. Here arguments about differences in values or beliefs are experienced as struggles for dominance and control. Differences are not tolerated within the family and when they emerge they are accompanied by the imperative that someone must change. This is true not only for differences between adolescent and parents, but for differences between the parents themselves. The parents are initially able to maintain a facade of unity when they are joined in an effort to control the adolescent. In these arguments the father characteristically follows the mother's lead.

The adolescent is perceived as a persecutor by both parents when he is critical of them. The mother insists that he wants to change her when he criticizes and disagrees with her. Projection seems to be an important determinant of the delineation. The father takes back into himself qualities of brilliance and genius he has projected into his son, to defend against the threat he feels from the adolescent's critical attitudes. Authority in this family is closely tied to fantasies of omniscience and perfection and any criticism or argument threatens this illusion. The consequent threat to authority results in extreme defensive behaviour. The feeling of being bereft of authority results in great uncertainty in the conduct of independent behaviour.

As treatment progresses and the adolescent is in fact functioning independently, differences between the parents themselves become increasingly overt. These differences are accompanied by the same quality of anxiety and struggle which characterized the differences with the adolescent. The father is now regarded as the deviant by the mother and in their arguments both feel attacked and controlled. Here the adolescent is delineated as being like his father in his deviance. In both, difference constitutes an attack upon the mother. The model for identification provided by the father has been one of submission to the mother with characteristic suppression of differences. Identification is reinforced by explicit delineation of the adolescent as similar to his father when the father's thinking is revealed to significantly deviate from the mother's. This carries with it a built-in expectation that the adolescent will eventually acquiesce to the mother as the father has.

The adolescent identity crisis is rooted in identifications which do not support the adolescent's new struggle for independent functioning. The father has accepted the mother's definition of difference as an attack and has characteristically acquiesced to the mother. The adolescent is in a crisis of redefinition of the consequences of differences and the basis of authority for independent behaviour. He must define whether relationships may be maintained despite differences, whether authority exists without omniscience and whether control must be the central issue between people.

Conclusion

Evidence of struggle over independent functioning in this family have been elucidated through analysis of excerpts of family interaction. Analysis of content and dynamics of delineations allow inferences to be made about the unconscious assumptions of the family as a group and the consequences of these for adolescent development.

In the conjoint family sessions delineations having the aim of containment and control are regularly seen when thinking or action of one family member is perceived as independent of the control of other family members. Evidence has been presented which indicates that differences are interpreted within the family as attacks and imply a serious threat of loss and alienation. This is particularly true when differences and disagreements are expressed by the adolescent. His parents' delineations of him communicate their expectation of conformity and their intense antagonism to behaviour independent of their supervision. Similar reactions are seen within the family to disagreements between the parents.

This family group is characterized by disturbance over independent functioning of individual members. Anxiety over authority and control, sensitivity over disagreements and provocation of disagreements are all configurations which have been seen in family interactions. The consequences of these characteristics of family functioning for adolescent personality formation are particularly marked. In the adolescent the maturation of cognitive ego capacities allowing independent functioning makes him particularly vulnerable to the presence or absence of nutriment for these capacities in the family environment. The quality of such nutriment in the family system may be considered with reference to delineations and their dynamic determinants, and the unconscious assumptions of the family as a group.

Parental delineations of the adolescent in this family do not contain a reliable view of him as capable of effective independent action or thinking. We propose a relation between these parental delineations and the fact that the identity crisis of the adolescent himself is manifested in great anxiety over his capacity to exist independently from his parents. His profound doubt of his own ability to function independently is an aspect of his disturbance in identity. It is a reflection of parental delineations of him. This problem in identity is generalized in his view of himself as highly vulnerable to the control of others. The clinical picture he presents, that of a defect in ego autonomy, specifically of an impairment in the ego's autonomy from objects in reality, is found in a family where parental delineations do not contain within them the potentiality for the adolescent to become independent. Family experience thus does not integrate with the maturing cognitive capacities of the adolescent's ego, to promote a self definition of independent functioning. On the contrary, cognitive development crystallizes an identity in accord with the parents' view of him, in which the adolescent sees himself as helpless, dependent and vulnerable to outside control. Efforts to achieve greater independence through overt behaviour in defiance of parental requirements are accompanied by guilt and disorganizing anxiety.

Unconscious assumptions of this family which we infer from these excerpts may be summarized as follows: Independent thinking and action are threatening and must be discouraged; control over possible deviance must be exercised constantly; differences between members constitute attacks; attributes of authority are closely tied to fantasies of omniscience and may not be questioned; independent behaviour contains a grave threat of separation and alienation; the anxiety inherent in this threat may lead to personality dissolution or physical disorder; the dilemma for each family member is on the one hand loss of individuation and differentiation through suppression of independent functioning or, on the other hand, anxiety and alienation through independent behaviour and separation. These unconscious assumptions are internalized in the adolescent and impair his development of increased ego autonomy and individuation.

The internalizations under discussion represent more than delineations. Internalizations based upon identifications are also evidenced in behaviour from which unconscious assumptions are inferred. We assume that through identification, images of the parents are internalized during development which shape important characteristics of adolescent personality functioning. We have presented evidence that through delineation, projection into the adolescent of particular characteristics of the parents results in an active definition of him related to qualities of the parents themselves. Thus certain characteristics which have been learned by the adolescent in identifications are also actively imposed and dynamically reinforced in defensive delineations. We consider the interplay between identification processes and delineations determined by family dynamics to be of great importance in the final determination of ego identity in adolescence, and to be crucial in determining differences in personality characteristics between siblings related to the dynamics of role allocation in the family.

Although the family group differs from the small groups studied by Bion in important ways, his conceptualization of the group as a whole and of the unconscious assumptions which frequently determine the behaviour of group members facilitates an organization of observations of family interaction which elucidates unconscious assumptions and dynamics of role allocation. Unconscious assumptions and defensive delineations seek to hold the child and adolescent in relatively fixed roles through development. In this way they interfere with the primary task of the family with regard to adolescent development. They militate against increased ego autonomy and the establishment of an identity in the adolescent which allows individuation and separation from his parents.

References

Bion, W. R. (1961), *Experiences in Groups*, Tavistock Publications, London.

Blos, P. (1962), *On Adolescence: a Psychoanalytic Interpretation*, Free Press, Glencoe, Ill.

Erikson, E. H. (1956), The problem of ego identity, *Journal of American Psychoanalytic Association*, **4**, 56–121.

Erikson, E. H. (1962), Reality and actuality, *Journal of American Psychoanalytic Association*, **10**, 451–474.

Freud, A. (1936), *The Ego and Mechanisms of Defence*, International Universities Press, New York, 1946.

Freud, A. (1958), Adolescence, *The Psychoanalytic Study of the Child*, **13**, 255–278.

Inhelder, B. and Piaget, J. (1958), *The Growth of Logical Thinking from Childhood to Adolescence*, Basic Books, New York.

Jacobson, E. (1964), *The Self and the Object World*, International Universities Press, New York.

Loewald, H. W. (1960), On the therapeutic action of psycho-analysis, *International Journal of Psychoanalysis*, **41**, 16–33.

Rice, A. K. (1969), Individual, group and intergroup processes, *Human Relations*, **22**, 565–584.

Schafer, R. (1968), *Aspects of Internalization*, International Universities Press, New York.

Shapiro, R. L. (1963), Adolescence and the psychology of the ego, *Psychiatry*, **26**, 77–87.

Shapiro, R. L. (1966), Identity and ego autonomy in adolescence, *in: Science and Psychoanalysis*, Masserman, Ed., Grune and Stratton, Inc., New York.

Shapiro, R. L. (1968), Action and family interaction in adolescence, *in: Modern Psychoanalysis*, Marmor, Ed., Basic Books, New York.

Shapiro, R. L. (1969a), The origin of adolescent disturbances in the family: some considerations in theory and implications for therapy, *in:* Zuk, G. H. and Boszormenyi-Nagy, I., Eds., *Family Therapy and Disturbed Families*, Science and Behaviour Books, Palo Alto, pp. 221–238.

Shapiro, R. L. (1969b), Adolescent ego autonomy and the family, *in:* Caplan, G. and Lebovici, S., Eds., *Adolescence: Psychosocial Perspectives*, Harcourt Brace, New York; pp. 113–121.

Singer, M. T. and Wynne, L. C. (1965), Thought disorder and family relations of schizophrenics. III. Methodology using projective techniques *and* IV. Results and implications, *Arch. of Gen. Psychiatry*, **12**, pp. 187–212.

Turquet, P. M. (1971), Four lectures: The Bion hypothesis: the work group and the basic assumption group, Given at the National Institute of Mental Health, May 26th, May 28th, June 2nd, June 6th. Not published.

Wynne, L. C. and Singer, M. T. (1963), Thought disorder and family relations of schizophrenics. I. A research study, *and* II. A classification of forms of thinking, *Arch. of Gen. Psychiatry*, **9**, 191–206.

Zinner, J. and Shapiro, R. L. (1971), Projective identification as a mode of perception and behavior in families of adolescents, Presented at the 58th Annual Meeting of the American Psychoanalytic Association, Panel on Adolescent Development from the Perspective of Family Studies, Washington, D. C., April 29th—May 3rd. Not published.

The Reorganization of a University Department of Psychiatry: A Blueprint for Change

William Hausman

Of the various types of educational organizations existing on the American scene today one of the most complex is that of the clinical department in the medical school. Not only is the leadership of such a department faced with conflicting demands for priorities between clinical services, research and education, but the management task is compounded by the often-stated need for change in each of these areas, by unwieldy and occasionally inconsistent systems of governance of both clinical and academic staffs, and by critical and often antiquated economic systems that diffuse or undercut the authority of leadership and direction of faculty effort in many schools. That this view represents more than simply the lament of one who is attempting to manage such a system is attested to by the fact that within the past two years more than a quarter of all of the medical schools in this country have been searching for chairmen of their departments of psychiatry. Despite the obvious implications of such a situation these departments must be led, and there are gratifications to be had in attempting to meet the challenge. It is with the consequences of my decision to accept such a leadership role, with my approach to the task, and with the knowledge that has come from the experience that I will deal in this chapter. The reader is cautioned that the comments here represent, in a full sense, work in progress. Perhaps it is because of the little time I have spent on the job that I have the audacity to write at this time, but I believe that there is an advantage to exposing one's blueprint for scrutiny after 18 months of work. Two or three years from now I fully expect that my view will still be labelled as 'work in progress', but I am uncertain whether, at that time, I will be as willing to open my plans and experience to public view.

In July, 1969 I was appointed to my present position as Professor and Head of the Department of Psychiatry at a major midwestern state university. My background for such a position was unique in several regards, including the fact that of about 20 years in the field of psychiatry only the previous three years had been spent in a full-time position in a university department. Another aspect of my career, which has played a major part in my accepting this challenging position and which is basic to the purpose of this chapter, was my involvement with a number of activities associated with A. K. Rice between 1964 and 1969.

In 1964, while I was serving as Chief of the Behavioral Sciences Research Branch of the Army's Medical Research and Development Command, Dr. Rice was invited to Washington by Dr. David McK. Rioch, Director of the Division of Neuropsychiatry at the Walter Reed Army Institute of Research (WRAIR), to consult with him and the Commander of WRAIR on the organization of the Division. A preliminary visit by Rice to WRAIR early in 1964 led to a longer visit later that year in which those of us involved with the Army research programme in psychiatry had an opportunity to work with him as interviewees, as consultees, as colleagues and as students. The exciting process of studying the organization of a remarkable and creative programme opened new areas of inquiry and knowledge to many of us who worked with Rice, and led not only to an extensive reorganization of the Division, but also to the development of a new pattern of interests for several of the coparticipants. As a direct result of that reorganization I was transferred to the Division as a Deputy Director, in early 1965, in order to assist in implementing the reorganization plans.

Another phase of my relationship with A. K. Rice began in 1965, when I attended the Tavistock Institute's Group Relations Conference at Leicester, England (Rice, 1965) and, a few months later, the Advanced Training Group of the first American Group Relations Conference at Mt. Holyoke College. I was privileged to be appointed to Rice's staff at the second American Conference the following year and to be renamed to the staff of that conference for each of the subsequent years. Thus I had some role in each of six conferences, in England and the United States, that were directed by Rice. In addition to periodic informal meetings between 1965 and 1969, Rice and I were both members of the Group Relations Conference Board of the Washington School of Psychiatry, which was organized in 1967 to further the work of these conferences in this country.

The commitment that I have felt toward the principles of organization developed, taught and carried forward by Rice in his work with organizations, as well as in the various conference events that he innovated and demonstrated, was clearly to be tested in my undertaking the responsibility for departmental leadership, and it is on these particular issues that I will focus here.

In keeping with the purposes of this volume I will outline the process of departmental reorganization, with special reference to several concepts that are basic to Rice's work, namely the primary task; the open system approach, including the import-conversion-export model; boundaries; and task and sentient groups. Each of these concepts has as much relevance to the university and the medical school as it has to the large corporation, the research organization and the service agency. Further, the complexity of our Department of Psychiatry can best be understood and managed, in my view, only when these issues are clearly appreciated.

I will not attempt to define these concepts. The reader is referred to Miller and Rice (1967) and Rice (1963) for discussion and definition of these terms.

History of the Department

The details of the history of our Department of Psychiatry have been elaborated elsewhere (Malmquist, 1963; Baker and coworkers, 1953). The department was originally organized as a Division of the Department of Medicine. In 1941 that Division came under the full-time leadership of a neurologist, Dr. J. C. McKinley and, in 1943, it was established as a separate Department of Neuropsychiatry. It was renamed the Department of Psychiatry and Neurology, under a new department head, Dr. Donald W. Hastings, in 1946. From the time the department was organized as such, until his retirement in 1970, Dr. Starke Hathaway directed its Division of Clinical Psychology. The Division of Child Psychiatry, under Dr. Reynold A. Jensen, was transferred to Psychiatry, from the Department of Pediatrics, in 1952. Dr. Jensen resigned as Director of Child Psychiatry in 1968, after which that division had an acting Director. A search for a new department head was begun in 1967 when Dr. Hastings asked to be relieved of his administrative duties. In 1969 the Division of Neurology directed by Dr. A. B. Baker, was elevated to separate departmental status, although that division had actually operated as an autonomous unit for about 20 years (Hastings, 1968).

The Medical School, considered among the better schools in the country, has achieved national recognition largely for the quality of its clinical and basic research, especially in the Departments of Surgery, Medicine and Pediatrics. The first two departments, in particular, developed their reputations principally around the work of the very influential heads of these departments, who were among the foremost international leaders of their respective specialities for several decades prior to their retirement in the 60's and whose strong charismatic leadership played a large part in determining the culture of the Medical School over the years.

The orientation of the Medical School has been largely focused on biological studies, with a distinct underemphasis of the psychological and social aspects of medicine. The highly respected Director of the Division of Clinical Psychology in the Department of Psychiatry was nationally identified with the empirical approach to his field. As a result the 'softer' aspects of the field, such as psychoanalysis and social psychiatry, were not strongly in evidence as a frame of reference for either the theoretical or practical approaches to education. Community psychiatry service programmes in the state were also unrelated to the department's activities. Those of the department's alumni that have remained in the area are largely identified with the private practice of psychiatry.

Although the university is state supported and has had the only operating medical school in the state, the relationship between the department and the state hospitals and other facilities, such as the community mental health centres, that are wholly or partially supported by the state, has been minimal. The general orientation of medical practice in the state is conservative, and strongly identified with the private sector, either individually or in groups. The quality of medical care is high, although the distribution of physicians is irregular, as is true of most of the country, with undersupport of some of the more remote rural areas and the lower income sections of the cities.

The Department in July 1969

At the time I took on my position in the department it was composed of a full-time faculty of 47 including 22 psychiatrists and 25 psychologists. Of this number, 11 psychiatrists and 10 psychologists were at the university hospitals where the department is based, while the remaining full-time faculty were at a Veterans Administration Hospital and at two country hospitals, all of which were fully affiliated with the university although their faculties' salaries were paid by the individual hospitals. The department was divided into a Division of Adult Psychiatry, which had been headed by the previous department head in a secondary role, a Division of Child Psychiatry, a Division of Clinical Psychology and a research unit. This last group, although it did not have divisional status, operated relatively autonomously, occupying part of a floor of a building which is separate from the centre and clinical facilities of the department, although part of the Medical School complex. The department's clinical and teaching activities have largely revolved around three adult and one children's wards on the sixth floor of the main University Hospital building. Most of the departmental offices are also on that floor but, in addition, there is a small cluster of offices on the 14th floor and an out-patient clinic, which has been shared with Neurology, on the third floor of the same building. The wards, which had been built in stages, include 59 adult beds and 16 beds for children. The funding for the department has been derived largely from special state appropriations, which has paid most of the salaries of the clinical staff and some part of the faculty salaries. There also has been a special appropriation for the research unit. In addition, the medical school has provided some of the faculty salaries. Basic salaries, particularly for the psychiatrists, have been generally low, with the provision that the individual faculty members could earn up to their full basic salary in private practice, providing they did their work at the University Hospital. This 'geographic full-time' system has been the basis for the salary pattern in all of the clinical departments in the Medical School. In addition, some small federal grants have been awarded for training activities, and the department has received several research grants. At the time that I took the position as head of the department there were three open faculty positions in the department, including those for Director of the Division of Child Psychiatry and Director of Research. In addition, in the negotiations that preceded my appointment, it was agreed that three new faculty positions would be established and funded in the department. The departmental physical facilities are extremely crowded, with little provision anywhere in the Medical School area for expansion but with established construction plans for a series of new buildings to provide for teaching needs based upon current needs for 'catch up' faculty positions and for planned future expansion in the number of medical students. The 'catch up' positions were those faculty positions that had been recognized by the administration for some years as necessary for the various departments to gain if they were to have an adequate ratio of faculty to students to properly carry out their teaching responsibilities in the face of larger classes and more demanding curricula. In keeping with the plan for expansion, the Medical School entering class was enlarged from 165 to 220 students between 1969 and 1970, with a programme to continue with classes of about the latter size in the 1970's. The Department of Psychiatry has had about 26 medical fellows who have worked at the University Hospitals and at the affiliate hospitals while they secured their residency training. For many years, the University Hospital and Medical School has required that each resident in training also must be accepted as a graduate student by the graduate school during the time of his training.

The primary task of the department, at the time that I took on its leadership, appeared to be centred on its clinical service activities, although it was evident that the various components in the department each described its mission in somewhat different terms. It should be emphasized here, and will be apparent later in this chapter, that one of the major dilemmas in defining the primary task in this type of department is that each of the three functions of the department, research, teaching and clinical services, can, by some criteria, be considered as separate primary tasks. Further at various times each of these does take precedence in the mission of the department. I have attempted here to use Rice's (Rice, 1963; Miller and Rice 1967) definition of the primary task as the task that the enterprise must perform at any given time if it is to survive. The reader is encouraged to read the discussions of these authors on the issues of the single versus the multiple primary tasks, which has great relevance in this setting.

The import system of the clinical services has been based upon the referral from all parts of the state of several categories of private and public patients to the treatment units, with therapy approaches (conversion) centering largely on each staff psychiatrist's responsibility for the care of patients assigned to him. Export of the treated patient was back into his own community, with most followup care then assumed by the referring physician. The medical fellows generally came from other American or foreign schools or from the pool of local private practitioners of general medicine. The conversion process, in their case, included a basic focus on clinical training and practice; the export, as noted above, was largely into the private sector. With a few exceptions, the fellows did not follow the graduate school program to the point of gaining a degree at either the masters or the doctoral level.

The import of psychology interns was from the large University of Minnesota graduate programme in psychology and from similar programmes in other universities. They were trained for a year in a range of clinical treatment and diagnostic skills, and were exported to a variety of positions in this community and elsewhere. Medical student import was largely involuntary, through a series of clerkships that were required of junior students. They were assigned to the wards of the University and affiliated hospitals and to the out-patient clinic, with variable supervision, depending upon where the students were working. After their clerkships they were exported back into the general Medical School programme, with relatively little evidenced interest by the students completing the clerkship for further work in psychiatry at this centre. Although there were available options for senior medical students to take clinical electives relatively few took advantage of this opportunity.

The most clearly defined boundaries were between psychology and psychiatry. Here there seemed to be near coincidence of task and sentient boundaries although a few of the psychologists were involved in the training of psychiatrists and some psychiatrists in the training of psychologists. The research unit, almost wholly staffed by experimental psychologists, was not only separate from the clinical programmes, with almost no overlap, but also was quite distinct from and relatively uninvolved with the Clinical Psychology Division. The one significant area of overlap between the clinical and research fields was in psychopharmacology where a federally funded clinical research unit supported workers of both disciplines.

Challenge for Leadership

In taking on the responsibility for leadership in a department which, by my observations and those of senior administrators and others, needed to work toward the achievement of several kinds of significant changes, I was initially confronted with several important basic problems. It is evident that anyone who attempts to explore a system from any theoretical frame of reference, while at the same time he is working within it and is responsible for the products of the system, must of necessity be faced with great difficulty in objectifying his own role in the change process and in the evaluation of the intermediate and long range results of his efforts. Where, for instance, does he gain 'objective' and unbiased feedback as he plans and institutes changes? Ideally, he should seek outside expert guidance and evaluation. Such a process is costly and the financial resources available to me were, at best, limited and had to be expended within the department if we were to effect any of the changes that appeared indicated. Beyond this, the head of the department must himself be an instrument of change, while at the same time he must establish an ongoing positive relationship with the individuals within the department and its various components that will sustain the strength of needed existing activities (Rice, 1963). In anticipating the department's potential for change he also must be aware of the constraints inherent in the larger university organization. In this department, as in true in most universities, most of the senior faculty hold tenured positions and therefore are not subject to the sort of economic controls that are available to the corporation executive or to the director of many non-university service organizations. Even though various types of pressure can be exerted on the faculty and staff to effect change, the Head must, at the same time, recognize the need for meeting the ongoing responsibility of both service and educational programmes with a staff that is already inadequate in size to carry out all of the operations for which they are responsible.

I was also confronted with the very complex democratic system established by the faculty of the University (University of Minnesota, 1970) and the informal power structure which results from long-standing personal relationships among the various faculty groups and between faculty and administrators of the Medical School and University. In attempting to resolve specific issues that have arisen from time to time it has become evident to me, also, that many unresolved issues had existed within the department and between various members of the faculty and Medical School administration over the years. This was further complicated by the fact that the Dean of the governance structure known as the College of Medical Sciences, which had existed at the time of my appointment, resigned his administrative position when that college was eliminated at the time that the univesity health science units underwent a reorganization a year later, in the summer of 1970. The consequence of this action meant not only that the Medical School was faced with an indeterminate period of time without specific executive leadership, but also that many long standing conflicts within the faculty were potentiated in the absence of well-defined Medical School direction.

A related issue deals with innovation. Schulman (1969), in describing the reorganization of a large eastern Department of Psychiatry observes:

'Innovation is a basic personnel problem for all but the most moribund of organizations. Participants must be recruited and promoted who are flexible enough to appreciate demands for change and who can act on these demands to create a balanced program of innovation. But innovation is also a basic organizational problem in the sense that potential innovators are helped or hindered in their efforts by patterns of organization.' (Schulman, 1969, p. 4)

Any changes that offer the opportunity for innovation clearly threaten the *status quo* of the existing organizational alignments and thus the security system of the best-established faculty members and groups of faculty. The resulting process is likely to represent a strong counterforce to change, with the risk of neutralizing leadership effectiveness around the very issues that call for the most critical leadership functions. The gain from maintaining the *status quo*, principally in the comfort of senior faculty and in the stability of the institution, is more than offset by the loss of an element of greatest significance to the university—its freedom to experiment, to challenge and to create and test newer concepts. The consequences of this struggle between change and the *status quo* of the department are likely to be measured by its climate of inquiry, by its reputation and by its attractiveness to imaginative potential faculty and students.

It was immediately clear that no programme change could be established in the Department without redefinition and clarification of its primary task. Beyond this, much work had to be done toward gaining faculty acceptance of revised mission priorities. In my view the primary task of the department, if it is to carry out its responsibility to the University and to the State, is to develop a broadly based educational programme, with particular emphasis on the social aspects of the mental health field. The latter issue reflects recent trends in psychiatry as well as my own principal interests, which were recognized by the university administration and Medical School faculty prior to my appointment (Hausman and Rioch 1967; Hausman, 1970).

Because there are competing opportunities for psychiatric training in a large number of different types of institutions throughout the country, it is evident that a teaching hospital associated with a major university can best use its resources by establishing an effective balance between training for clinical practice and education in the academic areas of psychiatry. An essential secondary aspect of the mission of the Department is to establish the educational programme in such a way as to attract more interest from our own medical students as well as from potential graduate students and residents from around the country. In my view, the achievement of such objectives calls for a gradual shift in focus toward the medically-related and socially-related aspects of psychiatry and for greater exposure of all groups of students to the more scholarly aspects of the field (Romano, 1966). Such a shift of emphasis can be expected to help enhance the local and national reputation of the Department and has clear implications, at all levels of the import-conversion-export process, for all those involved in the department's educational programme.

Another important aspect of leadership in a changing department involves the boundaries between the orientation of the new Head of the Department, the culture of the school, and the philosophies and the experiences of the existing faculty. This is complicated by another type of import issue, the recruiting of new faculty members to fill the existing vacancies and to broaden the range of skills and interest beyond that previously existing within the department. Recruitment has involved the definition of priorities for new faculty roles while, at the same time, these new staff members must be integrated into the existing faculty group. Their differences from the 'older' faculty have had to be encouraged in order to facilitate the newer directions for the department, while at the same time the existing faculty members require well-merited support to maintain their effectiveness and the overall departmental morale. The implications of such a broadened approach to education on the department's reputation and on recruiting of outside students have been noted. It is also evident that if we are to attract more of the University's own medical students into the field of psychiatry and to contribute a more sophisticated awareness of the field to the education of those students going into other areas, new approaches to education must be developed.

While educational goals are being expanded, the limited number of individuals available for leadership and supervisory roles on the existing clinical services also have had to be increased. Thus the competing demands between educational and clinical service requirements are again evident. In the clinical area, the development of a new liaison service, in conjunction with the Department of Medicine, has resulted in some objections from the short-staffed psychiatric ward clinicians. When the residents were asked to take on a greater load of consultation activities on the medical and surgical wards we were confronted with the resistance from them and from the psychiatric ward staff because of the shift from the more traditional and familiar priorities in the department and because of the greater resulting work load. The concern of the residents has been reduced in large measure through instituting a series of teaching rounds or consultations each week, led by senior faculty members.

The Process of Change

In order for me to initiate the steps toward change, it has become important to understand the nature of authority in the unique organizational structure of a university academic department. While the designation of 'head' as opposed to 'chairman' seems to indicate a greater degree of authority, it has become evident that the structure of the University requires frequent consultation with the faculty before critical decisions can be made. The existing Executive Council of the department is the most apparent vehicle for such consultation, but it has been clear that other types of consultation were expected by those in and out of the Council. The complex organizational structure of the University, complicated by the absence of a Medical School Dean and by the long-standing informal structure of the department, school and university has made it particularly difficult to define the limits of authority inherent in my role. The overlapping functions of the faculty, particularly in their doubling as clinical staff, has further added to the complexity inasmuch as the lines of responsibility and authority in clinical services differ from those related to educational programmes. The two-year search for a new head, prior to my appointment, had left faculty and staff anxious about the change in leadership and it has been evident that the personnel of the department need strong support while, at the same time, they are being asked to consider significant changes in the programmes. The residents, too, have been faced with changes in educational priorities from those that had existed when they entered the programme. In their case possible new programmes, reflecting the interest and priorities of new departmental leadership, may or may not have been consonant with their expectations and felt needs when they applied for training.

Early in my tenure as department head I talked with each of the various staff and student groups in the department, and in each of these talks emphasized my expectations of change, with particular focus upon my interest in social psychiatry, while at the same time I assured the faculty that I anticipated no radical immediate shifts in ongoing programmes. In visits to various groups at the university, and at professional meetings in the broader community, I emphasized my intent to broaden the programme of the department toward gaining greater acceptance for and interest in psychiatry within the Medical School and the community while I hoped to reduce distance between the department, the private sector and the state mental health programme. I also was able to arrange for a selective series of distinguished speakers to visit the department as part of a new staff development programme.

When I took on the leadership of the department I was aware that the geographic-full-time salary system, as described above, tended to strongly reinforce the practice orientation of the faculty psychiatrists, to order the assignment of clinical cases toward meeting their economic needs and to limit the potential for development of programmatic treatment and educational approaches.

318

While the Medical School departments have not been able to develop completely state-funded strict-full-time salary systems, presumably because of financial constraints and a culture, personified by the attitudes of a number of senior faculty members, that emphasized the value of private practice, some departments have been permitted to organize partnerships among their members so that clinical fees can be collected by the partnership and redistributed as salary augmentation to their members. Because several departments in the school had already established this system, in most cases with a fair degree of success, I felt that this was a step that we must take if the department was to move toward greater emphasis on education. In order to allow for the variable use of academic, research and clinical skills in the individual faculty members, it was important, as I saw it, that salaries be based upon total contributions of the members to the department, whether in clinical, research or teaching areas, and therefore that income from patient fees had to be pooled. One practical constraint which may significantly affect the success of such a system, however, is that the motivation to recruit and treat private patients in order to derive the pooled income is strongest, of course, where all of the proceeds of such activities go back to the individual physician. The Medical School facilitated the initiation of such a programme for the psychiatrists by offering to underwrite some part of the possible financial deficits in this programme during its first year or two, while it was being developed. However, in 1966, when the Board of Regents indicated that such partnerships could be recognized, they specifically provided that no member of the faculty could be required to join them (Board of Regents, 1966). Accordingly, the head of the department is permitted only the opportunity to convince the members of the advantages of joining such a partnership. He has no authority to order anyone in the department to join, nor can he make membership in the department of any prospective faculty member contingent upon such membership. Although initially all but one of the psychiatrists in the department elected to join the partnership, the difficulties in this arrangement became dramatically evident when several of the new senior faculty members who joined the department in 1970 refused to join the partnership. Because their actions were based in part upon the attitudes these individuals held toward clinical partnerships as such, the department is now looking into alternative routes for collecting fees on private patients and channelling these back into salaries. This issue, which is still in limbo, is further compounded by the reduction of funds available from patient fees as the faculty devote more time to teaching and research, and from the reduced personal incentive for recruiting and treating private patients. Another problem inherent in the shift to a strict-full-time system for only a part of the faculty is that it tends to increase the division between the psychiatrists, who are included in the system, and the psychologists, and thus to reinforce and make less permeable sentient boundaries which have a minimal relationship to the task requirements of the department.

A second step in the change process has been that of my presenting to the staff, in as many ways as possible, the need to modify those departmental activities and attitudes that have conflicted with the new definition of the primary task. This has been attempted through developing new types of teaching conferences in the department, some of which are focused on administrative issues and some of which have been attempts to experiment with educational innovation. In addition, a 'Blue Ribbon Committee' was formed to study the clinical services in the department, toward coming up with a new format for these important activities. At the same time, the staff development programme was organized to facilitate continued faculty education. The students also have profited from this latter programme which offered, as a by-product, the possibility of enhancing recruitment through contacts with prominent workers in the field from various parts of the country.

The most concrete changes that have occurred during the first year and one half have been related to the reorganization of the clinical services in adult psychiatry. This process was initially limited to the adult services because at the time this phase of reorganization was occurring we were actively recruiting for a new Director of Child Psychiatry and it was felt inappropriate to make any administrative changes in that area prior to this appointment.

The basic concept behind the pattern of reorganization of the clinical services has been that of establishing clear boundaries between service-centred groups in terms of clinical approach and philosophy of treatment, in contrast with the more traditional system of differentiating simply between programmes for in- and out-patients in psychiatry and between the various disciplines. Out of the work of the Blue Ribbon Committee three adult clinical 'firms' evolved, each of which had its own staff, comprised of individuals from a number of different disciplines, with responsibility for the care of a group of patients who remain within the firm's jurisdiction as long at they are in treatment, whether they are classified as in- or out-patients. Each firm was initially assigned an interdisciplinary staff, headed by a psychiatrist, which was asked to define the purposes of the firm and its methods of operation. Space and human resources have been allocated to each firm in accordance with its task needs. One firm, which has had responsibility for a ward of 20 beds and part of the out-patient unit, has asked to be assigned patients who are appropriate for individual and family psychotherapy or who fall into the adolescent age group. The ward station that serves as the base for the firm's activities had been organized for an interdisciplinary programme a few years before my joining the department and it therefore had relatively little difficulty in approaching the interdisciplinary aspects of its task. Its greatest problem has been in clearly establishing lines of authority, which had been somewhat blurred by previous organizational patterns on that unit.

The second firm, which has responsibility for the largest ward (26 beds) and out-patient facilities, is largely organized around research studies and treatment in the area of psychopharmacology. The lines of authority in this particular firm had been well-established previously through the Early Clinical Drug Evaluation (clinical research) Unit that had been centred on that station. It has broadened its areas of interest and concern and seems to have had little difficulty in establishing newer directions and organizational stability. Two all-staff retreats during the past year have served as effective mechanisms for determining the direction of change and for resolution of resulting administrative issues in this unit.

The third firm has had most difficulty in reorganization, largely because it took upon itself the task of completely redeveloping its programme. It, too, has out-patient facilities and a small ward of 13 beds. That unit had served for many years as the closed ward for the department and as such had represented the principal point of importation of active or suicidal patients from outside and was the area to which other stations would export their difficult patients as the need arose. Prior to my joining the department the staff of this station had asked that the ward be opened, and it has been maintained as an open station since late 1969. In the reorganization, the firm's staff decided to use some of its facilities for training and service in the crisis intervention area. At the same time, it recognized that such activity was unlikely to make use of its full facilities and staff. In order to properly employ the diversified skills and interests of its staff members, it also agreed to take on general clinical responsibility for evaluation of new patients and for long-term treatment of a limited population. The multiple tasks of this firm, coupled with its internal differences between various factions of the staff and faculty over the implications of establishing a crisis programme, particularly when partially centred on non-psychiatrist professionals, has resulted in this firm's becoming a centre for intrastaff and interdisciplinary conflict. Although the staff of this firm are highly qualified, they do represent the potential for strong polarization of factions and an arena for open emergence of the otherwise covert conflicts between the various disciplinary groups, particularly between the more traditionally oriented psychiatrists, on one side, and nursing, psychology and social work on the other. Within each discipline, also, there are clear divisions between the more conventional workers and those seeking changes in roles and constraints. These issues, still being explored within the firm and between the firm and the rest of the department, appear to be moving toward resolution, although it is likely that the most controversial of its programmes will be deferred for the present. My impression is that although conflict and stress have been greatest for this staff it has moved furthest in the understanding of critical staff issues.

In group process terms, it is quite understandable that this third firm has been the focus for the greatest chaos in the department. In its marked shift in task it symbolizes most dramatically the changes represented by my leadership in the department. It also has most closely approximated, in its self-assigned task, my particular and often-stated interests in social psychiatry, my expressed wish, in the interest of patient care and training, for modifying the monolithic role of the psychiatrist, and my concern for upgrading the skills and responsibilities of the various non-physician groups that make up the treatment 'team'. In assuming its new programme, then, this firm may also have invited the brunt of the attack on what I represented in my new departmental leadership while the other firms were left relatively free of chaos in their tasks.

Recognizing that the increased specificity of clinical activity for each of the firms may result in a situation where some potential patients could 'fall between the cracks' and where the overall departmental responsibilities could come into conflict with the defined purposes of each firm, a Clinical Services Coordinating Council, consisting of representatives of each firm and of each of the various clinical disciplines, was created. A position of Chief of Clinical Services was created in the department and awarded to a senior psychiatrist. He has responsibility for clinical import and is assisted in this process through an Intake Committee that meets daily to make assignment to the firms of those patients recommended for admission by the officers of day or referred to the hospital by physicians and mental health agencies around the state (Anderson, 1971).

While each of the issues described above merits a more detailed discussion it is not the purpose of this chapter to elaborate on each of these new programmes. Rather, it is more appropriate to look at the problems of organization in an academic department whose mission must contain within it effective programmes in education, clinical services and research, no part of which can be slighted if the department is to be successful in its activities.

In viewing the overall organization of the department, at least two major overlapping structures must be defined. One of these describes the sentient groups and follows the time-honoured tradition of the divisional arrangement to include Divisions of Adult Psychiatry, of Child Psychiatry and of Clinical Psychology. It is evident that in an interdisciplinary department of this kind clear recognition of the sentient group boundaries must be made and that each disciplinary group should be encouraged to develop a distinct identity of its own. This, however, leaves the divisional status of the research psychologists unresolved. It is clear that these faculty members and their staffs should be incorporated into some divisional structure. Although we are in the process of changing the name of the Division of Clinical Psychology to one with a broader connotation, it is still evident, that there is a marked difference in identity and function between the experimental and clinical psychologists. Because of budgetary considerations, work location and task, the experimental psychologists' primary investment is clearly with the research unit. While this problem is still open, it is hoped that the advent of new divisional leadership in Psychology will help in its solution.

The other essential organizational purpose relates to task performance. It is clear that research, whether in the research unit or in other areas, must have defined leadership. Similarily, the clinical activities should come under someone responsible for all clinical services, and the educational programme should be co-ordinated if we are to make effective use of all resources and to avoid the costly separation of educational programmes in the department in order to maintain task-sentient boundary coincidence. We therefore have placed all responsibility for research on a Director of Research, and have asked the Chief of Clinical Services to take similar responsibility for clinical activities. The position of Director of Education has been assigned to the recently appointed

Director of the Division of Clinical Psychology. He will oversee the activities of the chairmen of the educational committees responsible for specific programmes for medical fellows, medical students, psychology graduate students, and on graduate studies and other educational developments in the department.

It is clear that neither type of structure alone adequately represents the functional organization of the department. Both sentient and task groupings must be identified, legitimized and developed with effective leadership in their own areas. If the major faculty sentient groups are to be asked to take on equivalent responsibility in education they must have representation on the department's Executive Council, and yet such representation does not allow for the major emphasis on task development. For this reason both structures have been recognized by the department leadership, and leaders of both task and sentient groups have been appointed to the Executive Council along with some 'at large' faculty members. Similarly, the opinion of the Executive Council has been sought prior to appointing individuals to these various leadership roles, just as the Council's concurrence must be solicited for new departmental faculty appointments and promotions.

Summary and Discussion

In undertaking the task of reorganization of a Department of Psychiatry in a major American state university medical school, I have first attempted to define my view of the changes needed in primary task and mission priorities. The nature and history of the department, formal and informal structure of the Medical School and University and other constraints on change have been described. The complexity of requirements upon departmental leadership has been outlined and illustrated in terms of the import-conversion-export process for each of the components with which the department must maintain significant task relationships. They include a patient population, students in three categories, and knowledge in the field. The first are the concern primarily of the clinical services, but are basic to the educational process and to clinical research as well as to a significant part of the department's funding. The various groups of students, while they are principally concerned with education, justify the department's existence at a medical school, make use of the clinical population in their training, assist in the care of patients, and may be involved in research, particularly if they intend to avail themselves of opportunities for seeking graduate degrees. The research staff, in its search for new knowledge, offers prestige to the department while it contributes to the educational and training efforts and may, at times, rely upon the patient population as research subjects.

The faculty members' responsibility is principally in the educational area, but their participation in the clinical programme is essential if the latter is to be maintained and to grow. Their progress on the academic ladder, at the same time, is largely contingent on their research and the quality and quantity of resulting publications. The department's intellectual climate is very much dependent on the faculty's continued opportunities for academic growth and the mechanisms available for exchange of information and ideas among them.

Within the department a number of professional staff members play a major role in clinical services although they do not hold faculty positions. These well-trained individuals in social work, nursing, occupational therapy and other fields also must be encouraged to grow and to develop both their intra- and interdisciplinary relationships if the clinical services are to reach their potential level of effectiveness and if the various student groups are to be trained realistically for leadership in the contemporary field of psychiatry. This inevitably leads to role-competition and role-diffusion on the clinical services. In my view this area of conflict must be made explicit and should be fed into the educational process as we seek administrative and conceptual resolution of such issues. We have attempted to explore such problems at the departmental level in clinical forums, at staff meetings of the firms and in other settings. Such issues mirror some of the major dilemmas of the medical delivery system nationally and thus require sophisticated attention in the educational institution.

All of these aspects of the field must be recognized and directed. When one adds to the equation the specific need for leadership in change, the complexity of the task becomes evident. Broadening the scope of the department's objectives, to add meaningful education, service and research in social psychiatry, in liaison psychiatry, in psychoanalytic psychiatry and in administrative psychiatry, to list just a few areas that need new or increased emphasis, inevitably creates stress upon the security systems of the various components of the department. Each of these issues must be addressed, cultivated and woven into the fabric of the reorganized programme of the department.

We have talked of the need for change in the department and have suggested a number of opportunities for innovation. There is always the hazard of attempting change for change's sake, in order to place one's imprint on the organization. Such limited motivation for innovation can, of course, be destructive in that the consequence of change can be expected to include some degree of conflict, as noted above. On the other hand, constructive innovation is essential to the health of the ongoing institution. Richmond (1969, p. 167) points out that 'all institutions—universities, industries, government—must undertake the process of self-renewal or undergo deterioration and decline. University medical centres are no exception'. John Gardner (1963, p. xiv) further elaborates on this theme when he observes that 'an institution may hold itself to the highest standards and yet already be entombed in the complacency that will eventually spell its decline'.

That support or inhibition of creativity and innovation in the institution is related to organizational direction and administrative style is illustrated by several authors (Kotin and Sharaf, 1967; Pelz and Andrews, 1966; Rosner, 1968). Rosner demonstrates that *activity control* tends to reduce staff creativity and that *visibility of consequences* tends to increase it. Both of these terms are derived from the work of Gordon and Becker (1964). Rosner defines *activity control* as 'the degree to which members of an organization use procedures or resources specified by their superiors'. *Visibility of consequences* is defined as the 'ability and willingness to measure the consequences of organizational progress in terms of organizational goals' (Rosner, 1968, p. 37). He maintains that there is an inverse relationship between activity control and creativity because the low tolerance for conflict in maximally controlled organizations leaves little room for creative activity. Kotin and Sharaf (1967) focus on change in administrative style in a mental hospital and the consequences of a shift from 'tight' to 'loose' style on the performance of the staff. They also present evidence that the tighter controlled organization manifests less conflict and less creativity.

Where controls are relatively loose, conflict and innovation both increase, although it is also likely that creativity will decrease when the staff moves beyond an 'optimal' level of conflict. When conflict becomes too intense, one can expect a sharp fall-off in creative activity as a result of the institution of security measures within the organization, through loss of key personnel and through higher echelon administrative action. In terms of the boundary control function of leadership (Miller and Rice, 1967), in the clinical academic department the latter two consequences of inordinate conflict are likely to require disproportionate attention by the department head to the boundary between himself and the environment, as manifested by the need for increased recruiting activities and by preoccupation with his relationships with the school administration. The increased security operations within the department are likely to reduce the permeability of both task and sentient boundaries within the department, creating a situation where response to departmental leadership is sharply attenuated. At the same time, as indicated above, the institution of particularly strong centralized activity control by the leadership is likely to reduce innovation within the faculty group and thus to delay or impair the sophisticated accomplishment of the primary task. The leader's position on the tight rope of activity control, therefore, may be gauged in part by maximal levels of innovation and by optimal levels of conflict.

While the level of conflict in the organization is in large measure related to leadership style, the level of innovation and creative activity has several additional determinants. Individual competence is, of course, a major factor, and thus is also a reflection of the leader's ability to discriminate, recruit and reinforce creative workers. Another determinant is defined above as *visibility of consequences*. This entails the development of, and encouragement of participation of the staff in, a variety of auditing activities. In our department these have included academically-oriented clinical conferences, regular faculty meetings, the Executive Council, research presentations by departmental investigators and clinical staff forums. The scheduling of such meetings is relatively simple; the major demand for leadership, in this context, is in aiming and maintaining the focus of these meetings on *visibility of consequences*. If successful this may represent a major interface between the creative activities for all three major subtasks of the department and an important basis for reinforcing innovation.

Conclusion

I have attempted to indicate some of the problems identified and actions taken in the first 18 months of my departmental leadership. The process has been difficult and has not been without its setbacks. Whether or not our efforts will achieve satisfactory results may take several years to determine, and even at that time it is likely that the judgment of effectiveness will vary with the observer. In my view, it will be measured by the later careers of our residents and other graduate students, by the rate and quality of applicants for training at our institution, by the patterns of patient referrals, by the quality of research output and by the influence on our graduating physicians of their education, as medical students, in psychiatry. Few of these objectives lend themselves to hard-nosed analyses, and whatever data are appropriate probably will not be available in less than four or five years' time. In the meanwhile we must rely on changes in staff and faculty attitudes, in effective use of educational opportunities, in interest of students in departmental electives and in expressed views of our students and faculty. It is far easier to evaluate progress from a single event, or a small series of statements, than to attempt to interpret the available data in terms of the field in which they are obtained and against the backdrop of an imperfect blueprint for change. At the same time, if the Department of Psychiatry is to achieve its potential, it is the latter type of sophisticated reading of the milestones of change that must be sought. It is my hope that the influence of A. K. Rice will be manifested not only in the theoretical constructs that serve as the framework for this blueprint but also, and most importantly, in the disciplined approach to complex data in the living organization that he so impressively personified and which, in a variety of ways, he attempted to convey to those of us who sought his counsel.

References

Anderson, R. (1971), Reorganization of University Hospital's psychiatric services, Submitted for publication in *Minnesota Medicine*.

Baker, A. B., Schiele, B. C., Hastings, D. W., and Jensen, R. A., (1953), Neurologic and psychiatric trends in Minnesota, *Minnesota Medicine*, **36**, April, 384–386.

Board of Regents, University of Minnesota (1966), Private consultation practice in the College of Medical Sciences, Policy statement. Unpublished.

Gardner, J. W. (1963), *Self Renewal: the Individual and the Innovative Society*, Harper and Row, New York.

Gordon, G. and Becker, S. W. (1964), Changes in medical practice bring shifts in patterns of power, *Modern Hospital*, **102**, February, 89–91.

Hastings, D. W. (1968), History—Department of Psychiatry and Neurology, *in* J. Arthur Myers, *Masters of Medicine*, Warren H. Green, St. Louis.

Hausman, W. (1971), Applications of the military model to civilian psychiatry, *The Journal of Psychiatric Research*, **8**, 513–520.

Hausman, W. and Rioch, D. McK. (1967), Military psychiatry, a prototype of social and preventive psychiatry in the United States, *Archives of General Psychiatry*, **16**, 727–739, June.

Kotin, J. and Sharaf, M. R. (1967), Intrastaff controversy at a state mental hospital—an analysis of ideological issues, *Psychiatry*, **30**, 16–24.

Malmquist, C. P. (1963), The development of psychiatry at the University of Minnesota Medical School, *The Journal—Lancet* (Journal of the North Dakota State Medical Association), **83**, 275–283, No. 7, July.

Miller, E. J. and Rice, A. K. (1967), *Systems of Organization*, Tavistock Publications, London.

Pelz, D. C. and Andrews, F. M. (1966), *Scientists in Organizations*, Wiley, New York.

Rice, A. K. (1963), *The Enterprise and its Environment*, Tavistock Publications, London.

Rice, A. K. (1965), *Learning for Leadership*, Tavistock Publications, London.

Richmond, J. B. (1969), Creative administration, *Journal of Medical Education*, **44**, 165–169, March.

Romano, J. (1966), Twenty-five years of university department chairmanship. *The American Journal of Psychiatry*, **122**, Supplement, 7–27, June.

Rosner, M. M. (1968), Administrative controls and innovation, *Behavioural Science*, **13**, 36–43, January.

Schulman, J. (1969), *Remaking an Organization*, State University of New York Press, Albany.

University of Minnesota (1970), *Faculty Information Bulletin*, University of Minnesota, Minneapolis.

Operant Conditioning and Organizational Design

Arthur D. Colman

This paper attempts to delineate certain meaningful relationships between two disparate theoretical and methodological frameworks concerned with human behaviour. The first, *operant conditioning*, was developed by B. F. Skinner and his colleagues at Harvard in the early 1950's. In the controlled setting of the laboratory, it attempts to delineate exact relationships between experimentally arranged environmental contingencies and the behaviour of animal subjects. Skinner found that by programming the form and frequency of the consequences of behaviour, environments could be designed to support highly predictable, long term, complex behaviour. During the past ten years, the principles and technology derived have been verified when extended to human behaviour. They have been applied to the design of therapeutic and educational institutions and other environments where the control and modification of human behaviour is at stake.

The second framework is *organizational theory*, specifically that developed under the leadership of the late A. K. Rice, Eric Miller and others at the Centre for Applied Social Research of the Tavistock Institute of London. Their view of an organization is as an open system, relating to the environment through multiple input, conversion and export processes. The organization's primary task, the task which is required for survival, determines the critical input, conversion and export systems, and the priorities of all other such systems within the organization. They have studied the behaviour of groups and inter-groups within the enterprise, feeling that these relationships impose critical constraints on task function. They are concerned with the effect of technology and technological innovation on the group and organizational structure and attempt to show how organizations may be designed to maximize primary task function, not only in relation to this technology, but also in cognizance of the influence of sentient systems and covert group processes on the human resources utilized.

It should be clear from these brief summaries that the two models approach human behaviour from very different vantage points, use a different language to describe their observations, and derive their data from different sources. Yet they are both concerned with a common problem—the analysis and design of task oriented human environments.

As a physician and psychiatrist, my concern with the concepts and methods for designing human environments and social space is a pragmatic one. I have been faced with the task of creating and running medical and psychiatric wards where the absolute priority was successful patient care. It is the practical applications of such concepts to the treatment environment, particularly psychiatric treatment, that remain the focus.

The paper's organization reflects this emphasis. Firstly, the relevance of an environmental design model to recently developing psychiatric treatment methods is discussed. Secondly, after a review of the definition of design and the changing emphasis within classic design fields such as architecture, the development and use of operant conditioning as a discipline of environmental design is detailed, particularly as it relates to the design of treatment environments for a variety of behaviour problems. Thirdly, the importance of an organization behaviour and design perspective is explored in relation to the introduction of a new treatment mode into the complex social matrix of a psychiatric ward and hospital. Finally, the relationship and the usefulness of each of these models in the planning of treatment environments is considered.

Until the past decade, psychiatry has concerned itself with elucidating intrapsychic phenomena in dyads or in the face to face group. This emphasis has greatly increased our sensitivity to human phenomena in normal and abnormal psychology, and has enriched other fields such as literature, anthropology and religion. Unfortunately, this emphasis tended to obscure the critical impact of intergroup processes and organizational structures on the direction and course of most psychiatric treatment. In particular, the treating professionals usually ignored the possibility of designing the organizations within and through which treatment took place. They proceeded along similar lines whether therapy was conducted on a hospital ward, out-patient clinic, or non-medical setting within the community. Therapists rarely concerned themselves with the question of whether or not the behaviour directed by the organizational structure was appropriate to the treatment task.

The importance of the contributions of Sullivan,[1] Rioch and Stanton (1953), Jones (1953) and Wilmer (1958) should be considered in this context. Their work in developing the therapeutic community concept has emphasized the treating potential of the entire social organization of the ward on patients' behaviour and the treatment situation. In particular, they focus on the critical role of staff communication patterns on the patient community and the impact of feedback from this community on staffs' treatment techniques and attitudes.

Unfortunately, the instructions for translating the tenets of the 'therapeutic community' into operational terms for designing the social organization on a specific ward are left vague. As a result, in most cases, ward leaders have continued to use the traditional medical model to design their wards. Specifically, this means programming therapeutic activities into allotted time slots, just as X-ray, physical therapy and laboratory procedures are programmed into the usual medical or surgical ward schedule. It is true that the names of the therapies on therapeutic community wards are often different from traditional ones. Community meetings, crisis resolution groups, milieu time and psychodrama, the techniques thought to enhance the therapeutic community style, are inserted into daily activities, where individual therapy, devalued for its tendency to complicate intrastaff relationships, has been withdrawn. Except in the hands of the most inspired leadership, the organizational structure has remained remarkably similar. In other words, despite the therapeutic community's emphasis on the treatment potential of the entire social organization rather than specific time-linked techniques, it has remained anchored to specific therapies; what it lacks is an alternative model for designing this new emphasis into the organizational structure itself.

The lack of design models has limited other types of treatment and patient care innovation as well. Recently, psychiatry has begun to study the community in which psychiatric illness develops and becomes labelled as deviant. Out of these studies, the new field of Community Psychiatry has developed. In the United States a great deal of money has been poured into community treatment models such as community mental health centres. The lack of availability of a design model for community treatment has placed the focus almost entirely on the *constraints* imposed by the community social network on effective therapeutic intervention. The results of programmes based on this theoretical stance have been disappointing. A typical course of events is for a group setting up a community centre clinic to rediscover and reverify the power of the preexisting social forces in whatever area they hoped to work (and change), and then to retreat, overwhelmed, to the comfort of the one organizational structure that they know and within which they can function. The all too familiar and increasingly upsetting outcome is for the community clinic to reside in the community setting, apart from the hospital only in physical distance. The clinic has been relocated, but functional design and therapeutic technique remain unchanged and often unsuited to the requirements of the new environment.

It is true that the constraints that organizations place on individuals, particularly on their ability to change facets of the organization to which they belong, are formidable indeed. For example, Menzies (1960) has shown that nursing roles and relationships in hospitals are deeply rooted in denial of the feelings related to death, fearful illness, maiming or craziness. Organizational relationships developed to serve this denial are especially difficult to change, particularly if rational, non-interpretive techniques are used. Psychiatry must become increasingly interested in concepts and procedures which shift and redesign irrationally determined rigid systems so that appropriate organizational structures can be matched to changing treatment technology.

The Webster's definition of design is 'the deliberate, purposeful planning of a settled, coherent programme for selecting the means and contriving the elements, steps and procedures which will adequately satisfy some need.'[2] Given this definition, it is semantically possible to talk about *designing* a treatment ward or other planned social environment if one considers humans and human groups as one of the critical design elements. Nevertheless, the concept of design is most often associated with rearrangement of physical elements to serve an aesthetic or functional purpose.

For example, on the campus of the University of California at Berkeley, there are many separate departments dealing with problems relating to changing physical and social dimensions in the environment, yet *the* School of Environmental Design trains architects. In fact, architects have always conceived of their designs as affecting human behaviour through the physical forms created. Until recently they have largely attended only to the aesthetic and technical elements of the buildings. With the development of physical materials of increasing plasticity, it has become technically feasible to transmute the most fanciful ideas into a reality of form. Questions of designing shapes to facilitate certain kinds of behaviours has become increasingly modish. There is an embarrassment that human figures are usually absent from their final plans, as if people react rather than interact with the physical environment. The architect of a new steeple-shaped church in San Francisco was recently criticized for continuing the vertical man–priest–god relationship rather than creating a building whose shape and planes would enhance man–man interaction. Designers of planned communities are supposed to build structures to support a special life-style among preselected groups with known behavioural problems and peculiarities. The work of Hall (1966) and Sommers (1969) in the use of space in everyday behaviours, and Calhoun (1966) and De Lauwe (1965) on the psychopathology of crowding, have begun to define a new field. Thus design for the architect is now also felt to include a discipline that will link physical space and the structure and behaviour of human groups.

Over the past 20 years, a science of behaviour called operant conditioning has developed which, viewed in its broadest context, holds considerable promise for the field of environmental design (Skinner, 1953). Scientists working in this discipline have tended to see their work as leading to a theory of behaviour which would apply across species and be capable of experimental verification. The argument between behaviourists and other psychological theorists has been rife for many years, frequently preventing useful intellectual cross fertilization. However operant conditioning may be an important theory for environmental design irrespective of its relevance to theoretical psychology.

Consider the experimenter's relationship to the 'Skinner Box', the hallmark of this field. An animal is placed into a cage which contains levers connected to food, water or electric-shock dispensers. An assortment of lights can be flashed on or off, with or without superimposed geometric patterns. The experimenter works from the premise that the consequences of the lever press will change the probability of the next lever press occurring. That is, if the animal presses the lever more frequently after a given consequence, such as food, the consequence is defined as positively reinforcing to the animal. Similarly if the behaviour decreases after a given consequence such as electric shock, it was punishing to the animal. The precise programming of these consequences over time (schedules of reinforcement) was found to determine the relative rate of behaviour (Ferster and Skinner, 1967). Using these principles, the experimenter is able to decide which levers will be favoured by the animal and which will be ignored. By predesigning the exact conditions under which reinforcement or punishment will occur, it is possible to predict, within prescribed limits for each species, the rate and pattern of the lever press behaviour.

The experimenter can go further in programming the behaviour of the caged animal. He can also arrange stimuli such as colours, light, sounds and even the presence, absence and behaviour of other animals, which will lead to positive reinforcement or punishment. For example, a monkey will quickly learn to press a lever if its effect is to drop a food pellet into his hopper. If a green light is paired with the food condition and a red light with the shock condition, it will learn to press the lever differentially in response to whatever light colour pattern the experimenter programmes. Using these and similar procedures, an environment can be designed in advance which will insure long chains of complex behaviour with a high degree of accuracy. In a sense, the operant conditioner has learned to design environments which lead to specific behaviours in the limited world of cage and experimental animal.

Under many circumstances, these same principles are quite as effective with individual humans as with animals. Behavioural pathology such as stuttering (Flanagan and coworkers, 1958), or self-destructive behaviour in mental retardates (Minge and Ball, 1967), have been brought under the control of environmental stimuli and reinforcements. Similarly, new behaviours such as simple verbal skills in autistic children, dressing and toilet training behaviour in severely retarded children and social skills in chronic schizophrenics, have been elicited and supported by environmental designing according to operant principles[3]. Of course, in work with humans, interpersonal reinforcements such as praise, attention and affection have potent reinforcing qualities which must be considered in the design.

Ayllon and Azrin (1965) described what they called a token economy which applied the operant design concepts to larger social units such as hospital words and classrooms. Their idea was to pay the patient in artificial currency for specified behaviour. The tokens were then exchangeable for privileges on or off the ward. Tokens, like money in the larger economy, became a generalized reinforcer linked to the individual's own preference in his environment. The ward manager, in conjunction with staff and other principals on the ward, decided which behaviours were appropriate (according to *his* therapeutic formulae) and linked them to reinforcers available on the ward.

For example, the therapist, therapeutic team or ward community, might decide that in order for patients to leave the hospital and return to the community, they needed a minimal repertoire of socially appropriate behaviour such as getting up in the morning, attending to personal hygiene, performing adequately at sheltered work programmes and so on. These required behaviours were then divided into measurable units which were assigned value in the token economy. When a patient performed one of the unit behaviours, he received a fixed number of tokens. The tokens earned could be used to buy ward privileges such as snacks, toilet articles, passes, television viewing time— whatever is found to be of value to the patient group. In this way, the ward environment is redesigned so that the patients are continuously rewarded when they engage in behaviours leading towards the therapeutic goal. With clinical experience, these behaviours can be chosen so that they elicit positive consequences in the outside world as well.

Wards based on procedures elaborated from this simple behavioural framework have been shown to be surprisingly successful with a large range of difficult psychiatric problems including chronic psychotics, senile dementia, adult and juvenile retardates and autistic children[4]. Though unified by a common theory and language, wards have developed unique techniques and character as a function of the patients' difficulties. Thus retardates may require more individualized programmes to extinguish socially abrasive problem behaviours such as soiling or regressed sexual behaviour, in comparison to long hospitalized psychotic individuals where eliciting and shaping human relationship skills may be the target repertoire. In all cases, however, the design procedures require a clear formulation of behavioural requirements linked through the artificial economy to the available reinforcements.

Operant conditioning had developed in the psychological laboratories of the universities and research institutes. In that environment as long as certain ethical and policy constraints are adhered to, the experimenter has virtual autonomy over his animal subjects. He also has a strongly authoritarian relationship with his laboratory assistants, who are usually his graduate students. At first, work using operant conditioning techniques with human subjects was also carried out in an experimental context, even if the laboratory had been moved to the clinical ward. However when the demonstration projects were handed over to regular ward staff who had been retrained in the new procedures but still were very much within the hospital organization, programmes often failed to catch hold.

Failures were usually blamed either on the intolerable constraints imposed by the 'rigidity' of the organization or on the previously ingrained 'old style' training of the staff. Where the experimenters had strong administrative backing, they could try various solutions including replacing the entire staff with the experimenter's men, compulsive recycling of the recalcitrant staff members in special training courses or the development of a token system for staff! Remedies such as these were short lived. They were modelled after the milieu of the research organization where local autonomy is structurally possible. They were untenable for the interlocking bureaucracy and interward group loyalties that so characterized the hospital social environment. Many hospital administrators lost patience with what had been promising therapeutic advances and a number of operant wards closed down. Where wards did function well, they characteristically existed as isolated, paranoid units, walled off from the rest of their host institutions, unable to communicate their useful technology to their immediate neighbours.

From the point of view of organization theory, the breakdown described is more or less predictable. The case might be described as follows: A new technology is introduced by an expert into an existing organization with the assumption that it will lead to a more effective treatment system. Staff is shown that the model works (by demonstration) and is trained in the same procedures. Yet no attention is given to the inevitable impact that technological innovation has on task performance and organizational structure. At the simplest level of analysis, the ward staff is threatened with loss of previously well defined job skills and their role relationships to authority. On traditional psychiatric wards, a major staff function is to mete out punishments and privileges to the patients. Insignificant daily events such as who goes out on pass, gets an extra dessert or is allowed to gossip in the nursing station after lights out, are the very fabric of the role status of the isolated and socially deprived patient, and the source of major interactions between them and staff. On the token ward, these functions are removed from staff authority. Patients' use of privileges such as evening passes will not depend on the favour in which they are held by the staff member in charge or even the staff-patient 'community'. Rather, their privileges will depend *only* on the number of tokens they have earned in ward activities. Staff members have lost an important part of their role function. Their anxiety will increase and they will resist the change.

Slightly less obvious is the impact of the new data system on staff. The record of tokens earned by the patient provides an objective measure of his behaviour, which, if the data system has been properly designed, will accurately reflect his progress towards the ward goal. Such new measures decrease the impact of subjective observations of patients by staff, such as nursing notes, on ward leadership, further shifting their conventional roles and power source.

It is little wonder that staff, frustrated in performance of its traditional work tasks and still bound as a strong sentient group, acts to sabotage the new system. In *Systems of Organization*, Miller and Rice describe this exact phenomenon:

'A group that shares its sentient boundary with that of an activity system is all too likely to become committed to that particular system so that, although both efficiency and satisfaction may be greater in the short run, in the long run such an organization is likely to inhibit technical change. Unconsciously, the group may come to redefine its primary task, and behave as if this had become the defence of an obsolescent system. The group then resists, irrationally and vehemently, any changes in the activities of the task system that might disturb established roles and relationships.' (Miller and Rice, 1967, p. 31)

In this context, the problem of introducing the token economy (or other therapeutic innovation) is valuably restated as follows: The primary task for the innovator is to introduce and test out the operant model in a clinical setting. Part of his task is to design an appropriate organization (or succession of organizations) to effectively introduce the new technology into the existing system. This will require more than simply an analysis of the reinforcement system of the treating staff and the design of a 'token economy' to control staff behaviour. The factors are far more complex if just because the sentient group to which staff belongs will extend beyond the boundaries of the treatment ward. (Obviously the replacement of regular staff by a group of known loyalty to the experimenter, and few ties with the host organization, is an attempt to deal with this problem.) If the organizational aspects of successful innovation are outside of the interest or skill of the experimenter, he may have to redefine

334

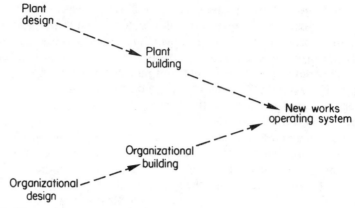

Figure 1. The setting-up process in the preliminary phase. (Based on Figure 26 in Miller and Rice, 1967, p. 144)

his position in relation to the task. A more appropriate role might be as consultant and director of research programmes run by a ward administrator more suited to the task of integrating a new system into the hospital environment.

Miller and Rice (1967) have developed a conceptual framework for understanding organizational process which seems to me to have practical importance for the kind of organizational design problems that continually face new treatment methods in the field of psychiatry. Their discussion of the structuring of innovation is a good case in point (Miller and Rice, 1967, pp. 135–157). They distinguish between a 'plant design system' which includes the provision of physical resources, and an 'organizational design system' which includes the provision of human resources in the form of people trained to occupy roles in the system, and given the task 'of establishing appropriate groupings within sentient boundaries that reinforce task requirements' (Miller and Rice, 1967, p. 137).

This dual process can be represented diagrammatically as they relate it to the development of a new steel works utilizing new equipment and technology (Figure 1). In their discussion of the setting-up process, Miller and Rice stress the needs for co-ordination of the two design systems, including the possibility of integrating them under one command if size allows. They also stress the requirement for affording maximum boundary protection to the setting-up organization, to prevent its being intruded upon by other sentient or activity group loyalties. The details of the specific steps required will of course vary with the technology being introduced, the structure of the host organization, the location of the experts within the system and so on. They do not imply that there can be a fully formulated blueprint for the new human organization prior to its actual operation any more than that the physical plant will be unaltered once work begins. The point is that both the technical and organizational aspects of any new systems must be well considered by the leaders.

The relevance of the ideas of Miller and Rice both on the specifics of innovation and the general organizational concepts from which their approach was derived, was apparent to me when I had the chance to design a new operant treatment system for delinquent men at Walter Reed General Hospital in Washington, D. C. (Colman, 1971). I was guided in this process by David Mc K. Rioch, then director of the Division of Neuropsychiatry at the Walter Reed Army Institute of Research, who first introduced me to their work. Following the Miller and Rice formulation, some months before the treatment ward was due to open, I organized a small work group whose task was to design the new ward. The team was equally divided between operant and organizational consultants, the latter having experience in running psychiatric wards in the Walter Reed setting from both a medical and nursing level. I was the leader of this group. We met frequently in both formal and informal settings and developed a strong sense of loyalty to the design task and to each other. Although it was hoped that some of the members of this team would go on to be principals in the operation of the ward, in order to insure sufficient insulation for their innovative task, no members except myself were committed to take part until after the design was completed. The design meetings early concentrated on the technical aspects of the token economy which included elucidating the behavioural requirements, and articulating these with the ward reinforcement system and a measurement system appropriate to the ward treatment goal. Later, the meetings increasingly focussed on organizational issues, particularly the effect of this new technical system on the existing staff roles and relationships. It became clear that the treatment system would necessitate new roles for staff members, as well as a redefinition of boundary relationships between leadership and staff, and staff and patients.

For example the behavioural requirements decided upon by the design team stressed education and group behaviour training rather than individual insight or recognition of feeling states. The point system provided a direct link between ward privileges and patient behaviour. It was predicted that staff, freed (or deprived) from its previous responsibility as gate keepers, insight givers and limit setters, would now need to invest themselves in other roles such as data collectors, tutors, course instructors and social reinforcers of target behaviours in patients. Therefore a critical part of the design team's task was to plan for appropriate training, leading to job satisfaction in these roles along with whatever general orientation to the new treatment model was deemed appropriate.

The final blueprint described the specifics of the token economy as well as the projected changes in the staff organization. It also included a temporally sequenced programme for reaching these endpoints. This plan included considerable opportunity for the staff members and the patients to redesign their own roles and relationships as the system unfolded.

By the time the ward opened, the design team had become a strong sentient group. It continued to meet during the first six months of the project's operation. Three of the six members continued as participants in the project. The design solution did in fact provide a sturdy framework for the technical and organizational changes which occurred as the ward developed. Inclusion of the patient group in the design plan decreased any ill effects of the changes on their course of treatment and, in particular, reduced their ability to use the ongoing changes as a way to frustrate and deflect their therapy as is so often the case during clinical innovation. The ward has been an effective therapeutic enterprise for four years despite two major changes in leadership.[5] Although I cannot prove a direct causal relationship between the setting up organization and the success of the project, my feeling is that it played a critical factor.

Operant conditioning proved useful in programming the social and institutional rewards in an environment so that specified behaviours become more or less probable. To what extent could this same behavioural technology have been applied to analyse the organizational problems of introducing and implementing a new programme into a complicated social system? The critical problem in technological transfer is probably in the area of social control. Operant techniques have always presupposed the ability to gain control of the critical reinforcing contingencies influencing the behaviour to be modified. Token programmes on wards or in institutional environments rely on the ability to manipulate the rewards in the system including the social rewards, such as attention and praise, which are part of the behaviour of personnel. Organizational design, however, relates as much or more to staff and administrative groups as it does to patients.

No matter how much self-government and decision-making capacity is delegated to a patient group, they are still in a dependent status relative to institutional staff, and are usually isolated from the potential sentient group of other patients. This cannot be said of hospital staff, most other employees and perhaps even the patients of the future. It is true that operant conditioning methods have begun to be useful in devising more effective reinforcing procedures using contingencies such as money rewards, time off, praise from the group leader and prestige roles in the hierarchy. Yet it is just these variables that are particularly subject to organizational influences such as the dynamics of intergroup relationships or the bargaining of professional pressure groups and unions. Group and intergroup processes add a complexity which operant conditioning (as well as most other psychiatric treatment techniques) has not as yet successfully considered.

It is in these areas that the organizational concepts discussed are so valuable. They provide tools for analysing conflicts between task and sentient groups, for delimiting boundaries between activity systems within the organization and its congress with the environment, for defining leadership role and authority relationships, and for selecting and organizing towards the primary task. Of particular relevance to psychiatry, the work of Rice and Miller suggests structural alternatives for designing organizations so that the inevitable intergroup relationships and the impact of technological change on these relationships do not become an overconstraint on the treatment task. Obviously these concepts could be equally well applied to the new more humanistically oriented treatment methods, as to the advances in scientific psychology, although the language of organizational theories may be felt to be less suitable to the former.

It is only necessary to point out that Rice has based the organization of the Group Relations Conferences, whose learning goals are felt to be achieved largely through an experiential and subjective mode, on just these concepts of organization design (Rice, 1965).

Notes

1. Sullivan's work at Shepard and Enoch Pratt Hospital from 1929 to 1931 is one of the most important modern studies in ward milieu treatment.
2. Webster's Third New International Dictionary, 1965.
3. In the past five years, a large literature has developed on the diverse applications of operant conditioning to behavioural disorders and change. See: the *Journal of Applied Behavioral Analysis* and Ulrich and coworkers (1966).
4. Professor Leonard Krasner at the University of the State of New York at Stoneybrook, New York has compiled a list of more than 200 centres applying operant techniques and token economy procedures to a variety of patient groups. Success obviously varies with each programme but generally effectiveness as measured by discharge rates, recidivism rates, or ward behavioural change has been comparable to other ongoing treatment modalities.
5. Follow-up of the first 48 patients admitted to the programme showed that 65 per cent of the men were successful, and were on duty or had been honourably discharged at least nine months after returning to duty. In a comparison group, only 28 per cent were successful while 72 per cent were in the failure category. Two years later, the success rate was above 80 per cent.

References

Ayllon, T. and Azrin, N. H. (1965), The measurement and reinforcement of behaviours of psychotics, *in Journal of the Experimental Analysis of Behaviors*, **8**, 357–383.

Calhoun, J. B. (1966), The role of space in animal sociology, *in Journal of Social Issues*, **22**, 46–58.

Colman, A. D. (1971), *The Planned Environment in Psychiatric Treatment: a Manual for Ward Design*, Thomas, Springfield, Ill.

De Lauwe, C. (1965), *Des Hommes et des Villes*, Payot, Paris.

Ferster, C. B. and Skinner, B. F. (1957), *Schedules of Reinforcement*, Appleton-Century-Crofts, New York.

Flanagan, B., Goldiamond, I. and Azrin, N. H. (1958), Operant stuttering: the control of stuttering behavior through response contingent consequences, *in Journal of the Experimental Analysis of Behavior*, **44**, 118–123.

Hall, E. T. (1966), *The Hidden Dimension*, Doubleday, New York.

Jones, M. (1953), *The Therapeutic Community*, Basic Books, New York.

Menzies, I. E. P. (1960), A case-study in the functioning of social systems as a defence against anxiety, Tavistock Pamphlet No. 3. (Reprinted in 1967 by the Centre for Applied Social Research, Tavistock Institute).

Miller, E. J. and Rice A. K. (1967), *Systems of Organization: the Control of Task and Sentient Boundaries*, Tavistock Publications, London.

Minge, M. R. and Ball, T. S. (1967), Teaching of self-help skills to profoundly retarded patients, *in American Journal of Mental Deficiency*, **71**, 864–866.

Rice, A. K. (1965), *Learning for Leadership*, Tavistock Publications, London.

Rioch, D. McK. and Stanton, A. H. (1953), Milieu therapy, *in Psychiatry*, **16**, 65–72.

Skinner, B. F. (1953), *Science and Human Behaviour*, Macmillan, New York.

Sommers, R. (1969), *Personal Space*, Prentice-Hall, Englewood Cliffs, N. J.

338

Ulrich, R., Stachnik, T. and Mabry, J. (1966), *Control of Human Behavior*, Scott Foresman, Glenview.

Wilmer, H. A. (1958), *Social Psychiatry in Action: a Therapeutic Community*, Thomas, Springfield, Ill.

Teaching and Learning for Responsibility: A Model of an Educational Approach for Meeting the Challenge of Change

Kenn Rogers

Introduction

This paper presents some reflections on the purposes and tasks of educational institutions, some observations on the present character and pace of changes in society and some comments on the implications of these changes for educational institutions, particularly at the collegiate level. But primarily, it relates some of the writer's teaching experiences at this academic level which suggest a particular way of directing students' attention to the social reality in which they live, and which provides opportunities to both student and institution for developing their own capacities to deal responsibly with social problems.

This teaching–learning approach is a developmental one. It is designed to provide opportunities for students to learn through their own actions—both in the classroom and in outside institutions—how conflicts between and within groups of people can be managed constructively and how to apply this learning to the development of responsible, creative and proactive approaches to social problems. The model for this approach can be called 'Teaching and Learning for Responsibility'. Learning itself is conceptualized as a response to social change occurring in a rapidly accelerated way.

Contemporary Social Problems

One of the strongest social forces, in the Western world and elsewhere, is a widespread distrust of, and disenchantment with, the policies and conduct of established institutions. In America this phenomenon is taking place in many segments of its society. There are the poor who seek to escape the dual vice of hard-core unemployment and inadequate welfare, and the youth who want an end to instability abroad and to corruption and hypocrisy at home. And there are those of all levels and ages who wish to free air, rivers, lakes and oceans from pollution, cities from slums, fellow citizens from malnutrition, drug addiction, poverty, uncontrolled technology and racism, and the other social ills that prevent the United States from truly realizing its potential.

Overtly, each of these groups espouses causes that call for social reforms. However, it is critically important to determine whether the various overt manifestations of these malfunctions represent social pathology itself, or whether they are not more accurately symptomatic expressions of such pathology.

The significance of this question can be demonstrated by reference to social events. For example, the doctrinaire belief that frustrated social mobility underlies the social pathology of the ghetto was exploded by the riots during America's 'hot summers' of the late 1960's. Analyses of social mobility criteria applied to the actual participants in those riots made nonsense of the 'riff-raff theory', i.e. that the poor, the unemployed, the 'underclass' express their frustration at being afflicted by social malfunctions by rioting. Most indices of socio-economic status, such as formal education, parental education, subjective social class, occupational level and status of residence area, did not relate to riot participation. In fact, the disorders attracted middle-class, working-class and lower-class people, educated and uneducated alike; three-fourths of those involved in the riots were fully employed, most of them earning good incomes in semi-skilled and skilled occupations (Fogelson and Hill, 1968; Sears and McConahay, 1969; U.S. Riot Commission, 1968). Indeed it was quite an eye-opener to learn that the 'riot-cry' for social change was not significantly related to a quest for social mobility.

More recently we have seen individuals and radical fringe groups express what they term *outrage* through acts of violence against people and property, i.e. kidnappings and bombings.

A favoured way to deal with pressing social problems is to appropriate monies for new social programmes which have a single purpose and which manifestly deny the usefulness of a system or ecological approach in which people's social behaviour is seen to lie at the interface between persons and their environment and therefore by definition is multidetermined. These social programmes are frequently designed to 'fix things', i.e. to provide a quick cure for a given social problem while disregarding the social pathology in which it is embedded. A closer examination of some of these programmes often reveals a desire to 'cool' a problem rather than to come to grips with it and all its complex ramifications, especially those occurring at the interface between personal, group and institutional dynamics.

The results of this particular approach are exemplified by a poorly conceived, but expensively implemented, programme for social change—the Pruitt-Igoe housing project in St. Louis, Mo. Intended to free people from the miseries of slum living, to bring Blacks and Whites together in 'vertical neighbourhoods', 'a roof over one's head' was constructed for some 10,000 people in 43 eleven-storey buildings. Almost from the start, the project was in serious difficulties. There was 'nothing to do, no provisions for services, no place for children in the winter, too many people on top of each other'.[1] Rainwater (1966), conducting social research in the project, indicated that the social strategy employed was unrealistic in the light of the day-to-day reality of Negro slum life. Examining 'the tangle of pathology which characterizes the ghetto', he found that when poor Blacks were encouraged to seek middle-class goals, they became subject to a kind of 'cultural depression', since these supposedly desirable goals were, in fact, unattainable. Rainwater suggests that an individual's inability to adapt to the reality of his economic, social and personal situation, results in emergence of what Erikson (1959) terms a 'negative identity'. Thus, unable to reconcile his conception of himself with his community's recognition of him, he decides: 'If I can't be somebody good, at least I'll be somebody, even if it's somebody bad'.

These data also represent the psychological phenomenon of 'self-hate', as developed by Horney (1950) and further illustrated by Putney (1964), in terms of present society examples. These authors suggest that a person's failure to perceive himself as a worthy human being depends more on his unconscious beliefs about himself than on external living conditions. This concept is supported by Frankl (1963), who described experiences in the Auschwitz concentration camp where some prisoners 'improved their health' while others, in the identical harrowing environment, quickly broke down, thus shortening their waiting period before being sent to the gas chambers. He ascribes these remarkable differences to the degree of the individual's will (or capacity) to see meaning in his life.

At Pruitt-Igoe, the acting-out, in the psychoanalytic sense, of this 'negative identity', or 'self-hate', brought on rampant crime and vandalism which drove out most tenants who could afford to leave the project. In 1971, 15 years after the project was fully occupied by 2800 families, 600 families remained, and those rather precariously. During a visit of HUD Secretary George Romney, conditions in the project were described thus: 'You can hardly get the smell of fresh air because the place is like a pigsty. People throw their garbage out the windows, in the halls. They use the stairways and the elevators for bathrooms. It's unbelievable'. Plans to demolish the housing project were deterred by the $31 million in outstanding construction bonds and by the additional $3.5 million needed for the demolition work itself (Associated Press, 1971).[2]

Yet the U.S. Congressional Programme to construct or rehabilitate a total of six million low-to-moderate income dwelling units during the years 1968–1978 stresses such factors as production efficiency, financing, land assembly, manpower and materials, as well as the political, social and economic constraints affecting the achievement of these goals (Cooper, 1971). By contrast, such critical determinants as the psychological needs of the people inhabiting those dwellings and of others in the affected communities, and the human and personal services they require, seem to be relegated to far less, if indeed any, importance. There is a refusal to accept that safe and sanitary housing by itself does not provide an adequate living environment and that, indeed, a total community culture must be the goal.

Between 1968 and 1972, the writer explored these and similar problems by conducting more than 200 intensive interviews with graduate students at The American University, Washington, D.C., and The City College of the University of New York, as well as with community leaders in Washington, New York and other major metropolitan areas. The investigation revealed a widely felt rage, often latent, at what the educational system is teaching students about our social institutions. There emerged a demand that practical experience gained in social institutions be recognized by, and integrated into, classroom learning. Moreover, there was a repeated emphasis on the need for educational experiences that would explicitly develop the students' system of values and thereby enhance their capacity for self-respect.

Argyris (1968) stresses the importance of combining thought with action in education. He agrees with Festinger (1957) that individuals prefer to reduce dissonance—the inconsistency between what one perceives to be his own attitudes and his behaviour—through changes in that behaviour or that cognition. Argyris[3] goes on to say 'that the way educational systems are managed says much about what the system really thinks of students. There is an ongoing clash between pronouncements of individual dignity and learning with the way we manage education'. He says that students are disenchanted with our lack of congruency; they resent the hypocrisy and they suspect that the values being taught are not workable since they are not being utilized in the existing educational system.

In essence, this youthful rage conveyed in word and action that 'early elementary education fails to teach students how to learn insightfully, and later advanced education does not develop their capacities to meet life's problems of today, let alone tomorrow's'. In the same vein, Levitas (1969) reports that one impatient youth stated: 'We itch, but we don't know where to scratch'. In summary, the learning offered in our formal educational systems, particularly about social institutions, is seen to be insightless and Pavlovian in character, and to stress a two-way, right–wrong logic; it is clearly inadequate for the needs of the learners. Even higher education that presents advanced computer technology and other tools of logical analysis does not seem to acknowledge, and often denies, the relevance of such human irrationality as prejudice and other destructive tendencies. Collegiate education in management, particularly, stresses 'the pursuit of progress' in terms of advancing the technology of product manufacture and marketing, and assigns low priority, if any, to problems of ethical, ethnic, political or social values.

Clinically, the persistence of such limited educational and social choices tends to foster in the recipients of this education an identity crisis, with its seemingly unanswerable questions: 'Who am I?' and 'Where am I going?' Indeed, some students—often those having keen insight into themselves and their environment—are barely able to verbalize these questions, let alone arrive at useful answers. Pointing to discrepancies in our value systems, they demand, often unconditionally, remedies that will alter their own authority position in society's institutions. Yet they seem to be aware, consciously or otherwise, that such changes are unlikely to occur as quickly and effectively as they would like. Some of them will act out their dilemma tonsorially, sartorially, pharmacologically and upon occasion they will rely on Molotov cocktails or dynamite as tools for instant social change.

These reactions can be seen as maladaptive tactics that deny the complexity of the social system and its various roles and values. In short, these students give the impression of suffering from a critical confusion about the identity of their roles and the principles that govern acceptable conduct in these roles. Erikson (1956) defines such an identity crisis as a stage in which the individual searches for some meaningful resemblance between what he has come to see in himself and what his sharpened awareness tells him that others judge and expect him to be.

There are those who argue that the demands for social reform far exceed what education can accomplish by itself. Others seem to take comfort in the recent general absence of the more spectacular variety of activism on college campuses. Yet 'campus unrest' did manifest itself on nearly 100 campuses in April 1972, in protest to the extended bombings of North Vietnam. Moreover, *Time* (1971a) reported that 'in the past three years U.S. high schools have become [even] more frequently troubled than college campuses...Almost two-thirds of the nation's high schools—expensive new suburban complexes as well as blackboard jungles of the inner cities—have suffered disruptions... ranging from peaceful sit-ins...to savage riots...' Indeed, the comparative calm on college campuses, termed by Yale University's President Kingman Brewster as an 'eerie tranquility', cannot be taken as an acceptance or subsiding of problems urgently demanding new approaches for social change.

Explicitly or implicitly, the educational institutions, then, stand accused of having fallen short of their responsibilities. Therefore, the critical issue is not whether, and to what degree, these accusations are justified or whether they are expressions of a generalized anger about social difficulties that is misplaced on educational institutions. The accusations exist and they warrant analysis and alternative actions. It is true that, whatever the merits of these protests, the protestors still manage to function in our society and, therefore, must have learned something from their education. However, considering what is needed and what could have been accomplished, there can be hardly a feeling of adequacy, even less of justified satisfaction, with the educational process as it exists in many institutions.

What appears to be needed is education in its intrinsic sense, designed to develop the learner's capacity for clearly defining and then dealing with problems. This educational process involves not only the traditional classroom and laboratory that emphasize analytic thinking within a framework predetermined by textbooks and instructors. It necessitates, beyond that, work with other real social institutions and an examination of their processes, including their internal contradictions, conflicts and inequities, to wherever that may lead. The latter experience invariably conveys to students a realization of the incompleteness of knowledge about human behaviour, of organizational difficulties often bordering on anomy and, if carried deep enough, of a sense of peril not only to the institutions examined but potentially to our nation, and perhaps to humanity itself.

A New Teaching Approach

This, then, makes education for responsibility a formidable task. It is the writer's belief and practice that we can begin to cope with this responsibility by presenting learning material that deals with social institutions in a broad cultural-professional perspective; a perspective that will lead to an understanding of contemporary society with its various ramifications and ambiguities. More specifically, as a university educator concerned with organizational behaviour, i.e. the ways in which individuals and groups act to carry out their tasks, this writer is engaged in a continuous process of creating and refining an approach for developing the student's capacity for assuming organizational and personal responsibility. It is a model for meeting the challenge of the plethoric changes—social, political, economic, technological, rapid and uneven in pace—that are prevalent in our crisis-ridden society.

The model's concepts are mainly derived from those developed by the writer's friend and teacher, the late A.K. Rice, whose work with, and writings about, enterprises and their organization (Rice, 1963, 1965, 1970a; Miller and Rice, 1967) have greatly influenced the writer's own work in this field and for which he herewith gives his acknowledgement and thanks. Other concepts are the writer's own, extended from those of Rice, or derived from his personal experience as executive in, and consultant to, a series of institutions. Others are taken from organization and learning theories. Critically important concepts making up this model are those of the *open system*, Rice's *primary task* and *import-conversion-export process*, and a working philosophy best expressed by President Kennedy: 'that what there is, is not good enough and that we can do better'.

The processes of the model's application, as they emerge in the classroom, are a confluence of several factors. Among them are capacity and willingness of the students to learn; the material they present for learning, acquired from their field research work, from their jobs or from other course studies; case histories from texts; and the Socratic Method used in examining all this material. Initially applied by the educator, the Socratic Method is adopted during the semester by many (though not all) students as a tool for sophisticated learning. Other factors affecting the teaching–learning process are both the educator's and the student's knowledge of the subject matter, and their abilities to perceive and use the classroom dynamics as those of a working institution.

This formulation, while general, nevertheless points to an important primary educational task: teaching and learning the tolerance of ambiguities and complexities when working with and for people. The educational model described here is a tool for performing this primary task.

Primary Tasks And Mission

Primary task is conceptualized by Rice (1963, pp. 198–202) as that task which an institution must perform to justify its existence and to survive. An institution may have several primary tasks which, when combined, form its overall objective or mission (Selznick, 1957). A university's primary task

345

might be to provide teaching, research and other services, perhaps including diagnosis and consultation to the community's institutions. Such a mission requires specific resources, human and material, and hence affects the institution's general priorities; more specifically, it affects those of its constituent parts: colleges, schools, departments, centres and programmes. The primary task and the resources allocated for its implementation, then, reflect the culture of the institution—the customary and traditional way of thinking and doing things, which is shared to a greater or lesser degree by all its members (Jaques, 1951, p. 251).

One aspect of the culture within a university is that members of its constituent parts may differ among themselves in the perception of their primary tasks. For example, the administration, led by the president, may endeavour to lift the university from the level of an academic 'bargain basement' to that of a high quality educational institution. In consequence, it may limit the scope of the university's operation and modify its resources accordingly. Yet within the university, one of the divisions may see as its primary task the 'production' of a large number of superficially trained students, perhaps justifying this with the greater revenue produced. There is certainly substantial evidence that the various parts of a university diverge in the perception of the primary task; some deans and department chairmen see themselves as heading fiefdoms. (Clark Kerr characterizes such a university as held together by its central-heating system.) But even beyond this, individual faculty members, who perform a largely self-supervisory function, will introduce diversity; and, depending on the culture of the teaching unit, this will be more or less integrated with the performance of other teachers and other courses.

This writer's perception of his own primary task or mission as an educator concerned with organizational behaviour is to provide, on behalf of the university, for students, faculty and the community, educational services designed to develop and enhance their competence in dealing with work in institutions. Implicit in this perception are several assumptions:

(1) Organizational problems do not differ in essence, whether they occur in private or public institutions or in those of mixed ownership. If there are essential differences in organizational problems, they tend to relate to the size and complexity of the institution rather than its ownership. The model, therefore, has a general application to all institutions—business, government, hospitals, industry, labour unions, schools, trade associations, etc. In short, it relates to all viable institutions where people gather to work.

(2) Discontinuities in our society require constant, conscious efforts to to understand our environment in depth. Reactions that are largely intuitive and pragmatic are no longer adequate or acceptable, and proactive interventions based on thorough diagnosis of the situation become increasingly requisite to organizational problem solving. Applied to the educational process, proactive interventions produce continuous feedback between student and teacher and among students themselves. This technique discourages the kind of teaching

that students often describe as boring or routine—an experience similar to that of the assembly-line worker between required visits to the time clock.

(3) Diffusion of education among broad groups in the community can reduce social and cultural differences, leading to a greater realization of our society's ideals. While it is true that social phenomena have multiple causes, many of which we do not know, let alone understand, one significant cause lies in the structures and processes of institutions. Consequently, providing learning opportunities for understanding these structures and processes, from which improvements may then be developed, is seen by the writer as a primary task of his role at the university.

(4) Task-oriented combination of traditional educational methods with organizational research, diagnosis and consultation links a university directly to the social development of the community in which it functions. This, then, provides a means to test innovative, theoretical approaches to social changes ultimately useful to the university and to its working environment. If successful, this may realistically benefit the university in these ways: (a) Improved teaching and learning processes offered to students; (b) An improved university image, as being concerned with society itself; and—not least—(c) Improved financial status, from augmented service contracts with government and private institutions and other research grants.

Thus, application of the teaching–learning model is designed to enhance the students' use of their education when functioning in society. Therefore, knowledge of organizational process *per se* is treated as a *sina qua non*. It represents the raw material for developing students' capacities to make and implement decisions designed to reach objectives of their own, of their institutions and ultimately of society itself. Most important, they learn to accept responsibly the consequences of these decisions.

The Ecology of Institutions

To say that change—even rapid change—is an outstanding characteristic of our environment, whether technological, economic, social, political or psychological, has become a shibboleth; at times it will anaesthetize even those concerned with the theory and practice of organizational behaviour. But in fact, most of our social problems and dislocations do not arise from change *per se* but rather from the fact that different parts of our society and its institutions are changing at different rates. This observation is not surprising to students of Bertalanffy's *open system* concept (Bertalanffy, 1950, 1951, 1956), according to which there is a constant interchange of inputs and outputs that continuously effect changes both within the institution and in its environment as well. Because of this constant and often uneven change, it is hazardous to predict with any accuracy what institutions are likely to become, within even one generation. This differs considerably from classic laboratory conditions which, with their controlled constants, lend themselves to the making of highly probable predictions.

There is also an important difference between so-called pragmatic reactions to changes and the proactive interventions that facilitate change. One rather dramatic example of this difference is observed in the changed attitude of the United States government toward outer space. When the first Soviet satellite was launched on October 4, 1957, leaders in the American government denied the importance of this historic event. Defense Secretary Wilson called it 'a neat scientific trick'.[4] Senator Wiley dismissed it as 'a great propaganda stunt and nothing to worry about'.[5] Rear Admiral Bennett, Chief of Naval Operations, described the satellite as a 'hunk of iron almost anybody could launch'.[6] Clarence R. Randall, President Eisenhower's adviser, called it a 'silly bauble'. The President himself was reported at the time to be in fine spirits, playing golf in Gettysburg with a neighbour.[8] It is difficult to see these 'pragmatic reactions' to a historic discontinuity as anything but defences against future shock, i.e. the stress people feel upon contact with developments which may have been predictable for some time, but for which they are unprepared, and which consequently shock them when they arrive (Toffler, 1965, 1970).

In contrast, some three years later, President Kennedy, choosing to intervene proactively, announced: '. . . I believe that this nation should commit itself to achieving the goal, before this decade is out, of landing a man on the moon and returning him safely to the earth' (Public Papers of the President, 1961). Well within that decade, the first American walked on the moon and returned. It resulted in 'a research bonanza of some 215 pounds of moon rocks and soil, along with thousands of frames of exposed still and movie film. . .[The astronauts] Young and Duke spent a few minutes more than 71 hours on the moon. . . this was longer by about four and one-half hours than any other crew's stay on the moon. They completed three extravehicular activities, or moonwalks, totalling 20 hours, and that, too was a record' (Newsweek, 1972)*. During the previous mission, the Apollo 15 crew roamed the moon for more than 17 hours, almost as long as did Apollo 11, 12 and 14 astronauts combined. They travelled 17.5 miles in the first car man has ever driven on the moon, took the first walk in deep space and returned with a record-breaking haul of more than 170 pounds of lunar rocks[9] (Time, 1971b).

It is the implication of this kind of change that makes such institutional management education a rather risky business today and of questionable validity for the future. On a broader scale effects of changing conditions can perhaps be appreciated best when considering in the United States, the comparisons shown in Table 1; from this the changes in the ecology of institutions appear to be formidable indeed.

Anatomy of the Model

The organizational relationships stressed in this model lean heavily on Rice's concept of the *import-conversion-export process* (Rice, 1963, pp. 12–14), which he sees as applicable to the work of any institution. An educational institution—for example, a university—*imports* (enrolls) students who assume

Table 1. Changing conditions in the United States

During the early 1950's	While in the early 1970's
Atomic energy largely meant bombs. No nuclear plants had yet been built.	22 atomic reactors are in operation; 55 are being built and an additional 44 are planned.
Foreign automobiles were just a curiosity on American roads which were still mostly two-lane highways.	There are about 45,000 miles of high-speed multiple-lane highways on which travel over six million imported cars.
Airlines were pioneering the first non-stop transcontinental service. The planes were propeller driven.	Transcontinental air travel is a form of mass transportation. The airlines use huge jumbo jets. The development of supersonic transport was halted by Congress because of environmental concerns.
Intercontinental missiles did not exist.	The United States is calculated to have 1054, the Soviet Union 1510 intercontinental missiles.
Transistors did not exist as yet, nor did institutions other than business use computers.	The computer industry has been the fastest growing major business in the world. Computers play a role in all phases of American life and business, highlighted by their sophisticated part in the U.S. moon landings. The development of transistors and miniaturized electronic equipment contributes in increasing measure to industrial, business and governmental operations, as well as making possible America's space explorations.

that its educational processes will develop their capacities for particular social and vocational skills and enable them to function more effectively in society than before. The *conversion* process involves the university teaching students and providing them with learning opportunities. Students then leave the university *(exports)* either having acquired skills in varying degrees or having failed.

The standard of skills attained by the university's 'exported' students directly affects its future, insofar as its reputation for quality education attracts new students and other sources of financial support. The importance of this factor becomes strikingly apparent when it is realized that universities, both private and public, are competitive enterprises. Indeed they compete among themselves and with other similar institutions for several things:

(1) *Human resources* (faculty, administrators, trustees).

(2) *Clients* (students, organizations who contract with the university for special institutes or for research).

(3) *Material resources* (foundation grants, research funds, alumni donations).

(4) *Prestige* (difficult to define operationally, but strongly affecting acquisition of all other resources).

In this educational approach students have the role of clients contracting with the university for services, usually specified in catalogues and other publications. Teachers have the role of professional consultants to students, fulfilling the university's contract with students by advising, teaching and helping them to acquire the desired skills. In this non-traditional relationship students and faculty, on behalf of the university, are perceived as *inter-dependent* partners in a contractual agreement, each with their own separate authority and responsibility, each *different* in capacity from the other, and *neither superior* to the other.

This kind of relationship differs substantially from that of traditional cultures, in which the administration and faculty view students as their 'products'. The students are then perceived as, and at times actually are, rather cynically striving for a certificate or diploma which they believe will provide them with at least a starting salary in their careers that is substantially higher than they could otherwise expect. Learning itself, the acquisition of lasting knowledge and insight, then, becomes a by-product, albeit a welcome one, of the educational process.

This latter kind of culture might well be viewed as a collusion to subvert the purpose of education. Its teaching processes are characterized by the intent to inculcate in students a set of beliefs and values that stress only order and rationality—values which students dare not question, let alone reject, without the risk of getting poor grades. Little recognition is given to the management of conflict, which even without resolution, would lead to increased institutional effectiveness and to personal growth and maturation for those working in these institutions. Not unexpectedly, the teaching culture and the faculty–student relations will mirror one another. Faculty are all too easily viewed by students as 'lords in a feudal system', while students questioning the system of educational forcefeeding and its superior–subordinate authority structure are perceived by faculty as 'aggressors'. Of course, this system does protect some members of the faculty from being surpassed by very bright students—at least while they are at the university.

The Conversion Process

The conversion process employed in this educational approach, based on Rice (1970b), consists of four primary tasks. They are:

(1) Dissemination of knowledge
(2) Discovery of knowledge
(3) Development of problem-solving capacity
(4) Development of capacity to assume responsibilities.

Clearly, these four tasks are interdependent and can be integrated into one mission; the development of students' capacities to make and implement decisions designed to reach their own objectives, those of their institutions and

350

ultimately of society itself, and to accept responsibly the consequences of these decisions.

Dissemination of Knowledge

Dissemination of knowledge operationally consists of the teacher's communicating to students what is known. Such information, necessary even at the university level, is complemented by the educator's guiding students in examining that which is only partially known. In doing so, however, this approach carefully avoids forcing students to memorize generalizations from survey texts or teachers' lectures. The reason for avoiding memorization is that it tends to inhibit thinking about scientific inquiries, not to mention carrying them out. It also fails to provide opportunities for growth and maturation, as well as a honed capacity for the innovative thinking that is needed when working in other institutions.

Discovery of Knowledge

Discovery of knowledge operationally involves rediscovery of what is already known and discovery of genuinely new knowledge. This is best accomplished via field research. Discovery is an integral part of this educational approach and is discussed later in more detail.

Development of Problem-solving Capacity

Development of problem-solving capacity implies the assimilation or use of acquired knowledge while thinking clearly about a related issue. This demands that opportunities be provided for the student to think for himself, to have his ideas questioned by his peers and by his educator, and in turn for him to doubt and question their ideas. To acquire this capacity for inquiry, students need continuous practice, along with guidance, in terms of formulating a self-critical approach and communicating its results—all of which lead to an appreciation of the complexity of concepts and objects. The criterion for testing the achievement of this task is an assessment of how cogently the student thinks and what he can learn—not how much he knows.

Development of Capacity to Assume Responsibilities

Development of capacity to assume responsibilities is essential to life in a changing world. It is highly unlikely that students can acquire once and for all the knowledge and skills that not only will prepare them for their first jobs, but will protect them against professional obsolescence. This fact has been acknowledged in the Killian Report (1963), which shows that the average engineer is obsolescent only ten years after his degree, and that he requires further education if he is not to become obsolete. It is safe to say that similar conditions prevail in the disciplines dealing with institutions. Moreover, this need for relearning, for changing jobs and perhaps even professions, becomes multiplied by the increasing longevity of our population.

Developing the capacity to assume responsibilities necessitates not only the student's ability to test his values by himself, with his colleagues and with his educator, but to decide for himself what to retain, amend or reject. He must then identify with a tradition or with a future not yet charted, although it may be discernible in skeletal structure. The educator's task is to demonstrate to students the inevitable consequence of whatever decisions they make. This, of course, requires an appreciable degree of self-discipline on the part of both student and educator, each taking responsibility for himself.

Areas in which the development of problem-solving capacity and the capacity to assume responsibility may find practical expression are:

(1) At work, in family relationships and in social milieux;

(2) In making considered judgements of people and events;

(3) In managing conflicts and adapting to change when faced with: (a) The necessity to determine priorities among problems, (b) the risks in trying to solve these problems and (c) the frustrations resulting from failures to reach attempted goals;

(4) In continuous examination of one's own values and those in the environment;

(5) In the ability to plan one's own career.

These areas represent only this educator's view. Although broad, they are by no means exhaustive.

Traditionally, dissemination and discovery of knowledge and some form of problem-solving have been taught in the classroom, while learning to assume responsibility has been largely left for individuals to acquire as best they can. For the past 25 years or so, teaching and learning for responsibility have been offered primarily in educational structures other than universities, such as the Tavistock Institute of Human Relations, London; the National Training Laboratories, Washington, D. C.; and by some of their offshoots—conferences, institutes and workshops. The educational model described here, however, has been developed to combine all four previously stated teaching–learning tasks; therefore it can be effectively applied to learning in traditional classroom settings. One important difference, however, between traditional teaching and the new model lies in the extra demand made on the educator by the latter. When using this approach, the teacher must be able to integrate group processes as they occur in the classroom into the traditional learning experiences.

The Model's Physiology—Its Strategy and Tactics

To work effectively in institutions, an individual needs both vocational and social skills. Among the former might be accounting, banking, marketing, nursing, production. However, it is on the social skills in particular that this model focuses, and emphasis is given to concepts dealing with:

(1) An institution's organizational structure: the way its members group themselves to carry out their tasks;

(2) An institution's culture: its traditional way of thinking and doing things;

(3) The personalities of its members, singly and in groups; the hopes and fears determining their expectation of how they will be treated by others, and the beliefs and attitudes on which they base their own code of behaviour towards others.

Directly intertwining vocational and social skills, this educational approach aims at developing skills that are related to real, living people and that can be used for innovative action. By contrast, in the traditional compartmentalization of knowledge, each subject is only peripherally related to others, and is perceived at only the superficially observed level. Such training tends to produce students with vocationally limited insights, who are poorly qualified for effective social change or personal growth.

Strategically, the approach is used to enhance students' awareness of their responsibilities when working with others towards the accomplishment of tasks. The aim, therefore, is to bring together their experiences, thoughts, emotions and intellect without neglecting one for another.

Operationally, the educator opens the first class-session with a request for students to complete anonymously two unfinished sentences: 'I expect from the course...' and 'I expect from the instructor...'. He studies these responses carefully and, in the second session, brings them back to the students, together with requisite comments. The rationale for this is that participatory planning for teaching and learning is desirable, but it is useful only if students are aware that their expectations can be met solely in the context of reality constraints. One of these constraints is their contract with the university; another, the purpose of the course; another, their own contributions. This initial procedure helps to ward off unrealistic expectations and the ensuing disappointments.

Next, students receive a course syllabus containing the following:

(1) A statement of the *Purpose of the Course*, relating its primary tasks specifically to the subject matter;

(2) A list of the *Main Topics* that will be examined;

(3) A suggested and extensive *Reading List*, leaving the responsibility for its use to students; prescribed texts are avoided, whenever possible, as they frequently represent an intellectual crutch, which hinders students' growth;

(4) The stated requirement for an *Action* or *Field Research Paper* dealing with a topic chosen by the individual student, in which he is to demonstrate his ability and understanding in applying subject-related concepts to institutional problems in a real-life situation.

It should be noted that the selection of a research topic causes extraordinary anxiety in some students. Some will try to manipulate the educator into prescribing a topic for them and this only shortly before the paper is due. When unsuccessful, they threaten to drop the course, and a few do so. These students apparently consider themselves incapable of assuming the responsibility of making choices for themselves, in spite of extensive help given them in discussing possible topics. The rationale for insisting that a student select his own research topic, in spite of the anxiety it causes—or perhaps more relevantly because of it—is based on a reality in today's culture. This is the common preference for leaving things alone until they become serious problems, rather then examining them before they become hardened and difficult even to deal with, let alone to resolve.

In personal terms, one research study might involve a student's capacity to examine his environment for career opportunities long before they are formally presented by corporate recruiters on campus. A research study on an institutional topic might relate to the organizational process by which a dean of a school at the university is chosen and the potential effects of this on the students' and the university's primary tasks. Other topics might deal with the gap between police and community, or between law enforcement officers and offenders in correctional institutions; with racial conflict in public housing; with problems between landlords and tenants, between small retailers, large chain stores and their customers, or with facets of a particular international conflict.

In each instance, the student is required to state in operational terms the study's primary tasks and, after an examination of the constraints in the situation, to suggest a plan of operation, together with several alternatives for approaching the attainment of these tasks. Each detail must be supported by a rationale derived from the analysis of the given situation. The need for alternative approaches arises from the assumption that there is no single 'right way' to solve a problem and the fact that a particular implementation policy appears to be reasonable is no assurance that the dynamics of the implementors will enable them to adhere to it.

In pursuing this primary task, experience has demonstrated that the Socratic Method, a time-honoured teaching process, is particularly appropriate. Using this educational stance, which is designed to help students analyse familiar, yet complex, concepts, the educator does not 'spoon-feed' students, but insists that they assume responsibility for their own work; in the process, they learn to cope with the accompanying frustrations. In operation, the educator (or perhaps a student) states a concept and asks for its meaning; in so doing he offers students opportunities to test their understanding of it. The opening question is never directed at a particular student, so that anyone may assume responsibility for leadership of his colleagues. If several students wish to participate, each is given an opportunity, and the educator's task is to guide them into a co-operative and reality-seeking dialogue among themselves, or, when he considers it useful, between the students and himself. If only one student takes up the opening question, the educator asks the entire class whether or not they agree with their colleague and, most important, why they do so.

For example, if the concept to be analysed is that of a 'manager', students may offer a definition memorized in another course. Examining it, they may find it wanting. In the course of the discussion, some students may express their own aspiratons to become managers. Yet they themselves and others may also express their dislike of being managed. Some of them may come to realize that the concept of a manager has in itself no particular connotation and that what very likely have affected their reality judgement were their feelings about managerial tasks, such as 'rewarding' or 'disciplining'. And so the discussion continues.

When the students arrive at a definition of the concept satisfactory to them, the educator poses questions designed to test this definition in the context of other concepts and in terms of real situations taken from the students' own experiences, either on the job, or preferably, in the 'here and now' of the classroom. During this dialogue, students usually depart from their earlier generalities and begin to commit themselves to operationally defined specifics. These specifics are then tested, preferably by students but, if necessary, by the educator, in terms of another set of circumstances. Often these specifics break down. Thus the dialogue proceeds, each new attempt producing a change, hopefully closer to reality, until a mutually agreed upon, operationally defined meaning of the concept is reached. Even this is examined again and often it is found not altogether satisfactory but is accepted, considering the limitations of available knowledge.

This process causes frequent and considerable frustration, even resentment, among students, especially early in the course. They express their feelings in various ways. At one extreme, they make comments clearly unrelated to the subject matter. These comments are explored until the students see them as designed to use class-time for purposes other than learning, thereby depriving themselves and their colleagues of the educational services they contracted for with the university. The other extreme—an overt refusal to participate in the learning processes—expresses itself in pregnant silences on the part of the entire class, lasting usually from 30 to 50 seconds, rarely over 90 seconds. Another not infrequent reaction is that students tell the educator to 'stop this educational approach' since it is alien to the culture of the university, or that it is 'not useful' since they were trained in other courses to give back what instructors have presented in their lectures. Most students, however, learn to value this educational stance; semester after semester, about 85 per cent of them rate it as good to excellent on a four-point scale (excellent, good, fair, poor).

The students' resistance is viewed here as an expression of their mental health and as part of the educational process. Indeed, students are not seen as either recalcitrant or stupid. Like all people, they do not behave against their own best interest without good cause. New learning presents them with problems of personal adjustment, both intellectual and emotional. Some of them resist insightful learning when it upsets their established pattern of thinking.

These patterns, satisfactory or not, are familiar to them and provide a degree of security; unless they can fall back on habit, they feel as precarious as the Fiddler on the Roof. Tradition, of course, is an integral part of our culture, and students learning new concepts often find themselves subject to two incompatible demands: one, to be progressive, desirous of change and improvement; the other, the desire to find instant solutions to problems. These demands militate against analysis, planning and the facing up to problems that are potentially insoluble or, at best, only partially soluble. Indeed, in this culture, accepting *a priori* potential failure is often viewed as if it were Original Sin.

Using the Socratic Method—consistently probing and testing each assumption offered by student or teacher—results in students' learning to distinguish between fantasy and reality, in deciding what experiences, knowledge and meaning to accept or reject, and in examining the values on which they are based. Obviously, the loss of some of their fantasies about social concepts is painful at first. However, with the majority of students, this process eventually effects greater internal strength and often exhilarating pleasure in this kind of learning. The existence of complexity in our social environment and its institutions is thereby demonstrated, making it intriguing and at the same time frustrating. In the same way, students' preoccupation with formulae and two-value dogma tends to be devalued.

For the educator, the use of the Socratic Method has at least a two-fold implication. For him, it represents:

(1) A significant and workable aid in helping students to test for themselves and, when necessary, to reconceptualize the social events in their environment, through which they learn to process information less affected by fantasy and other defences than before;

(2) A defence against being seduced by students into playing the role of a charismatic teacher who sways students to accept his teaching on emotional grounds, and on whom they can depend for obtaining course credits, preferably with an A or B grade.

Some comments on the latter point are appropriate here. Cautioning students not to try to be like him (but to be themselves) often makes the educator appear as an unloving person: this is not always easy or comfortable for him. Yet, while a teacher perceived as a loving person may facilitate learning processes, the writer believes that the educator who colludes with students to enhance their charismatic dependence on him is unethical and destructive of genuine growth, his own and theirs. The rationale for this is simple and often self-evident. While some students may *wish* to be like the teacher, they may not be *able* to be like him, and it would probably be of less than no value, anyway. For then both the educator and the students would lose the challenge of mutual critical stimulation which demands that all use more of their capacity, and thus develop further.

Both for the students and the educator, therefore, the Socratic Method represents a psychological sacrifice. It demands of both a rational examination of the conceptual frame of behaviour that successfully enabled them to reach and hold their professional position at that point in time. It denies customary escapes into fantasies and other conventional wisdom. In short, it affects their self-esteem—generally a painful experience. Indeed, the pains incurred in this process can be likened to those of growing up. But unlike physical growth, which implies aging and finally death, intellectual growth means staying alive and becoming even more alive. It is thus a reality-oriented endeavour toward the very thing sought by Ponce de Leon, in a fantasy-led endeavour.

Case problem solving represents another stance used here. However, in contrast to the generally practised cognitive-rational approach that deals only with the case material, this approach also focuses on the feelings that arise in the discussions between and among students and educator. Based on the behavioural science findings that small groups reflect much of what occurs in large institutions, the classroom is treated as a microcosm of society. Beyond textbook reality, the real-life behaviour of all people engaged in problem solving has rational, task-oriented thought mingled with irrational, non-task-oriented feelings.

In this context, several kinds of behaviour are displayed by students: a desire for dependence on the teacher or on other students to provide required solutions; feelings of despair and futility about their own capacity to make relevant contributions; jealousy, envy and rivalry with other students; favour-currying with the teacher; efforts at scapegoating other teachers, coursework or family, who are represented as having prevented students from doing their work. All these are interfering with the task of solving the case problem. Much of this behaviour is covert, some of it unconscious; all of it is subject to examination.

Therefore, it is important for students preparing themselves for working with others to learn to discern, within groups, the task-oriented behaviour from other kinds, and the overt agenda from the hidden. To make them aware of this, the analysis of the case continuously focuses on the content of the case and on the group processes emerging among students as they examine it. Difficulties that students experience in dealing insightfully with the case are then linked to their displayed differences in beliefs and attitudes. After some examination, these differences are usually acknowledged overtly. This, then, legitimizes the now-provided variance in their personal styles and makes a wide range of solutions to the case problem acceptable. While each student is responsible for his own recommendations, he can now respect other analyses and interpretations of data that differ from his, even though he would not accept them for himself. This educational stance differs substantially from that of concentrating solely on data experienced by desiccated persons described in the text. The traditional stance disregards the personal feelings and assumptions of student and teacher, while the proposed approach emphasizes what should occur and what is occurring, in the total context of textbook and classroom.

A final educational tactic is designed not only to stimulate students' awareness of organizational responsibility but also to provide opportunities for them to test and experience it. This relates to the evaluation of the educational work. The educator accepts students as responsible partners in the educational endeavour; therefore, each time he evaluates their work, he reminds them of their right to question the rationale for his evaluation. At the end of the course, he asks students to evaluate, anonymously and in writing, the course itself and his work with them in several of its aspects. So that they can use this information for improved task performance, students are also requested to provide a rationale for each of their judgements. When the final evaluations are made, students may discuss them with the educator and, if they wish, may challenge his rationale. If a student is not satisfied with the explanation, he is sincerely encouraged to follow the university appeals procedure, and to appeal the decision to the administrators to whom the educator is responsible. Thus, they assume responsibility for the evaluation of their own work and for their evaluation of the teacher's performance of his task.

Summary

An educational model, considered useful by the writer for meeting the challenge of change, has been presented. It is perceived as an open system and some of its elements were discussed in detail: the ecology in which it is used, the primary tasks and mission for which it is used, the strategy and tactics employed, and the organizational relationships which are adhered to. The educator eschews training, inculcating or indoctrinating. Nor does he attempt to establish harmony of thought where none exists, but rather he acknowledges irrational, non-task-oriented behaviour and he values complexity. In consequence, there is stress on the importance of directly intertwining the learning of both traditional vocational and social dynamics skills.

It is conceded that social learning often involves sacrifices: giving up familiar ways of dealing with problems, social misconceptions, conventional wisdom that leads to stereotyping, defensiveness and excessive social conformity. Considering the rapid and uneven changes occurring in our society, the future of which is already visible in its skeletal outlines and which indicates an undetermined mixture of promise and threat, the writer has described his attempt to help students become aware of their experiences, so that they cannot only identify changes and adapt to them, but beyond this, can potentially cause changes. This, then, demands both the overt recognition that changes, as we experience them, entail risk-taking and the acceptance of the spirit of President Kennedy's statement (in *The New Yorker* in 1963) that 'We cannot [simply] discharge our responsibility by the announcement of virtuous ends'.[9]

Notes

1. A personal communication from the Research Department of the Department of Housing and Urban Development (HUD).

2. Since then demolition of the project has been undertaken by dynamiting its vacant buildings.
3. A personal communication.
4. *New York Times*, October 9, 1957.
5. *New York Times*, October 8, 1957, p. 11.
6. *New York Times*, October 5, 1957, p. 2.
7. *Washington Post*, October 22, 1957.
8. *New York Times*, October 6, 1957, a United Press report from Gettysburg, Pa.
9. Quoted in the Talk of the Town, *The New Yorker*, November 30, 1963.

References

Argyris, C. (1968), Some consequences of separating thought from action, *Ventures*, Yale University Graduate School Magazine, **8**, 66–72.

Associated Press (1971), *Release on the Pruitt-Igoe Public Housing Project*, May 24.

Bertalanffy, L. (1950), The theory of open systems in physics and biology, *Science*, **3**, 27–29.

Bertalanffy, L. (1951), General systems theory, *Human Biology*, **23**, No. 4, December.

Bertalanffy, L. (1956), General systems theory: a new approach to unity of science, *Human Biology*, **28**, No. 4, December.

Cooper, J. R. (1971), *Can the 1968–78 National Housing Goals be Achieved?* Urbana-Champaign: Committee on Housing Research and Development, University of Illinois at Urbana.

Erikson, E. H. (1956), The problem of ego identity, *Journal of the American Psychoanalytic Association*, **4**, 56–121.

Erikson, E. H. (1959), The problem of ego identity, *in Identity and the Life Cycle*, *Psychological Issues*, **1**, No. 1, pp. 101–164.

Festinger, F. L. (1957), *A Theory of Cognitive Dissonance*, Row, Peterson, Evanston, Ill.

Fogelson, R. M. and Hill, R. B. (1968), Who Riots? A Study of Participation in the 1967 Riots, *in Supplemental Studies for the National Advisory Commission on Civil Disorder*, Washington, D. C.: U.S. Government Printing Office, pp. 216–248.

Frankl, V. E. (1963), *Man's Search for Meaning*, Washington Square Press, New York.

Horney, K. (1950), *Neurosis and Human Growth*, Norton and Co., New York.

Jaques, E. (1951), *The Changing Culture of a Factory*, Tavistock Publications, London.

Killian, J. R., Jr. (1963), The crisis in research, *The Atlantic Monthly*, March, 1963, p. 71.

Levitas, M. (1969), *American in crisis*, The Ridge Press, New York, p. 174.

Miller, E. J. and Rice, A. K. (1967), *Systems of Organization*, Tavistock Publications, London.

Newsweek (1972), *Home Run*, May 8, p. 87.

Public Papers of the President (1961), May 25, p. 205.

Putney, G. and S. (1964), *The Adjusted American: Normal and Neuroses in the Individual and Society*, Harper and Row, New York.

Rainwater, L. (1966), The crucible of identity; the negro lower class family, *Daedalus*, **95**, pp. 172–216.

Rice, A. K. (1963), *The Enterprise and its Environment*, Tavistock Publications, London.

Rice A. K. (1965), *Learning for Leadership*, Tavistock Publications, London.

Rice A. K. (1970a), *The Modern University*, Tavistock Publications, London.

Rice, A. K. (1970b), *Innovation and Change in Indian Universities*, an unpublished study.

Sears, D. O. and McConahay, J. B. (1969), Participation in the Los Angeles Riot, *Social Problems*, **17**, No. 1, 3–20.

Selznick, P. (1957), *Leadership in Administration*, Row, Peterson, Evanston, Ill.

Time (1971a), *Battlefield Communique*, August 16, p. 38.

Time (1971b), *Apollo 15*: A Giant Step for Science, August 16, p. 28.

Toffler, A. (1965), The future as a way of life, *Horizon*, **7**, No. 3, pp. 109–115.

Toffler, A. (1970), *Future Shock*, a Bantam Books, New York.

U. S. Riot Commission (1968), *Report*, New York Times Company, New York, p. 132.

Epilogue

W. G. Lawrence and E. J. Miller

Authorship of these last few pages is shared between the editor of the volume, who for many years worked closely with Rice, and a colleague whose encounters with him had been more remote—in the setting of group relations conferences—and who is a relative newcomer to the group in the Tavistock Institute that Rice had built up.

The death of a person who has been innovative and influential in his thinking sets in train a number of processes. For those closest to him there is the task of mourning. In its early phases at least, this carries the risk of deification. His writings become sacred texts; actions are determined by what he would have said, he would have done. These more immediate mourners tend to be sustained in this process by others in the wider circle of the dead person's influence. There is a 'Rice approach' which they are pressed to defend, explain and conform to—and to account for their deviation if they fail to conform. They exist—or at least run the risk of coming to believe that they exist—only in relation to him. Independent lines of thinking are to be suppressed; or, if they are expressed, they are labelled heretical. And, as we know well from the history of religions, there are often mutual accusations of heresy among the disciples themselves. Schismatic processes occur, as each follower asserts his own version of the truth, derived from his own distinctive relationship with the authority, and correspondingly interprets and elaborates the texts in his own way. The task of mourning is not effectively complete until the mourner is able to reassert in identity of his own, in which not only can the debts and the differences be acknowledged, but also quite distinctive points of view, which have nothing to do with the relationship, can be stated and heard.

Those who later join the founder's institution become embroiled in contingent processes and problems. For a time, the primary task is diverted, tacitly or overtly, to mourning. To the extent that the survivors and heirs have been dependent on the founder and therefore need to sanction new leadership and new structures, this temporary reformulation of the primary task is necessary to permit the work of the institution to continue in the longer term. To the extent that an element of deification occurs and that, whatever formal re-arrangements may have been made, the survivors continue to behave as if real leadership remains vested in the dead founder, the longer-term work suffers. Newcomers to the institution then find themselves caught up in several types of confusion: between the words and deeds of the founder and those attributed to him by the mourners; between the nominal new leadership and the 'basic assumption' leadership still vested in the deity and the bible; between factions among the disciples; between the stated and actual tasks. Added to this is uncertainty about their own motives for joining, about their image of the institution to which they wanted to belong—an image affected by their own unique view of what the founder stood for and how important he was to their scheme of things. What is certain is that the joining will be stressful. Confusion about the relation between past and future is particularly likely to be projected into them; they will be the ones who do not understand, who get things wrong; or alternatively they will be caught up in the schisms. To defend their conceptual identity they may also become the advocates of killing off the past and denying the inheritance.

At the same time the institution may well make constructive use of the dialogue between the mourners and the newcomers in hastening the process of establishing its working identity for the next phase. The process is one of examining the continuities and discontinuities of ideas and testing them against reality. The reality-testing that leads to the reconstitution of individual and institutional identities occurs in work. As one engages externally with different sectors of the environment and in new problems, effective work requires a constant retesting of assumptions, a mobilization of old and new resources in changing arrays. To put it more simply, one reacquires the capacity to think and learn.

In describing in this way the kinds of things that have been happening to ourselves and to our own institutions, we are also saying something of wider relevance. We are talking about the recurring theme throughout the volume: the transactions between individual processes and institutional processes. We are illustrating those institutional processes that affect the way in which ideas and concepts are developed (or stay frozen) and are transmitted. And more generally we are putting forward a view of man in relation to his society.

At this stage it does not seem to us to be fruitful to defend Rice, to correct apparent misinterpretations of what he said, or on the other hand to offer critiques or definitive judgements about his contribution to the understanding of organization. What is important is to try to be as clear as we can about where we ourselves stand. Yet paradoxically we find ourselves needing to say in the same breath that this seems to us to be precisely what Rice himself stood for. It is for each person to extract his own meaning from the situations he is in; and, beyond that, it is for each person to modify the situations in a way that gives him meaning. 'My authority for what I say and do is that I am right.' We heard Rice say this, or something like it, many times. You then (it follows) have the responsibility to exercise your own authority to declare whether that or something else is right for you.

Here therefore we are very much in the realm not of concepts as such but of values in relation to concepts. And, as Rogers says plainly in his contribution, the values have to do with man in relation to organizational change and social change. The assertion is that the individual is a self-managing being. And indeed much of our own activity is directed towards learning how to work with others so that they can discover this potentiality within themselves.

It is clear that this particular view of man is itself a product of contemporary society and our perception of its problems. The idea of individuality itself has not been the same in other eras or in all societies. Correspondingly concepts of personality are products of their times. Many of Freud's concepts are plainly less universalistic and more derivative from the particular pattern of family that was developing in western industrial society than he and his earlier followers believed. It has been pointed out by Greer (1970) and others, for example, that the concept of 'penis envy' as an inherent female personality characteristic is plainly linked to social values about the roles and relationships of women and men in a setting of increasingly segregated nuclear families. Moreover, the concept is of such a kind that while it may help to explain female behaviour in that particular culture it also tends to reinforce the prevailing cultural values by implying that this is what women are intrinsically like.

The idea of man (and woman) as a self-managing individual correspondingly belongs precisely to the current era of protest, of the questioning of cultural assumptions. The institutionalized 'protest' permitted by democratic voting procedures and parliamentary oppositions is seen as less and less credible—as preserving the *status quo* and inhibiting rather than promoting radical change. Accordingly, women's groups, black groups, student groups and many others pursue their more radical goals, varying in the quality of argument and the quantity of violence, but similar in their vehemence.

Apart from the vehemence itself, one common thread in the protest is that in the systemic complexity of this rapidly changing world, the individual experiences increasing impotence. He feels he is at the mercy of events and actions far outside his control. Structures and values inherited from the past no longer work: in particular, they no longer serve to give meaning to the individual's life. So while on the one hand the idea of individuality is valued and there is increasing encouragement 'to do one's own thing', on the other hand, the individual's capability to modify the institutions around him in a way that would give him more social space, more choice, is felt to be diminishing.

In his book, *From Death Camp to Existentialism*, Frankl (1959) came to the conclusion that what is primary in man's make-up is his will to meaning—not will to pleasure or will to power—and that a man will die if the meaning of his life is taken away. Today, he says:

'...man is threatened by existential frustration, by frustration of his will-to-meaning, by his unfulfilled claim to a meaning for his existence, by his existential vacuum, by his 'living' nihilism. For nihilism is not a philosophy which contends that there is only nothing and therefore no being; nihilism says that being has no meaning; a nihilist is a man who considers being (and, above all, his own existence) meaningless. But apart from this academic and theoretical nihilism there is also a practical, as it were, single 'living' nihilism: there are people who consider their own lives meaningless, who can see no meaning in their personal existence and therefore think it valueless'. (Frankl, 1959, p. 108)

Whether 'will-to-meaning' is an inherent human characteristic or a product of contemporary culture is disputable; the phenomena he describes are all too evident. Many people who, perhaps because of their differential life-chances and the use they have made of them, feel particularly ineffectual against the monolithic structures of society, are in effect nihilists. The relational counterpart of such nihilism is alienation, in terms of an incapacity to take up roles and engage in role-relationships.

Corresponding to the recognition of this problem, an increasing range of 'cures' have been offered and become more and more popular in the last decade. In some, such as encounter groups, the emphasis is on the removal of inhibitions against self-expression. The notion of 'self-actualization', implying that the individual is the possessor of a set of latent talents that can be brought into flower, has become attractive. The message of Thomas A. Harris, in *I'm O.K.— You're O.K.*, is not greatly different from Norman Vincent Peale's in the 1950's: one has to develop faith in oneself, a conviction of one's own importance. Alongside this thrust towards self-expression, there has been the growing participation in sensitivity groups that are designed to help the individual to discover and correct those aspects of his behaviour that make him less acceptable than he might be to others. Again there are echoes of Dale Carnegie. But whereas *The Power of Positive Thinking* and *How to Win Friends and Influence People* provided prescriptions that the reader was to study and apply on his own, the more recent trend has been towards group experience. Participants can try out new behaviour in a setting supportive of personal change.

Obviously all these techniques and movements are fulfilling an important need in staving off the experience of nihilism and alienation. The question is how far they are addressing themselves to symptoms rather than to the underlying problems. It may well be that, having come from institutions which do not satisfy the will-to-meaning, the participants have found new groups that do; but that still leaves the institutions as nihilistic in their effects as they were before. Organizational development programmes have become the popular mode of tackling institutional change, but too often they appear to serve as palliatives without fundamentally affecting the *status quo*. As Kahn pointed out in his paper, the idea of hierarchy and the concentration of power at the top remain largely unquestioned and unthreatened.

Our view is that this questioning has to be pursued with both vigour and rigour. It is the latter quality, as we said earlier, that has been missing in many protest movements. The starting-point for the rigorous examination is the individual himself in his own institutional roles.

The infant behaves as if he has no doubts about his authority: he is right. That inner sense of rightness gets progressively eroded by processes of socialization, or conditioning. (Note the way in which these two words, which refer to the same process, have acquired quite different values: socialization as a positive control over individual waywardness; conditioning as a negative control over individual creativity; yet waywardness is a prerequisite of creativity.) Examination of one's institutional roles demands an examination of these processes. This does not imply regression to an infantile posture of protest. What it does demand is a consideration of the compromises that are involved in struggling to be both an individual and a member of society.

Culture can be seen in one sense as that patterning of such compromises which currently prevails in a society. Some patterning is essential to any human inter-action: there must exist some consensus about the meanings we place on objects in our environment if we are to communicate with one another at all. However, the symbols that are necessary for communication may change more slowly than the features of the environment to which they refer. Symbols are assembled in theories, myths and ideologies, which are even more insensitive to change. They are thereby reassuring, and when they are built into the structures of relationships, they provide the participating individuals with mechanisms of defence against anxiety: see the Introduction to Part I. Organization and its accompanying culture then have the dual functions of facilitating the perfor-mance of a task and of satisfying individuals' defensive needs—of which the will-to-meaning itself may be one.

These intertwining processes on the one hand further the maturation of the individual. They support the development of the ego function, through which he can achieve some regulation of what he projects onto the outer world from his inner emotional system and what he introjects from outside. On the other hand, these same processes simultaneously subject the ego to attack in that the defensive social systems resonate directly to primitive inner needs for unchal-lenged security, so bypassing, as it were, the ego function.

The self-managing individual is constantly struggling to be alert to this by-passing process. He is refusing to allow cultural assumptions to remain untested and he is disentangling the cobweb of myths and mysteries of our social institu-tions. He has to differentiate between what is conventionally agreed to be reality and what is reality for him. Thus, whereas it is widely accepted that the search for scientific objectivity requires the individual to suppress subjective judgement, we would turn this proposition on its head and postulate that objectivity is essentially the clarification of one's own subjectivity.

But as he examines more closely what is inside and what is outside and tries to regulate the boundary between them, the individual is confronting those very cultural forms, hitherto taken for granted, that provide the defensive structures and thus confronting his own primitive inner needs that these struc-tures satisfy. In giving up an external definition of 'reality' and substituting his own, he is therefore giving up elements of certainty and security and substi-tuting uncertainty and insecurity.

Our argument is that the resultant disorder and chaos are the necessary risks and costs of undertaking change. Social change inescapably starts with self. It requires the individual to re-examine the boundary between inside and outside and to take a different and riskier stance towards his environment. This is not to imply that he may not work for change in concert with others. As Rice said, however,

'It is ... unfortunately true that innovation and change seldom appear to result from democratic process. Innovation and change occur when creative men and women exercise leadership'. (Rice, 1970, p. 90)

To sum up, therefore, we see much of our own work as directed towards helping individuals to discover their capacity for self-management, so that as they work in their various roles in various institutions, they are not merely reacting and adapting to environmental pressures but consciously acting upon their environment and shaping it into what they want it to be.

References

Frankl, V. E. (1959), *From Death-camp to Existentialism*, Beacon Press, Boston.
Greer, G. (1970), *The Female Eunuch*, MacGibbon and Kee, London.
Rice, A. K. (1970), *The Modern University*, Tavistock Publications, London.

Author Index

Le Sieur, F. G., 81
Levinson, D. J., 93, 94, 217, 218, 220, 221, 232
Levitas, M., 342
Lewicki, R. J., 63
Lewis, H. C., 224
Lieberman, S., 73
Likert, R., 79, 81, 123, 124, 125, 128, 129, 137
Litchman, C., 116
Litwak, E., 157
Lockwood, D., 154, 155, 157
Loewald, H. W., 289
Lofgren, L. B., 94, 235
Lorsch, J. W., 14, 137, 138, 148, 154, 157, 187, 210
Lupton, T., 3, 6, 88, 90, 91, 121, 136, 141, 144, 145, 148
Lynton, R. P., 227

Mabry, J., 338
McConahay, J. B., 340
McCord, C. G., 232
McDermott, J. F., 223
McGregor, D., 79, 81, 124, 129
McLaughlin, C., 219, 229
Macleod, K., 4
McLoughlin, Q., 74
Mahler, M. S., 235
Malmquist, C. P., 311
Mann, F. C., 74
Mansner, B., 122, 123
March, J. G., 2, 99, 100, 101, 110, 154, 155
Marx, K., 70
Mathiesen, T. L., 250
May, R., 274
Mayntz, R., 85
Mee, J. F., 212
Mensching, G., 278
Menzies, I. E. P., 20, 251, 329
Merrifield, J., 220, 232
Merton, R. K., 67
Michael, D. N., 82
Milgram, S., 76
Miller, E. J., 1, 8, 19, 20, 46, 50, 67, 69, 90, 92, 100, 107, 153, 158, 169, 170, 173, 191, 208, 219, 235, 254, 263, 264, 281, 287,

310, 313, 324, 333, 334, 336, 344, 361
Miller, J. G., 69
Milner, M., 271, 272
Minge, M. R., 331
Mooney, J. D., 263
Morris, P., 256
Morris, T., 256
Morrison, R. L., 249
Morse, N., 81
Mott, P. E., 74
Mouzelis, N. P., 5
Mouton, J. S., 126, 128
Mumford, E., 152
Murray, H. A., 19, 70, 100, 103, 107, 108, 116, 123, 136, 277
Myers, J., 231

Nadel, S. F., 274
Naylor, J. C., 100, 103, 105, 107, 108
Newsweek, 347
North, D. T. B., 139
Norton, N. M., 224

O'Brien, G. E., 100, 101, 229
Olsen, M. E., 107, 117
Owens, A. G., 100, 101

Palmer, B., 95, 261
Paul, W. J., Jr., 122
Pelz, D. C., 323
Perrow, C. A., 100, 154, 155, 162, 170, 188, 191, 247
Perry, F. A., Jr., 111
Pheysey, D. C., 106
Piaget, J., 289
Piven, F. F., 232
Platt, J., 154, 155, 157
Poggi, G., 89
Pollock, A. B., 19, 70, 100, 103, 107, 108, 116, 123, 136, 277
Porter, L. W., 99, 100, 112
Posner, M. I., 105
Public Papers of the President, 347
Pugh, D. S., 106, 174
Putney, G & S, 341

Quinn, R. P., 78

Subject Index

374